THE HOUSEHOLD HANDBOOK

THE HOUSEHOLD HANDBOOK

Everything you need to know for a safe, smooth-running home

Lawrence, Ardley, MacMillan, Murfitt, Nilsen, Maxwell, Eaton, Jones, Westland & McHoy

southwater

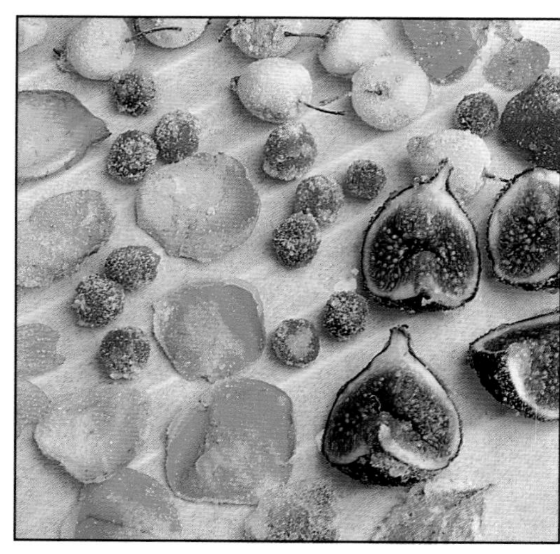

This edition is published by Southwater

Distributed in the UK by
The Manning Partnership
251–253 London Road East
Batheaston
Bath BA1 7RL
tel. 01225 852 727
fax 01225 852 852

Published in the USA by
Anness Publishing Inc.
27 West 20th Street
Suite 504
New York
NY 10011
fax 212 807 6813

Distributed in Canada by
General Publishing
895 Don Mills Road
400–402 Park Centre
Toronto, Ontario M3C 1W3
tel. 416 445 3333
fax 416 445 5991

Distributed in Australia by
Sandstone Publishing
Unit 1, 360 Norton Street
Leichhardt
New South Wales 2040
tel. 02 9560 7888
fax 02 9560 7488

Southwater is an imprint of Anness Publishing Limited
Hermes House, 88–89 Blackfriars Road, London SE1 8HA
tel. 020 7401 2077; fax 020 7633 9499

3 5 7 9 10 8 6 4 2

Publisher: Joanna Lorenz
Project Editor: Jane Royston
Designers: Patrick MacLeavey & Partners
Jacket Design: The Bridgewater Book Company Limited
Typeset by MC Typeset Limited

Previously published as *The Illustrated Hints, Tips & Household Skills*

Contents

INTRODUCTION

Managing your home is a complex process: from making the right decorating decisions through cooking quick and delicious meals to creative flower arranging, it's essential to know what to do to save time and money, and to keep your home running smoothly and looking great. Here, in one indispensable volume, thousands of useful ideas are presented to help you do just that.

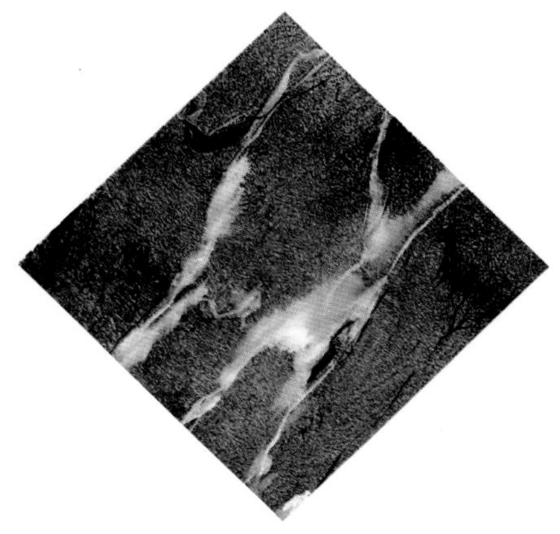

Home Basics shows you, step by step, the best ways to paint walls and woodwork, hang wall coverings, tile walls and surfaces, and how to add special features to your rooms from shelving to decorative mouldings. *Problem Solving and Repairs* includes vital advice on family health, including emergencies and first aid, safety and security in the home, simple home repairs, coping with appliance breakdowns, and ideas for insulating and ventilating your home effectively.

Cleaning and Home Hints offers hundreds of tips to keep your home, clothes and belongings spotless and in tip-top condition – from vacuuming and dusting to getting rid of household smells and problem stains.

The section on *Home Cooking* is a comprehensive guide to cooking techniques, from preparing asparagus and filleting fish to making perfect pastry and decorating birthday cakes, with delicious step-by-step recipes for family meals and entertaining. Finally, *Perfect Home Skills* covers the extras that make your home special: beautiful soft furnishings; ideas for trouble-free home entertaining; creating stunning floral displays with fresh and dried flowers; and caring for houseplants.

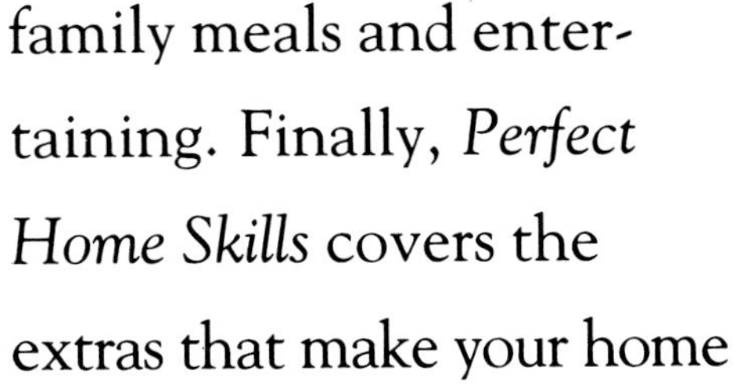

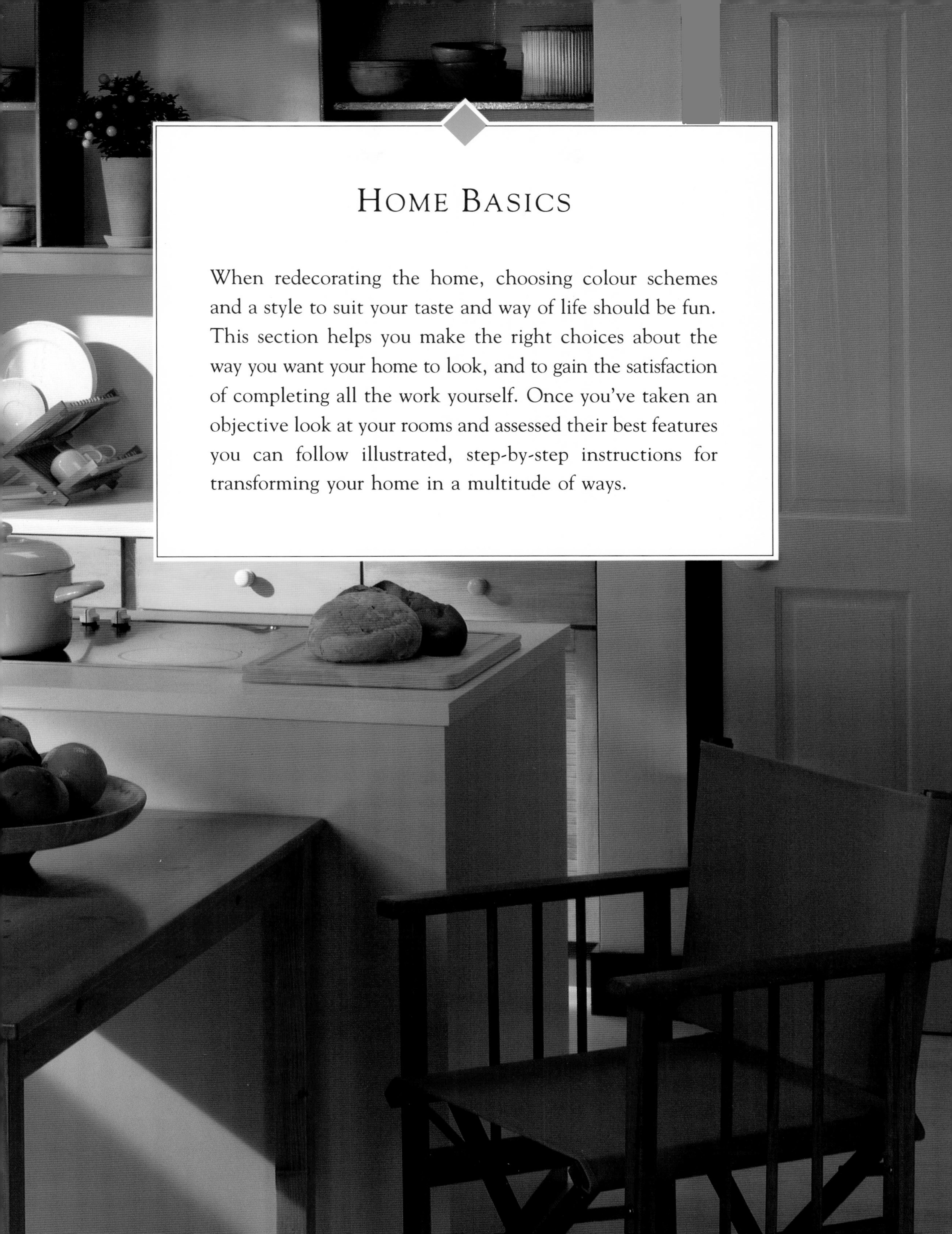

Home Basics

When redecorating the home, choosing colour schemes and a style to suit your taste and way of life should be fun. This section helps you make the right choices about the way you want your home to look, and to gain the satisfaction of completing all the work yourself. Once you've taken an objective look at your rooms and assessed their best features you can follow illustrated, step-by-step instructions for transforming your home in a multitude of ways.

Decorating Decisions

ASSESSING YOUR HOME

The best way to get an objective view of your home's interior condition is to imagine that it is up for sale and to view it in the role of a prospective purchaser. The aim of the exercise is not to give rise to a severe bout of depression on your part, but to determine what exists in the home and what could be done to change or improve it.

Start at the front door, and step into the hallway. Is it bright and well-lit, or gloomy and unwelcoming? A lighter colour scheme could make a narrow area appear more spacious, and better lighting would make it seem more inviting. Decorating the wall opposite the front door would make a long hall appear shorter, while changing the way the staircase is decorated could make it a less – or more – dominant feature. Is the staircase well-lit, for safety's sake as well as for looks? Opening up the space beneath the stairs could get rid of what is typically an untidy gloryhole (storage room), taking up space without saving any. Lastly, are the wall and floor coverings practical? The hall floor is bound to be well-trodden, and needs to be durable and easy to clean as well as looking attractive.

ABOVE Choose an integrated decorating scheme for the hallway, stairs and landing area. Bring down the apparent ceiling height using a dado (chair) rail or decorative border.

BELOW The living room has to be light and airy during the day, yet cosy and comfortable in the evening. The fireplace and a central table provide the main focal points here.

Now move into the main living room. This is always the most difficult room in the house to decorate and furnish successfully because of its dual purpose. It is used both for daily life and to entertain visitors. It must be fresh and lively by day, yet cosy and peaceful in the evening. One of the chief keys to success is flexible lighting that can be altered to suit the room's different uses, but the decorations and furnishings all have their part to play too.

Look at the colour scheme. How well does it blend in with the furnishings, the curtains and drapes, and the floor covering? Are there any interesting features such as a fireplace, an alcove, an archway into another room – even an ornate cornice (crown molding) around the ceiling? Some of these features might benefit from being highlighted – with special lighting, for instance – while other less-attractive ones would be better disguised.

Next, examine how the room works. Are 'traffic routes' congested? Are the seating arrangements flexible? Are there surfaces on which things can easily be put down? Does any storage or display provision look good and work well? Can everyone who is seated see the television? Does everyone want to? Assessing the room in this way reveals its successes and failures, and shows how to eliminate the latter.

Continue the guided tour with the dining room – or dining area, if it is part of a through room. This is often the least-used room in the house, so its design tends to be neglected. As it is generally used for just one purpose – eating – it needs to be decorated in a way that avoids visual indigestion. Warm, welcoming colour schemes and flexible lighting work best in this

LEFT Bedrooms are the most private of rooms, and their colour schemes and furnishings should reflect the personal tastes of their occupants.

BELOW The kitchen is the engine room of the house. It must be well-planned with plenty of work and storage space, and be pleasant to work in and easy to clean.

location; strident patterns and harsh colours are to be avoided.

Now turn to the kitchen. Whatever type of room this is, the most important consideration is that it should be hygienic, for obvious reasons. Are the various surfaces in the room easy to keep clean, and to re-decorate when necessary? Are there dust and grease traps? Is the lighting over the hob (burners) and counter tops adequate? Is the floor covering a practical choice? As the kitchen is often the hub of family life, it needs to be functional but adaptable, and also pleasant to be in so that the cook does not mind the time spent slaving over a hot stove.

Bathrooms have their own special requirements, mainly revolving around combining comfort with a degree of waterproofing, especially if there are young children in the family. Are the decorations and floor covering suitable? How well do they complement the bathroom suite? What about the space available within the room? Could congestion be relieved by moving things around, or by moving them out altogether? Having a shower instead of a bath, for example, could create lots of extra space. Could a second bathroom be created elsewhere in the house? Otherwise, putting washbasins in some of the bedrooms could take the pressure off the family bathroom during the morning rush hour.

Lastly, bedrooms. In most, the bed is the focal point of the room, so the way it is dressed will be the main influence on the room's appearance. The colour scheme also has its part to play in making a bedroom look comfortable and relaxing; remember that the room's occupant will see it from 2 viewpoints – on entering, and from the bed – so take this into account when making your assessment. What about the ceiling? In the one room where people actually spend some time staring at it, does it deserve something a little more adventurous than white paint? Is the floor covering warm to the touch of bare feet? In a child's room, is it also capable of withstanding the occasional rough and tumble or a disaster with the finger paints? Lastly, is the lighting adequate for all requirements? Most bedrooms need a combination of subdued general lighting and brighter local task lighting for occupations such as reading in bed, putting on make-up or tackling school homework. Some changes here may make the room function much more satisfactorily.

Once your tour around the house is complete, you should have a clear picture of its condition and how well it works, and some ideas as to how it might be improved. Above all, you will have viewed it as a whole, not just as a series of individual rooms. That is the first step towards creating an attractive, stylish and, above all, practical home.

ABOVE The bathroom needs tailoring to family requirements. A double vanity unit such as this one would provide valuable extra washing facilities for a busy couple or a growing family.

LIGHTING FOR THE LIVING ROOM, DINING ROOM AND BEDROOMS

The key to success with any lighting scheme is to ensure that it meets two criteria: it must give light where it is needed, and the effect it produces should enhance the room's appearance by creating a balanced mixture of light and shadow. The type of light fittings chosen has a major part to play, and so does the positioning of the fittings. The illustration on the opposite page (bottom) shows how both the type and positioning of ceiling lights can create different lighting effects on room walls.

The living room is one of the most difficult areas to light successfully, because of the many different uses to which the room is put. The aim should be to provide background lighting that can be bright or dim according to the mood of the moment, and then to add separately controllable feature lighting to highlight the room's focal points, and local task lighting where required. The accent is on flexibility. Choosing fittings in keeping with the style of the room will help to ensure that its lighting looks good by day or night.

The dining room has slightly different needs. The main requirement is a table that is well-lit without glare, which you can achieve with a rise-and-fall fitting or carefully targeted downlighters. The background lighting should be subdued, preferably under dimmer control – note that fluorescent lights cannot be easily dimmed. Additional lighting from wall lights or wall washers can be used to illuminate the serving and carving area, and uplighters for dramatic effect.

Bedroom lighting requires a combination of restful background lighting and easily controllable local lighting to cover separate activities including dressing and undressing, applying make-up, reading in bed, or perhaps watching television.

Background lighting can be provided by wall lights, by table lamps on bedside tables, by recessed downlighters or, very appropriately for bedrooms, by the wall- or ceiling-mounted fittings known as uplighters, which throw light on to the ceiling and completely conceal the lamp when viewed from below. The general light level can be lower than for the living room, as long as the task lighting does its job. Bright, glare-free lighting is needed at a dressing table, and light from above to check clothes.

ABOVE Recessed downlighters are the ideal light source for a child's room, providing good illumination of play and storage areas yet remaining safely out of harm's way.

ABOVE A rise-and-fall fitting provides glare-free light over the dining table, while a free-standing uplighter casts a gentle glow across the ceiling.

RIGHT An opaque shade on a bedside light prevents glare while providing gentle background uplighting and enough down-lighting for reading at bedtime.

ABOVE For lighting with minimal glare, team an opaque central fitting with strip lights behind pelmets (valances) to light up a cornice (crown molding) and the ceiling surface above.

OPPOSITE Pastel-shaded lamps in opaque lampshades help to create soft background lighting effects that complement the room's colour scheme.

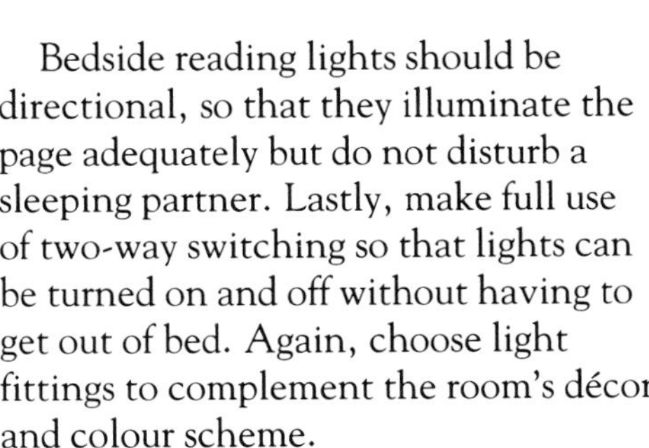

Bedside reading lights should be directional, so that they illuminate the page adequately but do not disturb a sleeping partner. Lastly, make full use of two-way switching so that lights can be turned on and off without having to get out of bed. Again, choose light fittings to complement the room's décor and colour scheme.

Children's bedrooms, especially nurseries, have some slightly different requirements. Good task lighting is essential for jobs such as changing or dressing a baby, and young children will want a higher overall lighting level than that in an adult's room when playing. They may also need a low-wattage night light for comfort and safety. Finally, older children will want portable task lighting for activities such as hobbies and homework.

WASHING WALLS WITH LIGHT

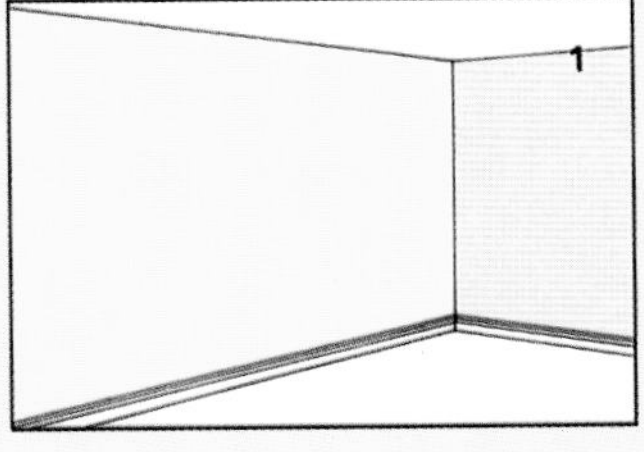

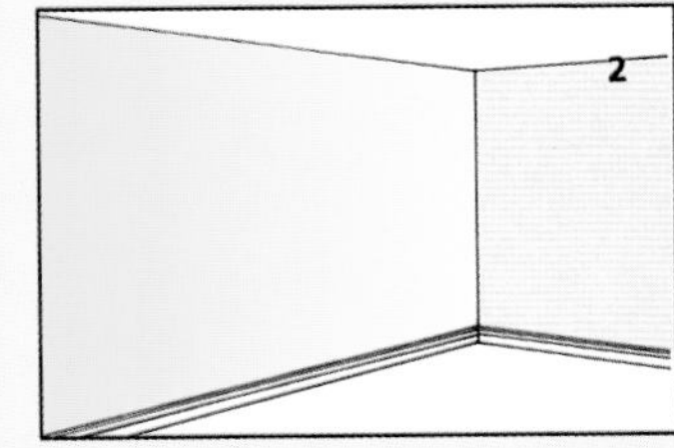

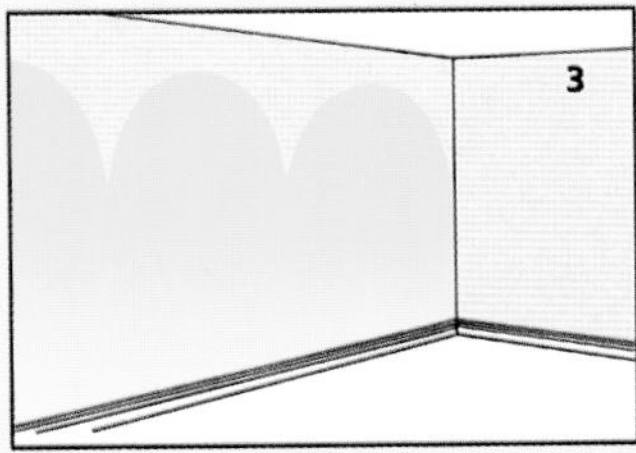

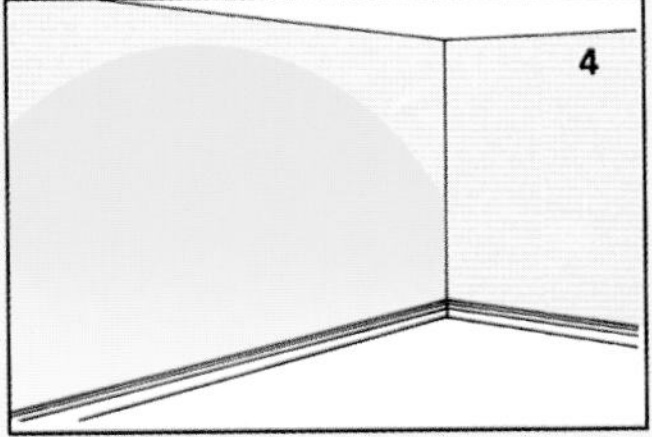

A row of wall washers of the same wattage creates a perfect wash (**1**), while decreasing wattages along the row give a graded wash (**2**). A row of downlighters can create a scalloped effect (**3**), while a single downlighter casts a parabola (**4**).

LIGHTING FOR THE KITCHEN, BATHROOM AND HALLWAY

The kitchen poses special lighting problems, mainly owing to the wide use of the fitted kitchen. In the old days most food preparation was done on a central table, so a central light was generally adequate. Now almost every task is carried out close to the perimeter of the room, making a central light – still the standard fitting in many homes – useless, and condemning the cook to working in his or her own shadow. What a modern kitchen really needs is lighting tailored to provide good illumination at each of the main work stations – the cooker (stove), the sink and the food-preparation area. There should also be a reasonable level of general background lighting, plus lighting to illuminate the insides of cupboards (closets). All of these requirements can only be achieved by separate, flexible and independently controllable light sources.

If the cooker has an extractor hood over it, containing a downlighter, this will illuminate the hob (burners) satisfactorily. Otherwise the aim should be to provide ceiling-mounted lights, positioned so that they shine directly on the hob without casting a shadow. The same is needed over the sink. Ideally each of these lights or sets of lights should have its own switch so that it can be turned on and off as required. For counter tops below wall-storage units, lighting is best provided by strip lights fixed beneath the wall units and shielded by baffles to prevent glare. Walk-in cupboards and open display units can be lit by recessed downlighters, and base units by small interior lights with automatic switches worked by opening the doors. If the kitchen is also used for eating, it is a good idea to provide a rise-and-fall fitting or recessed downlighters over the table so that the rest of the kitchen lighting can be turned off – not least to hide cooking debris during the meal.

The bathroom is much less demanding. The basic requirement is for a modest level of background lighting, provided by a close-mounted central light or some recessed fittings. If the washbasin area is used for shaving, add a wall strip (fluorescent) light over the basin to provide good, glare-free illumination there. Do not install a fluorescent light if this area is to be used for applying make-up, however, as even the best types of this lighting give a slightly inaccurate rendering of some colours. There may also be a need for a splashproof recessed light fitting in a shower cubicle.

LEFT The kitchen is difficult to light because most tasks take place around the perimeter of the room. Lights positioned above the counter tops are the perfect solution.

LEFT In the bathroom, enclosed fittings are a must for safety reasons. A central fitting with an opaque diffuser will cast a soft overall light.

ABOVE The hallway and stairwell need good illumination for safety reasons. Here, recessed downlighters illuminate every tread of the staircase and highlight the hall's features.

When you are thinking about the lighting in the different areas of your home, the landing, hallway and stairwell should not be forgotten. The latter is one area of the home in which good, bright lighting is essential; the safety aspect is more important than mood here, ensuring that all parts of the staircase are clearly lit without glare. For the best effect, fittings should be positioned so that the treads of the stairs are well-lit but the risers are in shadow. Make sure that any suspended fittings do not impede passage up and down the staircase, and check that any recessed fittings are readily accessible – it is irritating to have to get a ladder out to reach a high-level fitting whenever a lightbulb happens to fail.

LEFT Wall-mounted downlighters can also be used to light a staircase, casting the risers into shadow and making the treads clearly visible.

CHOOSING PAINTS, VARNISHES AND STAINS

Paint works by forming a film on the surface to which it is applied. This film has to do three things: it must hide the surface underneath; it must protect it; and it must stay put. All paint has three main ingredients: pigment, binder and carrier. The pigment gives the film its colour and hiding power. The binder binds the pigment particles together into a continuous film as the paint dries, and also bonds the film to the surface beneath. The third ingredient, the carrier, makes the paint flow smoothly as it is applied to the surface, and evaporates as the paint dries.

By adjusting the ratio of pigment to binder, paint manufacturers can produce paints that dry to a flat matt finish; to a silky sheen (eggshell); or to a high gloss. The choice depends on personal preference, tempered by the condition of the surface: high-gloss finishes highlight any imperfections, while matt finishes disguise them.

Paint types

Water-based paint has the pigment and binder suspended in water as tiny droplets. It is usually called emulsion (latex) paint. Solvent-based alkyd (oil or oil-based) paint has pigment and binder dissolved in a petroleum-based solvent, and takes longer to dry than water-based paint. Because of growing awareness of the risks of inhaling solvents, the use of this paint is declining in popularity and is already legally restricted in some countries.

Paint also contains a range of other additives to improve its performance. The most notable is one that makes the paint thixotropic or non-drip, allowing more paint to be loaded on to the brush and a thicker paint film to be applied; one coat of this is often sufficient.

Paint systems

A single coat of paint is too thin to form a durable paint film. To provide adequate cover and performance there must be a paint system consisting of several coats. What these are depends on the type of paint used, and on the surface being painted.

The first coat is a sealer, which is used where necessary to seal the natural resin in wood, or to prevent the paint from soaking into a porous surface. The second coat is a primer; this provides a good key to which the paint film can stick. On metal surfaces, this also stops the metal corroding or oxidizing. A primer can, in addition, act as a sealer. The third coat is the undercoat, which builds up the film to form a flexible, non-absorbent base of uniform colour close to that of the fourth and final layer, the top coat, which gives the actual finish and colour.

On walls, the system consists simply of two or three coats of the same paint, unless there is a need for a sealer or primer to cure a fault such as high alkalinity or excessive porosity. The first coat is a mist coat of thinned paint.

ABOVE Blues and greys are cool, fresh colours that particularly suit a well-lit children's room. The brightly painted ladder provides the perfect contrast. Painted surfaces need to withstand some rough treatment in a location such as this.

BELOW The yellow water-based paint chosen for the walls of this kitchen creates a basically warm colour scheme that is off-set by the gloss paint in cool colours selected for the woodwork. Solvent-based (oil) paint is ideal for surfaces which need washing down regularly.

A primer is also used if walls are being painted with solvent-based paints.

On woodwork, the first step is to apply a liquid called knotting (shellac) to any knots to prevent resin from bleeding through the paint film. Then comes a wood primer, followed by an undercoat and then the top coat. To speed up the painting process, paint manufacturers have now perfected combined primer/undercoats, and self-undercoating gloss paint which just needs a primer.

On metal, a primer is generally needed. A zinc-phosphate primer is used for iron or steel, and there are special primers for aluminium. This is then followed by an undercoat and top coat, as for wood. Copper, brass and lead can be painted directly, as long as they are thoroughly de-greased with white spirit (paint thinner).

Varnishes and wood stains

Varnish is basically paint without the pigment. Most types of varnish contain polyurethane resins and are solvent-based (like oil paint), although water-based acrylic varnishes are becoming more popular. Varnishes are available with a satin/silk or a high-gloss finish, either clear or with the addition of small amounts of colour.

Varnish is its own primer and undercoat, although it is best to thin the first coat with about 10 per cent white spirit (paint thinner) for solvent-based types, or water for acrylic types, and to apply it with a lint-free cloth rather than a brush so that you can rub it well into the wood grain. When this first coat has dried, 'key' or roughen it by rubbing very lightly with fine-grade sandpaper, dust it off, and then apply a second, full-strength coat. For surfaces likely to receive a lot of wear, it is advisable to key the second coat as before and apply an additional coat.

Wood stain, unlike both paint and varnish, is designed to soak into wood. It may subsequently be sealed with clear varnish to improve the finish and make the surface more durable. Wood stain is available in water-based or solvent-based types in a wide range of colours and wood shades. Different colours can also be blended to obtain intermediate shades, and the stain can be thinned with water or white spirit as appropriate to give a paler effect.

Wood stain can be applied with a brush, a paint pad or a lint-free cloth. Quick work is needed to blend wet edges together, and to avoid overlaps which will leave darker patches as the stain dries. A water-based stain will raise fibres on the surface of the wood, which will spoil the evenness of the colour. The solution is to sand the surface perfectly smooth first and then to dampen it with a wet cloth. This will raise the surface fibres. When the wood is dry, sand off the fibres with fine-grade sandpaper, ready to receive the stain.

LEFT Coloured varnishes help to enhance the colour of the wood grain without obliterating it completely, as paint will do.

BELOW Varnish can be used to enhance the beauty of wood throughout the home, from floors and fire surrounds to storage units and other items of furniture.

CLEANING PAINTING EQUIPMENT

Wash tools and equipment in soapy water if using a water-based paint, and with white spirit (paint thinner) or a proprietary brush cleaner for solvent-based (oil) paint. Soak hardened paint in paint remover overnight, then wash out with hot, soapy water.

PREPARING SURFACES FOR PAINTING

Modern paints have excellent adhesion and covering power, but to get the best performance from them you must prepare the surface thoroughly. To prepare painted woodwork, use fine-grade sandpaper wrapped around a sanding block to remove 'nibs' from the paint surface and to key the paint film ready for re-painting. Wash the surface using a solution of strong household detergent or sugar soap (all-purpose cleaner). Rinse very thoroughly and allow the surface to dry completely.

Remove areas of flaking paint using a scraper or filling knife (putty knife), and then either touch in the bare area with more paint or fill it flush with the surrounding paint film by using fine filler (spackle). Sand this smooth when it has hardened. Use a clean cloth moistened with white spirit (paint thinner) to remove dust from recessed mouldings and other awkward corners.

If knots are showing through on painted woodwork, sand back to bare wood and apply knotting (shellac) to the knot, then prime and undercoat to bring the new paint film level with the surrounding paintwork. Sand between coats. Resinous knots may produce stains which can only be prevented by drying out the knots with a blowtorch.

Stripping paint

Every time a surface is re-painted, a little more thickness is added to the paint layer. This does not matter much on wall or ceiling surfaces, but on woodwork (and, to a lesser extent, on metalwork) this build-up of successive layers of paint can eventually lead to the clogging of detail on mouldings. More importantly, moving parts such as doors and windows start to bind and catch against their frames. If this happens, it is time to strip back to bare wood and build up a new paint system.

There are 2 methods of removing paint from wood and metal surfaces. The first is using heat, traditionally from a blowtorch but nowadays more often from an electric heat gun. The second is to use a chemical paint remover, which contains either dimethylene chloride or caustic soda. Heat works well on wood (although it can scorch the surface), but it is less successful on metal because the material conducts heat away as it is applied. Chemicals work well on all surfaces, but need handling with care; always follow the manufacturer's instructions to the letter.

Using a Heat Gun

1 Play the air stream from the heat gun over the surface to soften the paint film. Scrape it off with a flat scraper as it bubbles up, and deposit the hot scrapings in an old metal container.

2 Use a shavehook (triangular scraper) instead of a flat scraper to remove the paint from mouldings. Take care not to scorch the wood if you intend to varnish it afterwards.

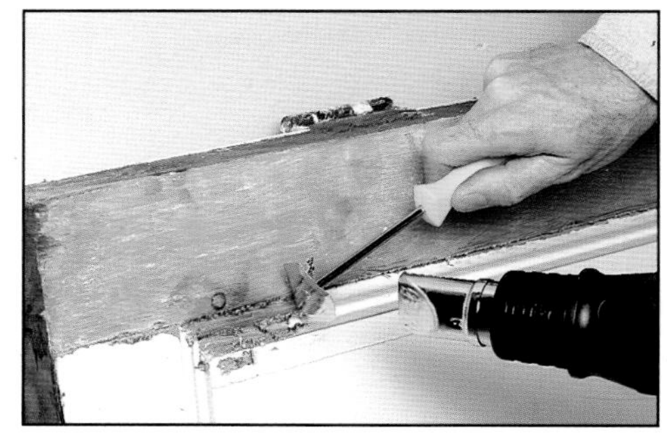

3 Remove any remnants of paint using wire wool soaked in white spirit (paint thinner), working along the grain. Use a hand vacuum cleaner to remove any remaining loose particles of paint.

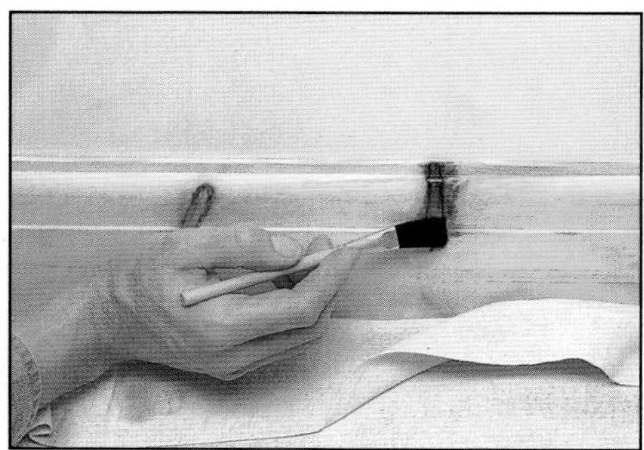

4 Sand the wood to remove any raised fibres, then wipe it over with a cloth moistened with white spirit. Seal the resin in any exposed knots by brushing on liquid knotting (shellac). Leave to dry.

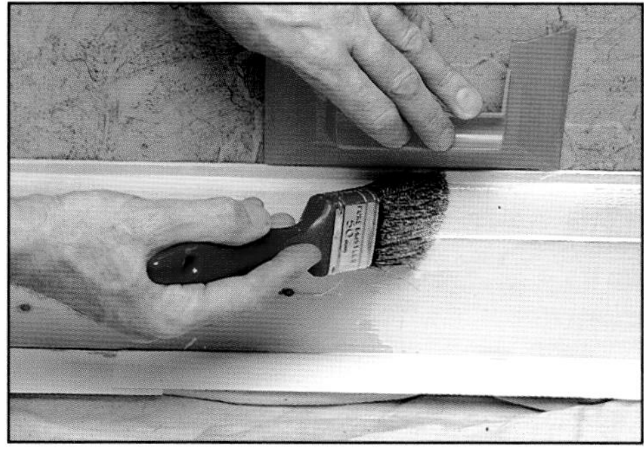

5 Apply a coat of either wood primer or a combined primer/undercoat to the stripped wood surface. This will provide optimum adhesion for the subsequent top coats, ensuring a really good finish.

Filling Defects in Wood

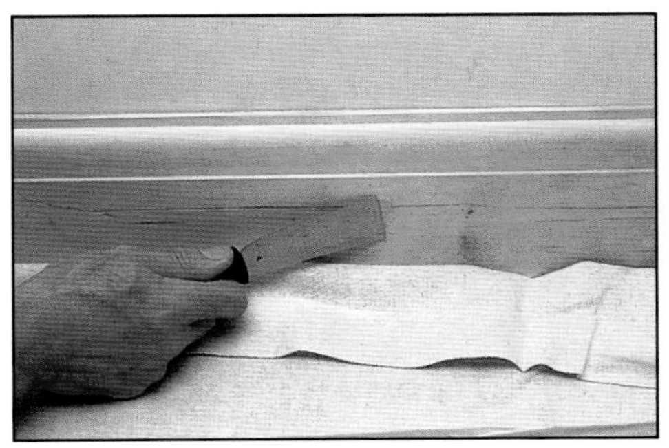

1 Fill splits and dents in wood using filler (spackle) on surfaces that are already painted, and tinted wood stopper (patcher) on new or stripped wood that you intend to finish with a coat of varnish.

2 Use the corner of a filling knife (putty knife), or a finger, to work the filler into recesses and other awkward-to-reach places. Smooth off the excess filler before it dries and hardens.

3 When the filler or wood stopper has hardened completely, use a piece of fine-grade sandpaper wrapped around a sanding block to sand down the repair until it is flush with the rest of the wood.

Using Liquid Remover

1 Wear rubber gloves and old clothing. Decant the liquid into a polythene (polyethylene) container or an old can, then brush it on to the surface to be stripped. Leave it until the paint bubbles.

2 Use a flat scraper or shavehook (triangular scraper) as appropriate to remove the softened paint. Deposit the scrapings safely in an old container.

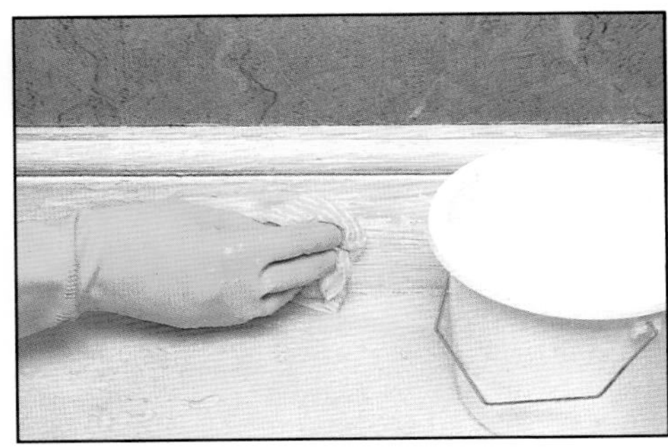

3 Neutralize the stripper by washing down the surface with water or white spirit (paint thinner), as recommended by the manufacturer. Leave it to dry.

Using Paste Remover

1 Paste remover is especially good for removing paint from intricate mouldings because it dries very slowly. Apply the paste liberally to the surface.

2 Give the paste plenty of time to work, especially on thick paint layers, then scrape it off. Wash down the surface with plenty of water to neutralize the chemical.

Home-made Paste Remover

Add caustic soda to water until no more will dissolve. Thicken to a paste with oatmeal and use as for proprietary paste remover. Be particularly careful when using this corrosive solution. If it splashes on the skin, rinse at once with plenty of cold water.

USING BRUSHES, ROLLERS AND PAINT PADS

The paintbrush is the most versatile and widely used tool for applying paint. Choose the brush size to match the surface that you are painting. For example, for painting glazing bars (muntins) on windows or narrow mouldings on a door, use a slim brush – or perhaps a cutting-in (sash) brush if you are painting up to an unpainted surface, such as glass, where a neat edge is needed. For expansive, flat areas, select a larger brush for quick coverage.

Get rid of any loose bristles in a new brush by flicking it vigorously across the palm of your hand before using it. Wash previously used brushes that have been stored unwrapped to remove any dust or other debris from the bristles, and leave them to dry out before using them to apply a solvent-based paint.

Paint rollers are generally used to apply water-based (latex) paints to large, flat areas such as walls and ceilings. Choose a sleeve with a short pile for painting plaster, a medium pile for painting embossed or textured wall coverings, or a long pile for sculpted surfaces such as those created with textured finishes (texture paints). Rollers can also be used to apply solvent-based (oil) paint to flat surfaces such as flush doors, but tend to leave a distinctive 'orange-peel' texture rather than the smooth finish left by a brush.

There are some drawbacks with paint rollers: they cannot paint right up to internal corners or wall/ceiling angles, so these need to be painted first with a brush or pad. They can also splash if 'driven' too fast, and the sleeves take a good deal of time and effort to clean thoroughly, especially if they have been used for a long period and there is dried paint in the pile.

Paint pads tend to apply less paint per coat than either a brush or a roller, so an additional coat may be needed in some circumstances, but they make it easy to apply paint smoothly and evenly with no risk of brushmarks.

Preparing the Paint

1 Wipe the lid to remove any dust, then prise it off with a wide lever such as the back of a table knife to avoid damage to the lip. Decant some paint into a paint kettle or small bucket. This will be easier to handle than a full container.

2 Remove any paint skin from partly used containers. Strain the paint into the paint kettle through a piece of old stocking or tights (pantyhose), or a piece of muslin (cheesecloth), to filter out any dirt.

Using a Brush

1 Tie a length of string or wire across the mouth of the paint kettle. To load the brush, dip it into the paint, but only to about one-third of the bristle depth. An overloaded brush will cause drips, and paint will run down the handle. Use the string or wire to scrape excess paint from the bristles.

2 Apply the paint to the wood in long, sweeping strokes, along the grain, until the brush begins to run dry. Load up the brush with more paint and apply it to the next area. Blend the paint using short, light strokes, again along the grain direction, so that no join is visible.

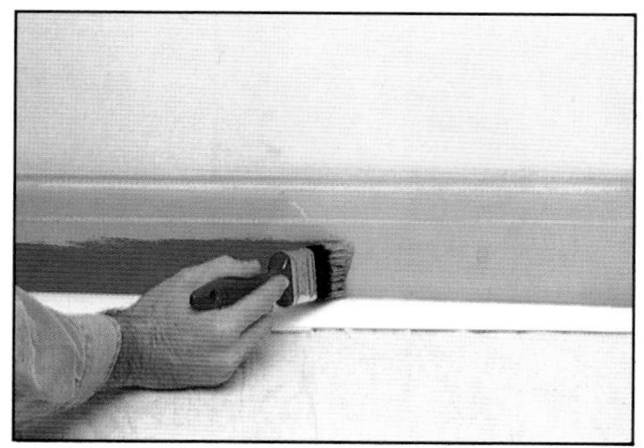

3 Repeat this process while working your way across the whole area to be painted, always blending the edges of adjacent areas together using light brushstrokes.

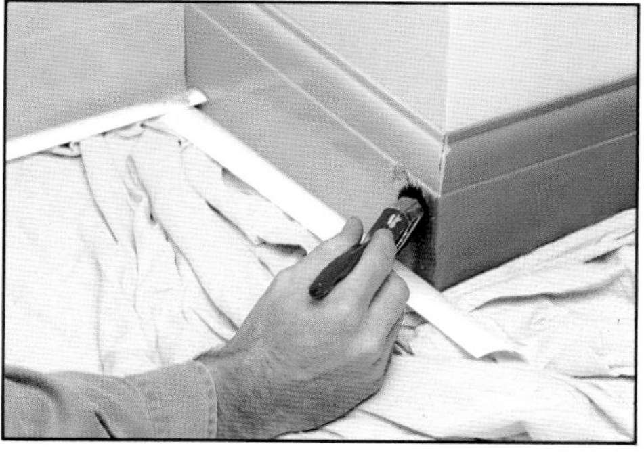

4 At edges and external corners, let the brush run off the edge to avoid a build-up of paint on the corner. Repeat the process for the opposite edge.

Using a Roller

1 Decant some paint (previously strained if from an old can) into the roller tray until the paint level just laps up to the sloping section. Slide a sleeve on to the roller.

2 Brush a band of paint about 5 cm/2 in wide into internal corners and wall/ceiling angles, around doors and windows, and above skirtings (baseboards).

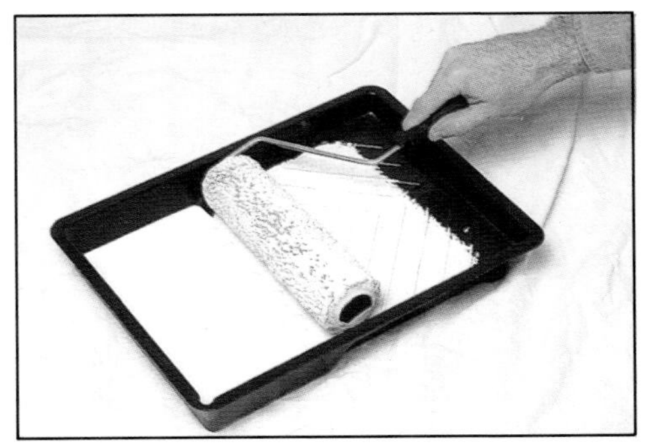

3 Load the roller sleeve with paint by running it down the sloping section into the paint, then roll it up and down the slope to remove the excess.

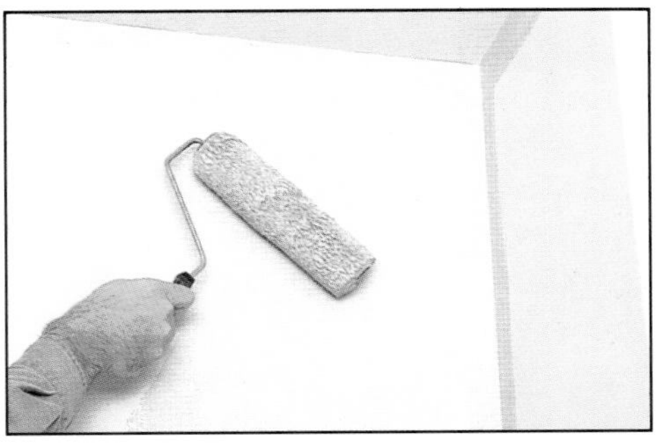

4 Start applying the paint in a series of overlapping diagonal strokes to ensure complete coverage of the surface. Continue until the sleeve runs dry.

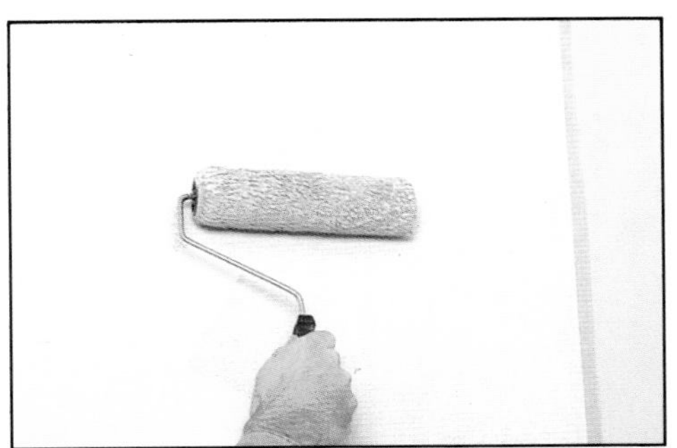

5 Re-load the sleeve and tackle the next section in the same way. Finish off by blending the areas together, working parallel to corners and edges.

Using Aerosol Paint

Aerosol paints and varnishes are ideal for hard-to-decorate surfaces such as wickerwork. Always follow the maker's instructions when using them.

Using a Paint Pad

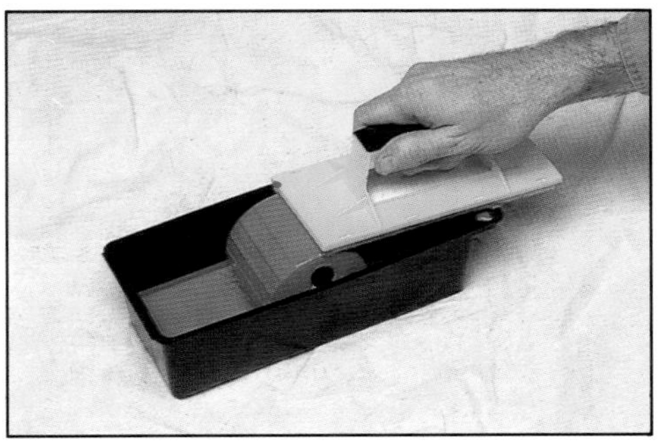

1 Pour some paint into the special applicator tray. Load the pad by running it backwards and forwards over the ridged loading roller.

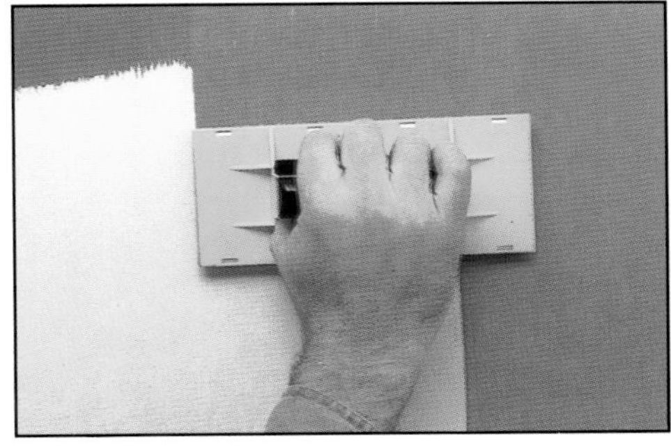

2 On walls, apply the paint in a series of overlapping parallel bands. Use a small pad or a special edging pad (see step 4) to paint right up to corners or angles.

3 Use smaller pads for painting narrow areas such as mouldings on doors or glazing bars (muntins) on windows, brushing out the paint along the direction of the grain.

4 Special edging pads are designed for painting right up to internal angles, and have small wheels which guide the pad along the adjacent surface as you work.

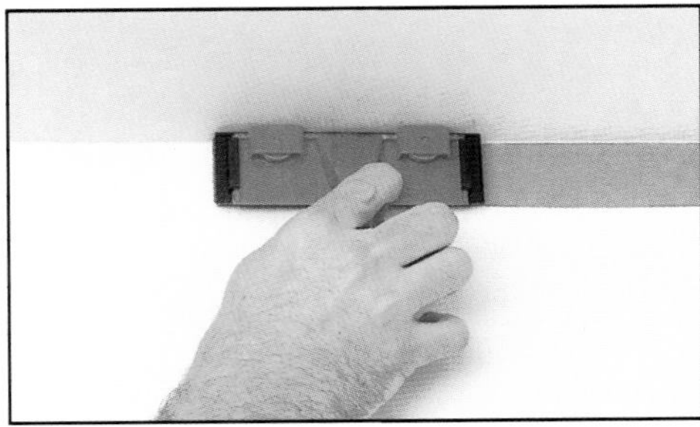

5 Some larger pads can be fitted to an extension pole to make it easier to paint ceilings and high walls. Make sure that the pad is attached securely.

SPECIAL PAINT EFFECTS

There is no need to stick to plain colour on painted walls, as there is a wide range of special paint effects that will enliven their looks. Some of these effects are purely decorative in their own right, while others imitate the appearance of different materials. All can be created with the use of inexpensive tools and materials, and practice and patience will bring about highly attractive results.

In sponging, rag-rolling and stippling, simple techniques are used to apply a second colour over another base colour so that the latter still shows through, providing a pleasing two-colour effect. For marbling, paint is cleverly used to copy the appearance of real marble.

For either finish it is essential to prepare the surface of the wall or woodwork thoroughly first (see the chart below right).

Glazes

Most special effects are applied as a tinted glaze that is semi-transparent and allows the underlying base colour to show through. Water-based glazes are made from water-based (latex) paint diluted with water or a proprietary emulsion glaze until the required level of translucency has been achieved. Use coloured paints or tint white paint to the required shade with artist's acrylics. Water-based glazes produce a thinner, more open, coat of colour and they dry extremely quickly, which means they are not suitable for the fairly complex technique of marbling.

Scumble is the main component of solvent-based (oil) glazes and is generally diluted with a mixture of 1 part linseed oil to 2 parts white spirit (paint thinner). However, the proportions can be varied: a higher proportion of scumble will increase the definition of the effect and will retard the drying time; more linseed oil produces a smoother texture; white spirit thins the glaze and speeds up the drying time. Once you have mixed the glaze, pour off a small quantity and add the colour to this, using either eggshell paint or artist's oils. When you have mixed the correct colour, gradually add this to the main quantity of glaze until the required level of transparency is achieved. Solvent-based glazes have a rich, hardwearing finish and the slower drying times are particularly suited to some special effects.

When working over large areas – more than about 2 sq m/22 sq ft – 2 people will be needed to achieve the best finish: one to apply the glaze and the other to work it. This is the only way to maintain a wet edge and therefore to avoid noticeable joins between one area of colour and the next, for a really professional finish.

Stencilling

This is slightly different from the other techniques, as the stencil produces a clearly defined shape on the surface. It is very simple to do, and you can create designs in more than one colour – including wonderful 3-dimensional effects – by using different stencils. Ready-cut stencils are available in a range of designs, but it is easy to create designs of your own using special waxed paper (see opposite).

PREPARING SURFACES

The method of preparation will vary depending on whether you are using water-based (latex) paints or solvent-based (oil) paints for the final effect. Taking care and spending a little time at this early stage will help to ensure a satisfying end result.

Once the preparation is complete, apply your chosen base colour. Use eggshell for a good opaque and non-porous surface if you are using either a water- or a solvent-based finish and, when dry, gently rub it down with fine-grade sandpaper.

Surface	Water-based effect	Solvent-based effect
Bare plaster	Prime with diluted water-based paint	Prime with proprietary primer or PVA adhesive (white glue)
	Apply 1–2 water-based undercoats	Apply 1–2 solvent-based undercoats
Painted plaster	Wash down, repair defects and sand solvent-based finishes	Wash down, repair defects and sand solvent-based finishes
	Apply 1–2 water-based undercoats	Apply 1–2 solvent-based undercoats
Hardboard	Prime with diluted water-based paint	Prime with proprietary primer
	Apply 1–2 water-based undercoats	Apply 1–2 solvent-based undercoats
Bare wood	Apply knotting (shellac) to knots	Apply knotting (shellac) to knots
	Prime with diluted water-based paint	Apply proprietary primer
	Apply 1–2 water-based undercoats	Apply 1–2 solvent-based undercoats
Painted wood	As for Painted plaster	As for Painted plaster
Varnished wood	Strip and prepare as for Bare wood	Strip and prepare as for Bare wood

CUTTING A STENCIL

To cut a stencil, you will need tracing paper, some special waxed paper for stencils (available from art stores), a pencil, a pin and a scalpel or sharp utility knife. Trace or draw the pattern, and then enlarge or reduce it on a photocopier if necessary. Tape the trace to the stencil paper and prick through it to mark the design outline on the paper. Join up the marks in pencil. Alternatively, transfer the trace on to the stencil using carbon paper. Cut out the design carefully, leaving ties to bridge the separate areas of the design. Allow a large margin above and below the design so that the stencil is sufficiently strong. Reinforce any accidental cuts with adhesive tape.

1 Affix the stencil to the surface with masking tape, aligning it with a true horizontal pencil guideline. Dip the stencilling brush in the paint and dab off the excess on a paper towel. Use a pouncing action to apply the paint, to minimize the risk of colour seeping under the stencil.

2 When the paint is touch-dry, release the stencil, wipe off the wet paint and re-position it further along the wall to create the next section of the pattern.

Sponging

This technique involves dabbing irregular patches of paint on to the base coat. You can apply two or more different sponged colours in this way. You must use a natural marine sponge to create this decorative effect; man-made sponges do not work. Soak the sponge in water first until it swells up to its full size, and then wring it out ready to start applying the paint.

1 After testing the effect on an offcut of board, dip the sponge in the paint and apply light pressure to leave overlapping splodges of colour.

2 Allow the first application to dry, then go over the surface again and add more colour if necessary to deepen the contrast with the base colour.

3 If you will be applying a different second colour, allow the first colour to dry and then use the same technique to apply the new colour over the top of it.

SPECIAL PAINT EFFECTS (continued)

Stippling

For an attractive mottled appearance, try stippling; apart from being used as a decorative finish in its own right it can also be used to obliterate brushmarks in the base coat beneath other broken-colour effects. The only item of specialist equipment that you will need to create this effect is a stippling brush.

1 Brush on the glaze over the base coat, applying a generous layer. Do not worry about leaving brushmarks; the stippling will obliterate them.

2 Hold the stippling brush with the bristle tips parallel with the surface, and simply hit the paint film. Clean paint from the brush regularly by wiping it with a dry cloth.

Rag-rolling

Another simple 2-colour effect, rag-rolling involves brushing a diluted second colour over the base coat and then using a rolled-up 'sausage' of cloth to remove some of the second colour before it starts to dry.

The technique works best with a base coat of eggshell paint and a top coat of eggshell paint diluted with white spirit (paint thinner). Use lint-free cotton or linen rags and change them frequently before they become soaked with paint.

1 Once the base coat is completely dry, lightly brush on the second diluted paint colour in bands across the surface. As you do this, aim to leave a random pattern of brushstrokes that allows the base colour to show through.

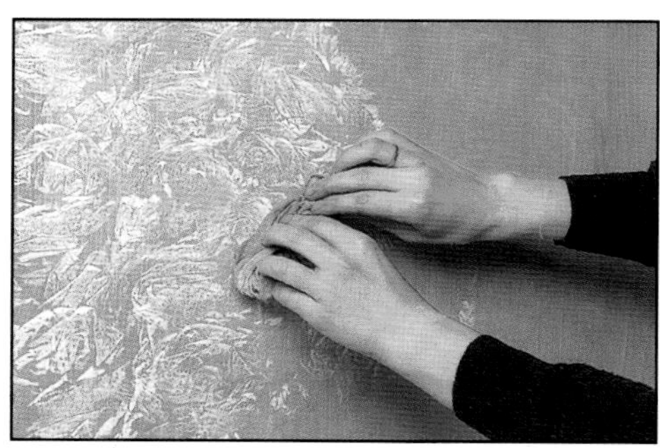

2 Roll the rag sausage across the surface in a continuous motion. Vary the direction for a random effect and touch in small areas by just dabbing with the cloth. Replace the rag at regular intervals.

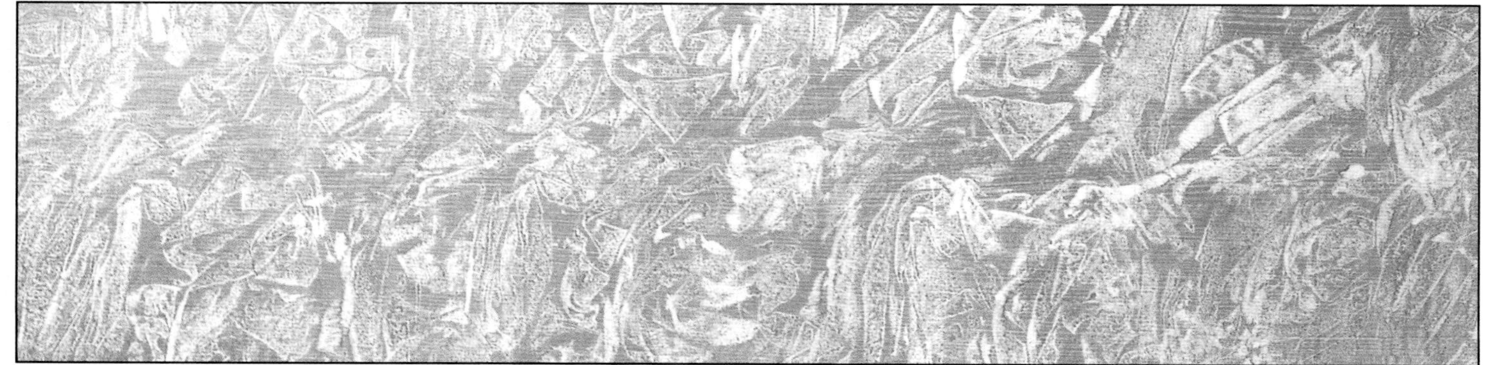

Marbling
As its name implies, marbling copies the appearance of marble. It is a relatively difficult technique to master, but the results can be quite spectacular. For a first attempt, choose a piece of real marble to copy. For best results, work with a solvent-based (oil) glaze, applied over an eggshell base coat. Add the veining details with artist's oils.

1 Either brush out the glaze or apply it with a pad of lint-free cloth. Only a relatively thin coat is needed.

2 Use a dusting brush (as here) or a special stippling brush to stipple the surface of the wet glaze. Add more colour to the glaze mixture, apply it selectively to some areas in order to create contrast and then stipple the glaze again.

3 Working on the wet glaze, draw in the main areas of veining with an artist's paintbrush and a mixture of glaze and artist's oils. Use different weights of line to create a natural-looking effect.

4 Use the softening brush again to soften the outlines of the veining and to blend it into the background. Wipe the brush regularly to avoid smudges.

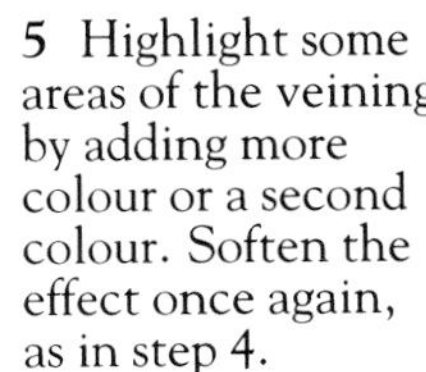
5 Highlight some areas of the veining by adding more colour or a second colour. Soften the effect once again, as in step 4.

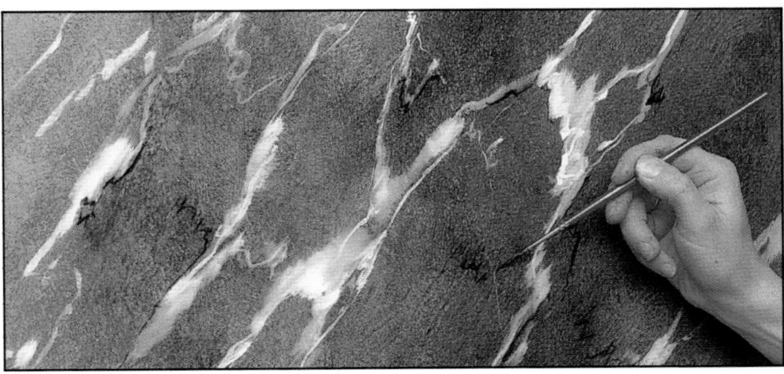

VARNISHING SPECIAL PAINT EFFECTS

Some special paint effects, especially graining and marbling, should be sealed with a coat of clear varnish for protection once the effect has dried completely. Use satin varnish rather than gloss unless you require a particularly polished effect – such as on a wooden trim or similar surface, for example. When this has dried, burnish the surface with a soft cloth and add a little wax polish to create a sheen, if you wish.

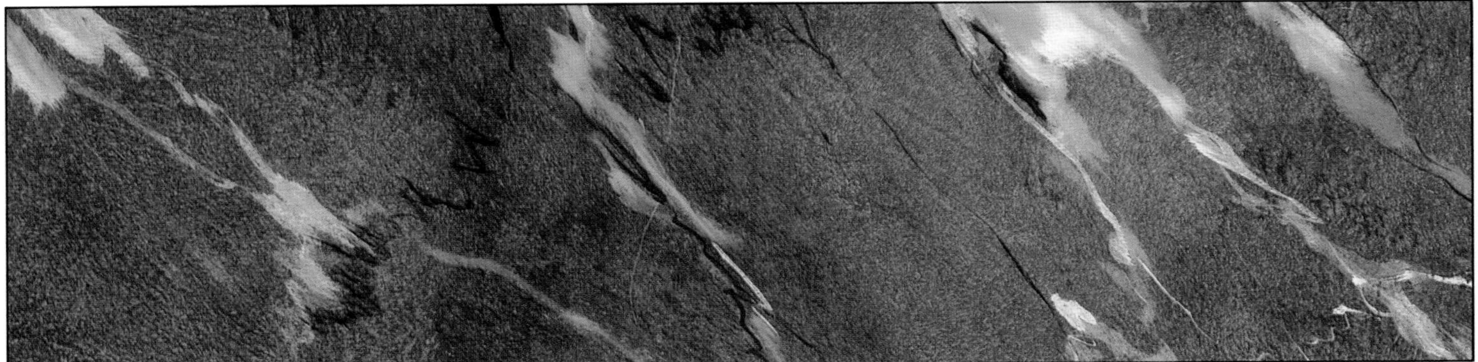

PAINTING DOORS AND WINDOWS

The main problem with painting doors – or indeed any woodwork with a large surface area – involves keeping what professional decorators call a 'wet edge'. Obviously the door has to be painted bit by bit, and, if the edge of one area begins to dry before this is joined up to the next area, the join will show when the paint dries completely.

The secret of success is to work in an ordered sequence, as shown in these illustrations of flush and panelled doors, and to complete the painting job in one continuous operation, working as fast as is reasonably possible.

Windows are more difficult to paint than doors because they contain so many different surfaces, especially small-paned types criss-crossed with slim glazing bars (muntins). There is also the additional problem of paint straying on to the glass. The ideal is a neat paint line that covers the bedding putty and extends on to the glass surface by about 3 mm/⅛ in to seal the joint and prevent condensation from running down between putty and glass.

Remove the window hardware before you start painting. On casement windows, tap a nail into the bottom edge of the casement and into the lower frame rebate and then link them with stiff wire to stop the casement from swinging about.

For the best results, remove sash windows from their frames before painting. Modern spring-mounted windows are easy to release from their frames. With older cord-operated types, remove the staff beads (window stops) first to free the sashes. Although quite a major task, take the opportunity to renew the sash cords (pulley ropes). This makes it possible to cut the cords to free the window.

PAINTING A PANELLED DOOR

1 Tackle a panelled door by painting the mouldings (1) around the recessed panels first. Take care not to let paint build up in the corners or to stray on to the faces of the cross-rails at this stage. Next, paint the recessed panels (2).

2 Paint the horizontal cross-rails (3), brushing lightly inwards towards the painted panel mouldings to leave a sharp paint edge. Feather out the paint thinly where it runs on to the vertical stiles at each end of the rails.

3 Finish the door by painting the vertical centre rail (4) and the outer stiles (5), again brushing inwards towards the panel mouldings. Where the rail abuts the cross-rails, finish with light brushstrokes parallel to the cross-rails.

VARNISHING WOOD

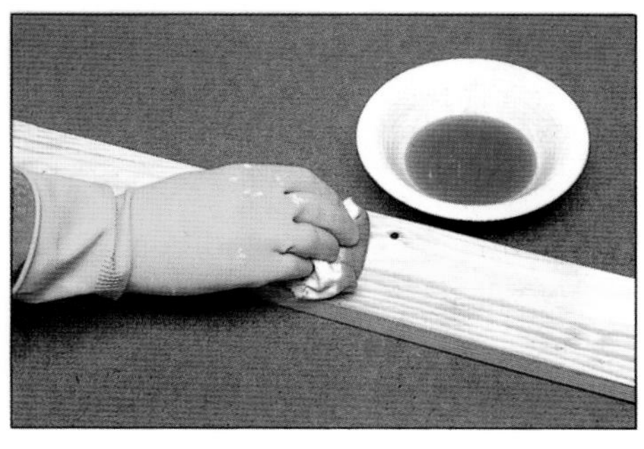

1 On bare wood, use a clean lint-free cloth to wipe the first coat on to the wood, working along the grain direction. This coat acts as a primer/sealer. When it is dry, sand it lightly and then wipe off the dust.

2 Brush on the second and subsequent coats of varnish, applying them along the grain and linking up adjacent areas using light brushstrokes.

USING STAIN

Test the stain on an offcut of the same wood, or in an inconspicuous area. If necessary, dilute it. Use a clean lint-free cloth to apply stain to bare wood. If the result is too pale, apply further coats when the first is dry. Avoid overlapping parallel bands of stain; the overlap will show up as a darker area when the stain dries.

Painting a Flush Door

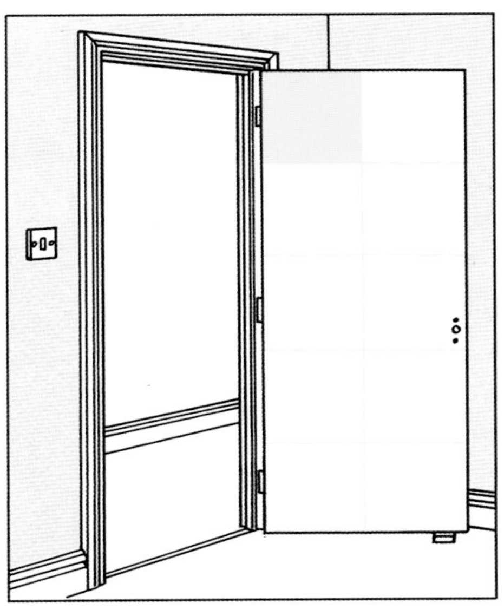

1 Remove the door furniture and wedge open the door. Divide it up into 8 or 10 imaginary squares, and start at the top by filling in the first square. Brush the paint out towards the door edges so that it does not build up on external angles. Paint the next block at the top of the door. Blend the 2 areas with horizontal brushstrokes, then with light, vertical laying-off strokes.

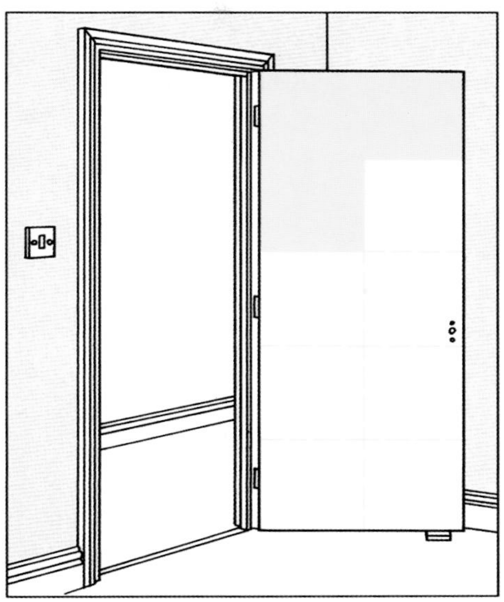

2 Continue to work down the door surface block by block, blending the wet edges of adjacent blocks together as you paint them. Always aim to complete a flush door in 1 session to prevent the joints between blocks showing up as hard lines. Replace the door furniture when the paint is touch-dry.

Painting a Casement Window

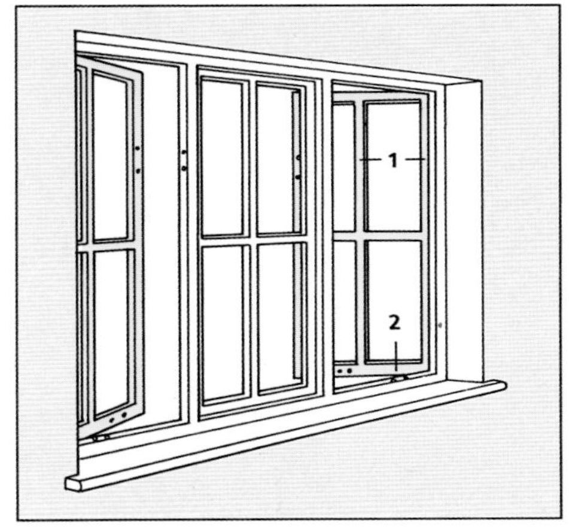

1 Remove the window furniture from the opening casement and wedge the window open while you work. Tackle the glazing bars (muntins) and edge mouldings first (**1**), then the face of the surrounding casement frame (**2**), and finally the hinged edge of the casement. Paint the other edges from outside the house.

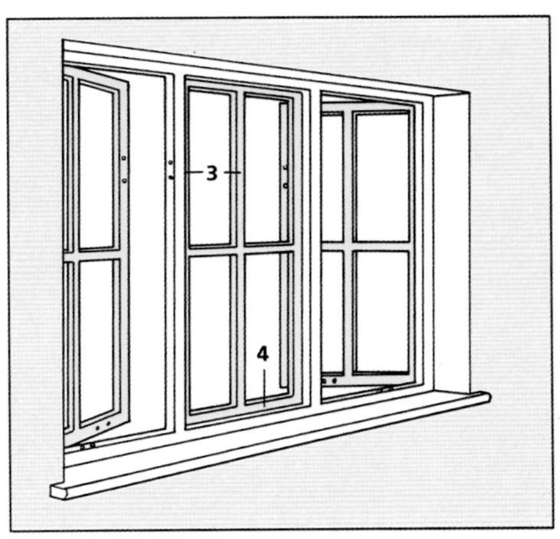

2 Move on to paint the glazing bars and edge mouldings (**3**) of the fixed casement. Use masking tape or a paint shield to ensure neat, straight edges here and on the opening casement; the paint should overlap the glass by about 3 mm (⅛ in). Paint the face of the surrounding casement frame (**4**).

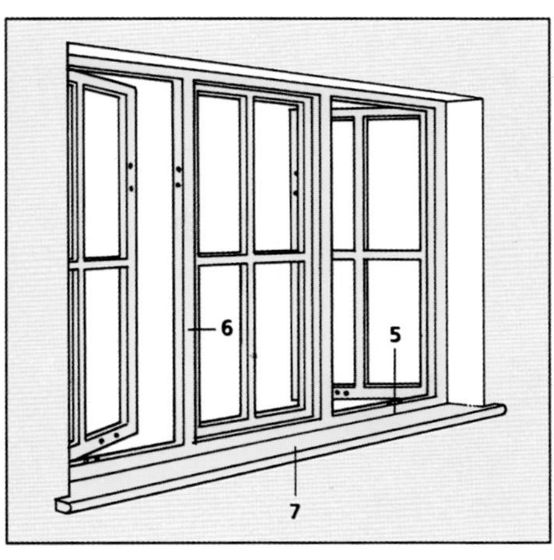

3 Paint the outer frame (**5**), then the centre-frame member between the opening and fixed casements (**6**). Complete the job by painting the window sill (**7**), followed by the rebate into which the opening casement closes.

Painting around Glass

1 Stick masking tape to the glass with its edge 3 mm/⅛ in from the wood. Paint the surrounding wood, removing the tape when the paint is touch-dry.

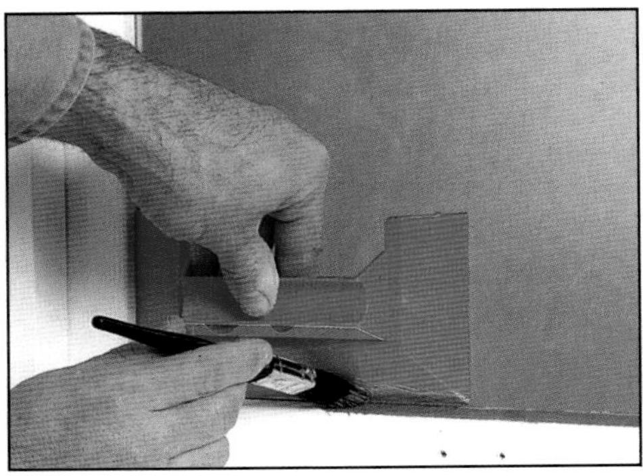

2 Alternatively, hold a small paint shield against the edge of the glazing bar (muntin) or the surrounding moulding while you paint. Wipe the shield regularly to prevent smears.

CHOOSING WALL COVERINGS

Wall coverings fall into 2 basic groups: those with a printed design or a surface material that is decorative in its own right, and those with a surface texture or embossing that is designed to be painted over once the coverings have been hung on the wall.

Printed wallpaper is exactly what its name implies – paper with a coloured design printed on it. It may also be embossed or have a distinctive surface texture. Cheaper types may be awkward to hang, tearing easily or stretching so as to make accurate pattern-matching difficult. The strongest printed wallpapers are called duplex papers, and are made by bonding 2 layers of paper together during the manufacturing process. Most printed papers can be wiped with a damp cloth if they become stained. All are easy to strip, making them a good choice if you like to re-decorate regularly.

Washable wallpaper is a printed wallpaper which has a thin, clear, plastic coating applied over the design during manufacture to render it water- and stain-resistant. As with printed types, the surface may be embossed or textured. Washable wallpapers are also widely available in ready-pasted form. The plastic surface will withstand gentle washing and sponging with a mild detergent, but not prolonged scrubbing. Choose washable wallpapers for rooms in which they will be subject to moderate wear, or for hot, steamy conditions such as those found in the kitchen and bathroom. The main drawback of these papers is that they are difficult to remove.

Vinyl wall coverings consist of a plastic film on to which the design is printed, laminated to a paper backing. Again, the surface may also be textured or embossed, or may have a metallic appearance – the so-called vinyl foils. The result is a wall covering that is much tougher than a washable type; it can be scrubbed to remove stains and

ABOVE Contrasting wall coverings can help to change the proportions of a room. Here a border at picture-rail level provides a natural break, and the darker wall covering above it helps to lower the ceiling, emphasizing the country-style décor.

LEFT In a bathroom, a vinyl wall covering resists steam and splashes well and is easy to wipe clean. Foamed types offer excellent imitations of materials such as ceramic tiles.

marks, although care must be taken not to lift the seams by oversoaking the surface. Vinyl wall coverings are widely available in ready-pasted form, and are extremely easy to strip as the plastic layer can be peeled off dry, leaving the paper backing behind on the wall. This backing can then be wetted and removed easily.

Tougher still are the foamed-vinyl wall coverings, which have a surface layer aerated with tiny bubbles to produce a slightly cushioned feel. The surface may be heavily textured or embossed to imitate materials such as ceramic tiles and wood grains, and is warm to the touch, making it a good choice for any rooms that are prone to mild condensation.

Flock wall coverings are either printed papers or vinyls on which parts of the design have a raised pile – of fine wool or silk fibres on paper types and of synthetic fibres on vinyls – that closely resembles velvet. The paper types are quite delicate and must be hung with care, but vinyl flocks are extremely tough and hardwearing.

Yet another printed wall covering is made from foamed polythene (polyethylene) with no paper backing. This is hung by pasting the wall and then brushing the covering into position direct from the roll. The surface can be washed, but is relatively fragile and will not withstand repeated scuffing or knocks. The material can be simply dry-stripped from walls and ceilings, like the plastic surface layer of a vinyl wall covering.

An alternative to a printed surface design is a texture. This can be achieved with a paper-backed fabric wall covering. The most common of these is hessian (burlap), but other materials include silk, tweed, wool strands, grasscloth and linen, offering a range of softly tinted or boldly coloured wall finishes. With the exception of hessian, these types of wall coverings are comparatively expensive to buy. They can also be fairly difficult to hang and to remove for re-decorating, and so are really best used for decorating or highlighting small and relatively well-protected areas such as alcoves.

The other kind of textured wall covering is intended for overpainting. These materials are generally known as relief wall coverings or 'whites'. The cheapest is woodchip paper, also known as oatmeal or ingrain, which has small chips of wood sandwiched at random between a heavy backing paper and a thinner surface layer.

ABOVE A frieze with a 3-dimensional design is an unusual way of filling in above a picture rail. The embossed panels are butt-joined to form a continuous strip.

LEFT A low-relief wall covering is the ideal cover-up for a less-than-perfect wall surface, and is available in a wide range of random and regular designs.

Vinyls are also made as relief wall coverings, with a plain white aerated plastic surface layer that is moulded during manufacture into a range of random or repeating patterns.

Other relief wall coverings are embossed to produce a random or regular surface pattern. Those with a relatively low-relief design are generally two-layer duplex papers; those with more pronounced embossing are made from stronger paper containing cotton fibres rather than wood.

All the different types of relief wall coverings can be painted with either water-based (latex) or solvent-based (oil) paints after hanging. You will need the help of a steam wallpaper stripper to remove them.

There is an additional type of wall covering: lining (liner) paper. As its name suggests, this is a plain paper used for lining wall surfaces that are in poor condition, or that have uneven or zero porosity, before a decorative wall covering is hung. It comes in weights from 55 g per sq m/360 lb per sq yd up to 90 g per sq m/600 lb per sq yd, and in 2 grades, white and extra-white. The latter can also be used as an economy wall covering, and is hung in the usual way and then overpainted.

MEASURING UP AND PREPARING SURFACES

Measuring up

The first job is to estimate how many rolls of wall covering you will need to decorate the room. If you are using a material that comes in standard-sized rolls, measure the room dimensions and refer to the charts given here for the number of rolls needed to cover the walls and ceiling (these allow for a typical door and window area). If you are using a paper-backed fabric covering of a non-standard width, measure up each wall, and ask the supplier to estimate the quantity you will need; such materials are too expensive to waste. Wall coverings in the USA vary in width and length, but are usually available in rolls sized to cover a specified area, allowing for trimming.

Stripping old wall coverings

It is always best to strip all old coverings before hanging new ones. Even if the old material looks sound, hanging a newly pasted wall covering over it may cause it to lift from the wall, creating ugly bubbles that are impossible to disguise. This also applies to the backing paper that remains after dry-stripping a vinyl wall covering; there is no guarantee that it is bonded to the wall, so hanging another covering over it could give very poor results.

Once you have cleared the room and spread dust sheets (drop cloths) over the floor and any remaining furniture, the next step is to identify the type of wall covering to be removed. An ordinary printed paper will absorb water splashed on it immediately; other types will not. To distinguish a washable from a vinyl, pick and lift a corner and try to dry-strip the covering. The printed plastic layer of a vinyl wall covering will peel off, but the surface of a washable paper will not come off unless it is a duplex paper made in two layers. To strip a washable paper, score the plastic coating with a serrated scraper or toothed roller, then soak and scrape as for a printed wallpaper (see opposite), or use a steam stripper. With paper-backed fabric wall coverings, it is often possible to peel the fabric away from its paper backing; try this before turning to more complicated methods.

Preparing the surfaces

Once you have removed the previous wall and ceiling decorations, the next task is to prepare the surfaces so that they are as near-perfect as possible for successful paperhanging.

Put down plastic sheeting on the floor, and cover any light switches and socket outlets (receptacles) with masking tape. Wash down the bare wall and ceiling surfaces with strong household detergent or sugar soap (all-purpose cleaner), working from the bottom up on walls, and then rinse off with clean water, working this time from top to bottom on walls. Leave the surfaces to dry thoroughly.

ESTIMATING WALL COVERINGS (CEILINGS)

Distance around room m	ft	No. of rolls
10	33	2
12	40	2
14	46	3
16	52	4
18	59	5
20	66	5
22	72	7

ESTIMATING WALL COVERINGS (WALLS)

	Distance around room																	
Height	9 m 30 ft	10 m 33 ft	12 m 40 ft	13 m 42 ft	14 m 46 ft	15 m 50 ft	16 m 52 ft	17 m 56 ft	19 m 62 ft	20 m 66 ft	21 m 69 ft	22 m 72 ft	23 m 75 ft	25 m 82 ft	26 m 85 ft	27 m 88 ft	28 m 92 ft	30 m 98 ft
2.15–2.30 m / 7–7½ ft	4	5	5	6	6	7	7	8	8	9	9	10	10	11	12	12	13	13
2.30–2.45 m / 7½–8 ft	5	5	6	6	7	7	8	8	9	9	10	10	11	11	12	13	13	14
2.45–2.60 m / 8–8½ ft	5	5	6	7	7	8	9	9	10	10	11	12	12	13	14	14	15	15
2.60–2.75 m / 8½–9 ft	5	5	6	7	7	8	9	9	10	10	11	12	12	13	14	14	15	15
2.75–2.90 m / 9–9½ ft	6	6	7	7	8	9	9	10	10	11	12	12	13	14	14	15	15	16
2.90–3.05 m / 9½–10 ft	6	6	7	8	8	9	10	10	11	12	12	13	14	14	15	16	16	17
3.05–3.20 m / 10–10½ ft	6	7	8	8	9	10	10	11	12	13	13	14	15	16	16	17	18	19

Numbers are based on a standard roll size of 10.05 m/33 ft long and 52 cm/20½ in wide. The measurement around the room includes all windows and the doorway.

Next, repair any defects such as cracks, holes and other surface damage that may have been concealed by the previous decorations, or even caused by their removal. Finally, 'size' the walls and ceiling with a coat of diluted wallpaper paste to even out the porosity of the surfaces and improve the 'slip' of the pasted wall covering during hanging. Leave to dry.

CUTTING TO LENGTH

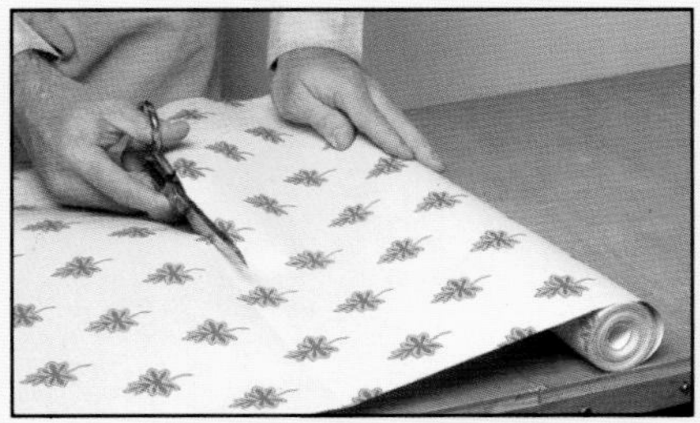

For quick calculations, mark the length of the pasting table at 30 cm/12 in intervals. Measure the length of wall covering that is needed for the drop, including trim allowances, mark this on the paper and then cut the first piece to length.

STRIPPING WALLPAPER

1 To strip a printed wallpaper, wet the surface with a sponge or a plant spray gun. Wait for the water to penetrate, and repeat the spraying if necessary.

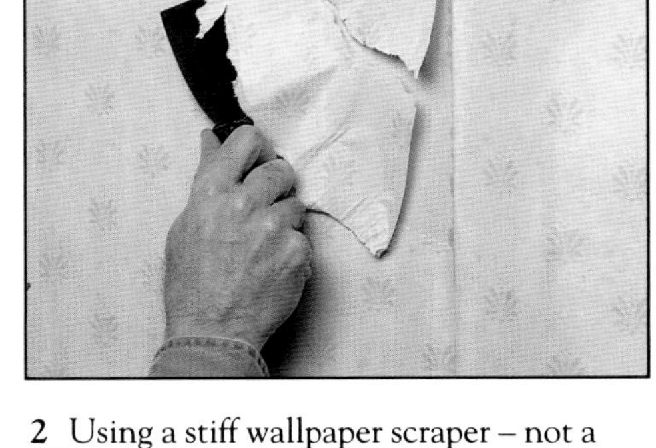

2 Using a stiff wallpaper scraper – not a filling knife (putty knife) – start scraping the old paper from the wall at a seam. Wet it again as you work if necessary.

3 Turn off the power before stripping around switches and other fittings, then loosen the faceplate screws to strip the wallpaper behind them.

4 After removing the bulk of the old wallpaper, go back over the wall surface and remove any remaining 'nibs' of paper with a sponge or spray gun and a scraper.

PASTING A WALL COVERING

1 Face the light to make it easy to spot any unpasted areas – they look dull, not shiny. Apply a generous band of paste down the centre of the length.

2 Align 1 edge of the wall covering with the edge of the table, then brush the paste out towards that edge from the centre band. Draw the length across to the other edge of the table, and apply paste out to that edge too. Check to make sure that there are no dry or thinly pasted areas.

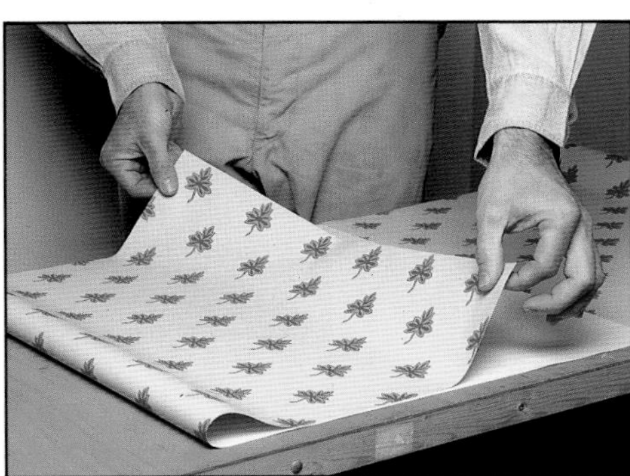

3 Continue pasting until you reach the end of the table. Lift the pasted end of the wall covering and fold it over on itself, pasted side to pasted side. Slide the paper along the table so that the folded section hangs down. Paste the rest of the length and fold the other end over on itself as before.

HANGING THE FIRST LENGTH

The first length of wall covering must be hung correctly if the decoration of the rest of the room is to go according to plan. The first thing to do, therefore, is to decide on exactly where to hang this. The usual starting point is close to the door, just less than the wall-covering's width away from the frame, so that the inevitable pattern discontinuity that will occur on returning to the starting point can be concealed on the short join above the door. If you are using a wall covering with a large design motif in a room which has a chimney breast (fireplace projection), it is preferable to start paperhanging on the chimney breast itself so that the design can be centred on it. When papering only part of a room, the starting point should be just less than the width of the wall covering from one corner of the room, to allow the edge of the covering to be trimmed accurately into the corner angle.

Next, use a roll of wall covering as a yardstick and mark off successive widths around the room walls with a pencil to check that there will not be any joins on external corners such as the sides of window reveals. If these occur, move the starting point along by about 5 cm/ 2 in and then re-check the positions of the joins all round.

Finally, mark a true vertical line on the wall at the chosen starting point, using a pencil and a plumb bob and line. Failure to do this could result in the pattern starting to run seriously out of alignment as you hang successive lengths, with disastrous results.

Other paperhanging techniques
As well as the traditional method of pasting the wall covering on a pasting table and then hanging it, you may sometimes also need to use 2 other techniques. The first is hanging ready-pasted wall coverings, which are growing in popularity, and the second is hanging speciality wall coverings.

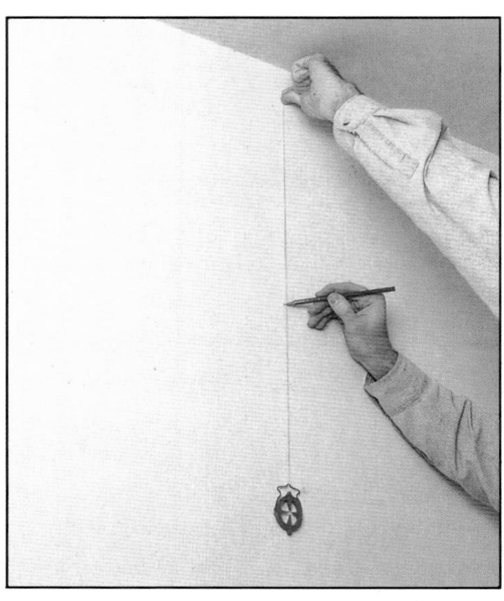

1 At your chosen starting point, use a plumb bob and line to mark a vertical line on the wall surface. Join up the pencil marks using a straightedge.

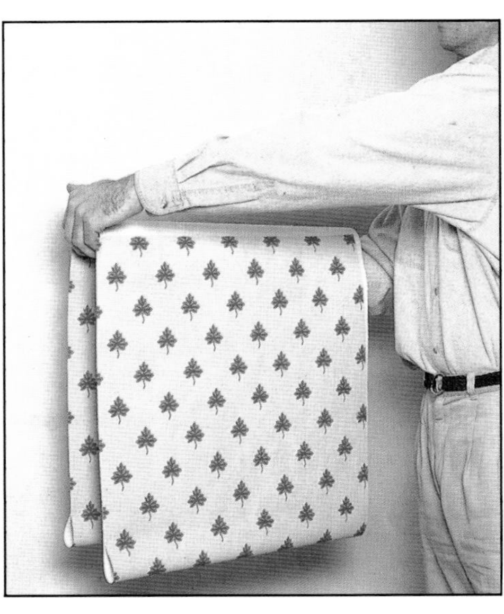

2 Fetch the first length of pasted wall covering, having left it to soak for the time recommended on the label. Carry it draped over your arm.

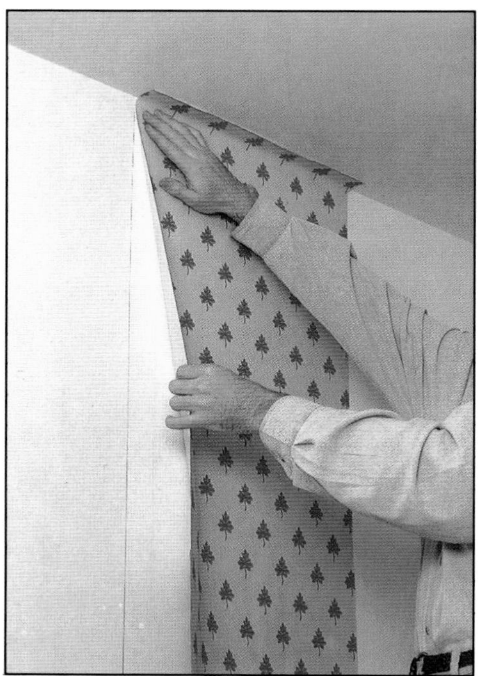

3 Unfold the upper flap and press the top edge of the length against the wall. Slide it across the wall until the edge lines up with your marked line. Use a paperhanging brush (or a sponge for washables and vinyls) to smooth the covering into place, working from the middle outwards.

4 Use a pencil or the curved back of paperhanging-scissors blades to mark the trimming line at ceiling level. Do the same at floor level.

5 Peel the end of the length away from the wall so that you can trim the excess using scissors. Brush the end back into place. Repeat at the bottom.

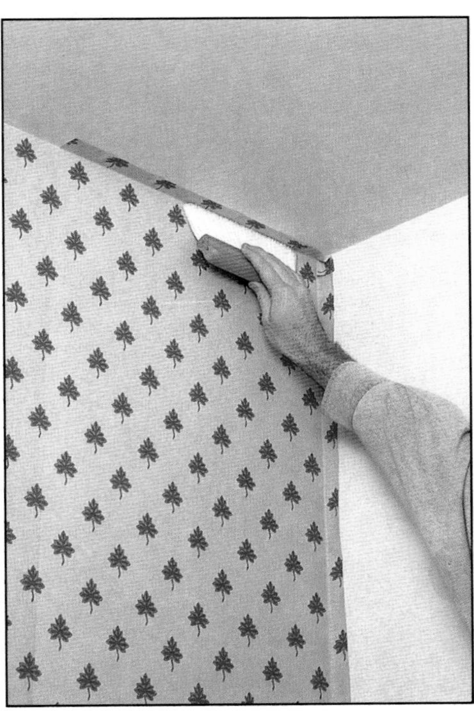

6 Hang the next drop with the lengths exactly edge to edge. Brush the wall covering into the wall/ceiling angle and into the internal angle.

7 On flat wall coverings, run a seam roller down the joins to ensure that they stick securely. Never use a seam roller on embossed or relief wall coverings, as this will ruin the pattern.

Hanging ready-pasted wall coverings could not be easier. The back of the wall covering – usually a washable or vinyl type – is coated during manufacture with an even layer of dried paste. To activate this, simply cut the length that you need, roll it up with the top of the length on the outside of the roll, and immerse it in water. Special soaking troughs are sold by most wall-covering suppliers, and are intended to be placed next to the skirting (baseboard) beneath the point at which the length is to be hung. Fill the trough with cold (not hot) water, immerse the length and then draw it upwards on to the wall so that all the excess water drains back into the soaking trough. Hang and trim the covering in the usual way.

Many speciality wall coverings are designed to be hung by pasting the wall itself, rather than the covering, which some people find easier. Some types of coverings also have untrimmed edges, which need to be cut after overlapping adjoining lengths, but this is simple to do.

Hanging a Ready-pasted Wall Covering

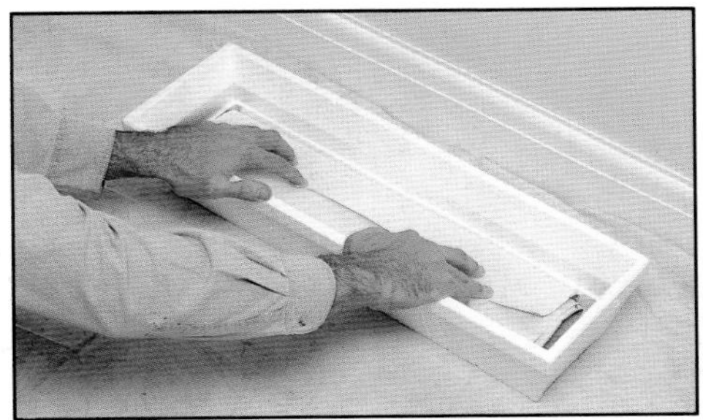

1 Place the trough next to the wall, fill it with cold water and immerse the rolled-up length in it, with the top end outermost, for the recommended time.

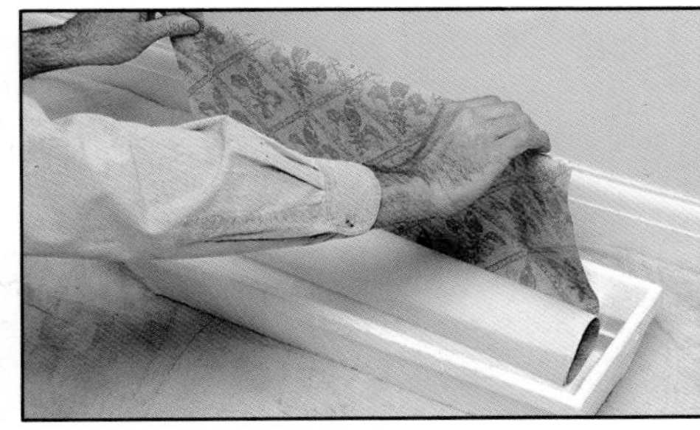

2 At the end of the soaking time, grasp the top end of the length and draw it upwards so that the excess water runs off and back into the trough.

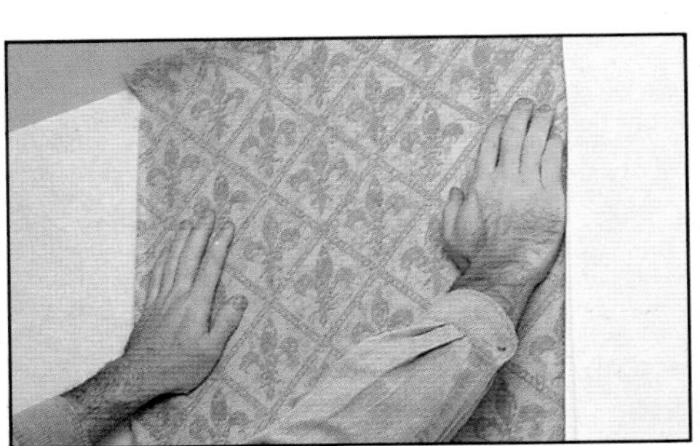

3 Slide the top of the length into position on the wall, aligning it with a marked line or butting it up against its neighbour. Take care not to step in the trough.

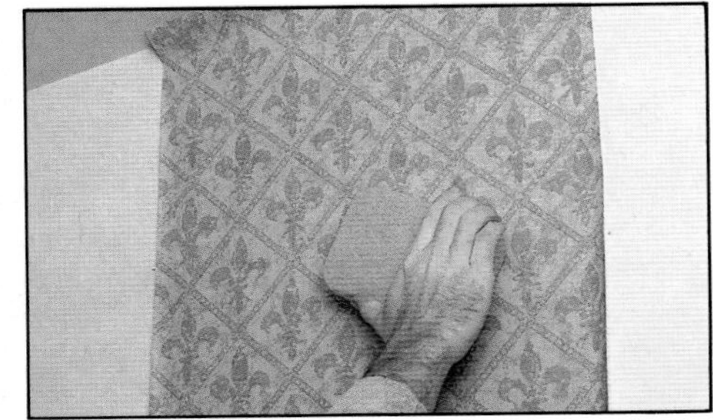

4 Use a sponge rather than a paperhanging brush to smooth the length into place on the wall – this will help to absorb excess water from the surface.

PAPERHANGING AROUND CORNERS

In a perfect world, rooms would have corners that were truly square and truly vertical, and it would be possible to hang a wall covering all around the room in a continuous operation, simply turning the lengths that ran into the room corners straight on to the adjoining walls. In reality, corners are seldom square or true, and, if the covering were hung in this way, lengths would be vertical on the first wall but could be running well off the vertical by the time they returned to the starting point. This would be visually disastrous, with vertical pattern elements out of alignment at corners, and sloping horizontal pattern features.

The way to avoid these problems is to complete each wall with a cut-down strip that only just turns on to the next wall. Then hang the remainder of the strip with its machine-cut edge against a newly drawn vertical line on the second wall, so that you can trim its other edge to follow the internal angle precisely. Any slight discontinuity of pattern will not be noticeable except to the very closest scrutiny, and the remaining lengths on the second wall will be hung truly vertically. The same applies to paperhanging around external corners.

PAPERING TIP

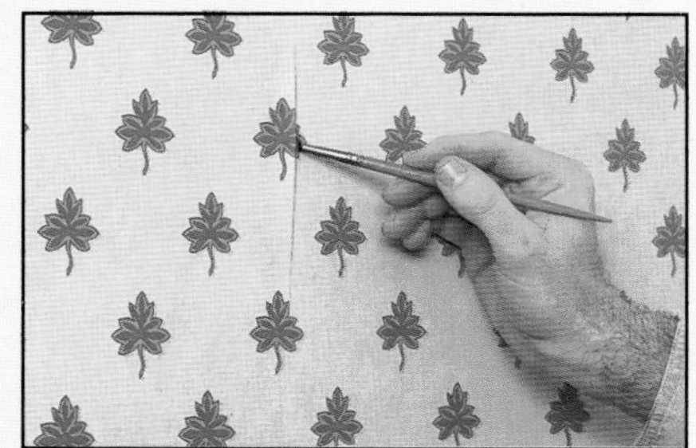

If a seam refuses to lie flat because it was inadequately pasted and has begun to dry out, brush a little paste underneath it and roll with a seam roller.

Papering an Internal Corner

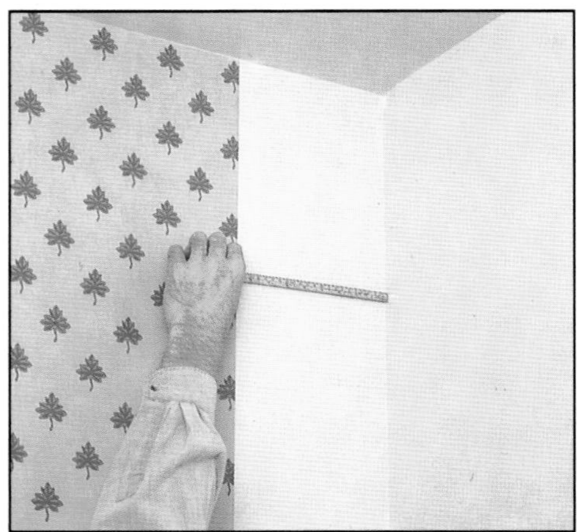

1 Hang the last full length before the corner of the room, then measure the distance to the corner from the edge of the length and add about 12 mm/½ in.

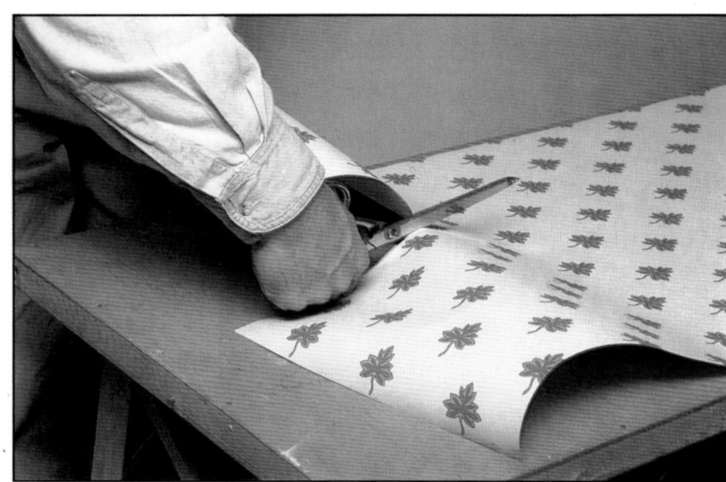

2 Use a pencil and straightedge to mark a strip of the required width, measured from the relevant edge (here, the left one), and cut it from the length.

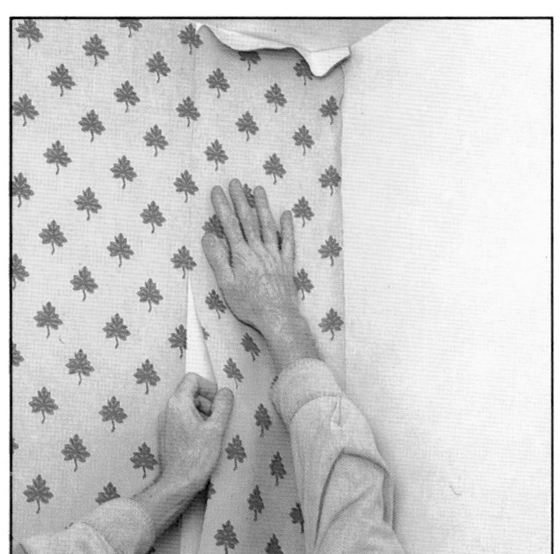

3 Paste the strip and hang it in the usual way, allowing the hand-cut edge to lap on to the adjoining wall. Trim the top and bottom edges as usual.

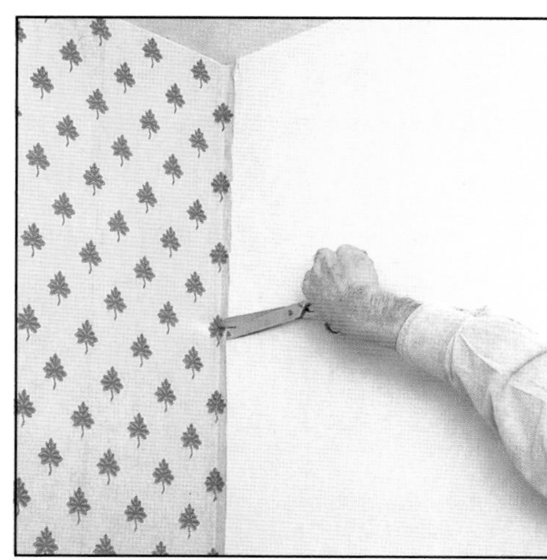

4 Brush the tongue into the internal angle. If it will not lie flat because the corner is out of true, make small release cuts in the edge and brush it flat.

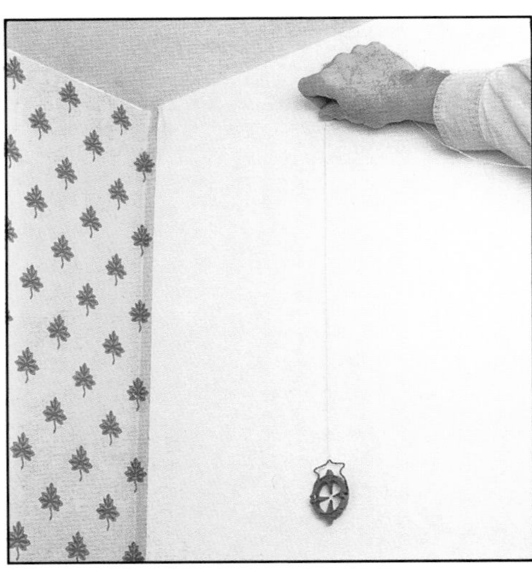

5 Measure the width of the remaining strip, subtract 12 mm/½ in and mark a fresh vertical line on the adjoining wall at this distance from the corner.

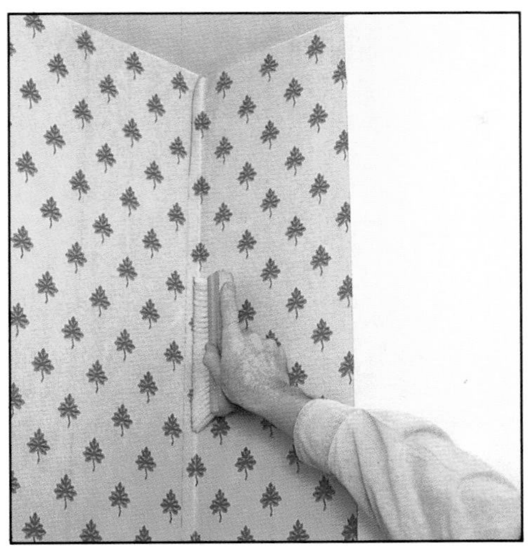

6 Hang the strip to the marked line, brushing the wall covering into the angle so that it just turns on to the surface of the first wall.

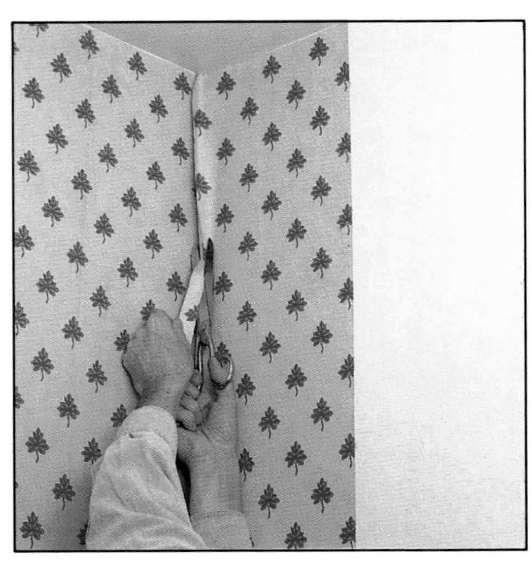

7 Use the back of the scissors blades to mark the line of the corner on the wall covering, then cut along the line and smooth the cut edge back into the angle. Use special overlap adhesive when using washables and vinyls on all lap joints.

Papering an External Corner

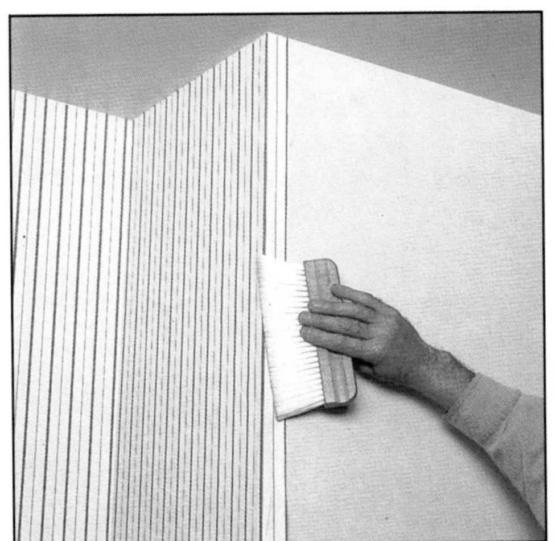

1 Plan the starting point so that lengths turn external corners by about 2.5 cm/1 in. Brush the paper on to the next wall, making small cuts so that it lies flat.

2 Carefully tear off a narrow strip of the wall covering along the turned edge to leave a 'feathered' edge that will not show through the next length.

3 Mark a vertical line on the next wall surface, at a distance from the corner equal to the width of the wall covering plus about 6 mm/¼ in.

4 Hang the next full length to the marked line, with its other edge overlapping the feathered edge of the strip turned from the previous wall.

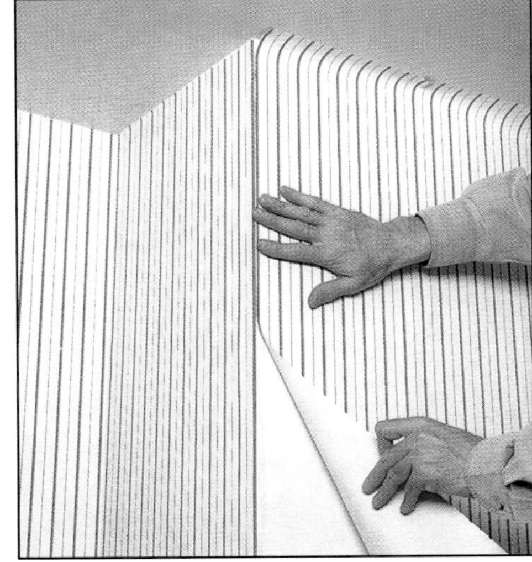

5 Brush this length into position, trim it at the top and bottom as before, and run a seam roller down the overlap (do not do this on embossed or textured wall coverings). Again, use a special overlap adhesive with washable and vinyl coverings.

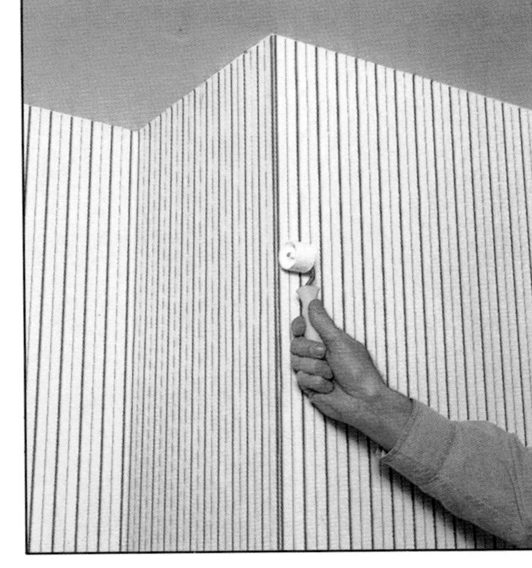

PAPERHANGING AROUND DOORS AND WINDOWS

Paperhanging on flat, uninterrupted walls is quite straightforward, calling only for the basic positioning and trimming techniques. Turning corners is only slightly more difficult. The trouble is that rooms also contain doors and windows, as well as wall-mounted fittings and fixtures such as light switches and socket outlets (receptacles). Paperhanging around these obstacles can be fairly tricky, but there are procedures for dealing with them successfully.

Doors and window frames fitted flush with the internal wall surface present few problems; all that is necessary here is to trim the wall covering so that it finishes flush with the edge of the architrave (trim) or casing. Where the window or door is recessed, however, you will need to do some careful patching-in of extra pieces in order to cover all the surfaces of the reveal. It is also important in this case to select the correct starting point, to avoid joins between lengths falling on the external corners of such reveals; always check this point before beginning paper-hanging, and adjust the starting point by about 5 cm/2 in if it will occur.

Paperhanging around electrical fittings (fixtures) is fairly easy. Always turn off the power supply to the accessory first. The idea is to make diagonal cuts over the faceplate, cut away most of the resulting triangular tongues and tuck what remains behind the loosened faceplate. Do not do this with vinyl foils, which can conduct electricity; instead, simply trim the covering flush with the edges of the accessory faceplate. In the USA, it is possible to remove wall plates and socket outlets separately without disconnecting the wall receptacles or switches, which makes the task of paperhanging around them much simpler.

Papering around a Flush Door or Window

1 On reaching a flush door or a window frame, hang the previous length as normal. Then hang the next length to overlap the door or window frame.

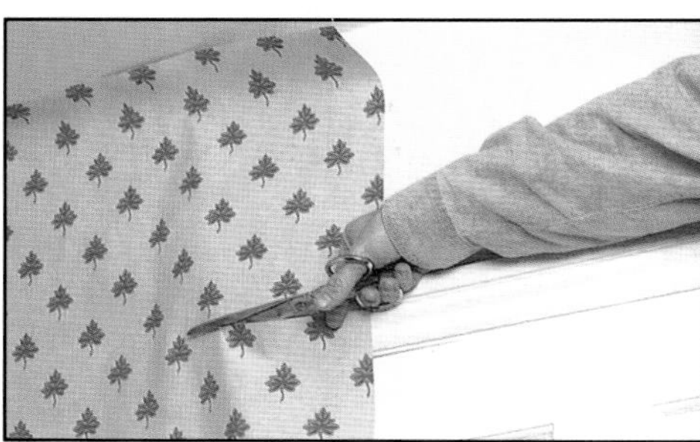

2 Cut away the unwanted wall covering to within about 2.5 cm/1 in of the edge of the architrave (trim) or window casing, and discard the waste strip.

3 Press the covering against the frame so that its corner is visible, and make a diagonal cut from the waste edge of the paper to the mark.

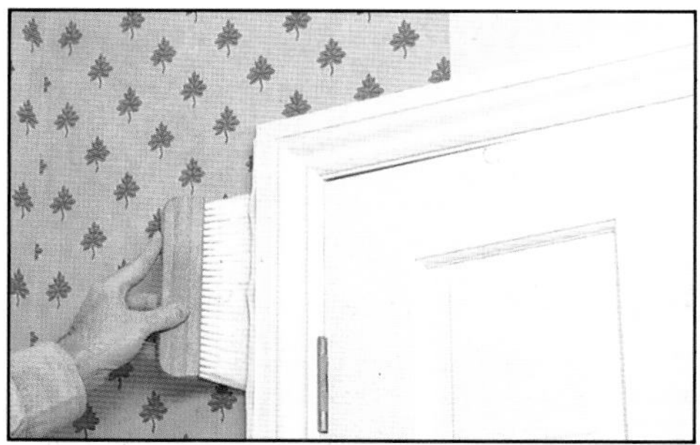

4 Use a paperhanging brush to press the tongues of paper well into the angles between the wall and the door architrave or window casing.

5 Carefully peel back the tongues and cut along the marked lines with paperhanging scissors. Brush the trimmed edges back into position.

Papering around a Recessed Door or Window

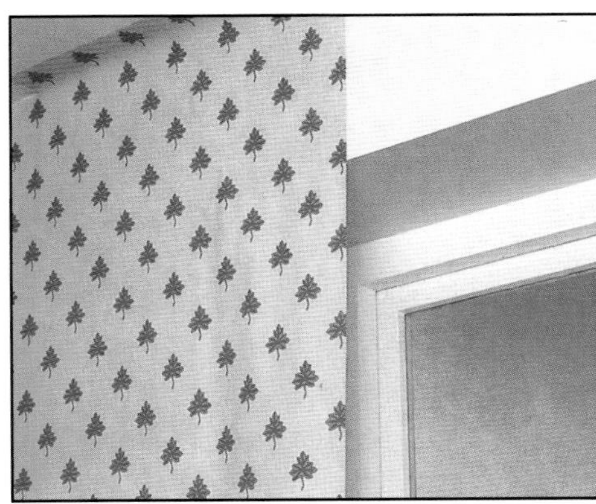

1 On reaching a recessed door or window frame, hang the previous length as normal. Then hang the next length, allowing it to overlap the recess.

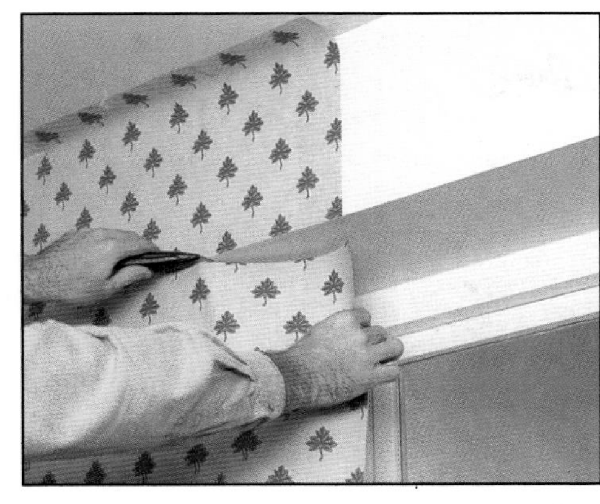

2 Carefully make a horizontal cut into the overlapping edge, level with the underside of the reveal, to allow the central portion of the length to cover the side wall.

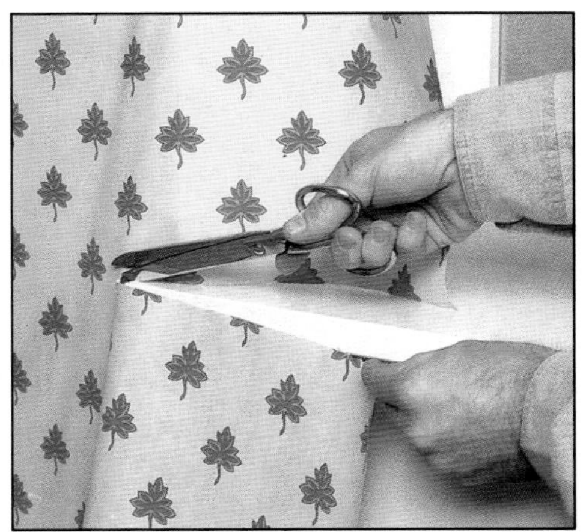

3 On a recessed window, make a similar cut lower down the length, level with the top surface of the window sill. Trim it to fit round the end of the sill.

4 Cut a patch to fit on the underside of the reveal, big enough to turn on to the adjoining wall and frame surfaces. Press it well into the internal angles.

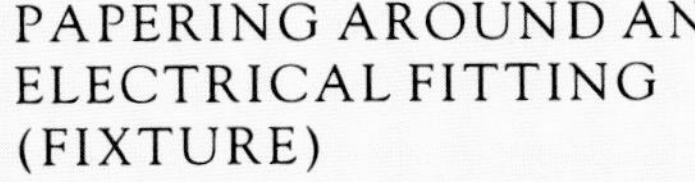

Papering around an Electrical Fitting (Fixture)

Always turn off the power supply before you begin. Make diagonal cuts in the paper towards the corners, trim off the triangles and tuck the edges behind the loosened faceplate.

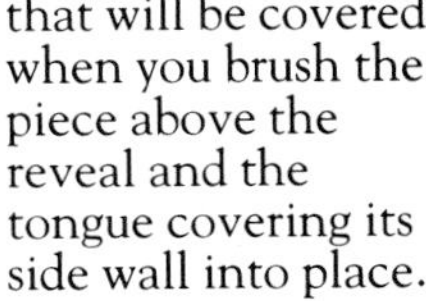

5 Tear along the edges of the patch that will be covered when you brush the piece above the reveal and the tongue covering its side wall into place.

6 Trim the edges of the patch and tongue to meet the frame neatly. Hang full widths when you reach the other side of the reveal, and repeat steps 1–6.

CHOOSING WALL AND FLOOR TILES

Ceramic tiles provide the most durable of all finishes in the home, whether they are used for walls, floors or work tops, and there has never been a bigger choice of colours, designs, shapes and sizes. Vinyl, lino and cork tiles offer alternative floor finishes to ceramics. They have the same advantages of ease of laying small units, combined with a surface finish that is warmer to the touch and also less noisy underfoot than their ceramic counterparts.

Ceramic tiles for walls

In today's homes, the surfaces that are tiled more often than any others are walls, especially in rooms such as the kitchen and bathroom where a hard-wearing, water-resistant and easy-clean decorative finish is required. Tile designs tend to change with fashions in interior design. Plain tiles, often with a simple border frame, are always popular, as are tiles which create a frieze effect when laid alongside one another. Some sets of tiles build up into larger designs (known as feature panels), which can look quite striking when surrounded by plain tiling.

The surface of ceramic wall tiles is no longer always highly glazed, as was traditionally the case. There are now semi-matt finishes available, too, often with a slight surface texture that softens the somewhat harsh glare of a high-gloss surface.

Tile edges have also changed over the years. Once special round-edged tiles were used for the exposed edges of tiled areas, and plain ones with unglazed square edges (known as field tiles) were used elsewhere. Nowadays tiles are either the universal type or the standard square-edged variety. The former have angled edges so that, when butted together, they leave a gap for the grouting, which fills the spaces between them. The latter, as their name suggests, have square edges and so must be positioned with the aid of spacers.

Tiles for floors and work tops

Ceramic floor tiles are a popular choice for 'heavy traffic' areas such as porches and hallways. They are generally thicker and harder-fired than wall tiles, to enable them to stand up to heavy wear. Again, a wide range of plain colours, simple textures and more elaborate designs is available. The most common shapes are squares and rectangles; hexagons are also sold in plain colours, and a popular variation is a plain octagonal tile laid with small square coloured or decorated inserts at the intersections.

Quarry tiles are unglazed ceramic floor tiles with a brown, buff or reddish colour, and are a practical choice for hallways, conservatories and country-style kitchens. They are usually laid in a mortar bed, and, once the joints have been grouted, the tiles must be sealed with boiled linseed oil or a recommended proprietary sealer. Special shaped tiles are also available for forming upstands at floor edges. Terracotta tiles look similar to quarry tiles but are larger, and are fired at lower temperatures and so are more porous. They need to be sealed in the same way as quarry tiles.

LEFT Many tile ranges include a variety of plain and patterned field tiles, teamed up with a complementary border tile, allowing the home decorator complete freedom to decide on the finished design.

BELOW Ceramic tiles provide a durable and waterproof floor surface for bathrooms. Here, coloured corner insets are used to set off the dazzling white octagonal tiles.

ABOVE Lino tiles offer a warm, attractive and durable alternative to cork or vinyl floor coverings in rooms such as kitchens and hallways. Borders can be used to frame individual tiles.

Mosaics

Mosaics are just tiny tiles – usually plain in colour, sometimes with a pattern – which are sold made up in sheets on an open-weave cloth backing. These sheets are laid like larger tiles in a bed of adhesive, and all the gaps, including those on the surface of the sheet, are grouted afterwards. Square mosaics are the most common, but roundels, hexagons and other interlocking shapes are also available. Mosaics intended for laying on walls and floors are made in different thicknesses, as with ordinary ceramic tiles.

LEFT Cork is the warmest of tiled floor coverings underfoot, and when sealed is also good-looking, hardwearing and durable.

Cork, vinyl and lino tiles

Cork tiles come in a small range of colours and textures. They feel warm and relatively soft underfoot, and also give some worthwhile heat and sound insulation. The cheapest types have to be sealed to protect the surface, but the more expensive vinyl-coated floor types can be walked on as soon as they have been stuck down, and need little more than an occasional wash and polish to keep them in good condition.

Vinyl tiles come in a very wide range of plain and patterned types. They are generally more resilient than cork and so can be used on floors subject to fairly heavy wear, but they are a little less gentle on the feet. Some of the more expensive types give very passable imitations of luxury floor coverings such as marble and terrazzo. Most are made in self-adhesive form and need very little maintenance.

Modern lino tiles, made from natural materials rather than the plastic resins used in vinyl tiles, offer far better performance than traditional linoleum. They come in a range of bright and subtle colours and interesting patterns, often with pre-cut borders.

TILING A WALL

For a large area of tiling – a whole wall, or perhaps even a complete room – the preliminary setting-out is by far the most important part. You must first plan precisely where the whole tiles will fall. It is best to use a device called a tiling gauge – a batten (furring strip) marked out in tile widths – to work this out. The gauge is easy to make from a straight piece of timber about 1.2 m/ 4 ft long, marked off with pencil lines to match the size of the tiles. Use this to ensure that the tiles will be centred accurately on major features such as window reveals, with a border of cut tiles of equal width at the end of each row or column of tiles.

With a large area of tiling, 2 main factors are vital. First, the tile rows must be exactly horizontal; if they are not, errors will accumulate as the tiles extend across the wall, throwing the verticals out of alignment. Second, the tiles need some means of support while the adhesive sets; without it, they may slump down the wall.

The solution is to fix a line of battens across the wall just above the level of the skirtings (baseboards), securing them with partly driven masonry nails so that you can remove them later. The precise level will be dictated by setting out with the tiling gauge, but will usually be about three-quarters of a tile width above the skirtings. Do not rely on this being level; it may not be. Draw out the line in pencil first, using a spirit level, and then pin the battens up and check the level again. Use vertical battens as necessary – next to a door architrave (trim) that is not truly straight, for example – to ensure vertical alignment.

Once all the necessary setting-out work has been done, the actual technique of fixing tiles to walls is quite simple: spread the adhesive evenly and press the tiles into place. Apply enough adhesive to fix 10 or 12 tiles at a time. When all the whole tiles are in place,

FIXING WHOLE TILES

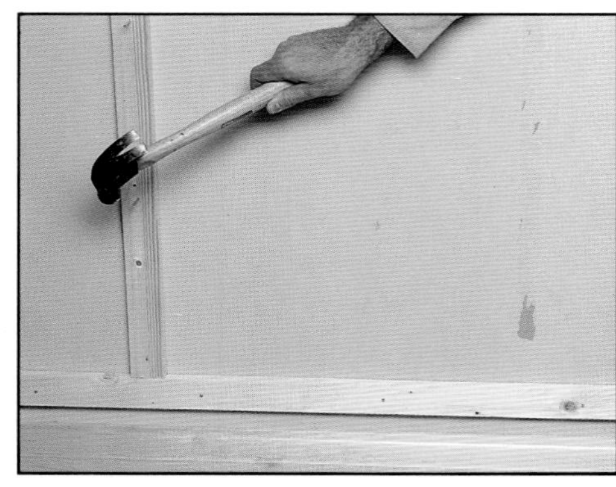

1 When tiling a large area, pin vertical and horizontal guide battens (furring strips) to the wall to help keep the tile columns truly square and aligned.

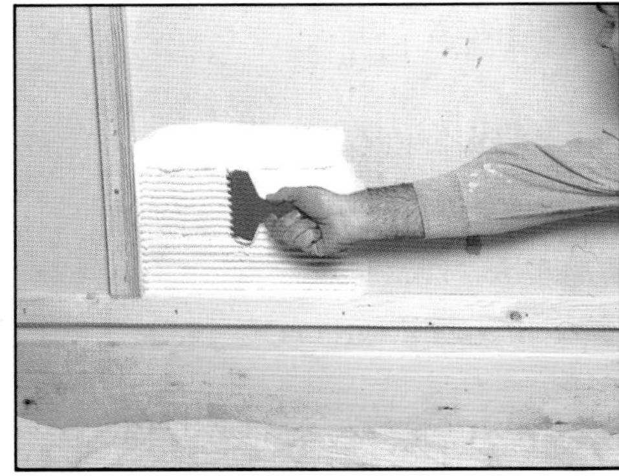

2 Use a notched spreader to scoop some adhesive from the tub and spread it on the wall. Press the teeth against the wall to leave ridges of even height.

3 Place the first tile on the tile support, with its side edge against the pencilled guideline or vertical guide batten (furring strip) as appropriate.

4 Add a tile spacer against the tile corner and position the second tile. Add more tiles to complete the row, then build up succeeding rows in the same way.

CUTTING TILES

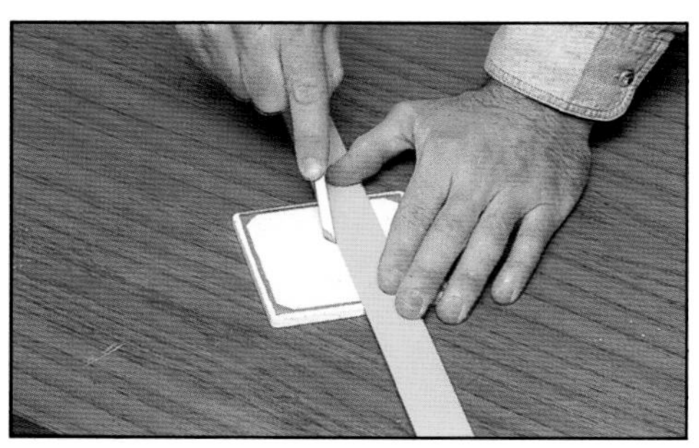

1 Use a pencil-type tile cutter and a straightedge to make a straight cut. Measure and mark the tile width needed and score a line across the glaze.

2 Place a nail or matchstick (wooden match) under the scored line at each side of the tile, and break it with downward hand pressure on each half of the tile.

you will need to tackle any cut tiles required at the ends of rows, and along the base of the tiled area beneath the horizontal tile support. Remove this, and the tile spacers, only when the adhesive has set; allow 24 hours. The final stage is to fill in the joint lines with grout. This can be bought in powder form or ready-mixed. Use a flexible spreader (usually supplied with the grout) to apply it.

Most ceramic wall tiles have 2 glazed edges, making it possible to finish off an area of tiling or an external corner with a glazed edge exposed. Alternatively, finish off tiling by edging it with wooden mouldings or plastic trims bedded into the adhesive.

Completing the Wall

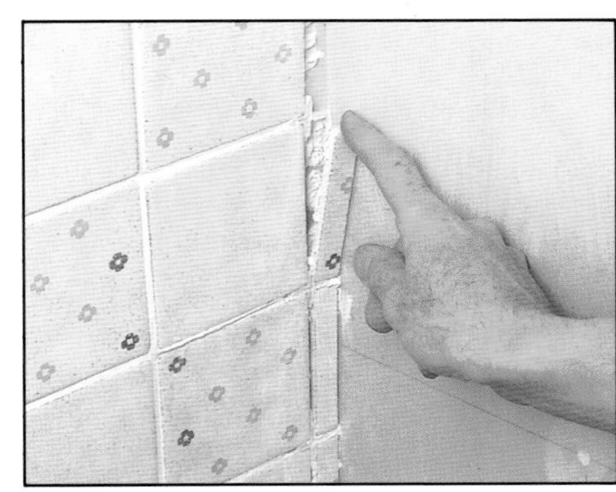

1 Measure, mark and cut the sections of tile needed to complete each row. Spread adhesive on them and press into place. When tiling adjacent walls, place all the cut pieces on the first wall. Repeat on the second wall, overlapping the cut pieces.

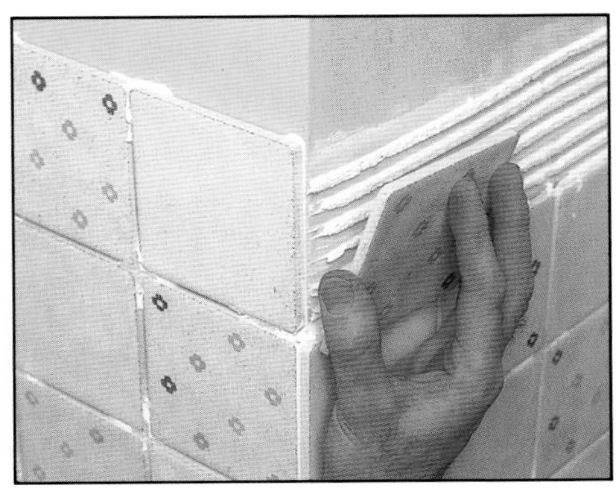

2 When tiling external corners, always set out the tiles so that whole tiles meet on the corner. Overlap the tiles as shown.

Grouting the Tiles

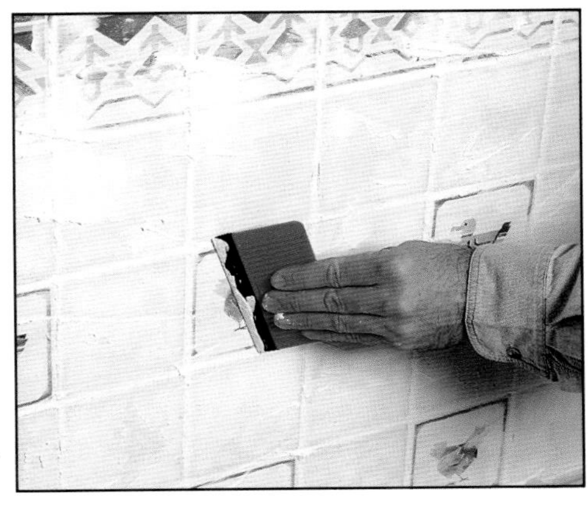

1 Apply the grout to the tile joins by drawing the loaded spreader across them at right-angles to the join lines. Scrape off any excess grout and re-use it. Use a damp sponge or cloth to wipe the surface of the tiles before the grout dries out.

2 Use a short length of wooden dowel or a similar implement to smooth the grout lines to a gently concave cross-section. Allow the grout to harden completely, then polish the tiles with a dry cloth to remove any slight remaining bloom and to leave them clean and shiny.

3 Use a cutting guide, or a tile-cutting jig if you prefer, especially for cutting narrow strips. This type holds the tile securely and also guides the tile cutter accurately.

4 The traditional way of making a cut-out in a tile is to score its outline and then gradually to nibble away the waste material with pincers.

5 An alternative is to use a special abrasive-coated tile saw. This is indispensable for making internal cut-outs – to fit around pipes, for example.

LAYING FLOOR TILES

Both glazed ceramic and quarry tiles can be laid directly over a concrete floor, as long as it is both sound and dry. They can also be laid on to a suspended timber floor, but only if it is strong enough to support the not-inconsiderable extra weight (it is advisable to check this with a building surveyor). In this case, cover the floorboards with exterior-grade plywood, screwed down or secured with annular nails (spiral flooring nails) to prevent it from lifting; this will provide a stable and level base for the tiles.

You will need specially formulated adhesive for laying glazed ceramic floor tiles – this should be a waterproof type in bathrooms and a flexible type if you are tiling on a suspended floor. Lay quarry and terracotta tiles on mortar over a solid concrete floor, or in thick-bed tile adhesive over plywood.

You should lift old floor coverings before laying ceramic or quarry tiles, but, if a solid floor is covered with well-bonded vinyl or cork tiles, you can leave these in place. Remove any wax polish used on them, then tile over them using tile adhesive.

Setting out a tiled floor

Like a tiled wall, a tiled floor needs careful setting-out if the end result is to look neat and professional. This is especially important with glazed ceramic and quarry tiles, and patterned vinyl and lino tiles, but matters rather less with plain vinyl or cork tiles where the finished effect is of uniform colour and the joins between the tiles are virtually invisible.

The necessary setting-out is, fortunately, much easier with floor tiles than it is with wall tiles, as you can dry-lay the tiles on the floor surface and move them around until you find a starting point that gives the best arrangement, with cut border tiles of approximately equal size used all around the perimeter of the room.

LAYING CERAMIC FLOOR TILES

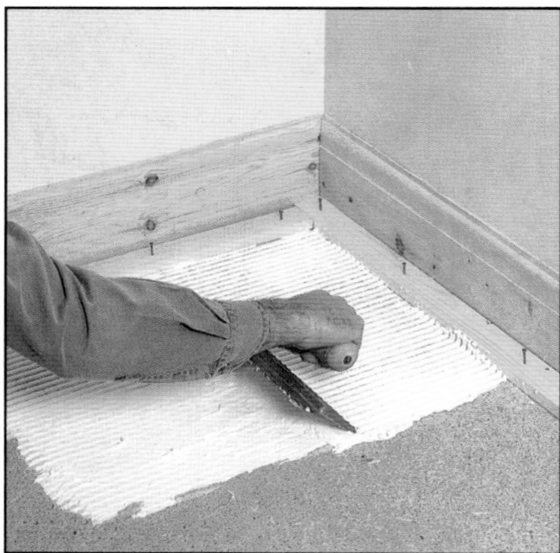

1 Pin (tack) tiling guides to the floor in the corner of the room at right-angles to each other, then spread some adhesive on the floor using a notched-edge trowel.

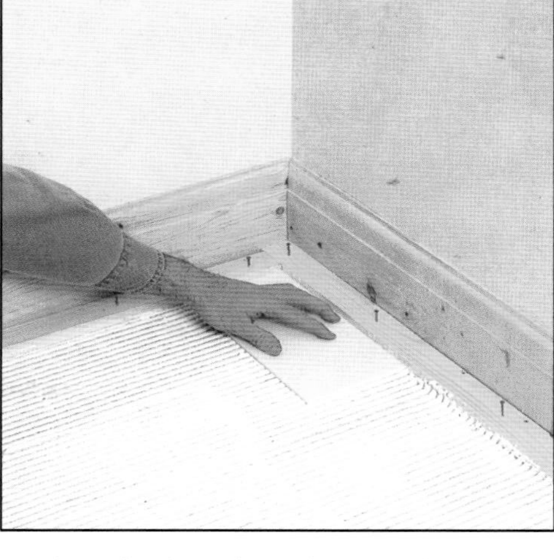

2 Place the first tile in the angle between the tiling guides, butting it tightly against them and pressing it down firmly into the adhesive bed.

3 As you lay the tiles, use tile spacers to ensure even gaps between them. Use a straightedge to check that all the tiles are horizontal and level.

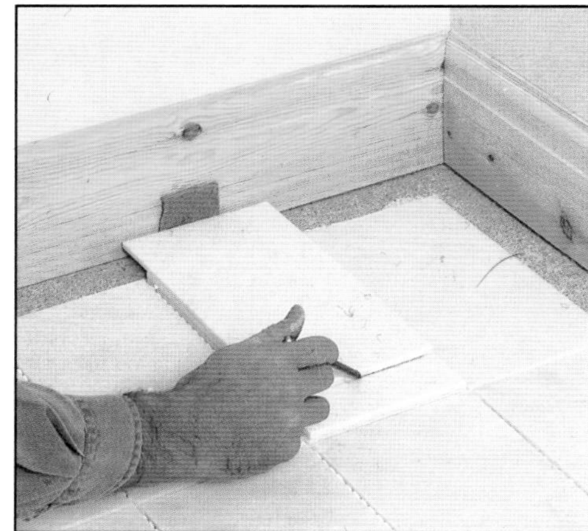

4 To cut border tiles, lay a whole tile over the last whole tile laid, butt another against the skirting (baseboard) and mark its edge on the tile beneath.

Start by finding the centre point of the floor, by linking the mid-points of opposite pairs of walls with string lines. Dry-lay rows of tiles out towards the walls in each direction, remembering to allow for the joint thickness if appropriate, to see how many whole tiles will fit in and to check whether this starting point results in over-narrow border tiles or awkward cuts against obstacles. Move the rows slightly to improve the fit if necessary, then mark the string lines using a pencil. Begin tiling in the corner of the room furthest from the door.

TILING TIP

Remember to take off and shorten room doors before laying floor tiles, and to remove sufficient depth to allow the door to clear both the plywood underlay (if used) and the new tiles.

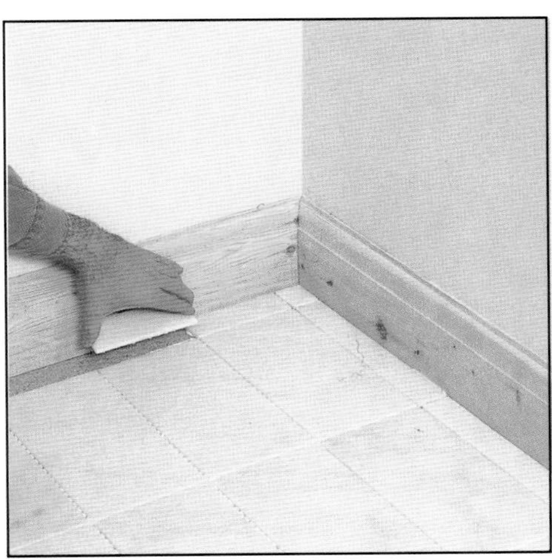

5 Cut the tile and use the exposed part of the sandwiched tile in step 4 to fill the border gap. Use the offcut to fill the next border gap if it is wider than the gap.

6 Use a squeegee to spread grout over the tiles and fill all the join lines. Wipe excess adhesive from the surface of the tiles with a damp cloth.

7 Use a piece of wooden dowel or a similar rounded implement to smooth the grout lines. Finally, polish the tile surface with a clean, dry cloth.

Laying Quarry Tiles

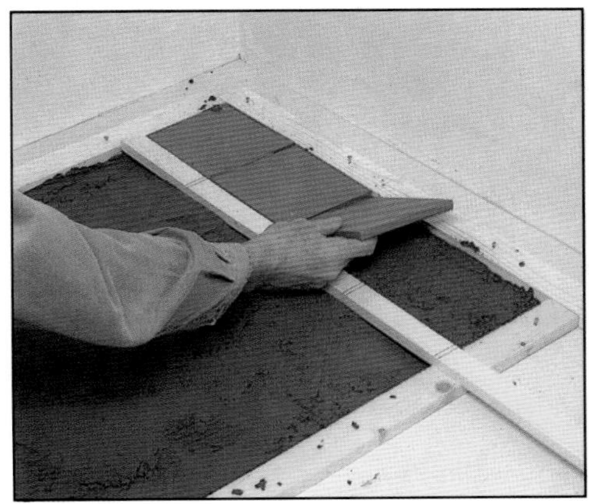

1 Add a third tiling guide to form a bay that is 4 tiles wide. Put down a thin mortar bed and place the first row of tiles, using a tiling gauge to space them.

2 Complete 4 rows of 4 tiles, then check that they are completely level. Tamp down any that are proud, and lift and re-bed any that are lying lower than the other tiles.

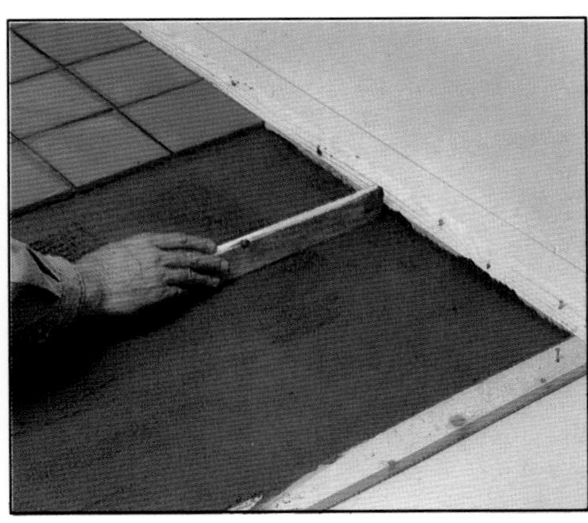

3 Complete the first bay, then remove the third tiling guide and re-position it another 4 tile widths away. Fill the second bay with mortar and tamp it down.

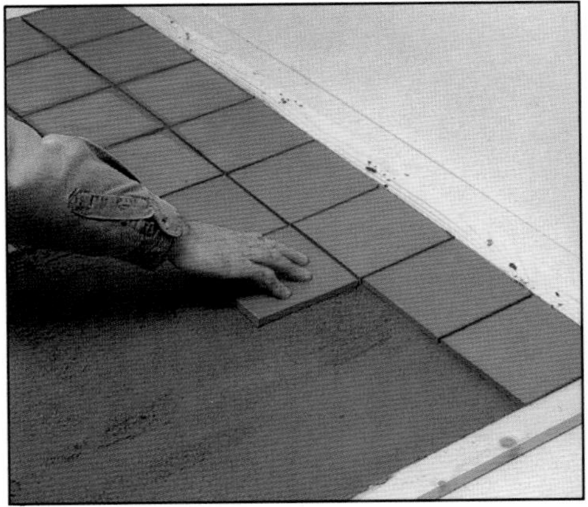

4 Complete the second bay in the same way as the first. Continue in this fashion across the room until you have laid all the whole tiles.

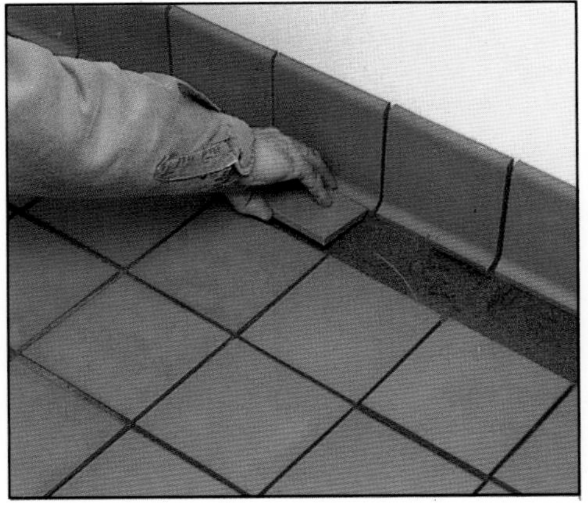

5 If you are installing a tiled upstand, place this next, aligning individual units with the floor tiling, then cut and fit the border tiles.

6 Mix up a fairly dry mortar mix and use a stiff-bristled brush to work it well into the joins between the tiles. Brush away excess mortar as you work.

COVERING FLOORS

CHOOSING FLOOR COVERINGS

In principle it is possible to lay any floor covering in any room of a home, but custom and the practicalities of life generally tend to divide up the home into 3 broad areas.

Access areas such as the hallway, landing and stairs need a floor covering that is able to cope with heavy 'traffic' and muddy shoes. Ideal choices for a hallway are materials with a water-repellent and easy-to-clean surface – for example, sheet vinyl, vinyl tiles, a wood-strip or wood-block floor, sanded and sealed floorboards, or glazed ceramic or quarry tiles. For stairs, where safety is paramount, the best material to choose is a heavy-duty carpet with a short pile, which can also be used on the landing.

Work areas such as the kitchen and bathroom also need durable floor coverings that are easy to clean and, especially in the case of the bathroom, water-resistant as well. Sheet vinyl is a popular choice for both rooms, but tiles of various types can also provide an excellent surface – sealed cork, with its warm feel underfoot, is particularly suitable for a bathroom. However, if you prefer carpet for these rooms, there are extremely hardwearing kitchen carpets available, with a specially treated short nylon pile that is easy to keep clean, and also water-resistant bathroom carpets that give a touch of luxury underfoot without turning into a swamp at bathtime.

Leisure areas – the living room, dining room and bedrooms – are commonly carpeted wall-to-wall. Do not be tempted to skimp on quality in the living room, which gets the most wear and tends to develop distinct 'traffic' routes. It is reasonable, however, to choose light-duty types for carpeting bedrooms.

Alternatives to carpets depend simply on taste in home décor. Options include sanded and sealed floorboards teamed with scatter rugs, or a parquet

ABOVE Plain – or almost plain – carpets are the key to simple yet sophisticated colour schemes. Neutral tones, here softly textured with a twist pile, can be offset with the subtlest of colour contrasts.

LEFT Natural mattings in coir or sisal provide a hardwearing floor covering. Available in a wide range of neutral shades and textures, as well as striped and check designs, they are at home in traditional or modern interiors.

perimeter to a fine specimen carpet. Sheet vinyl or cork tiles may also be worth considering for children's rooms.

Carpets

Carpets consist of fibre tufts or loops woven or stuck to a durable backing. Woven carpets are generally the most expensive. Tufted carpets are made by stitching tufts of fibre into a woven backing, where they are secured by attaching a second backing under the first with adhesive. Some of the less-expensive types have a foam underlay bonded directly to the backing; others require a separate underlay.

A wide range of fibre types is used in carpet construction today, including wool, nylon, acrylic, polypropylene and viscose rayon. Fibre blends can improve carpet performance; a mixture of 80 per cent wool and 20 per cent nylon is particularly popular for providing a combination of warmth, resilience, wear, low flammability and resistance to soiling.

Pile length and density affect a carpet's performance as well as its looks, and most are classified to indicate the sort of wear they can be expected to withstand. The pile can be cut, often to different lengths, giving a sculptured effect; looped (shag), that is, uncut and left long; corded, which means uncut and pulled tight to the backing; or twisted, which gives a tufty effect. A dense pile wears better than a loosely woven one that can be parted to reveal the backing. Carpet widths are described as broadloom, when more than 1.8 m/6 ft wide; or body (stair carpet), which is usually up to 90 cm/ 3 ft wide.

Carpet tiles are small squares of carpet of various types, designed to be loose-laid. Cheaper tiles resemble cord and felt carpets, while more expensive ones may have a short- or long-cut pile. The most common sizes are 30, 45, 50 and 60 cm/12, 18, 20 and 24 in square.

ABOVE Modern sheet linoleum has taken on a new lease of life, offering a range of sophisticated colourways teamed with stylish borders that are perfect for kitchens, utility rooms and hallways.

Sheet-vinyl flooring

This is a relatively thin material which provides a smooth, hygienic and easy-to-clean floor covering that is widely used in rooms such as kitchens, bathrooms and hallways. It is made from layers of plastic resins, with a clear wear layer protecting the printed design and frequently with an air cushion layer between this and the backing for extra comfort and warmth underfoot. It is fairly flexible and easy to cut for an exact fit; it is generally loose-laid, with double-sided adhesive tape used only at seams and edges.

Vinyl flooring is available in a wide range of designs, including realistic imitations of ceramic tiles, wood, cork and stone. It is sold by the linear metre (or yard) from rolls 2, 3 or 4 m/6 ft 6 in, 10 ft or 13 ft wide.

Wood floor coverings

These come in two main forms: as square wood-block panels made up of individual fingers of wood stuck to a cloth or felt backing for ease of handling and laying; or as wood-strip flooring – interlocking planks, often of veneer on a plywood backing. They are laid over the existing floor surface. Most types are tongued-and-grooved, so only occasional nailing or clipping is required to hold them in place. Wood-block panels are usually 30 or 45 cm/12 or 18 in square, while planks are generally 7.5 or 10 cm/3 or 4 in wide and come in a range of lengths to allow the end joins to be staggered from one row to the next.

BELOW Sanded floorboards can be further enhanced with a delicate stencilled border design. Always seal floorboards with several coats of good-quality varnish for a hardwearing finish.

LAYING A FOAM-BACKED CARPET

Laying a traditional woven carpet can be a difficult task for the amateur to undertake, because the carpet must be correctly tensioned across the room by using gripper strips and a carpet stretcher if it is to wear well. Because of the cost of such carpet, it may be considered best to leave the job to professionals. However, there is no reason why you should not get some practice by laying less-expensive foam-backed carpet in, for example, a spare bedroom. It is possible to disguise any slight inaccuracies that creep into the cutting and fitting process more easily here than when using smooth sheet floor coverings such as vinyl, so a job such as this would be an excellent introduction to the general technique of laying roll floor coverings.

Start by putting down a paper or cloth underlay on the floor, taping the joins and stapling down the underlay so that it cannot creep as you lay down the carpet. Unroll the carpet right across the room, with the excess lapping up the walls. Using a sharp utility knife, roughly trim the excess all around the room, leaving approximately 5 cm/2 in for final trimming. Carefully make small cuts at any external corners such as around a chimney breast (fireplace projection), and let the tongues fall back into the alcoves, then trim off the waste carpet neatly across the face of the chimney breast.

Next, press the carpet into internal corners and mark the corner point with a finger. Make cuts to remove the triangle of carpet from the internal angle. Finally, trim the perimeter by drawing a knife along the angle between the skirtings (baseboards) and wall, and secure the edges with double-sided adhesive tape. Fit a threshold (saddle) strip across the door opening to give a neat finish.

1 Before laying a foam-backed carpet, put down a paper or cloth underlay to keep the foam from sticking to the floor. Tape any joins and staple the underlay in place.

2 Stick double-sided adhesive tape all around the perimeter of the room, leaving the top backing paper on the tape. Unroll the carpet and position it so that it laps up the room walls.

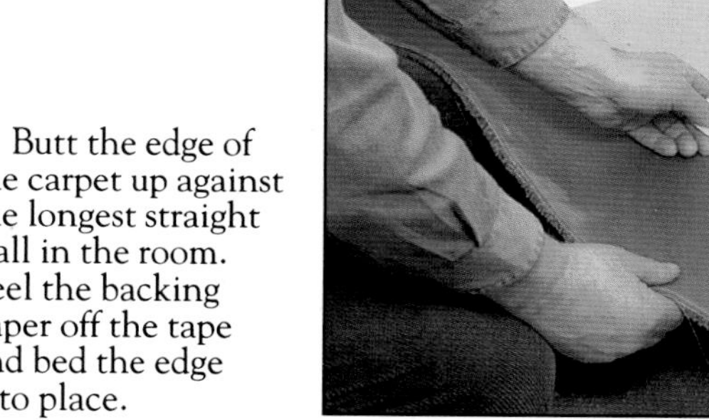

3 Butt the edge of the carpet up against the longest straight wall in the room. Peel the backing paper off the tape and bed the edge into place.

4 Work the carpet across the floor to the opposite wall to ensure that it is lying flat. Trim this edge against the skirting (baseboard) and then tape it down as before.

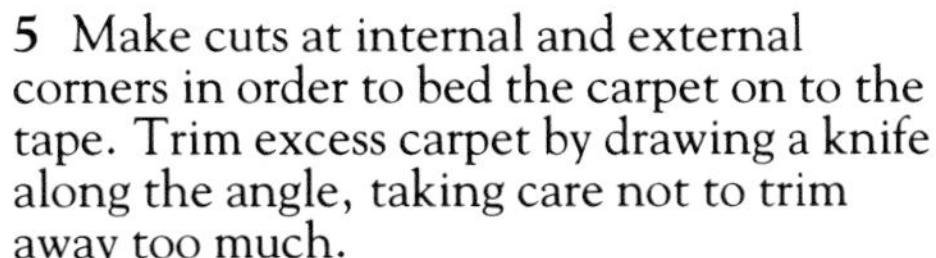

5 Make cuts at internal and external corners in order to bed the carpet on to the tape. Trim excess carpet by drawing a knife along the angle, taking care not to trim away too much.

6 Use adhesive seaming tape to join pieces of carpet together where necessary in particularly large rooms. Applied pressure from a wallpaper seam roller will ensure a good, lasting bond.

LAYING CARPET TILES

Carpet tiles are among the simplest floor coverings to lay, because they are highly tolerant of any slight inaccuracy in cutting to fit. The cheapest types are usually plain in colour and have a very short pile or a corded appearance, while more expensive tiles may have a longer pile and are available in patterns as well as plain colours. Most are designed to be loose-laid, with just the edges and door thresholds (saddles) secured with bands of adhesive or double-sided tape. This makes it easy to lift individual tiles for cleaning or to even out wear.

Most carpet tiles are marked on the back with an arrow to indicate the pile direction. Align these for a plain effect, or lay them at right-angles to create a chequerboard effect. When you are satisfied with the layout, lift the perimeter tiles and put down double-sided tape all around the room. Peel the backing paper off the top of the tape and press the tiles into place. Finish off the doorway with a threshold (saddle) strip.

CUTTING CARPET TILES

1 Measure the size of the cut tile required and mark the back accordingly. Cut the tile from the back on a cutting board, using a sharp utility knife and a metal straightedge.

2 After cutting cleanly through the backing, separate the 2 halves and trim away any frayed pile with scissors. Lay the cut tile in place.

LAYING SHEET VINYL

Sheet-vinyl flooring can be difficult to lay because it is wide and comparatively stiff to handle, and edge-cutting must be done accurately if gaps are not to be noticeable against skirtings (baseboards). Lengths of quadrant beading (a base shoe) can be pinned (tacked) around the perimeter of the room to disguise any serious mistakes.

Most rooms contain at least one long straight wall, and it is often easiest to butt one edge of the vinyl up against this first of all. Use a block of wood and a pencil to scribe the wall profile on to the vinyl and cut along this line for a perfect fit. Alternatively, simply press the vinyl into the angle between wall and floor, and cut along it using a sharp utility knife held at a 45° angle. Press the ends of the length neatly against the walls at right-angles to the first wall, make small diagonal cuts at internal and external angles, and trim the edges to fit there. Finally, stick down the edges and any seams with double-sided adhesive tape. Finish off the doorway with a proprietary threshold (saddle) strip.

The best way of achieving an accurate fit when laying sheet-vinyl flooring around unusual-shaped obstacles, such as washbasin pedestals and piping, is to make a template of the obstacle so that you can transfer its shape on to the vinyl. Use taped-together sheets of paper cut or torn to roughly the outline of the room and the obstacle. Tape the template to the floor, and use a block of wood and a pencil (or a pair of compasses) to draw a line on the template parallel with the outline of the obstacle.

Next, transfer the template to the vinyl, and use the same block of wood or compass setting to scribe lines back on to the vinyl itself. These lines will accurately represent the shape of the room and the obstacle. Cut along them and remove the waste, then stick down edges and seams as before.

1 Unless the wall is perfectly straight, carefully make a cut at the corner and then trim the adjacent edges of the sheet using a sharp utility knife along the angle of wall and floor.

2 At the door architraves (trims), make cuts into the edge of the sheet so that it will lie flat, and trim off the tongues. Use a similar technique for trimming around larger obstacles such as washbasin pedestals.

3 To join sheet vinyl edge to edge, overlap the 2 sheets so that the pattern matches, then cut through both layers against a metal straightedge. Discard the waste strips.

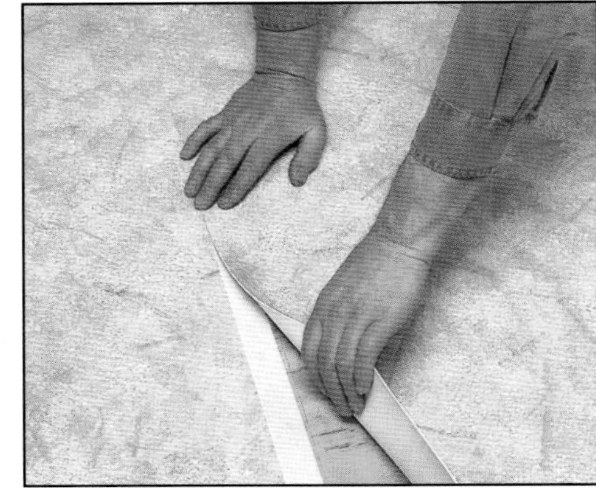

4 Place a strip of double-sided tape underneath the join line, peel off the backing paper and press the 2 cut edges firmly down on to the tape.

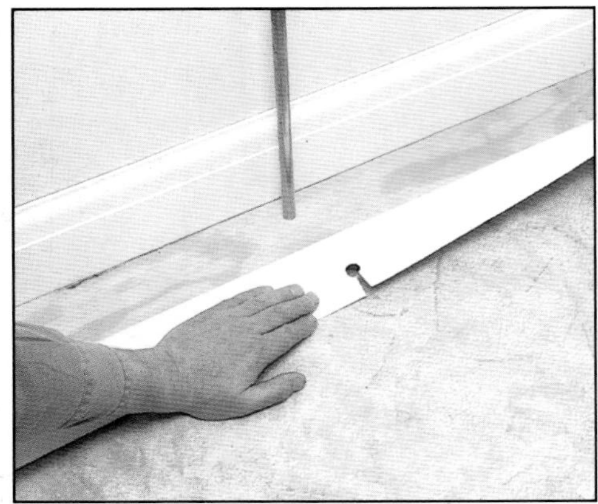

5 To fit the sheet around plumbing pipework, make a cut into it at the pipe position and then trim out a circle of the material to fit around it.

6 At the door opening, fit a threshold (saddle) strip to anchor the edge of the sheet. Here, an existing strip has been prised up and is being hammered down again.

Making Templates for Sheet Vinyl

PREPARING A TEMPLATE TO FIT AROUND OBSTACLES

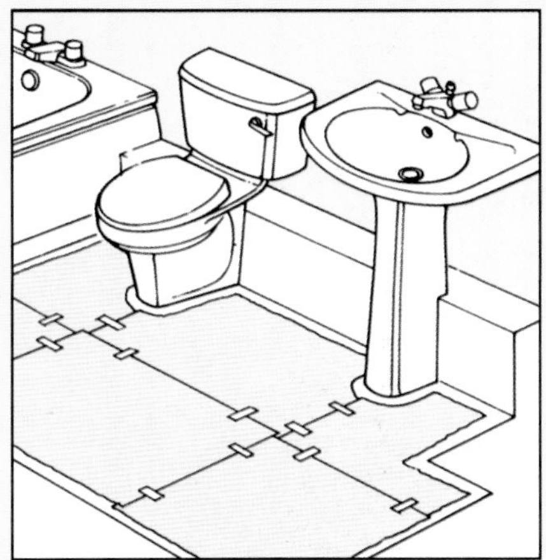

To make a cutting template for a room full of obstacles, such as a bathroom, tape sheets of paper together with their edges about 5 cm/2 in from the room walls all around. Tear in from the edges to fit the template around the obstacles as shown, ready for the outline of the room and the obstacles to be scribed on to the template.

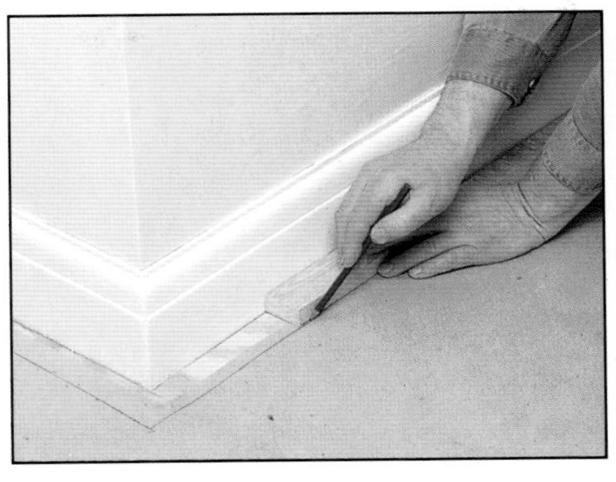

1 Use a block and pencil to scribe the wall outline on to the paper.

2 Tape the template over the sheet vinyl and use the same block with a pencil to scribe a copy of the room outline back on to the vinyl.

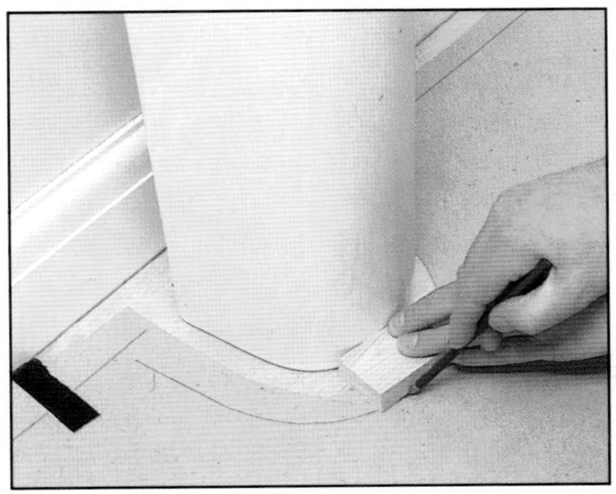

3 Use the same scribing technique as in step 1 to draw the outline of obstacles such as washbasin pedestals on to the paper template. Fix the pencil to the block with tape or a rubber band if you find that this makes it easier to use.

4 Repeat step 2 to scribe the outline of the obstacle on to the vinyl. Using a sharp utility knife, cut carefully around the outline of the obstacle. Make a cut into the waste area, test the cut-out for fit, and trim it slightly if necessary.

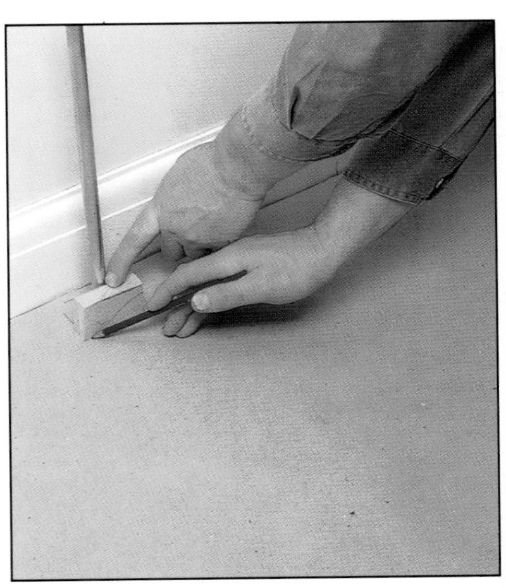

5 To make a cut-out around a pipe, use a slim block and a pencil to scribe the pipe position on to the template as four lines at right-angles to each other.

6 Place the template over the vinyl at the pipe position, and use the same block and pencil to mark the cut-out on the vinyl as a small square.

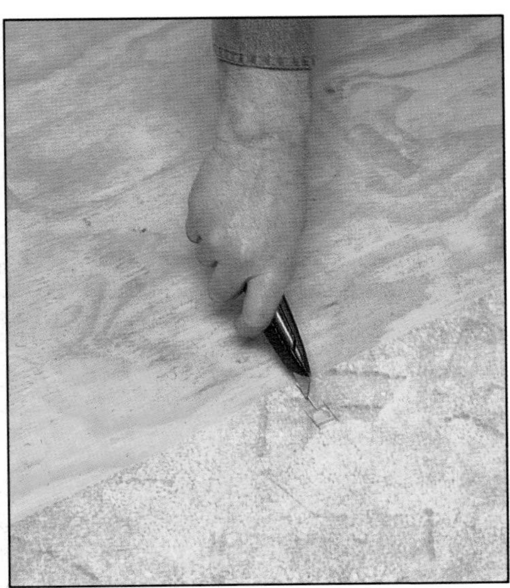

7 Use a pair of compasses or a pipe offcut to draw a circle inside the square. Cut carefully around the circle and cut into the waste area from the edge.

LAYING WOOD-STRIP FLOORING

All the hard work involved in putting down wood-strip flooring lies in the preparation; the actual laying, like so many decorating jobs, is simple and proceeds gratifyingly quickly.

The flooring is available in 2 main types: as solid planks, and as laminated strips with a decorative surface veneer. Lengths range from as little as 40 cm/ 16 in up to 1.8 m/6 ft, and widths from 7 cm/2¾ in up to 20 cm/8 in. Solid planks are usually 15 mm/⅝ in thick; laminated strips are a little thinner.

Both types are generally tongued-and-grooved on their long edges for easy fitting. Some are designed to be fixed to a wooden sub-floor by secret nailing; others are loose-laid, using ingenious metal clips to hold adjacent strips together. A wide range of wood varieties is available in each type. Laminated strips are generally pre-finished, as are some solid types, but others may need sealing once they have been laid down.

Always unpack the strips and leave them in the room where they will be laid for about a week to acclimatize to the temperature and humidity levels in the home. This will prevent buckling due to expansion, or shrinkage due to contraction, when the flooring is laid.

If the manufacturer recommends the use of a special underlay – which may be polythene (polyethylene) sheeting, glass-fibre matting or foam – put this down next, and tape or staple the joins together so that they do not ruck up while you lay the floor.

REMOVING OLD FLOOR COVERINGS

Generally speaking, old floor coverings should always be lifted before you lay new ones. This also provides an opportunity to inspect the floor itself and to carry out any repairs that may be necessary.

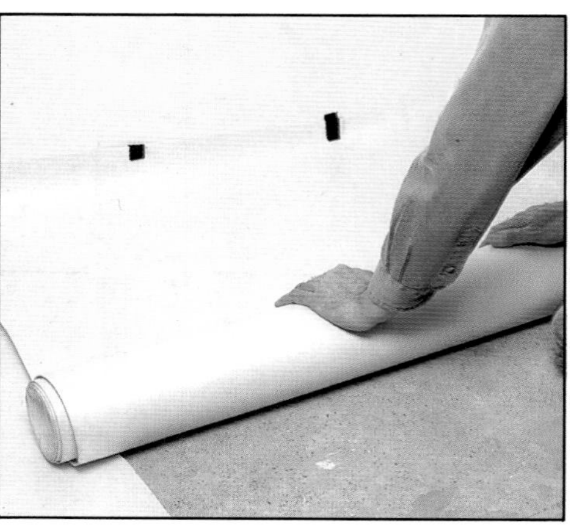

1 Make sure that the sub-floor is clean, dry and level, and remove the skirtings (baseboards) if necessary. Unroll the special underlay (if using) across the floor, taping 1 end to keep it in place.

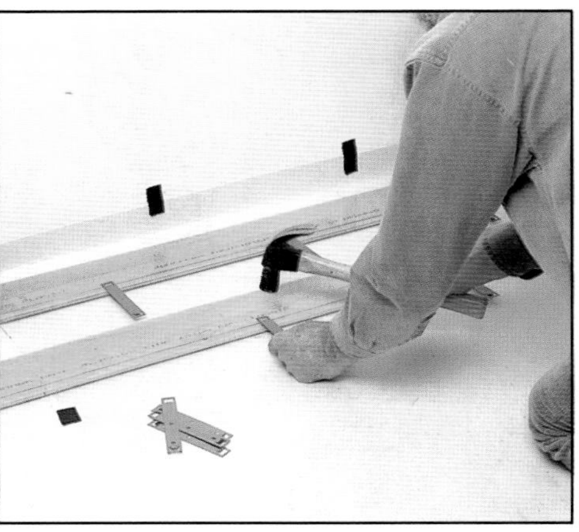

2 Prepare all the lengths of board by hammering the special metal joint clips into the grooves on the undersides of the boards, next to the tongued edges.

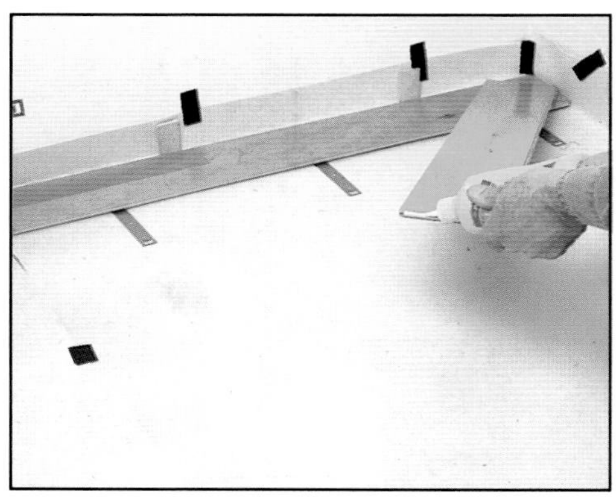

3 Lay the first length, clips outwards, against the wall, using spacers to create an expansion gap next to the wall. Glue the ends of butt-jointed lengths.

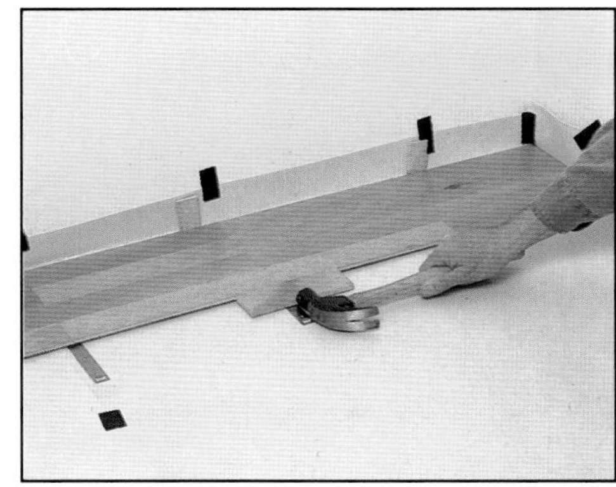

4 Position the second row of boards, tapping them together with a hammer and an offcut so that the clips on the first row engage in the groove of the second.

5 The last board is fitted without clips. Cut it to width, allowing for the spacers as in step 3, and apply adhesive along its grooved edge.

6 Insert some protective packing against the wall before levering the strip into place. Tamp it down level with a hammer and protect the floor with a board offcut.

ABOVE Hardwearing and elegant, wood-strip flooring is a practical choice for a living room, especially if teamed with a colourful rug.

7 Replace skirtings or pin (tack) on lengths of quadrant beading (a base shoe) to hide any gap. Weight down the board so that it fits tightly against the floor.

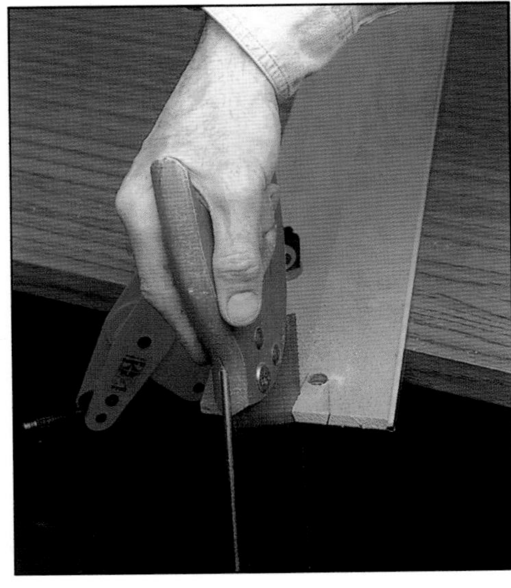

8 To fit a board around a pipe, mark its position and drill a suitable-sized hole. Cut out a tapered wedge, fit the board and then replace the wedge.

PUTTING UP DECORATIVE FEATURES

You can enhance the walls and ceilings of your rooms in many ways: for example, with decorative wood or plaster mouldings, fire surrounds, wall panelling, replacement doors, new door and window furniture, and curtain (drapery) tracks and poles. Pictures and mirrors provide the finishing touches.

Plaster mouldings

Perhaps the simplest type of ornamental plasterwork is panel moulding. This is a decorative strip used to outline areas on walls or a ceiling that will be treated in a different way to the rest of the room, especially as a way of highlighting pictures, mirrors or alcoves.

Panel mouldings are made in a wide range of profiles to suit every taste, from plain fluted and reeded effects to more elaborate versions such as egg-and-dart, flower-and-husk, Roman vine and Greek key. Corners can be mitred, or formed with matching corner blocks or special re-entrant curves.

Cornices (crown moldings)

These decorative plaster features were originally used externally in classical architecture at the edges of roofs, but were soon also used inside on the perimeter of ceilings. As with panel mouldings, a huge range of profiles is available, from authentic Greek and Roman forms through 18th- and 19th-century styles, and featuring such classic motifs as acanthus, dentil, swag-and-drop and egg-and-dart. Plain concave mouldings – known as coving – are also available, made either as a paper-faced moulding with a plaster core, or machined from wood.

ABOVE Ornamental plasterwork, such as cornices (crown moldings) and corbels supporting delicate arches, add a flourish to any décor, especially in period homes.

LEFT Decorative mouldings are very much in vogue as a means of breaking up large expanses of wall and displaying picture groups. The choice of paint colours is important in balancing the different, defined areas of wall.

RIGHT Wood panelling below dado- (chair-) rail level is a durable alternative to wall coverings. The natural divide can be highlighted with an attractive stencil border.

RIGHT Panelled doors can be made part of an overall colour scheme by highlighting the panel surrounds to match the other decorative mouldings in the room and to complement the soft-furnishing fabrics.

BELOW Window dressing adds the finishing touch to any room. Here, a festoon blind is suspended from a decorative wooden pole.

Wooden mouldings

Most wooden mouldings are machined either from softwood or from a cheap hardwood, in a wide range of cross-sections. The larger mouldings – architraves (door and window trims), skirtings (baseboards) and the like – are cut from softwood, while mouldings with smaller and more intricate profiles are made from hardwood. Mouldings can be given a coloured finish, or stained and varnished.

Skirtings (baseboards)

These boards are fitted to plastered walls at ground level to protect the plaster surface from damage by careless feet or furniture, and also allow floor-cleaning implements to be used right up to the floor edge without wetting or marking the walls. Until recently, the fashion was for low, plain skirtings, but in many homes there is now a switch back to more ornate types, often stained and varnished.

Dado (chair) and picture rails

These are horizontal mouldings fixed to wall surfaces, the former about 90 cm/ 3 ft from the floor and the latter a short way below ceiling level. The dado rail was designed to protect the plaster from damage by chair backs, and also provided a break in the walls' colour scheme. Traditionally, the area below the rail was panelled or finished in a relief wall covering, while that above it was papered or painted. The picture rail allowed pictures to be hung and moved about, and also provided a visual break in rooms with high ceilings.

Doors and windows

Replacing room doors is one way of giving a room a dramatic facelift, especially if the existing doors are out of keeping with the look of the room. New doors deserve new fittings, and again there is a wide range of handles, knobs and latches from which to choose, including various metallic finishes, wood, plastic and even glass and ceramics. The same applies to windows. Changing these is a bigger job than replacing a door, but simply fitting new stays and catches can give an old window frame a new lease of life.

Curtain (drapery) tracks and poles

One last fixture that deserves some attention is the hardware that supports the curtains (drapes). Curtain tracks and poles may be wall- or ceiling-mounted, and can be made of metal, wood or plastic in a range of styles and finishes. The simplest types of tracks are unobtrusive; more complex versions include cords or motor drives to move the curtains. Ornamental poles make a feature in their own right.

PUTTING UP A CORNICE (CROWN MOLDING)

There are 3 types of decorative cornice commonly used in today's homes. The first type is coving, a relative of sheet plasterboard (gypsum board), which consists of a concave hollow-backed plaster core sheathed in a strong paper envelope. It is fixed in place with adhesive. The second is moulded cornice; this is made either from traditional fibrous plaster or from modern foamed plastics to imitate the ornate decorative cornices often found in older buildings, and comes in a range of profiles. Plaster types must generally be secured in place with screws because of their weight, but plastic types can simply be stuck in position with adhesive. The third type is a machined wooden trim with a similar profile to plasterboard cornice, and is either nailed direct to the wall framing or to a nailing strip or batten (furring strip) in the angle of the wall and ceiling.

Apart from its decorative appearance in framing the ceiling, a cornice can also help to conceal unsightly cracks. These often open up around the ceiling perimeter as the ceiling expands and contracts with changes in temperature and humidity, or as the building settles.

FITTING A CORNICE (CROWN MOLDING)

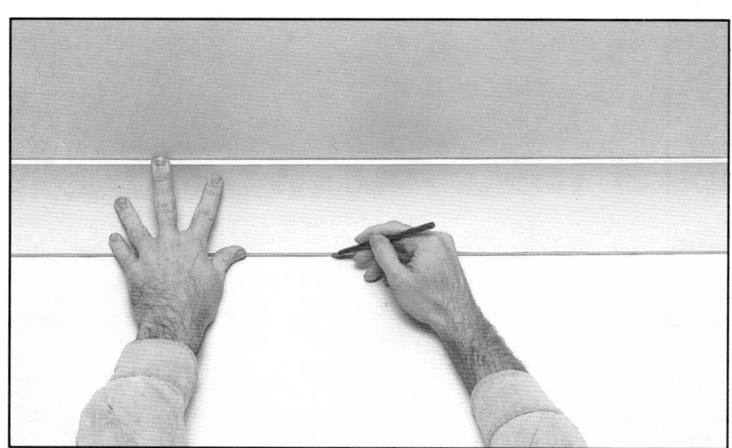

1 Hold a length of cornice squarely in the wall/ceiling angle and draw 2 guidelines on the wall and ceiling surfaces. Cut any mitred edges (see opposite page, below).

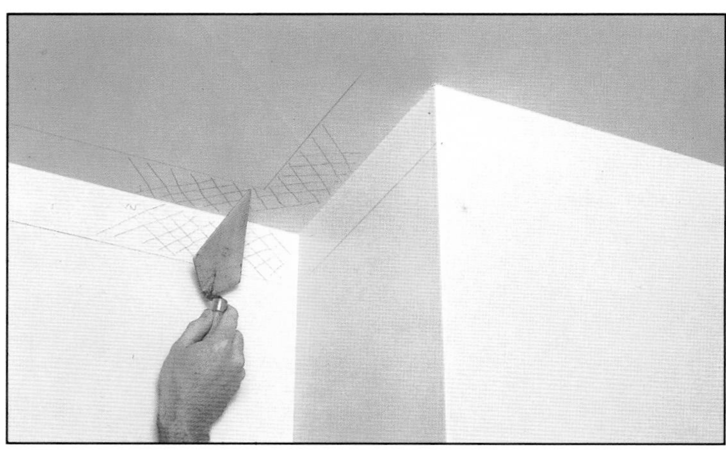

2 Remove any old wall coverings from between the guidelines by dry-scraping them. Cross-hatch painted or bare plaster to key the surface.

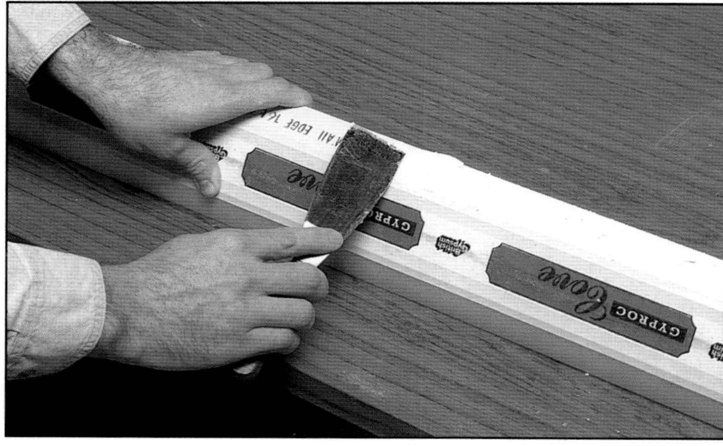

3 Either mix up powder adhesive or use a ready-mixed type. Using a flat scraper, 'butter' the adhesive on to both edges of the rear of the cornice.

4 Press the length into place between the guidelines, supporting it if necessary with partly driven masonry nails. Remove the nails (if used) once the adhesive has set.

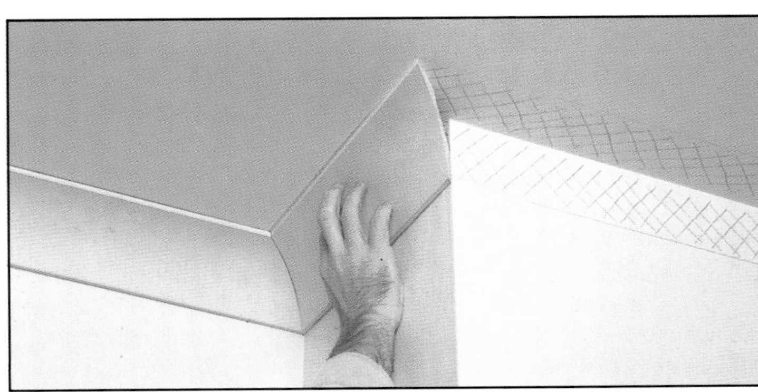

5 Fit the adjacent corner piece next. Here, the next section also incorporates an external mitre; measure and cut this carefully before fitting the length.

6 Complete the external corner with a further length of cornice, butting the cut ends closely together and ensuring that the length fits between the lines.

7 Fill any slight gaps at external and internal angles with a little cellulose filler (spackle), applied with a filling knife (putty knife) to leave a crisp, clean joint. Sand the filler smooth once it has hardened.

8 Before the adhesive sets hard, use a damp sponge to remove any excess from wall and ceiling surfaces and also to smooth over the filled joints.

Cutting a Cornice (Crown Molding)

1 Make up a large mitre block big enough to hold the cornice, and use this and a tenon saw to make accurate 45° cuts for internal and external corners.

2 Some cornice manufacturers supply a paper template that enables cutting lines to be marked accurately for internal and external corners.

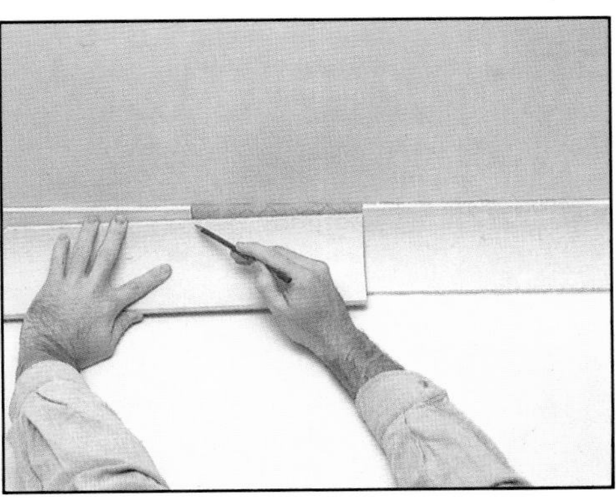

3 When using cut pieces to complete a wall, mark off the length required directly, square a line across the cornice with a pencil and cut it to length.

PUTTING UP A DADO (CHAIR) OR PICTURE RAIL

A dado (chair) rail is a flat-backed wooden moulding that runs around the room about one-third of the way up from the floor. Its primary purpose is to protect the wall surfaces from damage caused by furniture – especially chair backs – knocking against them. Once fitted, it can be painted, varnished or stained to complement or contrast with the room's colour scheme. It also serves as a visual break in the surface of the wall, as different treatments can be used above and below the rail – wallpaper above, for example, and wood panelling below.

The area below the rail, which is known as the dado (wainscot) was traditionally panelled or decorated with a relief wall covering and painted, while the surface above the rail was generally papered or painted in a plain colour. The wide range of decorative techniques in use today, however – including special paint effects such as sponging, rag-rolling, stippling and marbling (see pages 22–5) – offer great potential for interesting results.

A dado rail can be nailed to wood-framed walls after using a stud finder to locate the vertical members of the frame. On masonry walls, do not use masonry nails, as the rail may need to be removed in the future; use screws and wall plugs instead.

A picture rail is, as its name implies, used to support pictures. It is fixed to the wall a short distance below the ceiling, and has a curved upper edge designed to accept S-shaped picture hooks, from which the pictures can hang on wire, cord or chain. As large pictures (and also large mirrors) can be heavy, the rail must be securely fixed – with screws rather than nails. As with a dado rail, a picture rail can be decorated to complement or contrast with the wall covering. Its presence also allows the ceiling decoration to be carried down to rail level, a useful trick for making a high ceiling appear lower.

1 Start by deciding on the precise height at which to fix the rail, and use a pencil and spirit level to draw a horizontal line around the room.

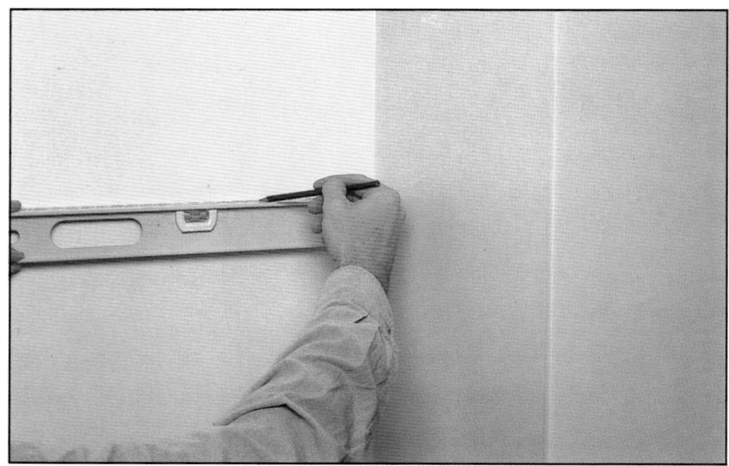

2 Alternatively, use a chalked string line pinned to the wall to mark the horizontal guideline on each wall of the room in turn.

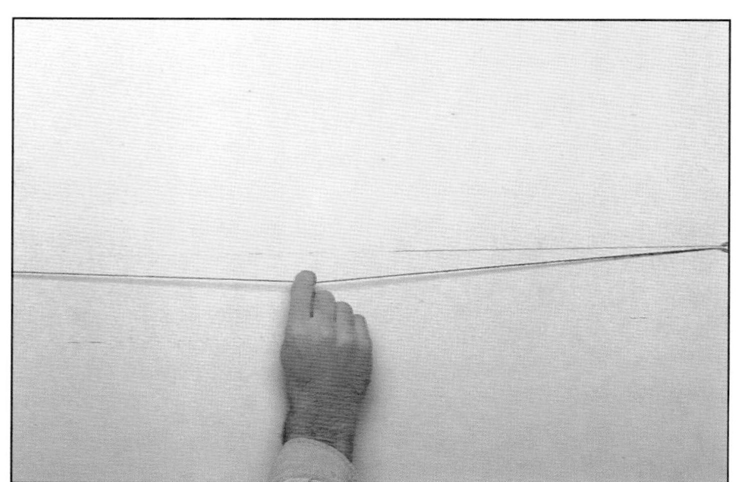

3 Drill clearance and countersink holes in the moulding at roughly 60 cm/2 ft intervals. Alternatively, counter-bore holes for wooden plugs instead.

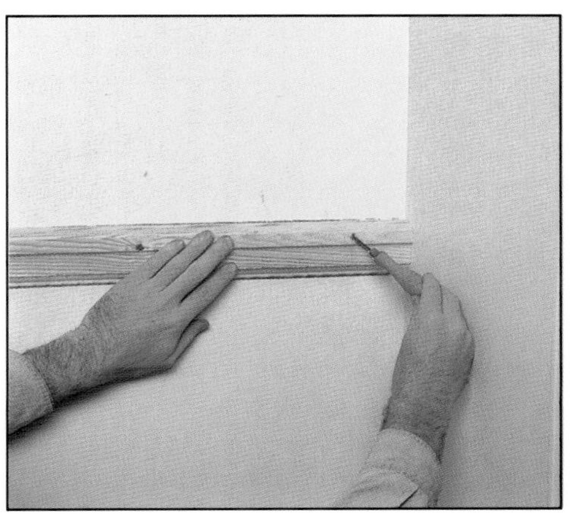

4 Hold the first length of rail up to the guideline and use a bradawl or similar tool to mark the fixing positions on the wall through the screw holes.

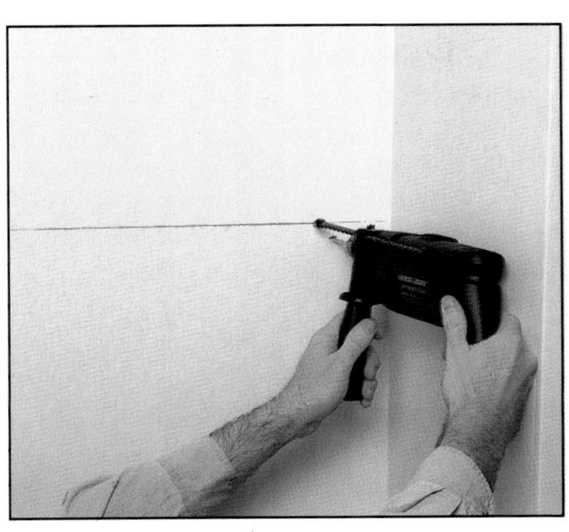

5 On masonry walls, drill holes for wall plugs. On wood-framed walls, use cavity fixings or locate the studs so that nails can go directly into them.

6 Drive in the first screw at one end of the length, then the next at the other end before driving in intermediate screws. This will keep the rail exactly on line.

MAKING ANGLED JOINS

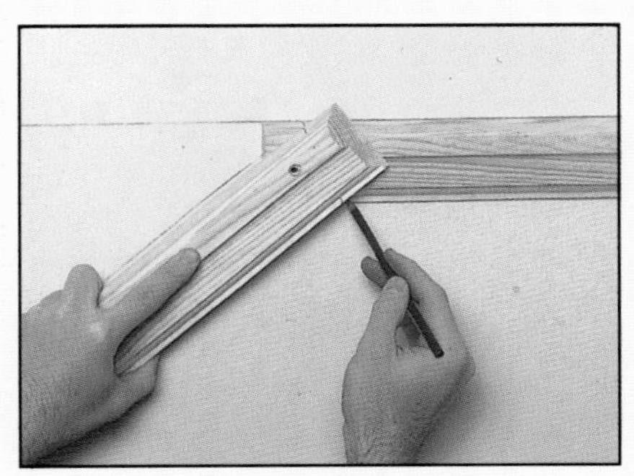

1 If you wish to fit a dado (chair) rail down a staircase, draw guidelines parallel with the flight on the staircase wall and mark the 2 meeting rails.

2 Cut the ends of the 2 rail sections so that they will form a neat join line; this should exactly bisect the angle between the 2 sections.

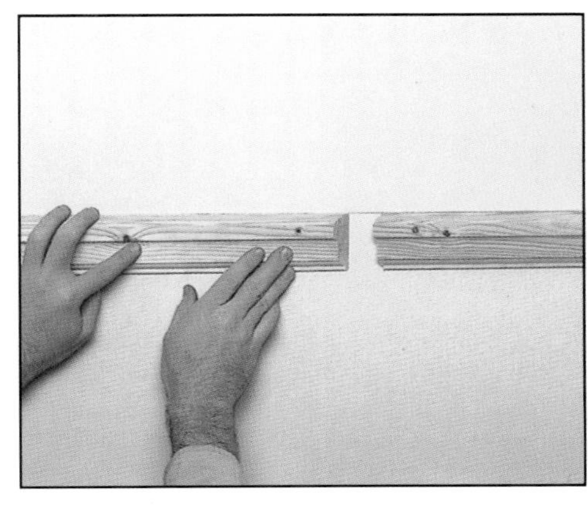

7 If lengths need joining along the length of a wall, make 45° mitre cuts on the meeting ends so that any shrinkage which occurs will not open up a visible gap.

8 Always use butt joins at internal angles. Scribe the rail profile on to the rear face of the length that will go on the second wall.

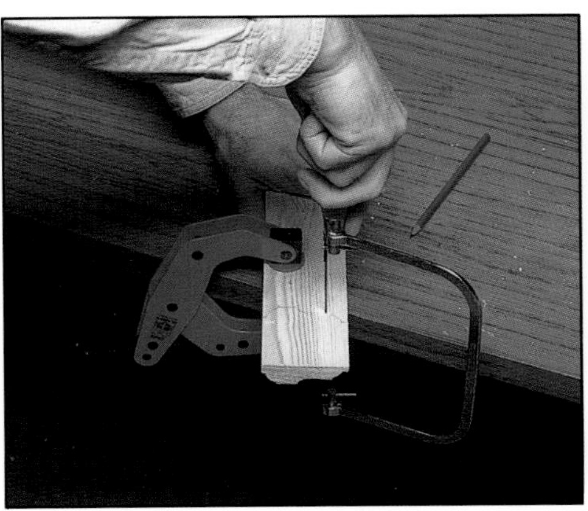

9 Cut carefully along the marked line with a coping saw, then fit the cut end so that it butts tightly against the face of the rail on the first wall.

10 Use mitred joints at external corners, cutting at just under 45° so that there is no chance of an ugly gap at the corner.

FITTING DOOR AND WINDOW HARDWARE

Door and window fittings can be ornamental as well as practical and secure. The simplest type of door catch is a spring-loaded ball which is recessed into the door edge. The ball engages in a recess in the door frame as the door is pushed closed, and retracts as the door is pulled open. This type of catch is inexpensive to buy and easy to fit.

A more positive action is provided by a mortise latch; this is also recessed into the door edge and has a projecting bolt that is flat on one face and curved on the other. As the door is pushed shut, the curved face hits the striking plate on the door frame and pushes the bolt back into the latch body. When the door is fully closed the bolt springs out into the recess in the striking plate, with its flat face providing a positive latching movement. The action of turning the handle rotates a spindle, withdrawing the bolt from the striking plate and allowing the door to open again. A mortise lock combines the same type of latch mechanism with a lockable bolt.

The most common items of hardware used on hinged windows are a rotating cockspur handle that is used simply to fasten the window, and a casement stay that props it open in one of several different positions. On sliding sash windows, the basic hardware consists of a catch screwed to the 'back' window that swings across to lock the 2 sashes together when they are closed.

SAFETY TIP

If you are fitting lockable window catches and stays, do not leave the keys in the locks in case they fall out as you open and close the window. Instead, hang them on a pin driven into the window frame. This will also ensure that they are readily available should the window have to be opened quickly in an emergency.

FITTING A MORTISE LATCH

1 To fit a mortise latch to a new door, use the latch body to mark the mortise position on the door edge, in line with the centre rail or lock block.

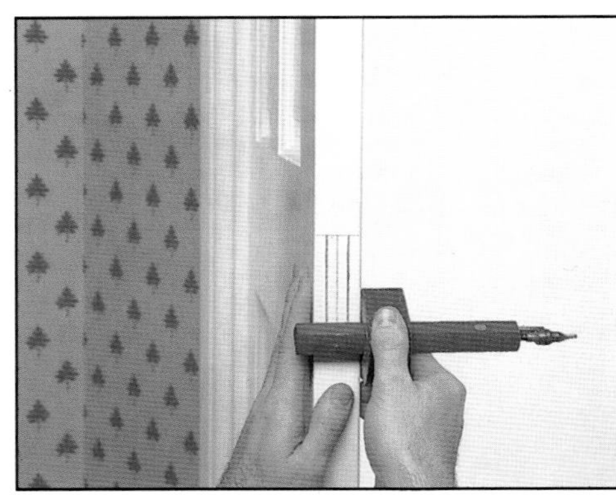

2 Set a mortise gauge to a setting just wider than the thickness of the latch body, and scribe the outline of the mortise centred on the door edge.

3 Use a flat wood bit in a power drill to make a series of holes between the guidelines, a little deeper than the length of the latch body.

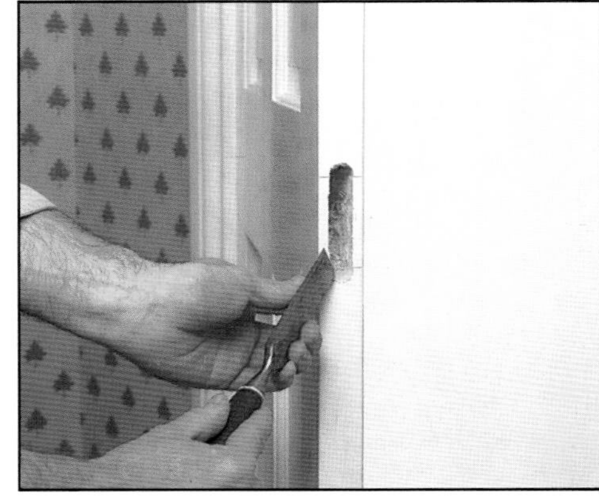

4 Chop out the waste using a chisel and mallet, then pare down the sides of the mortise and clean out the recess. Try the latch for fit in the mortise.

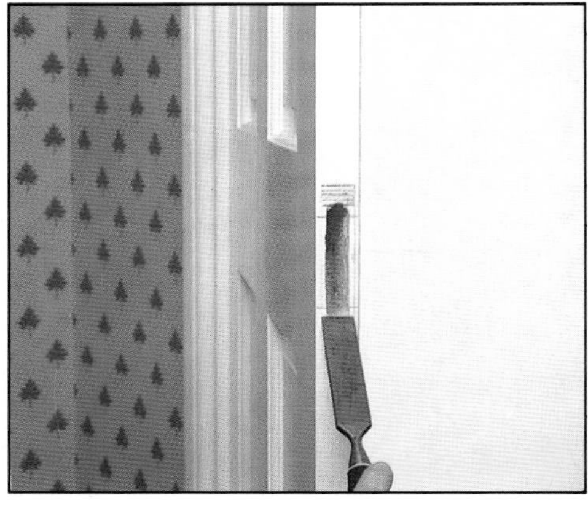

5 Draw around the latch faceplate on the edge of the door, then cut around the lines with a chisel and make a series of parallel cuts across the grain.

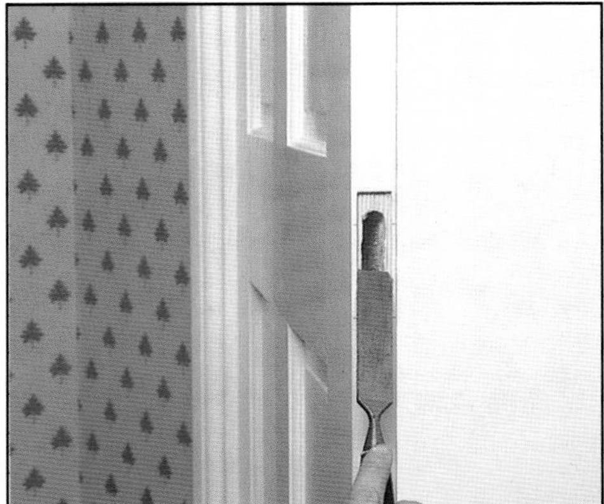

6 Carefully chisel out the waste wood between the marked guidelines, taking care not to let the chisel slip and cut beyond the ends of the recess.

7 Hold the latch body against the face of the door, in line with the mortise and with its faceplate flush with the door edge. Mark the spindle position.

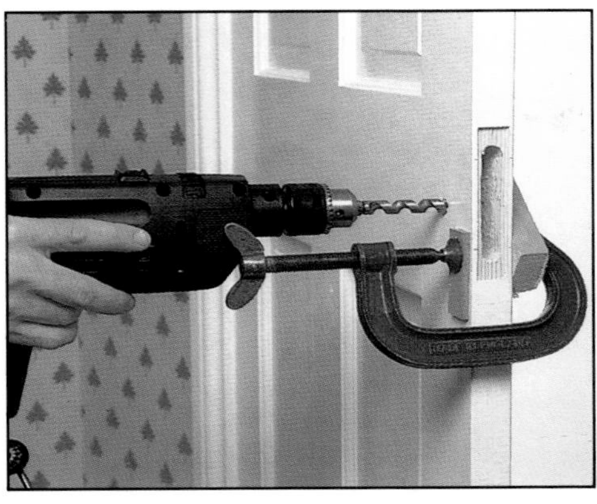

8 Clamp a piece of scrap wood to the other side of the door. Drill a hole large enough to accept the spindle through the door into the scrap wood.

9 Slide the latch into place in its mortise, and make pilot holes through the faceplate with a bradawl. Drive in the faceplate fixing screws.

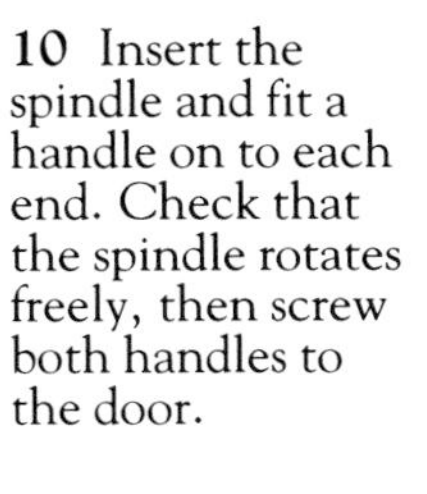

10 Insert the spindle and fit a handle on to each end. Check that the spindle rotates freely, then screw both handles to the door.

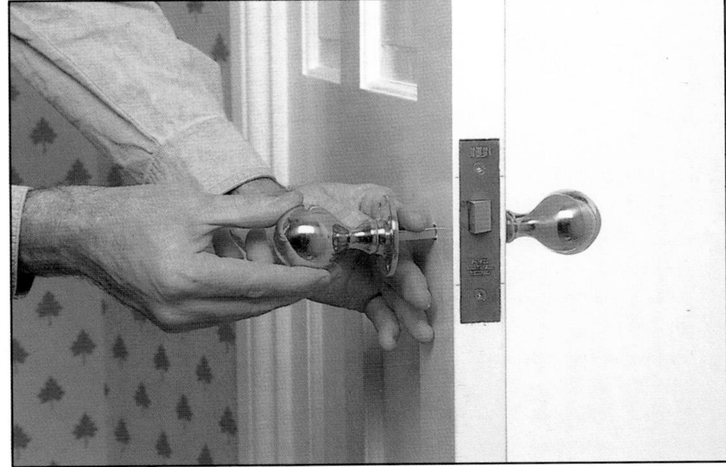

11 Close the door in order to mark where the latch bolt meets the frame. Chisel out the recesses for the bolt and striking plate, and screw on the plate.

Fitting a Window Handle and Stay

1 Decide where the cockspur handle should sit on the casement and make pilot holes through it with a bradawl. Screw the handle to the casement.

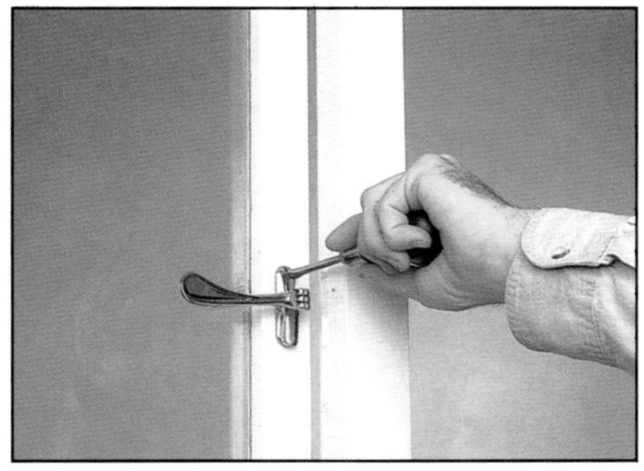

2 Fit the striking plate to the frame so that the cockspur will engage in it. Drill out the frame to a depth of about 20 mm/¾ in through the slot in the plate.

3 Fit the casement stay by screwing its baseplate to the bottom rail of the casement, about one-third of the way along from the hinged edge.

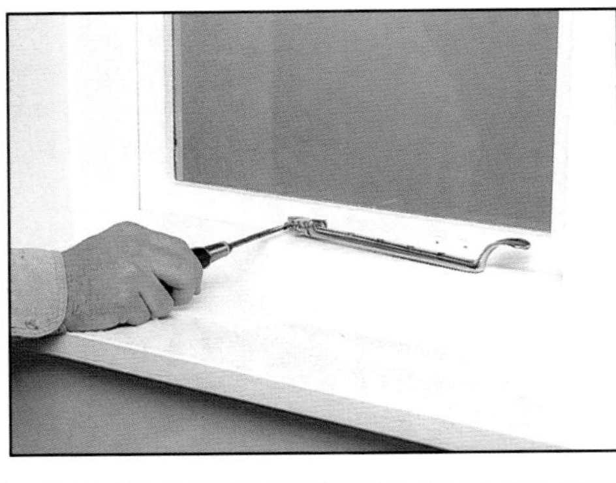

4 Open the window to find the correct position for the pins to sit on the frame. Attach the pins, then fit the stay rest on the casement rail.

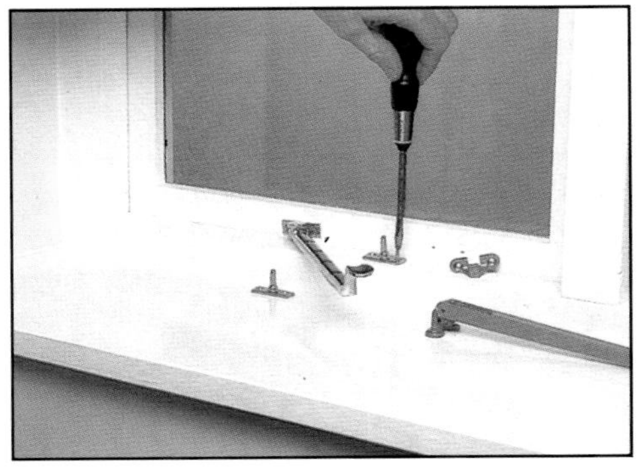

FITTING CURTAIN (DRAPERY) POLES AND TRACKS

There are many different methods of hanging curtains and drapes, ranging from simple rings on a wooden pole to complex tracks that are often cord-operated and may even be motor-driven. Poles may be wooden or metal, while tracks are either metal or plastic. Some are designed to be unobtrusive, others to be a definite design feature. The choice depends on the style of décor, and also to some extent on the curtains themselves, as some heading styles work better with one type than another. Check with the supplier to see which track style will work best.

Fixing curtain tracks can be tricky on a masonry wall. The top of the window opening may be bridged by a reinforced concrete or galvanized-steel beam, concealed behind the plaster. The problem lies in making firm fixings into this beam, as drilling concrete at a precise spot to take a wall plug and screw can be difficult, and you will need a cavity fixing such as a spring toggle for a steel beam. It is often easier either to fit the track above the beam, or to put up a wooden support strip first and then attach the track to that. If the worst comes to the worst, you could use a ceiling-mounted track. Fixing tracks to wood-framed walls, by contrast, could not be easier. You can fix the brackets anywhere on the wooden beam over the window opening.

TIP

Before you buy your curtain (drapery) pole or track, measure the width of the window carefully, and add extra width at the sides. The amount you add will depend on the bulk of the curtains, and how much space they will take up when they are open. With a narrow window, it is important to allow enough width for the pole or track so that the curtains do not obscure the window at all.

PUTTING UP A CURTAIN (DRAPERY) POLE

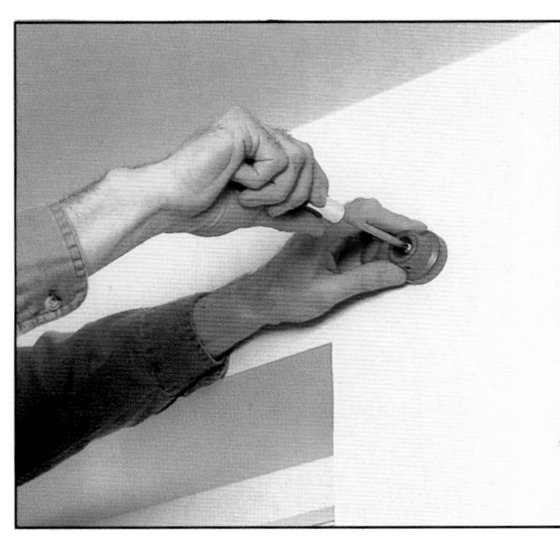

1 Draw a pencil guideline on the wall, and mark the bracket positions along it. Attach the bracket bases after drilling and/or plugging the holes.

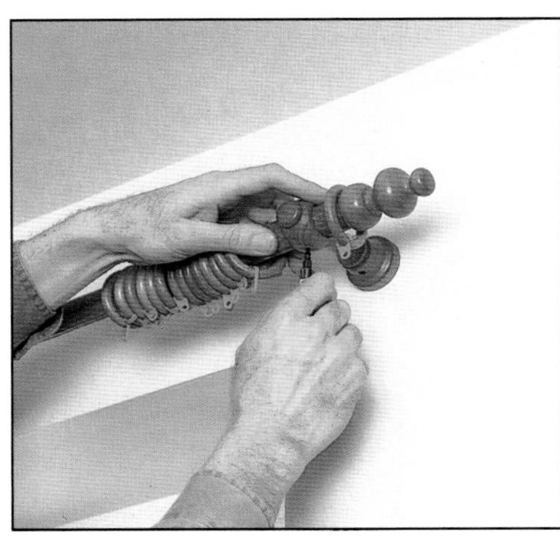

2 Slot in the bracket extensions and tighten the locking screws. Slide in the pole, fit the rings and finial, and screw through the brackets into the pole.

PUTTING UP A ROLLER BLIND (SHADE)

A roller blind, as its name implies, consists of a length of material – usually fabric – wound on to a roller that is mounted in brackets close to the window. It can be used instead of curtains and drapes for a simple, uncluttered effect, or in conjunction with them – for example if extra shade is required in a sunny window.

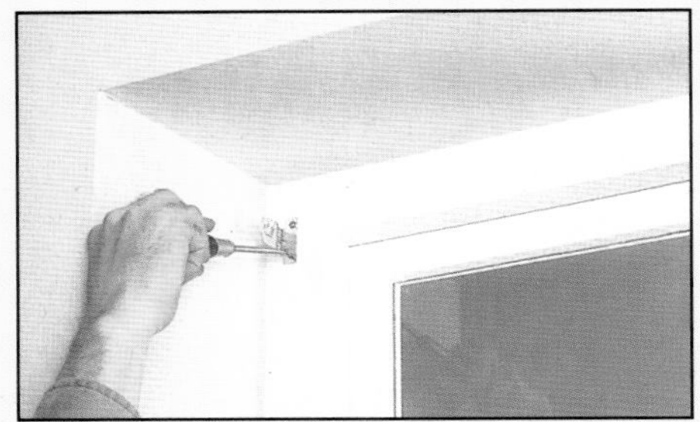

1 Screw the roller brackets to the frame close to the top corners, with the fixing flanges facing inwards so that you have room to use a screwdriver.

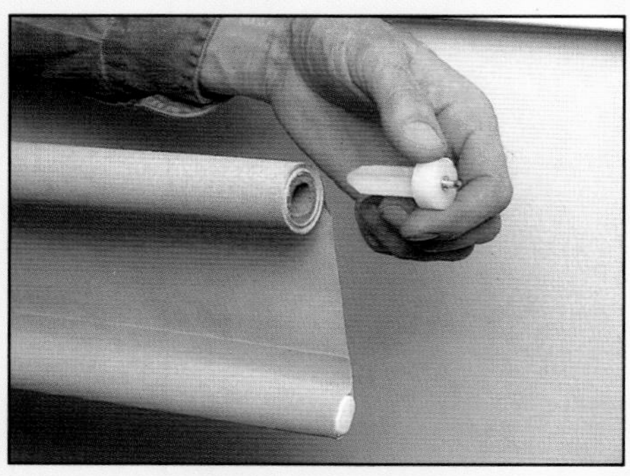

2 Cut the roller and fabric to the required width, and insert the pin caps at each end to match the brackets – one is round, the other rectangular.

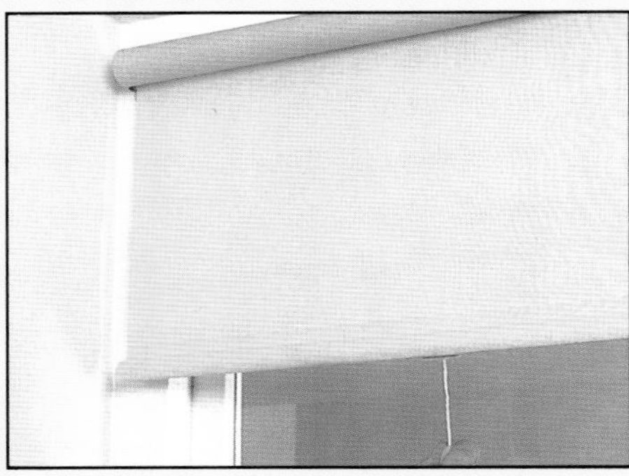

3 Hang the roller on its brackets, then pull it down to check the tension. If it will not retract, lift off the ratchet end, roll up the blind and replace it.

PUTTING UP A CURTAIN (DRAPERY) TRACK

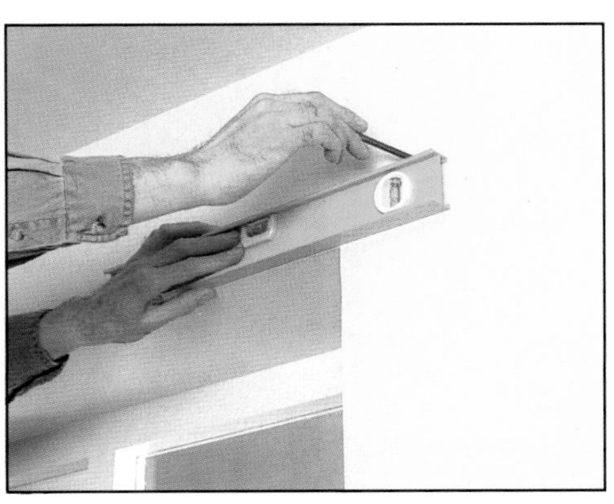

1 Decide at what level to fit the track, and use a pencil and spirit level to draw a guideline on the wall surface. Extend the line at the sides.

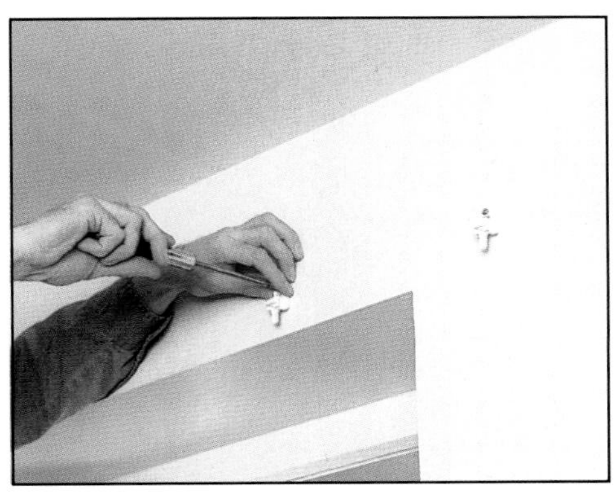

2 Drill holes for wall plugs in a masonry wall, or make pilot holes in a wood-framed one, at the spacings recommended in the instructions. Fit the brackets.

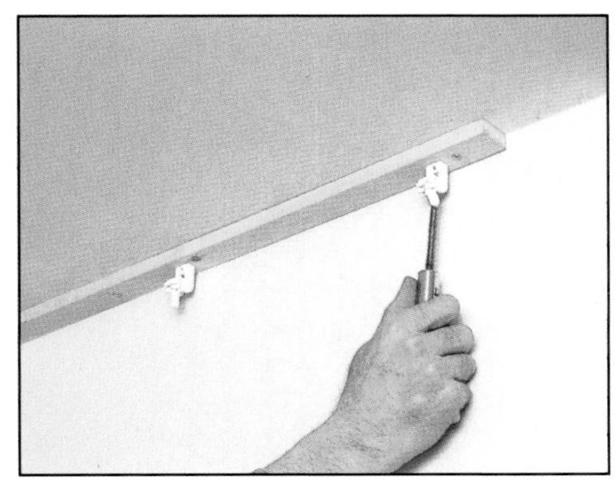

3 If you need to use a ceiling-mounted track, locate the joist or joists and screw a support strip into place. Attach the track brackets to the support strip.

4 If you have to fit lengths of track together to cope with wide windows, you must use special connectors that do not interfere with the runners.

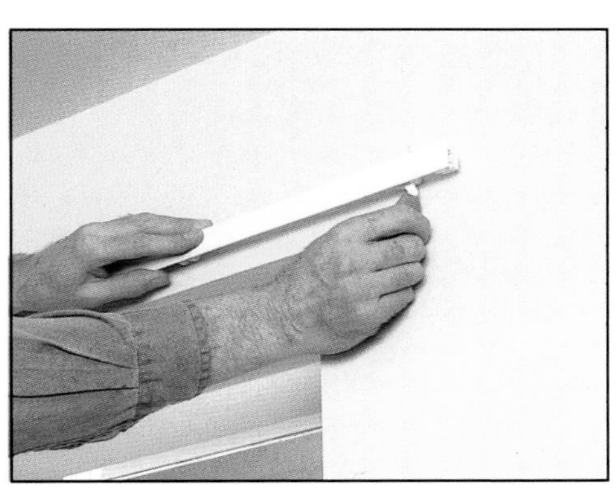

5 Mount the track on the brackets. Here, this is done by rotating a locking cam via a small lever; on other types there is a locking screw.

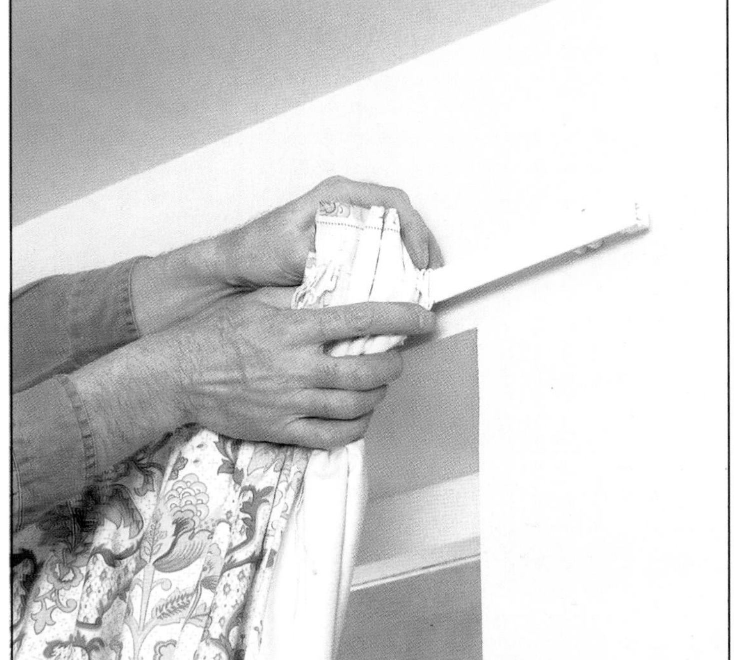

6 Fit the curtain hooks to the heading tape, then clip the hooks to the track. Some types have hooks on the track already, in which case you can simply hook on the curtains.

MAKING AN OVERLAP

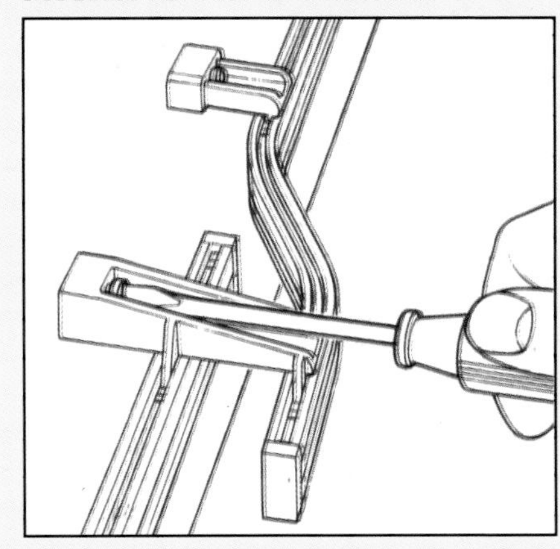

If you require a curtain overlap, form an S-bend on a length of track so that it overlaps the track behind. Clip the extension bracket to the tracks and screw the bracket to the wall.

INCREASING STORAGE SPACE

Apart from obvious places such as kitchen units (cabinets) and bedroom wardrobes (closets), there are many places in the house in which you can store items without spoiling the look of the room. Properly planned storage space can be not only practical and capacious, but positively elegant.

In the kitchen, storage is a serious business, and what you need and how you provide it will depend on what kind of kitchen it is and how you use it. The fully fitted kitchen is popular because it packs the most storage into the least space, whereas the farmhouse-style kitchen, with free-standing furniture, reduces the amount of storage space. There is, however, one big advantage with free-standing furniture: you can take it along when you move house.

In deciding what you want, analyse your storage needs thoroughly. Think about food, cooking utensils and small appliances for a start; all need a place close to cooking and food-preparation areas. Move on to items such as china, cutlery and glassware; do they need to be in the kitchen at all, or would the dining room be a better place to keep them? Then consider non-culinary items – cleaning materials, table linen and so on – and make sure that there is enough space for them.

Always make the best possible use of cupboard (closet) space. Fit extra shelves where necessary, use wire baskets for ventilated storage, hang small racks on the backs of doors and use swing-out carousels to gain access to corner cupboards.

In the living room, storage needs are likely to be leisure-oriented. There has to be enough room for books, cassettes, compact discs and videotapes, not to mention display space for ornaments. The choice is again between free-standing and built-in furniture, and is much freer than in the kitchen because in this room looks are just as important as performance.

Built-in furniture can make optimum use of alcoves and other recesses. A more radical option is a complete wall of storage units, which could include space for home-entertainment equipment as well as features such as a drinks cupboard (cabinet). While planning living-room storage, pay particular attention to working requirements for power points (receptacles), especially if you have a lot of hi-fi (stereo) equipment, and for any concealed lighting in the unit.

Storage needs in the dining room relate mainly to providing places for china, glassware and cutlery (flatware)

ABOVE Wall-mounted shelving in this hallway provides an unobtrusive home for the telephone.

LEFT Fitted kitchen units (cabinets) offer much more than a home for provisions and pots and pans. Tailor-made units can now store and display everything from wine bottles to the family china.

STORAGE IN THE HALLWAY

Simple hooks and an umbrella stand are the bare minimum, but consider having an enclosed cupboard (closet) that is built-in rather than free-standing. It is simple to 'borrow' some porch- or hall-floor space to create a suitable enclosure. If you fit the cupboard with a door to match others leading to the rest of the house, it will blend in perfectly. Make sure that the cupboard is ventilated so that any damp clothes will be able to dry.

LEFT An alcove is the perfect site for built-in shelving for books, or for display and storage cupboards (cabinets) for music cassettes and discs, videos, hi-fi (stereo) equipment and so on.

BELOW A beautifully tiled bathroom is further enhanced with an attractive vanity unit, which can offer valuable storage space for toiletries.

– especially any that is kept for special occasions. Think too about storage for table mats, cloths and other table accessories. Once again, the choice is between built-in storage units and free-standing furniture.

Now take a look at your storage requirements upstairs, starting with the bedrooms. Here the main need is for space to store clothes, and this is one area in which built-in (and ideally, walk-in) storage is the perfect solution. Space can often be 'poached' between bedrooms by forming a deep partition wall, accessible from one or both rooms; this can actually save money, as there will be no furniture to buy. An alternative if overall space permits is to create a separate dressing room, at least for the master bedroom.

Bedrooms built under the roof slope offer an unparalleled opportunity to make use of the space behind the room walls by creating fully lined eaves cupboards (closets). These are ideal for long-term storage of items such as luggage which may be needed only occasionally, as well as providing a home for toys in children's rooms.

Finally, look at the bathroom. Here requirements are likely to be relatively low-key – somewhere to keep toiletries and cleaning materials, for example. The choice is likely to be between a floor-standing vanity unit and some wall-hung cupboards (cabinets), although if space permits you might give some thought to the growing number of fully fitted bathroom-furniture ranges. Where space is very limited, make use of the 'hidden' space behind a removable bath panel to store small items such as children's bath toys.

USING THE ROOF SPACE

Except in older houses, the roof space is usually cluttered with all the woodwork that makes up a modern trussed-rafter roof and is of little use for storage. However, it is still worth boarding over the area immediately around the access hatch so that you can put luggage, boxes and the like there. If the roof construction permits, however, there is a chance to create an almost unlimited storage capacity. Fit a proper fixed ladder to allow both safe and easy access.

ABOVE Pull-out baskets are often more accessible than traditional shelving in kitchen base units (cabinets).

FITTING FIXED AND ADJUSTABLE SHELVING

Wall-mounted shelving is either fixed or adjustable. With fixed shelving, each shelf is supported independently using 2 or more shelf brackets, which are fixed both to the wall and to the underside of the shelf. With adjustable shelving, the shelves are carried on brackets, studs or tongues which are slotted or clipped into vertical support strips screwed to the wall.

Shelves can be made of natural wood or manufactured boards. Ready-made shelves are usually made of veneered or plastic-coated chipboard (particle board). The latter traditionally have either a white or imitation wood-grain finish, but pastel shades and bold colours are now more widely available. Otherwise, you can cut shelves from full-sized boards: chipboard, plywood, MDF (medium-density fibreboard) and blockboard are all suitable.

There are many types of adjustable shelving on the market, with uprights and brackets usually made of metal but occasionally of wood. All operate on broadly the same principle. Start by deciding on the position and spacing of the uprights; this will depend on what sort of shelf material you are using and what load it will carry. Hang the uprights on the wall, making sure that they are perfectly vertical and level with each other. Finally, clip in the brackets and fit the shelves.

You may also want adjustable shelves inside a storage unit. There are 2 options. The first involves drilling a series of aligned holes in each side of the unit, then inserting small shelf-support studs. The second uses book-case strip – a metal moulding with slots into which small pegs or tongues are fitted to support the shelves. You will need 2 strips at each side of the unit.

Using Shelf Brackets

1 Select the correct bracket spacing, then attach the shorter arm of each bracket to the underside of the shelf, so that it is flush with the rear edge.

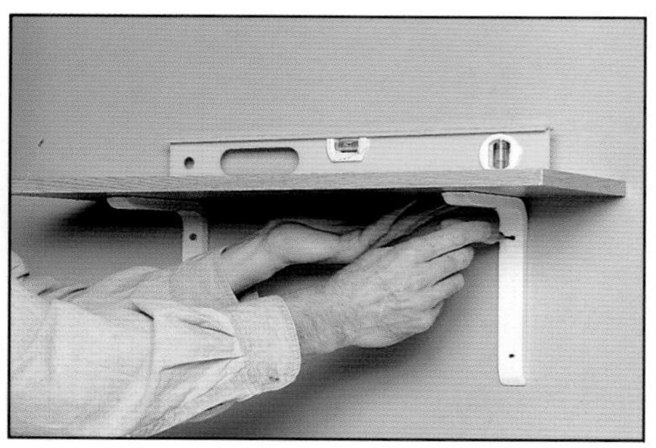

2 Fix the shelf to the wall with a screw driven through one bracket, check that it is horizontal and mark the remaining screw positions. Let the shelf swing downwards on the first screw, then drill the other holes.

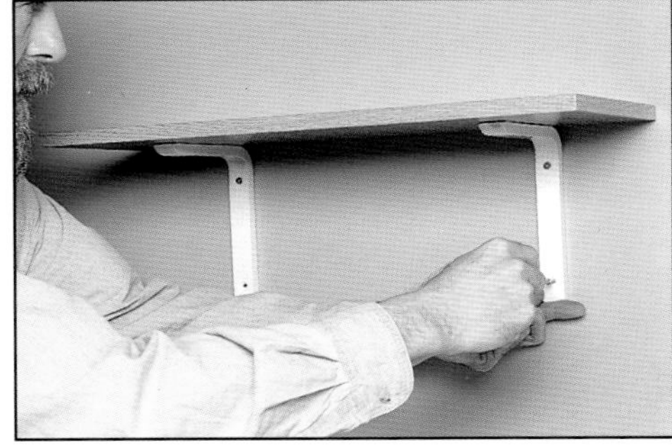

3 Insert plugs for masonry wall fixings if needed. Swing the shelf back up and drive in the remaining fixing screws. Tighten them fully so that the screw heads pull the brackets against the wall.

Putting up Adjustable Shelves

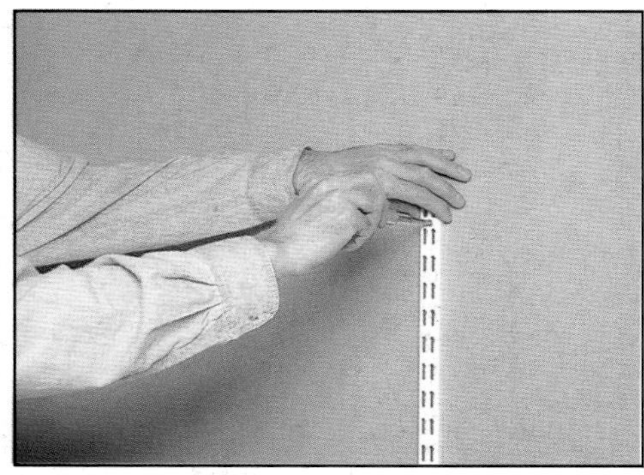

1 Decide where to position the shelves, then fix the first upright to the wall by driving a screw through the topmost hole. Do not tighten it fully.

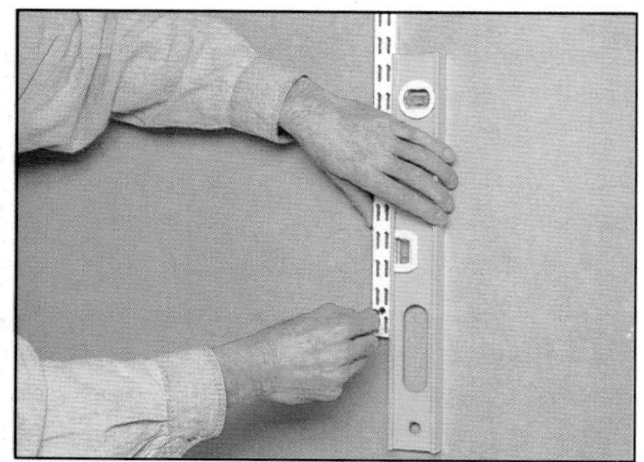

2 Pivot the upright until it is vertical. Mark the position of all the other fixing holes. Swing the upright aside, drill the rest of the holes and drive in the screws.

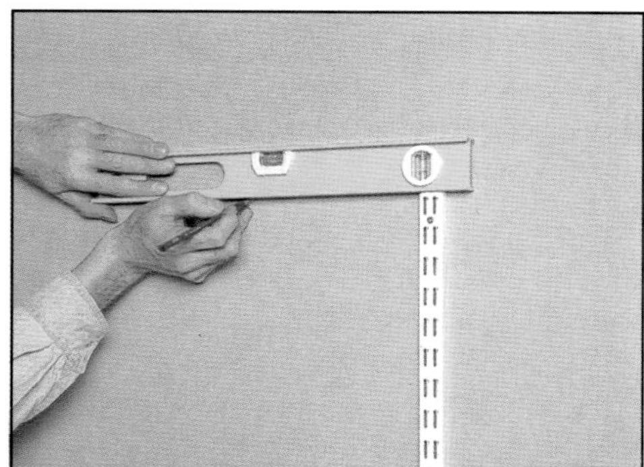

3 Use a spirit level to make a mark on the wall, level with the top of the first upright and at the required distance from it. Fix the second upright there.

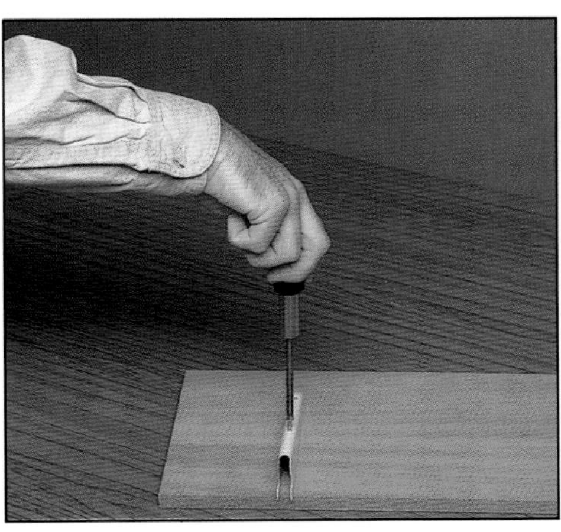

4 Mark the upright positions on the rear edge of each shelf. Align the back of each bracket with the edge of the shelf and with the mark, and screw it on.

5 If the shelves are to fit flush against the wall, cut notches at the upright positions to fit around them and then attach the brackets as shown.

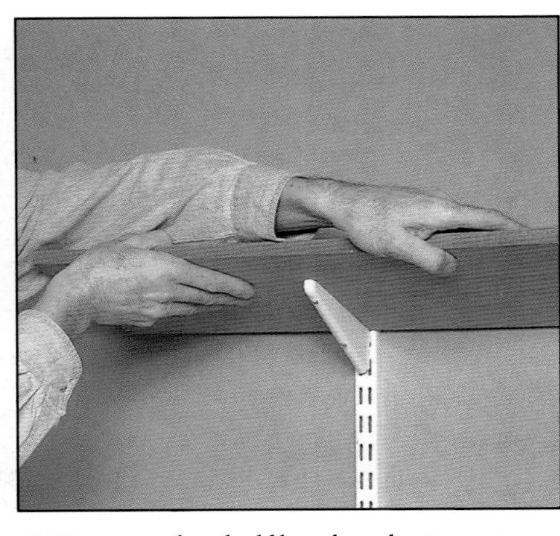

6 Position the shelf brackets by inserting their tongues into the slots in the uprights. The weight of the shelf will lock them in place. Adjust the shelf spacings as wished.

PLANNING SHELVES

Think of how to make best use of your new storage area. It is a good idea to make a rough sketch initially, in order to take account of factors such as the height of books or record sleeves, or the clearance that ornaments or photographs will require. Aim to keep everyday items within easy reach – in practice, between about 75 cm/2 ft 6 in and 1.5 m/5 ft above the floor. Position deep shelves near the bottom so that it is easy to see and reach the back. Allow 2.5–5 cm/1–2 in of clearance on top of the height of objects to be stored, so that they are easy to take down and put back.

Think about weight, too. If the shelves will store heavy objects, you must choose the shelving material with care – thin shelves will sag if heavily laden unless they are well-supported. With 12 mm/½ in chipboard (particle board) and ready-made veneered or melamine-faced shelves, space brackets at 45 cm/18 in for heavy loads or 60 cm/2 ft for light loads. With 20 mm/¾ in chipboard or 12 mm/½ in plywood, increase the spacing to 60 cm/2 ft and 75 cm/2 ft 6 in respectively. For 20 mm/¾ in plywood, blockboard, MDF (medium-density fibreboard) or natural wood, the bracket spacing can be 75 cm/2 ft 6 in for heavy loads, or 90 cm/3 ft for light ones.

Using Bookcase Strip

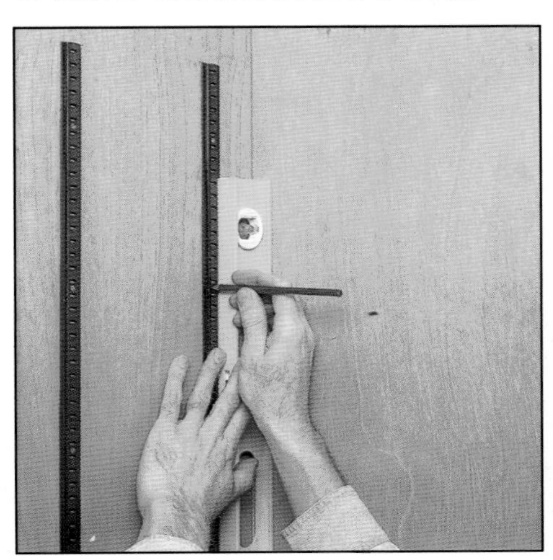

1 Mark the positions of the top ends of the strips to ensure that they are level, then mark the screw positions to a true vertical and screw on the strips.

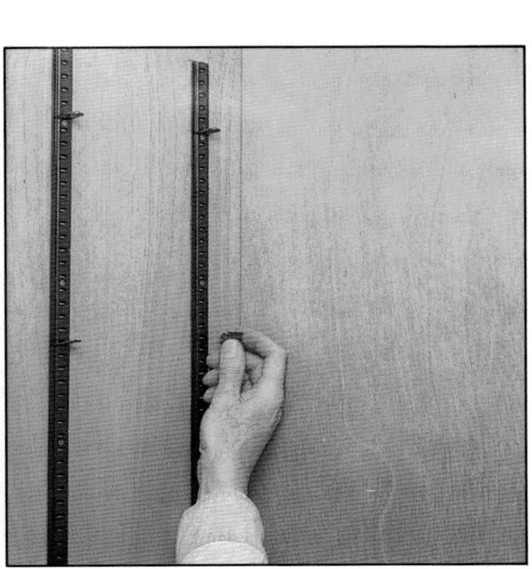

2 Insert pairs of pegs into the strips at each shelf position, checking that their lugs are properly engaged in the slots. Lift the shelf into place.

Using Shelf Supports

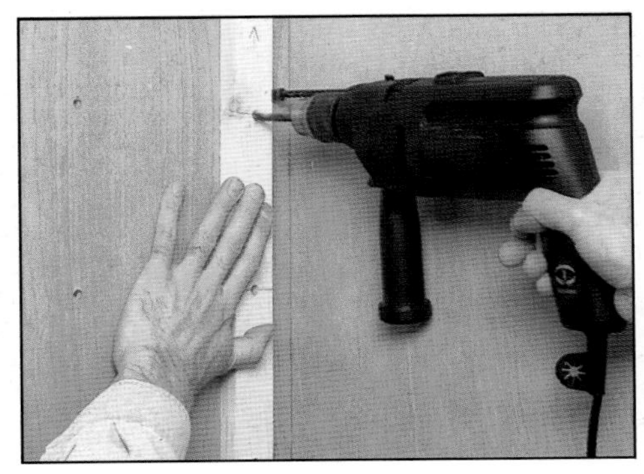

1 Use a simple pre-drilled jig to make the holes for the shelf supports in the sides of the unit. A depth stop will prevent you from drilling too deep.

2 Drill 2 sets of holes in each side of the unit, with the top of the jig held against the top of the unit to guarantee alignment. Insert the supports.

FITTING SHELVES IN AN ALCOVE

An alcove beside a chimney breast (fireplace projection) or similar protrusion makes a perfect site for shelves, as the back and side walls can be used as supports. Although it is easy to use fixed shelf brackets or an adjustable-shelving system to support shelves, it is cheaper to fix wood or metal support strips to the alcove walls and to rest the shelves on these.

If you are using wooden supports, cut their front ends at an angle so that they are less noticeable when the shelves are fitted. Paint them the same colour as the walls (or to tone with the wall covering) to make them even less obtrusive. If you use L-shaped metal strips for the supports, choose a size that matches the shelf thickness so that they will be almost invisible once you have fitted the shelves.

The actual job is quite simple. Mark the shelf level on the alcove walls, cut the supports to the required lengths and screw them to the walls. Then cut your shelf to size and slip it into place, so that it rests on the supports. You can nail, screw or glue it in place for extra stability. The only difficult part lies in making the shelf a good fit, as the alcove walls may not be truly square. Accurate measuring of the alcove width at front and back, plus some careful scribing of the rear edge of the shelf, will ensure good results.

FREE-STANDING SHELVING

A free-standing shelf unit is another possibility for an alcove. This type of unit is basically a box with internal dividers, and is best made using glued butt joints reinforced with hardwood dowels to provide rigidity. Cut the shelves and unit sides to length, drill the dowel holes and insert the dowels to make up the joints. Nailing on a plywood or hardboard backing panel will give the unit extra rigidity.

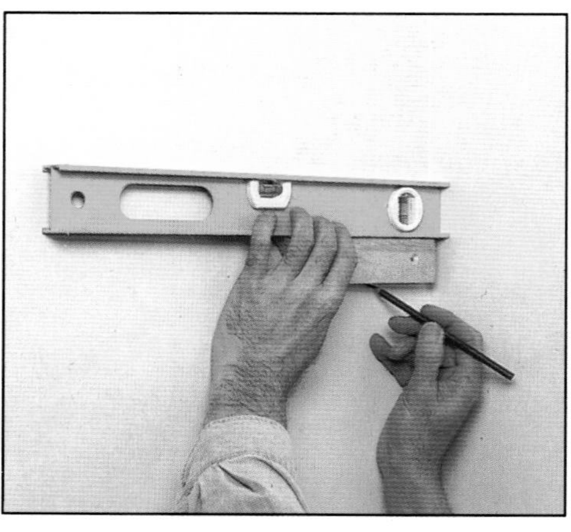

1 Decide on the shelf positions, then use a spirit level to mark the position of the first shelf support on one alcove wall.

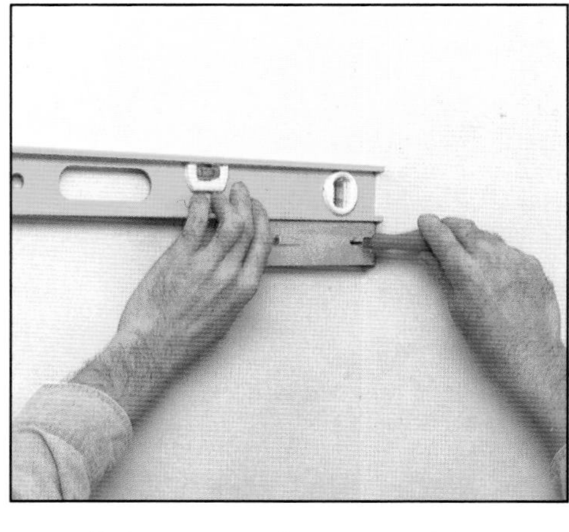

2 Drill clearance and countersink holes in the supports, and use the first one to mark the fixing hole positions on the wall. Drill the holes and fix this support.

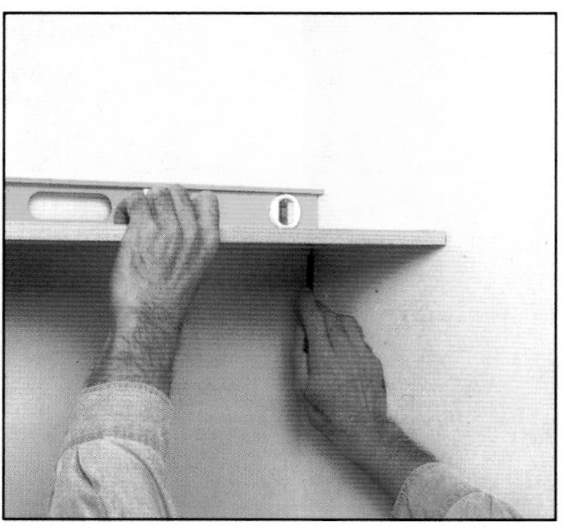

3 Rest a shelf on the first support, adjust it until it is level and mark the shelf position on the opposite wall of the alcove. Prepare the second shelf support.

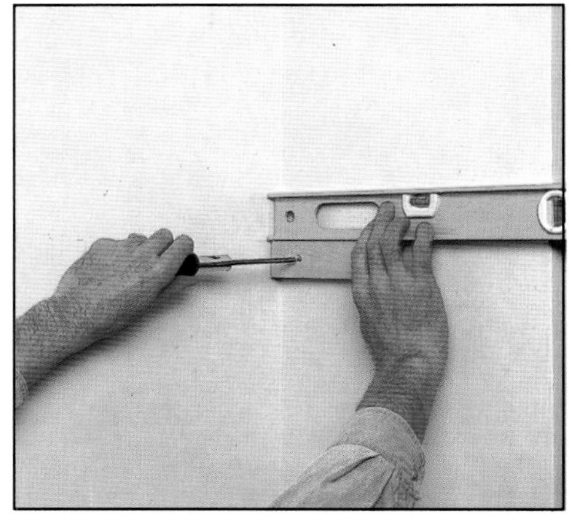

4 Screw the second support in place after using it to mark the positions of the fixing holes on the wall, as in step 2. Check again that it is level.

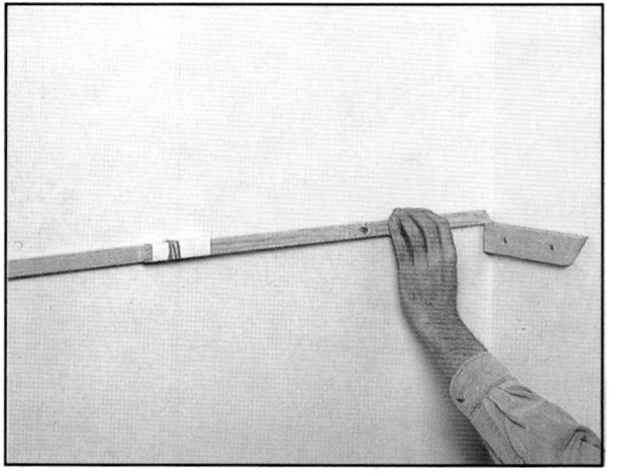

5 Make up a set of pinch rods from scrap wood, held together as shown with a rubber band. Extend the rods to span the rear wall of the alcove.

6 Lift out the rods carefully without disturbing their positions. Lay them on the rear edge of the shelf and mark on it the width of the alcove.

RIGHT Alcove shelving can be put to practical or decorative use. Here, painted shelves form a focal point in the room for the display of boxes and wicker baskets.

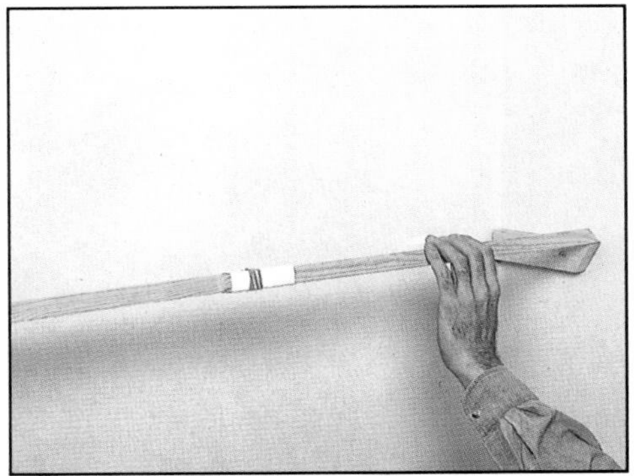

7 Repeat the operation in step 5 to measure the width at the point where the front edge of the shelf will be, then transfer the measurement to the shelf.

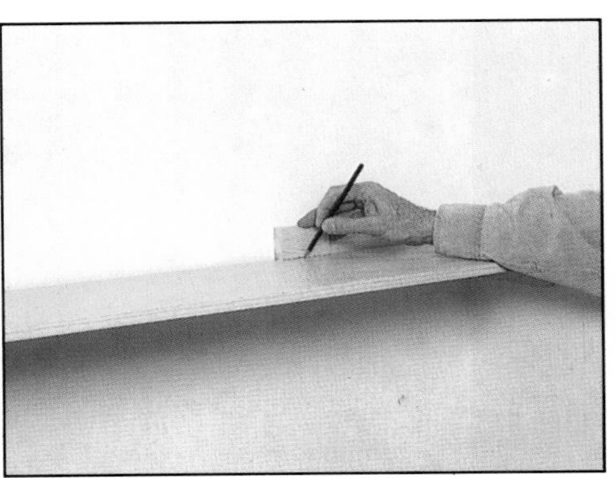

8 Cut the shelf to width and lay it on the supports. If the fit is poor against the back wall, use a block and pencil to scribe the wall outline on the shelf.

9 Saw carefully along the scribed line with a power jigsaw (saber saw). Sand the cut edge until it is smooth and then fit the shelf back in position.

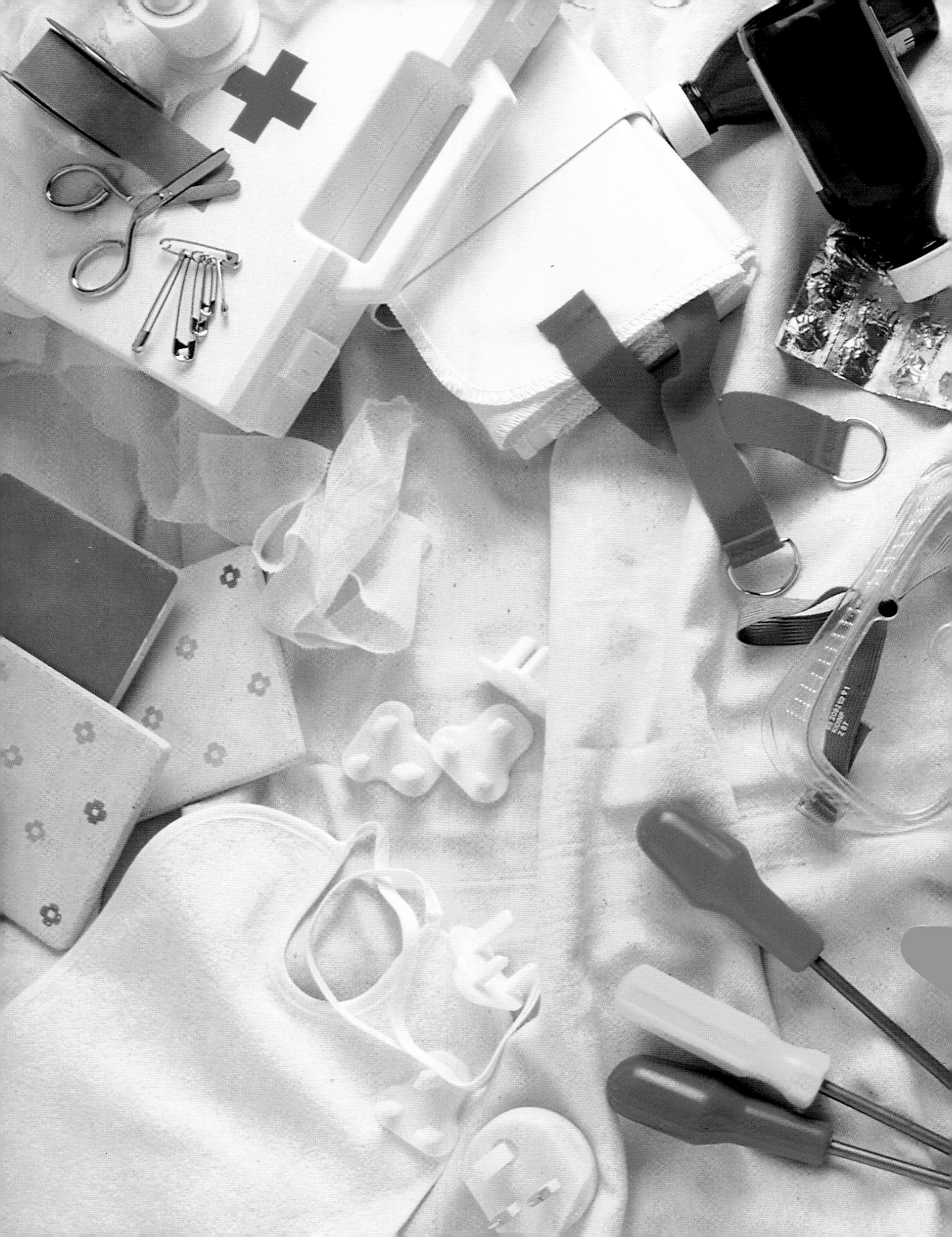

Problem Solving and Repairs

Taking the right action when an emergency strikes is as important as dealing with it quickly, and in this section you will find all the information to help you to cope with a multitude of common crises. Simple repairs on house items, replacing a broken window pane or unblocking a sink saves calling out expensive engineers or specialists. Reducing fuel consumption by installing effective insulation will also save money and reduce the harm to the environment.

SIMPLE FAMILY MEDICINE

Given time, the human body will heal itself from most minor infections and illnesses. Colds, coughs, stomach upsets and sore throats will all eventually clear up by themselves, but keeping the body rested, the temperature down and pain to a minimum all help to make the sufferer comfortable while giving the body's own defences time to work effectively.

There are numerous medicines and preparations that can be bought over the counter of a chemist (drugstore) which can help to alleviate the symptoms of minor ailments.

BUYING AND TAKING MEDICINES

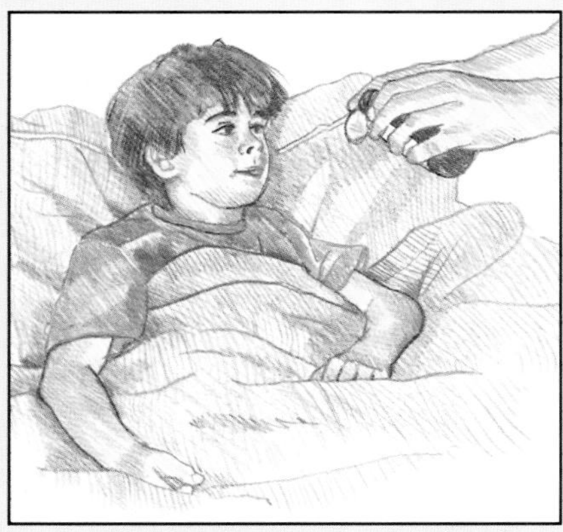

- Make sure that only the recommended dose is taken.
- Always ask the pharmacist for help and advice, and tell him or her if you are taking any other medication.
- Always read the directions on the packet and label.
- If you are pregnant, always consult your doctor before taking medicines.
- Keep all medicines locked away and out of the sight of children.
- Never tell children that the medicine you are giving is like a sweet or tastes nice – they may try to take more when you are not looking.
- Flush old and out-of-date medicines down the toilet or take them to your pharmacist for safe disposal.

Abdominal pain
This can be caused by indigestion, colic or wind, and antacids or charcoal tablets will help to relieve the symptoms quickly. Anyone suffering from abdominal pain accompanied by diarrhoea, vomiting or fever should be seen by a doctor.

Bad breath
Bad breath may simply be the result of smoking or eating spicy foods, but can also be caused by gum disease. Cleaning teeth regularly and using dental floss will ensure the health of gums and, with the use of antiseptic mouth washes, the problem should disappear. If gums are not the problem, there may be a digestive disorder and you should seek the advice of a doctor.

Chickenpox
In the first few days a slight fever may occur, which can be treated with paracetamol. Try to prevent a child from scratching the spots, as this may lead to infection. A daily bath or shower will prevent the spots from becoming infected, and calamine lotion applied afterwards will help to reduce and relieve the itching.

Colds
Resting as much as possible and taking plenty of fluids will help to clear up a cold quickly. Aspirin or paracetamol will help to reduce the discomfort and lower fever, and medicines containing decongestants will ease congestion.

Cold sores
After the initial infection, the virus that causes cold sores lies dormant in nerve cells until, under the right conditions, it re-activates and causes the familiar blistering. The blisters are highly contagious, so avoid touching them as the virus can easily be transferred. Cold-sore creams are available from chemists (drugstores). They should be applied when the symptoms of 'prickling' start, but before blisters appear.

Constipation
Lack of dietary fibre and exercise, and an insufficient fluid intake can cause constipation. Eat plenty of foods containing bran, wholemeal (whole grain) bread, vegetables, pulses and fruits. If the problem persists, it would be advisable to see a doctor.

Coughs
Numerous cough remedies are available, depending on the type of cough – ask your pharmacist for advice. Breathing in steamy air can help to loosen phlegm, and inhaling a few drops of eucalyptus oil in a bowl of hot water can have a cleansing effect.

Convulsions
Convulsions usually affect small children and are often the result of a high fever. These are known as febrile convulsions, and will only last for a few minutes at a time. Reduce the child's temperature by sponging with tepid water. Once the convulsion has passed, paracetamol elixir will help to reduce the fever. Always call a doctor even when the convulsion has stopped.

Earache
This can be the result of a heavy cold, or of an infection of the inner or outer ear causing pain and deafness. Aspirin or paracetamol will help the pain. See a doctor if fluid builds up behind the ear drum, causing it to rupture and the fluid to seep out.

Eye infections
Conjunctivitis is a common eye infection that results in sticky eyelids and sore, bloodshot eyes. Make up a dilute solution of 1 part bicarbonate of soda (baking soda) to 20 parts of boiled and cooled water, and use cotton-wool

(absorbent cotton) swabs to ease the sticky 'glue' from the eyelids. Use a fresh swab on each eye.

Food poisoning
The sufferer should have plenty of rest and only be given fluids for 24 hours. With an adult, call a doctor if the condition does not improve within this period. Food poisoning can be more serious with children and the elderly as they may become dehydrated, so they should be watched carefully. Call a doctor straight away if a baby is suffering from sickness and diarrhoea.

Hayfever
Hayfever symptoms can be similar to those of a common cold. Antihistamine medicines can be prescribed by your doctor, and air purifiers in the house can help to reduce airborne irritants.

Headaches
A doctor should be seen for long-lasting, acute and recurring headaches, as they could be caused by another ailment. However, a rest in a quiet room, a cold compress on the forehead and an analgesic will be sufficient to deal with most headaches.

Indigestion
This can be caused by eating too large a meal or rich and spicy foods, or by eating in a hurry or just before going to bed. For immediate relief take antacids. Alternatively, 2.5 ml/½ tsp of bicarbonate of soda (baking soda) dissolved in a glass of water will relieve indigestion.

Influenza
The symptoms of influenza often include fever, aching muscles, nausea, headaches, a cough, a sore throat and a running nose. A doctor may prescribe antibiotics to prevent a secondary infection from causing additional problems. Otherwise, rest in bed, plenty of fluids and an analgesic taken every 4 hours should help.

Note: the first symptoms of meningitis can be similar to those of influenza. If the symptoms shown are accompanied by vomiting, a stiff neck and joints, a skin rash, bruising or patchiness of the skin and an aversion to bright lights, call a doctor at once.

Insomnia
Irregular working hours, depression, stress or being in an unfamiliar room can lead to sleeplessness. A doctor can prescribe drugs to help, but try to restrict their use as it is easy to become dependent on them. A milky drink before going to bed can be relaxing – avoid coffee, tea and alcohol, as these are all stimulants which will only exacerbate the problem. A walk during the day in fresh air and a warm bath before going to bed may also help.

Measles
All children should be immunized against measles, but can suffer from the disease before then if they come into contact with an infected person. A blocked nose, fever and conjunctivitis are the first symptoms, followed a few days later by a red, blotchy rash spreading from the head downwards. Call your doctor to see whether the child should be seen. Otherwise, give plenty of fluids and paracetamol elixir to reduce the fever.

Mumps
This is a viral infection of the parotid glands, which are situated just in front of and below the ear. Discomfort and fever can be reduced by giving either paracetamol or aspirin, or paracetamol elixir to young children. The virus is usually infectious for up to 6 days before the swelling appears, and for 10 days after the onset of the swelling. Adult men can suffer from swollen testes and should visit a doctor.

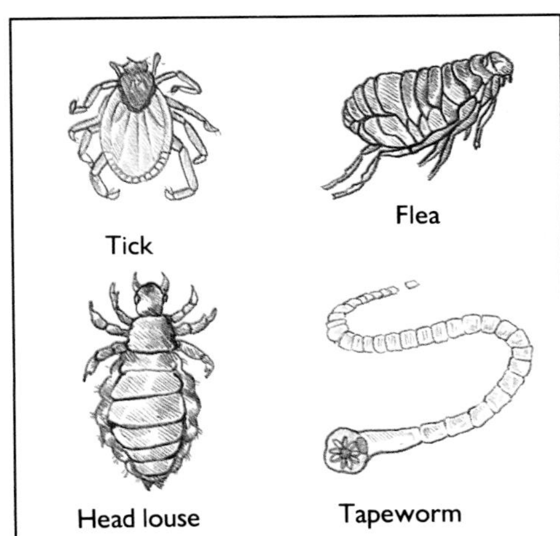

Parasites
At one time or another, most children and some adults suffer from parasites.
Head lice: these are tiny brown insects with 6 legs. They feed on blood and lay eggs (known as nits) which are attached to the base of the hair shaft. They are usually found behind the ears and cause irritation. If head lice are detected, the whole family should be treated with insecticidal shampoo.
Fleas: these are usually passed on to their host by cats, birds or other pets, or in infected bedding, carpets or upholstery. Treat animals with a veterinary insecticide. Where flea bites have occurred on your skin, use an antiseptic wash to prevent infection. Spray throughout the house with a flea killer and vacuum thoroughly.
Tapeworm: eggs can be seen in faeces. Consult your doctor, who will prescribe a suitable medicine.
Threadworms: live in the lower bowel and lay eggs around the anus, causing itchiness. The eggs are minute, but occasionally a fine, thread-like worm may be seen around the anus or on bedding. A doctor will prescribe a suitable medicine to eradicate them.
Ticks: these live in long grass and will latch on to humans and animals to suck blood. Remove ticks with tweezers, using a rocking motion to release them then wipe the area with an antiseptic.

EMERGENCIES AND FIRST AID

Increasing knowledge and advances in medicine constantly update first-aid techniques in the event of an emergency, but the emphasis remains on the prompt and proper care of the casualty by helping to alleviate pain and suffering. Whether first aid involves being able to deal with a suspected broken leg or stopping a nose bleed, it is vital to know the right steps to take in order to prevent further complications and to reassure the casualty that they are in good hands.

Learning basic first-aid techniques is straightforward and is something that everyone should do. Knowing how to act in some emergency situations may well make the difference between life and death.

Animal bites and scratches

All animals carry germs in their mouths and on their claws. When these penetrate the skin, the germs will be left in the muscle tissues and may cause infection if not cleaned thoroughly.

Hold the wound under warm running water and wash the affected area with soap for at least 5 minutes to remove any saliva or dirt particles. Gently pat the area dry, then wipe the wound with a mild antiseptic solution before covering it with a sticking plaster or sterile dressing. A serious wound should always be referred to hospital.

Broken bones

Always treat any doubtful cases of injured bones as if they were broken in order to prevent additional internal injuries. Do not attempt to move the casualty until the injured part is secured and supported, unless he is in danger. If the broken limb is an arm, it may then be reasonable to take the casualty to hospital by car, otherwise call for an ambulance immediately. Do not give the casualty anything to eat or drink, as surgery may be required if bones are badly broken.

TREATING A BROKEN LEG

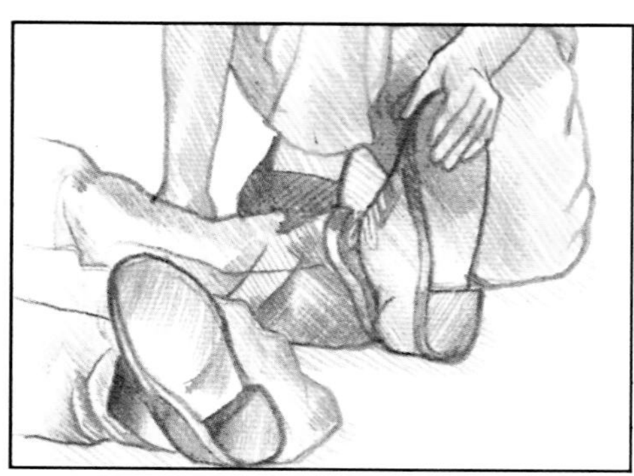

1 Ensure that the casualty remains still, and support the leg above and below the injury with your hands. Move the uninjured leg against it and place padding between the knees, ankles and hollows.

2 Using a scarf, tie or cloth, tie the feet together in a figure-of-8 to secure them, and tie on the outer edge of the foot on the uninjured leg.

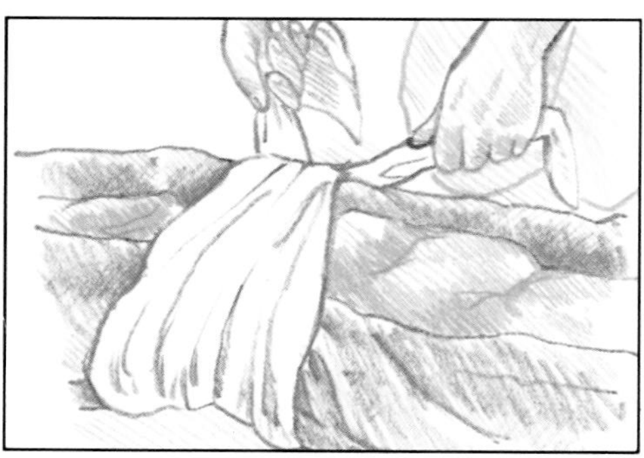

3 Immobilize the joints by tying both knees and ankles together. Tie additional bandages above and below the injured area.

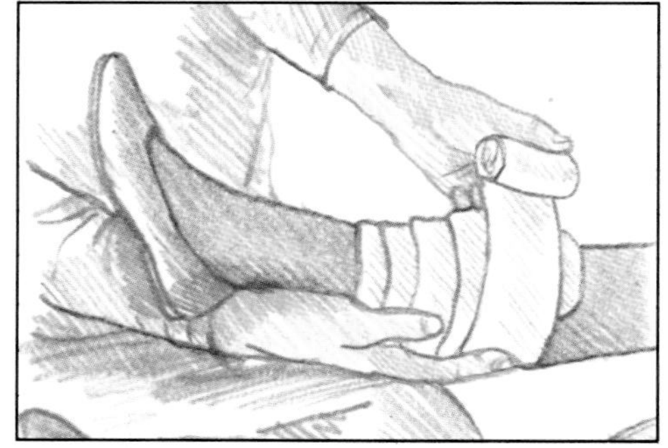

4 Should the bone protrude through the skin, cover the wound with a sterile dressing or clean pad, and apply pressure to control the bleeding. Use a bandage to secure the pad and immobilize the limb.

TREATING A BROKEN ARM

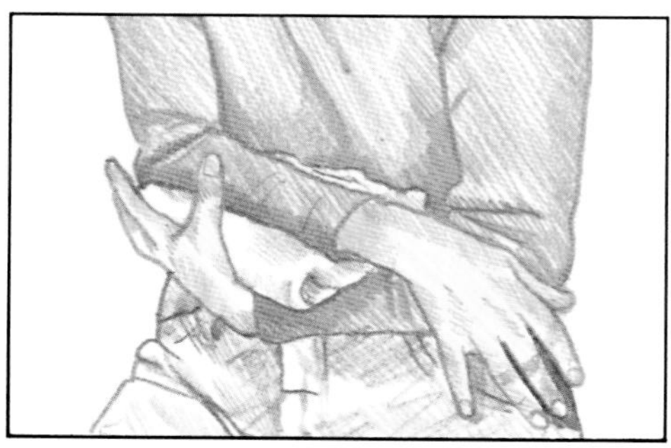

1 Sit the casualty in a chair and carefully place the injured arm across his chest in the position that is most comfortable. Ask him to support the arm or place a cushion underneath it to take the weight.

2 Use a shawl or piece of sheeting (approximately 1 sq m/1 sq yd in size) and fold it diagonally into a triangle. Slide this under the injured arm and secure by tying the ends by the collarbone on the injured side. Strap the arm to the body using a wide piece of fabric and tie as shown.

Burns and scalds
Immediately douse the burned or scalded area in cold running water. Gently try to remove any jewellery or constricting clothing from near the burn before it starts to swell. Keep the affected part in cold water for at least 10 minutes, then place a clean dressing over the burn and gently bandage it. Any injury larger than 2.5 cm/1 in will require treatment at hospital.

TREATING BURNS

- Never break blisters.
- Never use a sticking plaster.
- Never apply butter, lotions or ointment to the affected area.

Choking
Remove any food or false teeth from the mouth, but never attempt to locate the obstruction by putting your fingers down the casualty's throat, as this can push the obstruction further in.

If the casualty becomes unconscious this may relieve muscle spasm, so check to see whether he has begun to breathe. If not, turn him on his side and give 4 blows between the shoulder blades. Should this fail, place one hand above the other just below the ribcage and perform abdominal thrusts. If the casualty still does not start to breathe, call immediately for an ambulance and give the kiss of life (see next page).

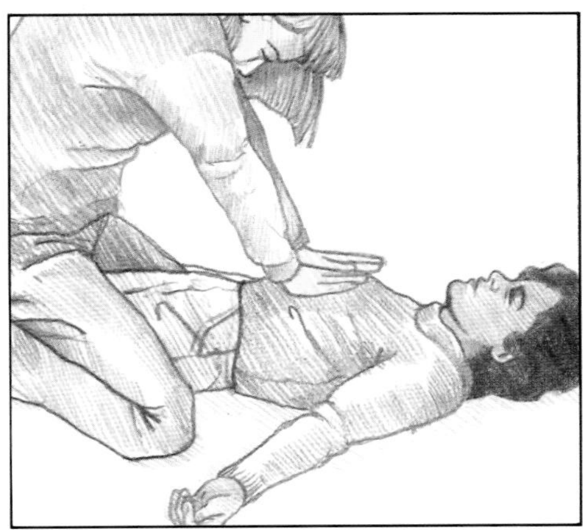

ABOVE If a choking casualty becomes unconscious, kneel astride him and, placing one hand above the other, perform abdominal thrusts.

DEALING WITH A CHOKING PERSON

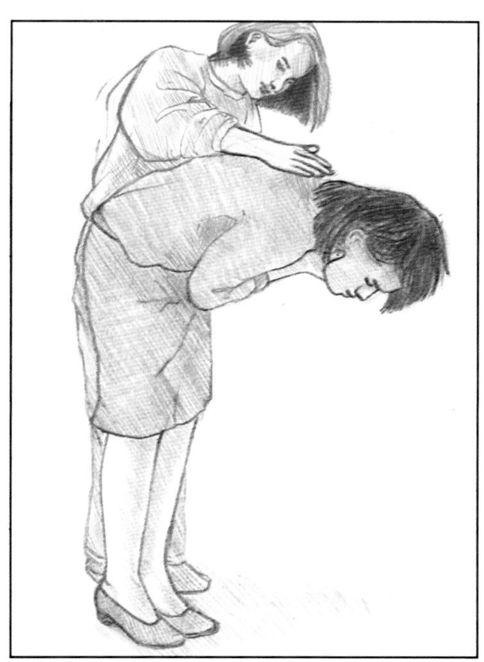

1 Bend the casualty forward so that the head is lower than the chest, and encourage him to cough. If this does not dislodge the object, sharply slap him up to 5 times between the shoulder blades using the flat of your hand.

2 If this fails, stand behind him and grip your hands together just below the rib cage. Pull sharply inwards and upwards from your elbows to deliver up to 5 abdominal thrusts. This action causes the diaphragm to compress the chest and should force out the obstruction. If the blockage still remains, repeat the process of 5 back slaps followed by 5 abdominal thrusts.

3 If a child is choking, place him across your knees with the head down. Holding him securely, slap smartly between the shoulder blades (using less force than that required for an adult) to dislodge the object. If the child continues to choke, sit him on your knees and, using just one clenched hand, perform gentle abdominal thrusts to avoid causing injury.

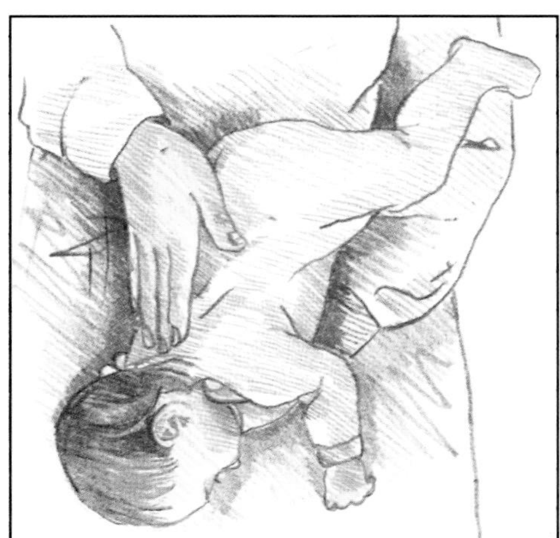

4 If a baby or toddler is choking, lay him along your forearm with the head down, using your hand to support the head. Use your fingers to slap the baby smartly between the shoulder blades, but remember to use less force than you would for an older child.

If the baby fails to start breathing, turn him over on to his back so that the head is tilted down. Using only 2 fingers, apply up to 4 abdominal thrusts just above the navel by pressing quickly forwards towards the area of the chest.

EMERGENCIES AND FIRST AID (continued)

Drowning
When carrying a drowning casualty, the head should be lower than the rest of the body to avoid inhalation of swallowed water. Lie him down on a blanket or towel. Turn the head to one side to allow water to drain from the mouth. If the casualty stops breathing, brain damage can occur in less than 5 minutes. It is vital to ensure that oxygen reaches the brain, and the kiss of life puts air into the lungs until they are able to breathe again by themselves.

Electric shocks
It is vital not to put yourself at the risk of an electric shock as well when dealing with a casualty. Immediately switch off the source of power at the mains. If you are unable to do so, stand on any good insulating material such as a thick book, a rubber mat or a pile of newspapers before attempting to help the casualty.

Use a wooden broom handle, walking stick or chair to push the casualty away from the source of electricity. Otherwise, without touching the casualty, a scarf or rope looped around their arms or feet can drag them clear. Once the victim is free from the electric current, place him in the recovery position or, if unconscious be prepared to resuscitate (see right). Treat any burns.

DEALING WITH ELECTRIC SHOCKS

- Do not touch the casualty until you are sure that the electric current has been switched off.
- Never use a damp or wet towel or a metal object to free the casualty, even when the power has been turned off.

GIVING THE KISS OF LIFE

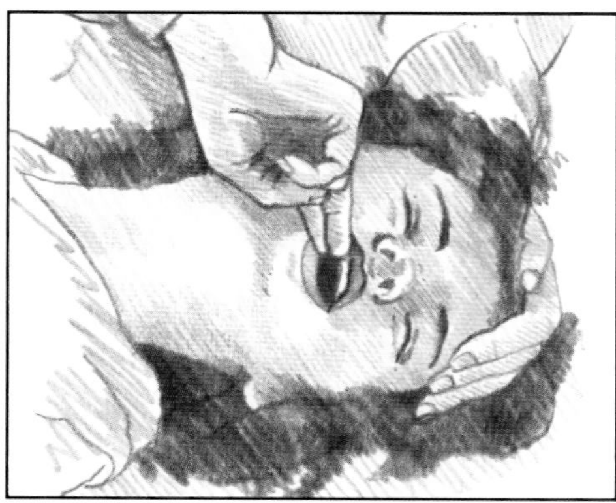

1 First turn the head sideways and remove any obstruction from the mouth.

2 Placing 1 hand on the forehead and the other under the chin, tilt the head back to open the airway.

3 Close the nose by pinching the nostrils together. Take a full breath and, placing your lips over the casualty's mouth, blow firmly into the mouth until you see the chest rising. (With a small child or baby, cover both the mouth and nose with your mouth.) Remove your lips to allow the air to be exhaled and the chest to fall fully. Repeat the sequence at the rate of 15–16 breaths per minute (for a small child or baby, take quicker and more shallow breaths to avoid injuring the lungs).

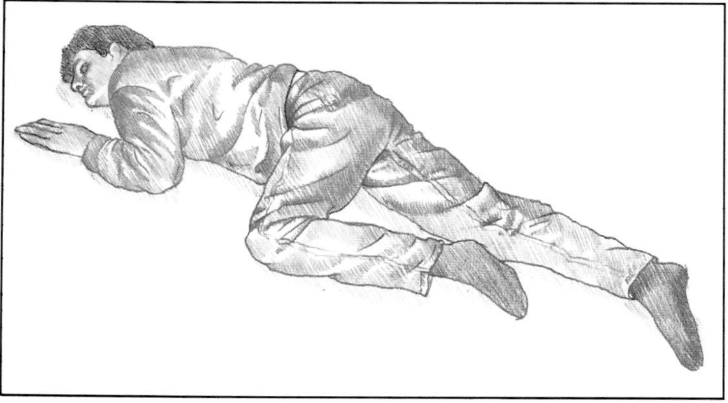

4 When breathing begins, place the casualty in the 'recovery' position. Tilt the head back to open the airway, adjust the uppermost arm so that the hand supports the head and bend the uppermost knee so that it is at right-angles to the hip.

Eye injuries
Do not attempt to remove any foreign body that is sticking to or into the eyeball. Cover the eye with a sterile pad, bandage both eyes to prevent them from moving and seek hospital treatment immediately.

Wash out any grit, dust or other small particles. Ask the casualty to tilt his head to the injured side, and rest a towel on his shoulder. Using your finger and thumb, hold the eyelid open and gently wash out the particles using a glass of clean, warm water.

Heart massage

When the heart stops beating, artificial circulation is vital in order to maintain a supply of oxygen to the brain. To enable this, heart massage needs to be administered intermittently with the kiss of life (see left) so that oxygen in the lungs can pass into the blood.

Insect stings

Remove a sting that is left in the skin by carefully pulling it out, using a pair of tweezers. Rinse the area under cold running water. Wine or vinegar can reduce the swelling caused by a sting from a jellyfish or sea anemone, but seek medical advice if the pain does not subside after a few hours.

Nose bleeds

Help the casualty to sit down so that his head is well forward. Ask him to pinch his nose just below the bridge and to breathe through his mouth. After 10 minutes the pressure can be released but, if the nose is still bleeding, re-apply the pressure for a further 10 minutes. Once the bleeding has subsided, gently swab around the nose and mouth with warm water.

FIRST-AID BOX

Always keep the following items of first-aid equipment in a clean container where you can find them in a hurry.

- Sticking plasters – either a box of assorted sizes or a strip that can be cut to the correct size.
- Crêpe bandages for bandaging wounds in awkward places, such as elbows, and to bind sprains.
- Sterile dressings in various sizes.
- Blunt-ended scissors for cutting bandages and dressings to size.
- Sterile cotton wool (absorbent cotton) for cleaning cuts and grazes.
- Antiseptic wipes and cream for cuts and grazes.
- Pain killers – keep paracetamol and aspirin that are suitable for both children and adults.
- Tweezers for removing insect stings or splinters.
- Antihistamine cream for treating insect bites and stings.
- Triangular bandage to make a sling.
- Safety pins to hold bandages or a sling in place.

GIVING HEART MASSAGE

Lie the casualty flat on his back and kneel at his side. Find his lowest rib and follow it up until it meets the base of the breastbone. Approximately 2–3 cm/ ¾–1¼ in above this point is where the pressure must be applied.

- Interlocking your fingers, place the heel of your lower hand just above the base of the breastbone. Keeping your elbows straight, press down on the heels of your hands to depress the breastbone by 4–5 cm/1½–2 in. Release the pressure without removing your hands.
- Repeat at around 80 compressions per minute.

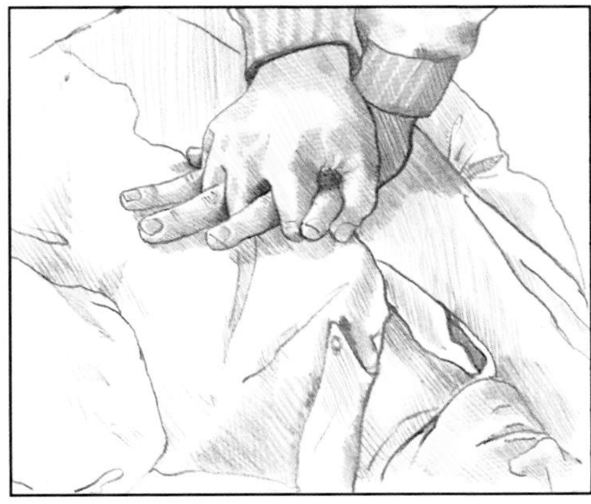

Puncture wounds

Any object that pierces the skin, such as a nail or a metal spoke, may not create a large entry wound but will cause damage deep in the tissues where infection can start. Occasionally, an unseen piece of an object may remain embedded, so ensure that the casualty is taken to hospital.

Start by stemming the flow of blood by applying pressure around the wound. If the bleeding is severe, raise the injured part above the level of the heart to slow the rate of flow, then cover with a sterile dressing and bandage.

Severe open wounds and cuts

The first priority with a wound of this kind is to control the bleeding, and also to prevent shock and infection before the casualty is taken to hospital. Ask someone to call for an ambulance immediately. Ideally, wear disposable gloves or protect yourself by ensuring that any sores or cuts are covered with a waterproof dressing.

Hold a sterile dressing or clean pad over the wound and apply direct pressure to the wound with your fingers. If there is an object such as glass or metal protruding, squeeze the edges of the wound around the object. Keep the injured part raised, as this will help to reduce the blood flow and minimize shock. Continue to apply pressure to the wound for at least 10 minutes to allow time for the blood to clot. If the dressing or pad becomes soaked with blood, place a fresh one over it – never remove the original dressing, as this will re-open the wound.

Sprain, strain and bruise injuries

A sprain or strain will cause swelling of the injured area, but raising the part and applying cold compresses or a bag of ice wrapped in a cloth will ease it. Wrap the area in thick padding, then bandage it firmly before resting it in a slightly raised position.

Bruising may take time to develop and often requires little more than a cold compress to relieve the pain. Severe bruising that develops quickly may indicate a deeper injury such as a fracture, in which case the casualty should seek medical advice.

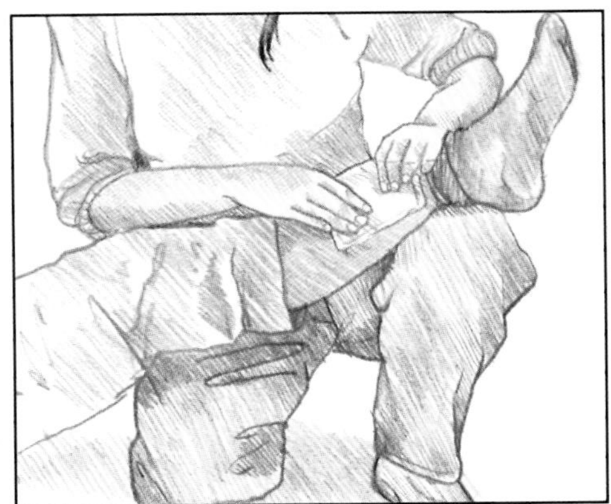

ABOVE Treat a puncture wound by raising the injured part above the level of the heart.

SAFETY AND SECURITY

HOME SAFETY

Unfortunately, accidents do happen, and often in what is usually considered to be the safest of places – the home. There are simple preventive measures that you can take to reduce the risks of serious injury, however, most of which are simply a question of common sense. Every member of the family should be fully aware of the dangers present in all areas of the home.

Just a little thought and planning as to the potential dangers can give peace of mind and, more importantly, reduce the risks of a serious accident occurring. The elderly are especially vulnerable to accidents in the home, as are children – particularly those under 4 years of age. If you have young children, or even grandchildren, who visit, look around your home to count the hazards lurking there; it is surprising how many there are. It is impossible to watch children every minute of the day, so it is vital that you make every effort to eliminate potential hazards, most of which can quickly be removed.

Different areas of the home present different safety issues – refer to the information given below and take the necessary action. Any safety products that you need to buy are relatively inexpensive, and will be a small price to pay for the creation of a safer home environment for all the family.

The hallway, staircase and landing

The first priority if you do not already have one is to install a smoke detector – or 2 if your home is on different levels – so that every member of the household can be quickly alerted in the event of a fire. Smoke alarms are inexpensive and widely available, and can save lives. Regularly check that the alarms are functioning properly by vacuuming the vents to remove dust and letting the smoke from a snuffed candle drift into them as a test. Alternatively, some alarms have a special button for testing on a weekly basis. Always follow the fixing and siting instructions supplied by the manufacturer, and replace batteries as soon as they run down – keep spares in the house so that you can fit them straight away.

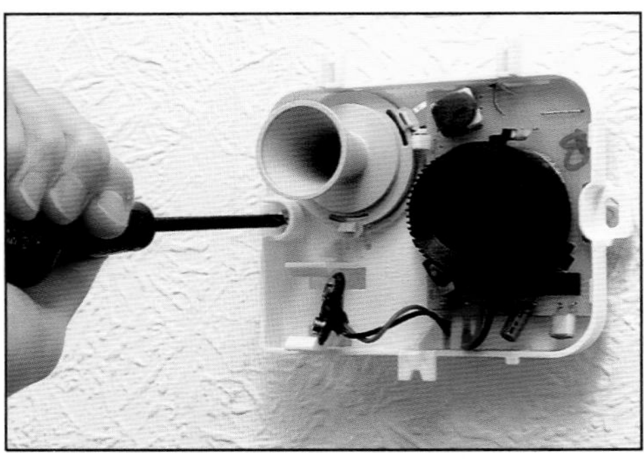

ABOVE A smoke detector can be installed easily by screwing the base to the ceiling, fitting the battery and clipping on the cover.

ABOVE Test the detector regularly and vacuum dust away from the sensor to ensure that it works efficiently at all times.

Sufficient lighting is vital on the staircase and in the hallway to avoid misleading shadows being cast on steps and stair treads. Rugs on polished floors can easily slip when trodden on, so attach special non-slip backing strips to prevent them from sliding. Make sure, too, that the carpet is securely fitted with no tears or gaping seams, as these can cause a serious fall.

The living room

Ensure that any glass-topped tables, patio doors and interior glass doors are fitted with toughened or laminated safety glass. You can buy a special safety film (available from DIY stores) that is invisible once fitted, but will prevent shards of glass from causing injuries should the glass shatter.

Never overload a socket outlet (receptacle) – ideally, there should only be one plug to one socket. If numerous electrical appliances are in use, be sure to use the correct adapter – ask your retailer for the one most suited to your needs. Avoid trailing flexes which can easily be tripped over.

- If anyone smokes in the household, insist that cigarette butts are placed in an ashtray that is washed out before going to bed. This will ensure that any smouldering ashes are extinguished and will leave the room fresher too. Ensure that an open fire is always covered with a fire guard whenever the room is unoccupied – even for 5 minutes.

The kitchen

Buy a kettle guard to hold a kettle safely in place so that it cannot be tipped or pulled. Alternatively, a 'curly' cord will prevent the hazard of a trailing flex but will still allow the kettle to be lifted.

ABOVE Fit a curly cord to prevent the risk of a trailing flex from a kettle.

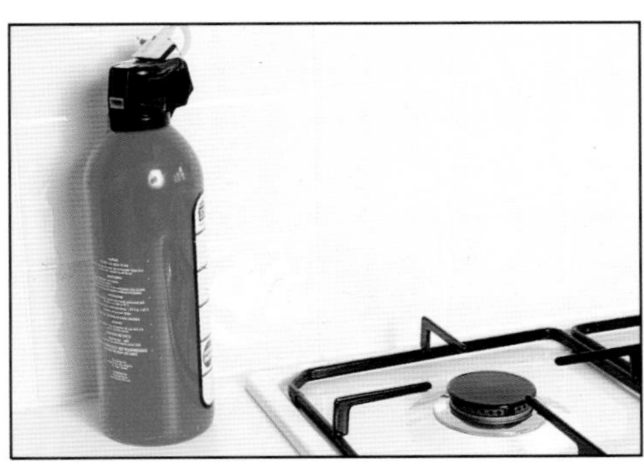

ABOVE Buy a fire extinguisher to keep in the kitchen or garage.

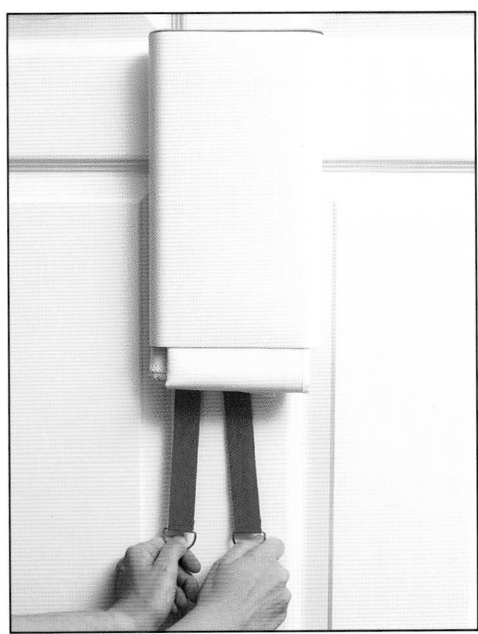

ABOVE Keep a fire blanket on the wall or back of a door so that you can reach it easily in the event of a kitchen fire.

Keep a domestic fire extinguisher in the kitchen, but do not position it too close to or above the cooker as a pan fire would make it inaccessible. Check that everyone knows how the extinguisher works and if possible choose one that is suitable for electrical fires. A compact fire blanket, hung on the wall, will suffocate flames from deep-fat fryers, which are a major cause of household fires. You should never throw water on this type of fire.

Take care not to stretch your arm over a gas cooker if you are wearing clothing with loose sleeves, such as a dressing-gown or baggy sweater – especially with synthetic fabrics. The gas could catch on to the fabric and cause a severe burn. Always turn saucepan handles inwards so that you do not inadvertently knock them, and so that loose clothing cannot catch them as you pass by.

ABOVE Turn pan handles inwards to avoid them being caught in loose clothing.

The bathroom

Prevent a slippery floor, bath or shower from causing falls by installing 'grab' rails at a height that can be easily reached. Modern baths often have an integral safety rail. If yours does not, fit a rail to the nearest wall. Mop up splashes of water and even body lotion on vinyl or tiled floors quickly, and always have a bath or shower mat on the floor so that wet feet do not slip. Non-slip rubber safety mats and stickers will prevent slipping while getting in or out of the bath.

Keep all electrical appliances away from sources of water where they are likely to get splashed or saturated with steam. Remember that even cordless gadgets can deliver a powerful shock if dropped into water. Replace flick switches with pull-cord light switches.

ABOVE Avoid slipping in a wet shower or bath by placing a safety mat or stickers on the surface.

Outside

Keep a check on the state of paving stones and paths, as a loose stone can easily trip an unwary visitor.

Never use petrol (gasoline) or any other household chemical to light a fire or barbecue. These can ignite with an explosion, causing burning debris to land on people, pets and possessions. Keep a bucket of water handy to douse a fire that gets out of hand.

When using outdoor electrical equipment, plug the appliance into a residual circuit breaker (RCD), which will cut off the power should the cable be accidentally cut or a fault occur. After finishing with any tools, make sure that you put them away in order to prevent children or pets from cutting themselves on sharp blades.

Wear safety goggles and a face-mask when clearing guttering situated above you, when drilling into masonry, or when applying paint or creosote, in order to prevent dust or specks from falling into your eyes, nose or mouth.

ABOVE Use an RCD (Residual Current Device) when using power tools – this will break the circuit should an electrical fault occur.

ABOVE Wear a pair of stout gloves and protective goggles when doing potentially dangerous jobs.

HOME SAFETY (continued)

IN THE EVENT OF A FIRE

- Immediately you discover a house fire, get everyone out safely – then telephone the fire services.
- With a pan fire, switch off the heat and cover the pan with a lid, plate, damp towel or fire blanket. Wait until the flames are extinguished and the pan is cool before touching it.

  With an electrical fire, before dealing with a burning electrical appliance or socket outlet (receptacle), switch off the electricity at the consumer unit. Put out the fire with a fire extinguisher or water.

  If a television or computer is on fire, switch off the electricity at the consumer unit or at the socket if you can reach it safely. Do not use water, as residual electricity may still be present. Always smother the flames with a rug or blanket to extinguish them.
- If a fire is too big to deal with without danger, leave the room immediately, closing the door firmly behind you. Ensure that everyone leaves the house, closing doors behind them to slow down the spread of smoke and flames. Telephone the fire services from a telephone box or from a neighbour's house.
- Smoke kills more people than flames do. It is vital to get out of a smoke-filled house as soon as you can.
- Smoke and heat rise, so if the smoke is very dense, crawl on your hands and knees and you should be able to see and feel your way to safety.
- A damp towel or cloth tied over your nose and mouth can help to reduce smoke inhalation.
- If you are trapped on an upstairs floor, open the window to call for help. A wet towel placed at the gap under the door will help to prevent smoke from penetrating. Double-glazed windows that are sealed create a barrier of astonishing strength. Do not attempt to smash them with your hands – instead, try to find a chair or other heavy object.

Child safety

In the kitchen: only buy detergent and cleaning chemicals with child-proof tops, as not all dangerous products have these. As many such products are often stored conveniently under the sink where youngsters can reach, fit cupboard (closet) locks as well. Ideally, store the cleaning materials in a high cupboard or on a shelf out of their reach. Never decant household cleaning agents or chemicals into other containers.

Never leave out knives and scissors once you have finished with them. Keep them safe and beyond reach in a wooden knife tidy, on a magnetic rack or in a lockable drawer.

Even if you make sure that pan handles are kept pointing inwards so that children cannot reach them, hob and cooker guards that clip to the edges are an additional safety measure for the one time they can.

A hot oven front can give a nasty burn to an unsuspecting child. Look for the cool-touch oven fronts that are available on many new ovens, or buy an oven guard which forms a neat but effective barrier between the heat and the child. If you are using a frying pan, avoid spots of hot fat landing on the floor where a child could easily slip – or even worse falling on a child standing nearby – by placing a spatter guard over the pan while you are cooking.

ABOVE Cover sockets (receptacles) with special covers to prevent young children from poking their fingers or pencils into them.

In the bathroom: when running a bath, even if you have mixer taps (faucets), run the cold water first, then top it up with hot water to bring the bath temperature to the correct degree. Always test the water first by dipping your elbow (which is as sensitive as a child's delicate skin) into it. Similarly, never turn on a shower while you are standing underneath it – switch it on first, check that the temperature is not too hot, and then step in.

Unfortunately, children can find the toilet a wonderful place for dropping in your toiletries and their toys. Keep them safe by fitting special lid locks which are easy and quick to open.

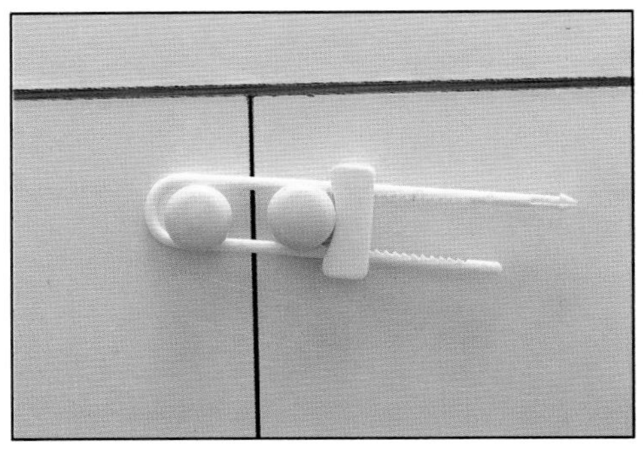

ABOVE Cupboard (closet) locks on bathroom cabinets keep small hands away from cleaning chemicals and medicines.

Always keep medicines locked away in a safe, dry place. Wall-mounted bathroom cabinets are ideal, and can be situated where children are unable to reach them. Flush old and out-of-date medicines down the toilet, or take them to your chemist (drugstore) for safe disposal.

On the staircase: discourage children from leaving toys or clothing on the stairs, as they can be a hazard.

Fit a safety gate at the bottom *and* the top of the stairs, so that babies cannot crawl up only to try going back once they find their way blocked.

Windows and doorways: fit safety locks to upstairs windows to prevent them from being opened by children.

Make sure that older members of the family know how to work them in the event of an emergency. In very hot weather, look for an extending safety gate that can also be used as a static barrier across both open windows and doorways.

In the bedroom: jumping on beds can be great fun but the consequences lethal if a child should crash into a pane of glass. Cover any potentially dangerous windows with special self-adhesive safety film, which will stop the glass from breaking into sharp, jagged pieces. Jumping on sofas can be equally hazardous if you have glass-fronted units or glass-topped tables, so ensure that these too are covered with sheets of safety film.

ABOVE Fit safety film to window panes, glass doors or tables to prevent shards of glass from causing injury if they break.

RIGHT A socket nightlight will provide children with a reassuring glow and help them to see their way out of the room at night.

Provide a nursery light or a simple night light that plugs directly into a socket outlet (receptacle) to give a soft, reassuring glow and to enable a child to find his or her way if they happen to wake at night.

Choose children's toys carefully, checking for any loose parts, sharp points and edges or rough joins, all of which can cause injury. Pulling any suspect parts is worth doing before you buy, to find out whether the toy comes apart and could hurt a child.

When re-painting a child's bedroom or toys, always be sure to use lead-free paints. If you are uncertain as to whether or not certain paints contain lead, ask a senior salesperson for advice or look for 'non-toxic' information on the label.

BELOW Choose children's toys carefully, checking for any loose parts or sharp edges.

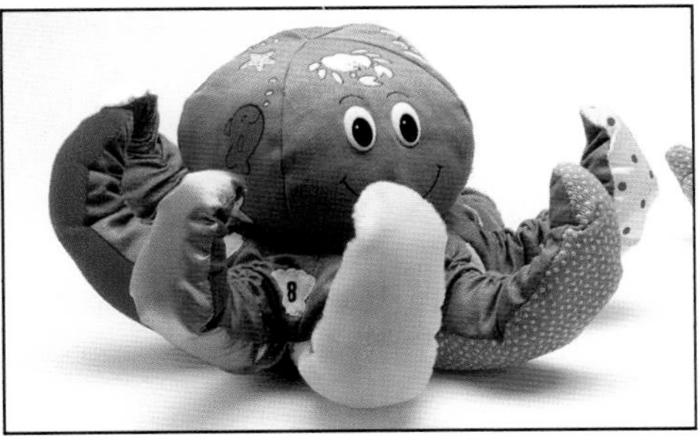

BELOW RIGHT Always place a fire guard in front of the fire – even if the fire is electric.

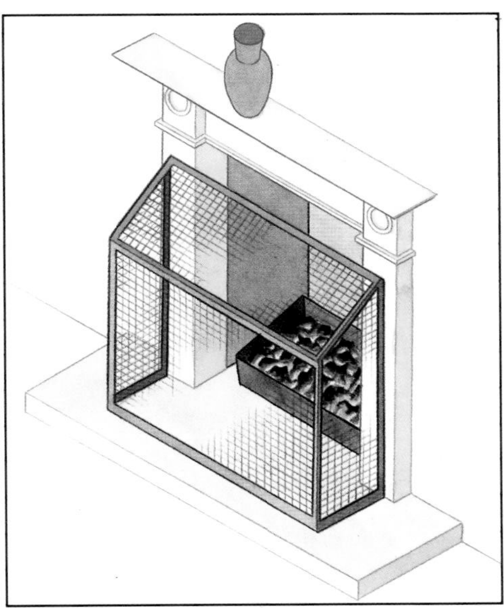

When young children are unwell, a portable baby monitor will alert you to all the sounds from the nursery, leaving you to move about freely while the children sleep.

In the living room: always place a fire guard in front of a fire – even an electric one, as children may be fascinated by the glow that it emits. If possible, choose a guard with a sloping top so that toys or drinks cannot sit on it.

Outside: swimming pools and ponds should be covered when not in use, or surrounded by a child-proof fence that cannot be climbed or crawled under. An unobtrusive wire cover can be placed over ponds and left in place throughout the year.

HOME SECURITY

Statistics show that domestic burglaries are on the increase, but many of these break-ins need not have occurred if just a few basic security measures had been taken. It is easy to prevent opportunist thieves from being tempted by the sight of open windows and doors by always being sure to close them both at night and even when you go out for a short time during the day. Even the most determined burglar who sets out with a crowbar to force an entry can be thwarted by sturdy locks, bolts and security floodlights. As well as giving peace of mind, a well-secured home can save money on insurance premiums and, more importantly, the anguish of losing your valued possessions.

Outside the house

Check that garden gates at the rear of the house close firmly, and can be secured if you go away for long periods. A garden fence with gaping holes can provide a discreet entry for a burglar, so be sure to keep this in good repair. Another frequent entry point is a garage – if attached to a house, this can allow a thief to force a door into the house unseen. Always fit secure locks to garage doors to minimize the risk of this happening. Padlock a garden shed if you have one in order to prevent tools from being stolen or used to gain entry to your home.

Remember that high shrubs and hedges at the front of your house may give privacy but can also screen a burglar from the street or neighbours. Large trees situated very close to a flat roof or window can also give an easy access route.

Fit a passive infra-red (PIR) floodlight to the front and back of the house. This will automatically switch on if activated by a passer by, making a pleasant welcome for a visitor but a strong deterrent for intruders. Choose one that has a variable light duration and an adjustable sensor for covering large or small areas. A bell box is another good deterrent – even a false one can deter an opportunist thief.

A spy-hole fitted in the front door discreetly lets people outside know that you can observe their movements while you are still secure behind the door. Always use the spy-hole before opening the door, and never open it unless you are sure of the identity of the person.

Door security

On a front door, replace a standard 'nightlatch' with a 5-lever mortise lock that cannot be opened without the key, even if the burglar can reach it via a broken pane of glass in the door. Remember, however, that good door locks are only as strong as the door that they are on, so choose a solid door and hinges so that both the opening and the hinged side will withstand an attempted forced entry. If you are in doubt, insert hinge bolts on the hinge side of the door. These fit into corresponding holes in the door frame, providing extra strength and preventing the door from being forced off its hinges. Even if the door does eventually give way, there is a good chance that the noise created by the burglar will have attracted someone's attention.

Fit a door chain or bar restraint to the front door. These both work in the same way by restricting the amount by which a door can be opened, giving you valuable time to assess the validity of a caller. A bar restraint is stronger than a chain, as it consists of a solid metal bar. Both require the door to be closed for the bar or chain to be released before the door can be opened to its full extent.

ABOVE Fit a strong mortise lock that can be locked from the inside to prevent a burglar from opening it through an adjacent broken pane.

ABOVE A door chain or bar restraint will allow you to see who is calling at the door without the risk of the door being burst open.

Fit French windows and casement doors with additional rack bolts at the top and bottom, which slide into the frame. Keep the key out of sight of intruders, but where it can be found by you and all the other members of the family in an emergency. Special patio-

door locks, which are fitted to the top, bottom or side of the door, prevent these doors from being slid open or lifted out of the frame. Look for the new 3-figure combination locks that do not need a key.

Window security

Most insurance companies now demand that key-operated window locks are fitted to all the windows in a house, and these do contribute greatly to security. Before buying window locks, however, check that they are suitable for the windows to which you intend to fit them. Measure the window frames before you go to buy, and check that they will accommodate the type of locks that you have in mind. In the case of very narrow frames, use a surface-fitted lock.

Sash windows can be fitted with dual screws, where a bolt passes through the inner frame into the outer frame to hold the 2 sections together; or with surface-fitted bolts that fit on the upper sashes and allow a small gap for ventilation. Replace existing handles with lockable ones that, once locked, cannot be re-opened without the key.

ABOVE Lockable window handles are useful for keeping children in and burglars out.

EMERGENCY ACTION

- A length of wooden dowel cut to the exact length to fit inside the bottom track of a patio door can wedge it closed. Similarly, if a dowel is placed vertically in the side runner of a sash window, it cannot be opened.
- Sink a screw into the wood frame beside a handle to prevent it from being opened.
- Stay-bars on casement windows can be secured by sinking a screw through a hole into the wooden frame.

When you are out

Light-sensitive fittings on interior and exterior lights sense when it is growing dark and turn on automatically. Time switches are also an excellent idea. These can be used to operate a number of appliances, making it appear as if the house is inhabited – televisions and radios create enough noise to be convincing. Electronic curtain controllers are also available, to close curtains automatically at a pre-set time. This will give the impression that the house is occupied.

ABOVE A time switch set to operate while you are out will give the impression that the house is still occupied.

Marking property

Ultra-violet pens are easy to use, and leave an invisible mark that will only show when placed under an ultra-violet lamp. Engraving scribers, ranging from simple carbide or diamond-tipped pens to electric engraving tools can be used to scratch a postcode, telephone

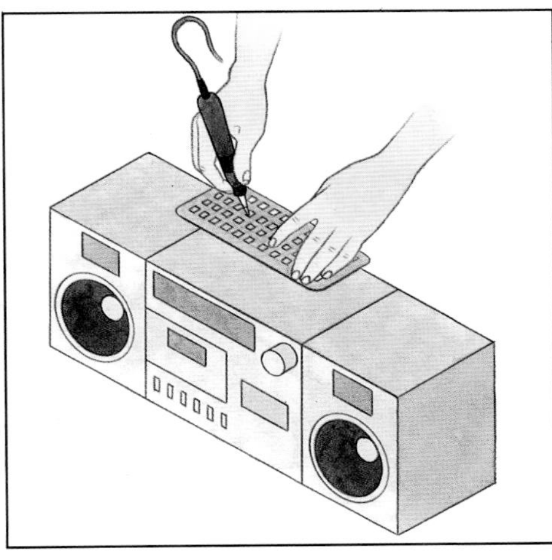

ABOVE Engraving scribers are an effective and easy method for marking hi-fi equipment.

number or other identifiable code. Use stencils with an engraver to give a neat, legible result. Another option is an etching kit, which is ideal for marking glass objects. Stencil transfers mask off the security code, and acid brushed over the surface etches the code.

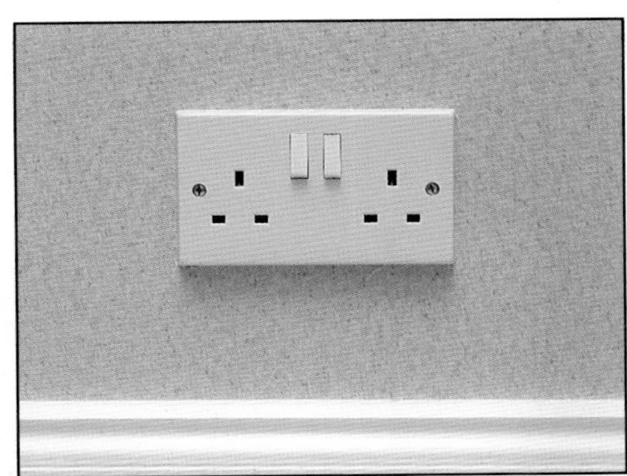

ABOVE A socket (receptacle) safe looks just like an ordinary socket, but is large enough to hold cash and jewellery in the box behind it.

SECURITY MEASURES

- If you return home to find signs of a break-in, do not enter but go straight to a neighbour's house to telephone the police.
- If you hear an intruder in the house or trying to break in, put on the lights and make a noise to alert them to the fact that you are there. If you are upstairs, do not go downstairs to investigate but telephone the police from your bedroom if possible.

REPAIRING HOUSEHOLD ITEMS

Being able to deal confidently with simple household repairs is an important part of running a home with the minimum of fuss and expense. Many common problems – blocked drains, overflowing cisterns or even noisy pipes – are often very easy to remedy if you are prepared to spend a little time and effort on them. More importantly, you will save a great deal of unnecessary expense by tackling the job yourself rather than calling out an expert to deal with it.

Renovating a bath

Acrylic: use a hard paint such as radiator enamel to paint out marks on this type of bath. Small chips in the surface can also be repaired using a 2-part car-repair filler (spackle). Mix the filler following the instructions on the packet and mix a little paint colour into the paste to blend with the bath. When the filler is hard, rub it down with wet-and-dry sandpaper, keeping this wet as you work.

Enamel: heavy limescale deposits can etch into the surface of a bath. Remove these using a chemical limescale remover applied with a brush. Chips in the enamel coating of a bath can lead to the metal rusting. Use limescale remover to shift any rust stains around the chips, and, when dry, sand with an emery cloth to remove loose particles. Re-paint with an enamel paint, blending colours if necessary to achieve a perfect match.

Repairing china

Clean new breaks thoroughly using methylated spirits and a lint-free cloth before gluing the pieces together with a cyanoacrylate (super glue). Badly repaired breaks will show in time. Start by removing the old glue in hot, soapy water, using an old toothbrush. Apply neat bleach to stains along the crack, using cotton buds (swabs). Rinse and repeat until the stain disappears.

REPAIRING A CLEAN BREAK IN CHINA

1 Having cleaned the broken edges thoroughly, apply a cyanoacrylate (super glue), following the manufacturer's instructions carefully.

2 Press the broken edges together for a few seconds, then apply strips of masking tape to hold the pieces securely. Leave to dry, and repeat with the other broken pieces.

Bond simple breaks in pottery with a 2-part epoxy resin or PVA (white) glue. Use cyanoacrylate adhesives for fine breaks and porcelain. Multiple breaks should only be glued piece by piece and allowed to dry between stages. Using acrylic paints, it is possible to 'hide' cracks and even to replace parts of a missing pattern if you fill the area with Plaster of Paris and carefully paint over it. Repaired china and pottery will never be as strong as it was formerly, so do not use it in an oven, or to carry hot foods or drinks.

An overflowing cistern

If the ball-float allows too much water into the cistern, the water could start to run out of the overflow pipe. Older-style Portsmouth-type valves can be adjusted by bending the metal float arm down. When full, the cistern's water level should be about 2.5 cm/1 in below the overflow. If the problem is caused by corrosion or scale, the Portsmouth valves may have failed and the washer may have worn away too.

Newer cisterns have plastic diaphragm valves. The float arm can be adjusted by the screw that is secured with a locknut. Release the locknut, then turn the screw towards the valve to reduce the amount of water. Re-tighten the locknut afterwards.

Radiator 'cold spots'

These are usually caused by air becoming locked inside the top of the radiator and preventing the water from reaching the whole of the inside. Hold a rag under the square valve and, using the radiator key gently release it until the air starts to hiss out. When the hissing stops and water starts to dribble out, close it up again. If the air released from the radiator smells of gas, it could be due to corrosion in the system. If this is the case, ask a central-heating engineer for advice.

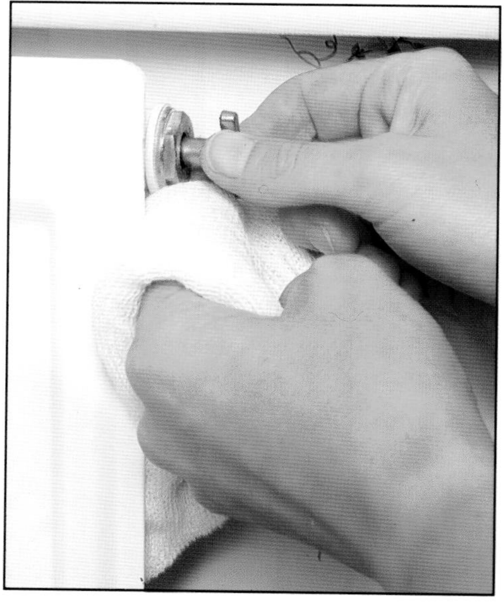

ABOVE Hold a cloth underneath a radiator valve to catch any drips as the air is released.

REPAIRING A DIAPHRAGM VALVE

1 If the rubber diaphragm has worn or its action been disrupted by debris in the water, turn off the water supply. Dismantle the valve and lay out the parts in the order they come off, to make re-assembly easier.

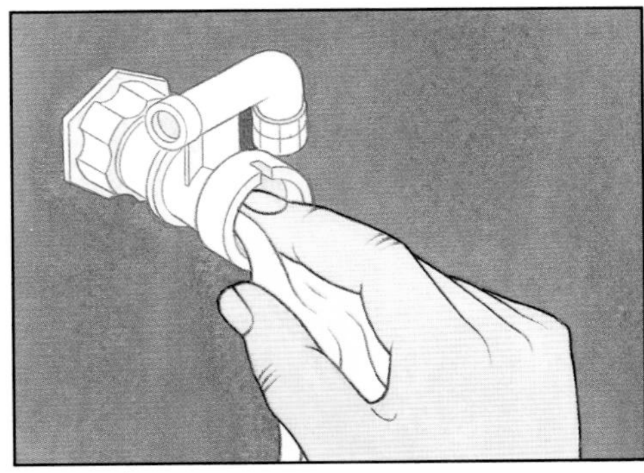

2 Clean the diaphragm in warm, soapy water or, if it is damaged, replace it with a new one. Turn on the water to flush out any debris and then replace the diaphragm, ensuring that the rim faces inwards. Re-assemble the valve.

REPAIRING A PORTSMOUTH VALVE

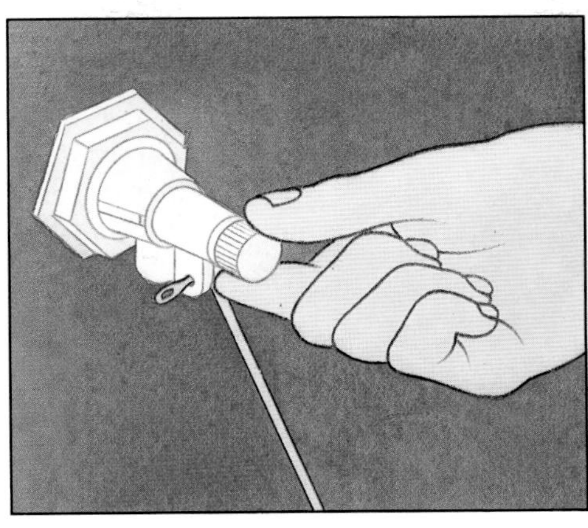

1 Turn off the water supply and unscrew the cap at the end of the valve. If the cap is tight or rusted, use pliers to loosen before taking it off.

2 Dismantle the valve by removing the split pin securing the float arm. If this is rusty it may snap, so have a spare split pin to hand.

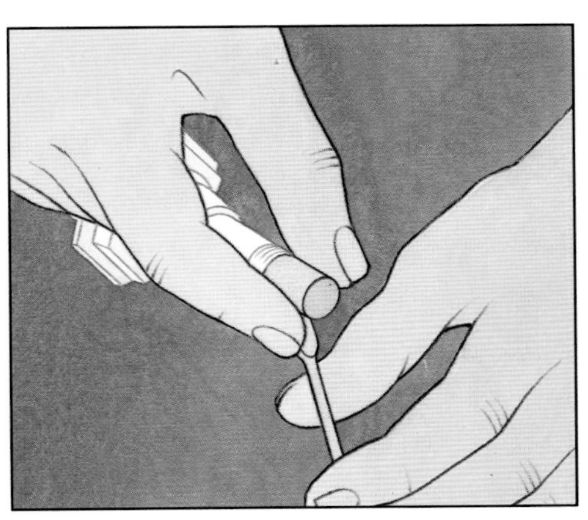

3 Push the valve plug out with a screw-driver and clean it thoroughly, inside and out, using wire wool.

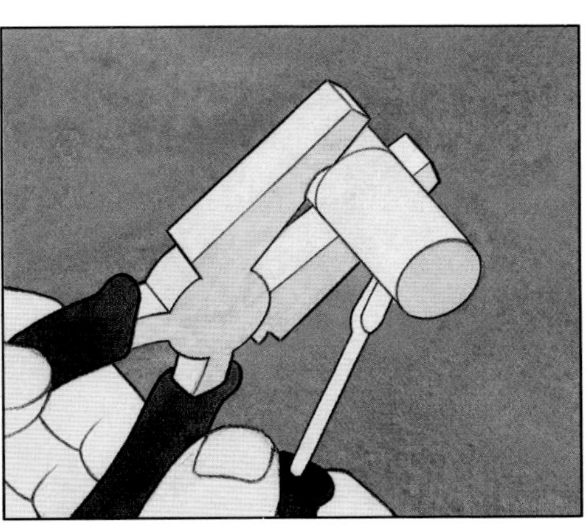

4 Unscrew the valve cap by turning a screwdriver in the slot of the valve plug and remove the washer. Replace the washer with a new one if necessary and re-assemble the plug and valve.

UNBLOCKING A SINK

1 LEFT If the water will not run out of the sink, place a sink plunger over the plughole and cover the overflow with a damp cloth. Pump the plunger hard up and down a few times to release the blockage.

If the blockage still remains, hold a large dish or other container beneath the U-bend under the sink. Keep the plug in the sink, then unscrew the U-bend, remove it for cleaning and then replace it.

2 RIGHT If the obstruction is not in the U-bend, probe a piece of thick wire or an unravelled wire coat hanger into the waste pipe to hook out the blockage.

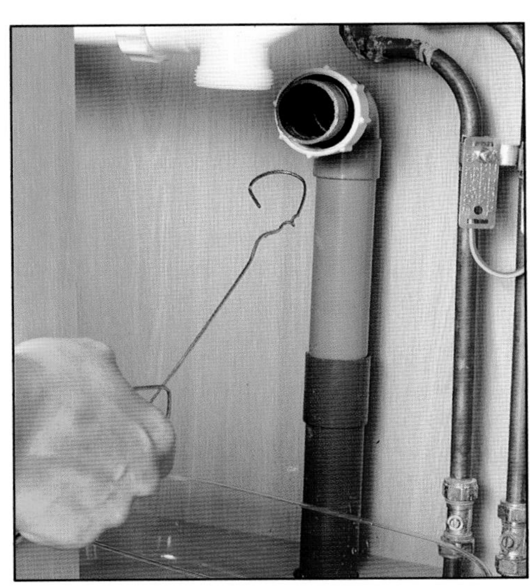

APPLIANCE BREAKDOWN

Before calling in a specialist to deal with an appliance that has stopped working, there are certain basic checks that you can carry out yourself to remedy the most commonly occurring problems. Always unplug an appliance while fault finding until you are ready to test it. With all appliances, first check the instruction manual under 'Fault Finding' and follow the recommendations for your particular make of appliance. Ensure that the plug or plugs are pushed in firmly and that the socket (receptacle) switch is on. This may seem an obvious point, but can easily be overlooked if the switch is hidden behind the appliance. Look to see whether the flex is loose or split – if so, switch off the power and replace the flex as soon as possible.

If all these things are in order, refer to the following list of simple checks and repairs that you can carry out yourself. If these are not successful you will have to call in an engineer.

A portable air conditioner

If an air conditioner is not cooling properly, or is operating erratically, it may be the incorrect size for the room. (If too small, it will operate continually and may ice up, making the room feel cold and damp.) Check to see whether the filter needs cleaning, or whether the seal or panels are out of position. Also check the internal evaporator and exterior condenser coils, and clean them as necessary.

If an air conditioner is not working at all, the thermostat control may be incorrectly set. Alternatively, if the machine has a water reservoir, this may need emptying.

A dishwasher

If the hose is leaking, it may be due to a loose clip, or the hose may be damaged. Ensure that clips are tight and secure, and either tape up the hose or replace it as necessary.

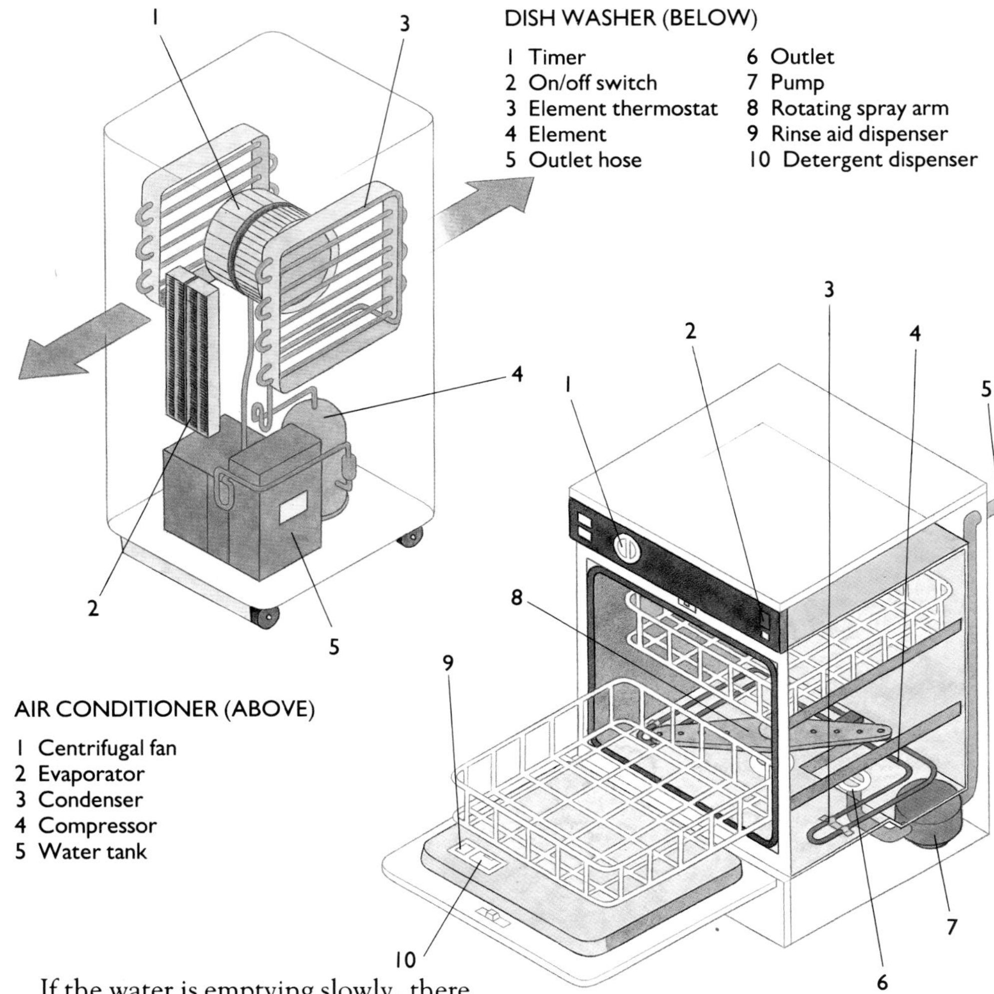

AIR CONDITIONER (ABOVE)

1 Centrifugal fan
2 Evaporator
3 Condenser
4 Compressor
5 Water tank

DISH WASHER (BELOW)

1 Timer
2 On/off switch
3 Element thermostat
4 Element
5 Outlet hose
6 Outlet
7 Pump
8 Rotating spray arm
9 Rinse aid dispenser
10 Detergent dispenser

If the water is emptying slowly, there may be a blockage in the pump or outlet filter. Disconnect the outlet hose and remove any debris. Prise out the filter and clean.

If the dishwasher is simply not cleaning the dishes properly, you may be using the wrong programme, or there may be a blockage in the spray arms. If the programme is correct, unscrew the central hub cap on the spray arm and wash it out if necessary.

A food processor

If a food processor only produces intermittent bursts of power, or the speed is erratic, the causes could be a worn drive belt, or food clogged inside the casing or commutator. Undo the machine casing screws and check the belt for nicks or signs of perishing.

FOOD PROCESSOR (BELOW)

1 Speed controls
2 Motor
3 Drive belt

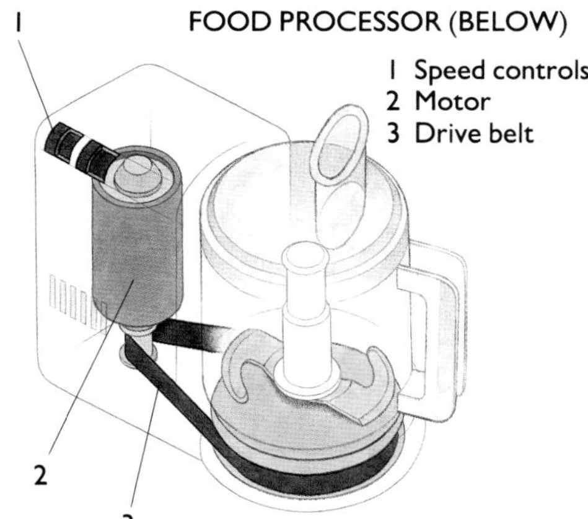

Clean the inside of the machine thoroughly using a soft, dry brush. The commutator contains lots of copper strips and is situated between the brushes in the motor. Clean gently with methylated spirits (denatured alcohol).

A kettle

If there is no power, and the kettle will not heat up, check for any loose wiring or poor connections in the lead and plug and re-wire as necessary. If this does not solve the problem, the cut-out device may have been triggered. Try re-setting the cut-out but, if it continues to trip, you will need to replace it. Another possibility is that the element is damaged, so check for hairline cracks. If the repair is likely to be costly, however, it may be easier simply to replace the kettle.

A refrigerator

If the problem is poor cooling, causing the ice box to melt, the causes are likely to be a faulty door seal or a faulty condenser, or it could be that the fridge simply needs de-frosting. Check the door seal for perished or damaged areas, and replace it if necessary. Check the condenser by turning the temperature control to the lowest setting. Leave the door open for 5 minutes, then see whether the motor comes on when you shut the door. If nothing happens, the condenser is probably faulty and you will need to call in an engineer. You should de-frost the refrigerator approximately every month.

If the refrigerator temperature is too cold, causing some foods to freeze, the problem may simply be an incorrect thermostat setting, or the thermostat may be faulty.

A tumble drier

If a drier is particularly noisy when in use, the drum bearings may be worn or the fan could be loose. Check the condition of the front and rear bearings, and that the large fan on the main motor is secure and not rotating independently. Check the fan for damage and replace it if necessary.

If loads of washing are not drying properly, the cause may be a blocked filter, or it could be that you are simply overloading the machine. Remove the filter and clean away any fluff. Place a smaller quantity of laundry in the drum before re-starting the drier.

A washing machine

If the problem is leaking water, the causes could be a faulty hose or hose connection, a perished door seal, a blocked outlet or a faulty pump. Switch off the machine and remove any washing from inside. Check that the filter is not blocked, check the outlet hose for any blockage, and check the pump by switching to the rinse cycle. Check the hose and connections for any leaks, and make a temporary repair with adhesive tape if possible to prevent further leakage. Examine the door seal and replace it if damaged, or see whether garments or an object have been caught in the door gasket.

If the problem is that the machine is not emptying, the causes could be a faulty pump, or a blocked filter or outlet hose. Switch off the machine, and drain down the system following the instruction manual. Open the filter and remove any debris or objects using an old toothbrush. Also check the pump chamber and remove any blockage.

If the drum of the machine will not turn, the reason may be a slack or broken drive belt.

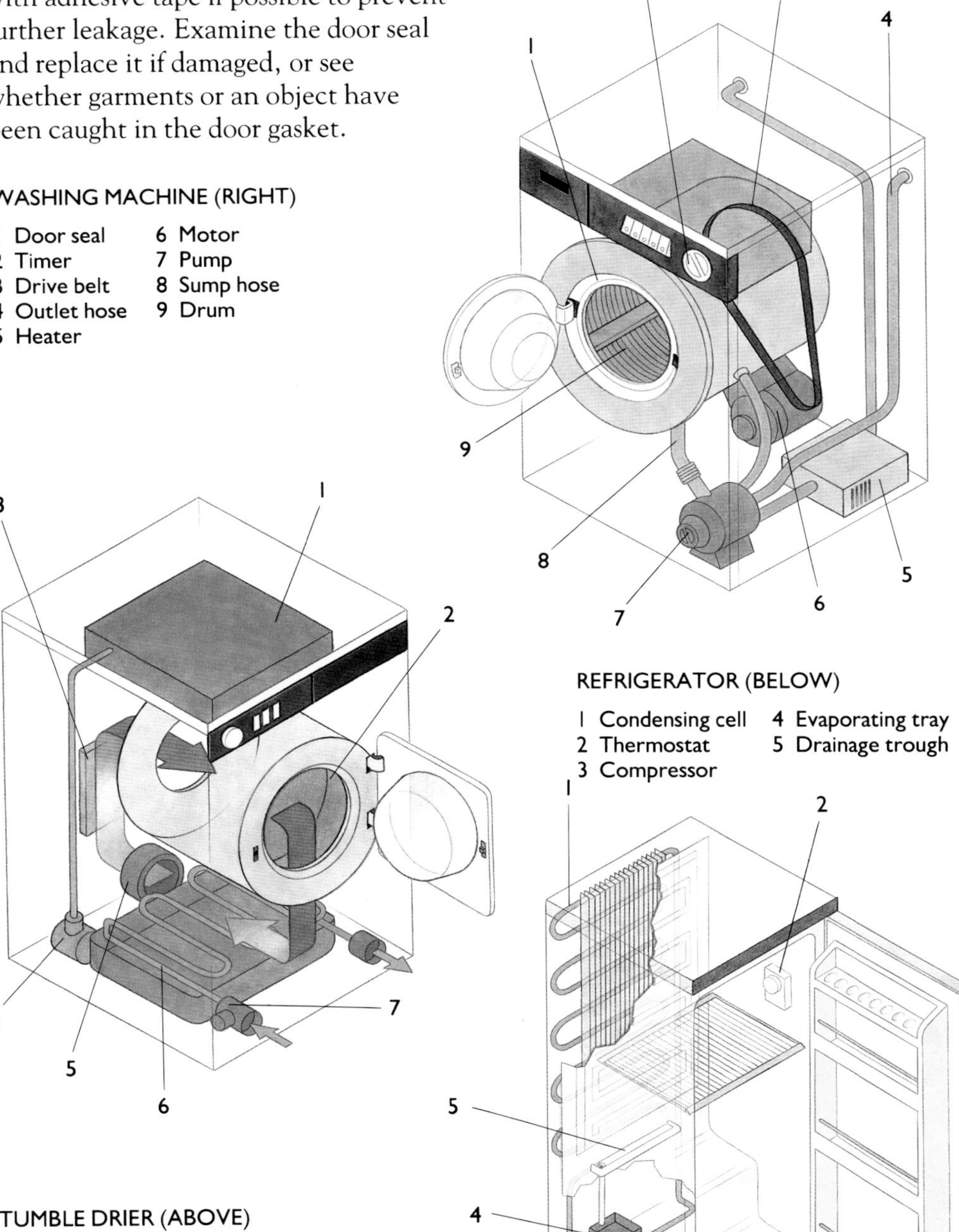

WASHING MACHINE (RIGHT)

1 Door seal
2 Timer
3 Drive belt
4 Outlet hose
5 Heater
6 Motor
7 Pump
8 Sump hose
9 Drum

TUMBLE DRIER (ABOVE)

1 Reservoir tank
2 Circulating drum
3 Heater unit
4 Pump
5 Circulator fan
6 Cool metal ducting
7 Air vent

REFRIGERATOR (BELOW)

1 Condensing cell
2 Thermostat
3 Compressor
4 Evaporating tray
5 Drainage trough

REPAIRING WALLPAPER AND CARPETS

It is a simple matter to repair minor damage to painted walls and ceilings and then to cover it up with a fresh coat of paint. With wall coverings, patching damage or curing paperhanging defects requires a different approach.

The most common form of damage to a wall covering is an impact that leaves a jagged tear. If the torn part is still attached, brush some paste on to its rear face and press it back into place. Use a seam roller to apply pressure to the flap and roll it flat.

If the torn part is missing it will be necessary to patch the damage. If there are some offcuts from the original papering job, cut a patch from them. If not, cut and dry-strip a patch from an out-of-sight area behind a piece of furniture to use for the repair. Tear around the edges of the patch, holding it face-down, to create a thin 'feathered' edge, then paste it, place it over the damaged area and flatten it with a seam roller. If the paper is a thick 2-layer duplex type, try to peel away the backing paper to reduce the thickness of the patch and make it less noticeable once it is in position. Feather the edge and paste in position.

Another common problem, blistering, is the result of inadequate pasting during paperhanging. It is a relatively simple task to slit blisters open and lift dry seams to apply a little fresh paste and stick the covering firmly back to the wall. With fragile printed or flocked wall coverings, take care not to get paste on the surface.

If a carpet becomes damaged in one area – perhaps as a result of a cigarette burn, for example – and you cannot remove the mark, trim back the pile of the carpet with a razor blade. If this does not work, the answer is to patch the mark with a new piece of carpet. Use a spare offcut if you have one available, or cut the patch from an area in the room that will not be visible, such as under a sofa.

PATCHING DAMAGED WALLPAPER

1 Cut a repair patch from an offcut of the original wall covering, or strip one from behind a piece of furniture. Check that the patch will cover the damage and match the pattern.

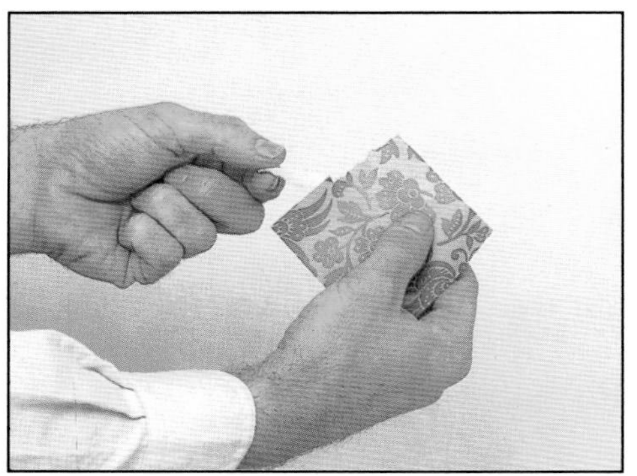

2 Carefully tear along the edges of the patch to reduce its thickness and create a thin feathered edge. Check that no backing paper is visible.

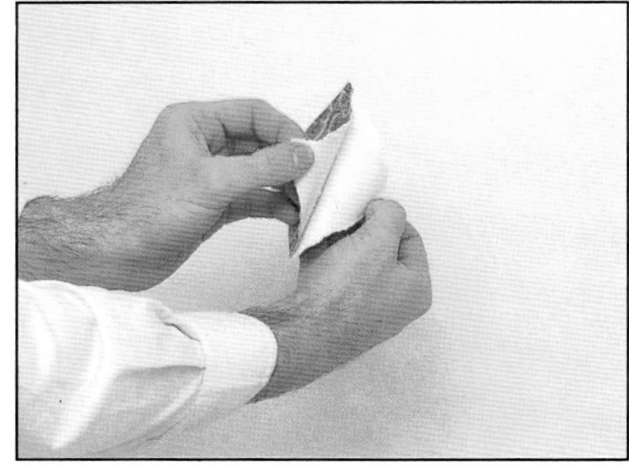

3 Some 2-layer duplex papers are too thick to use as a patch. Try to separate the backing paper at a corner of the patch and peel it off.

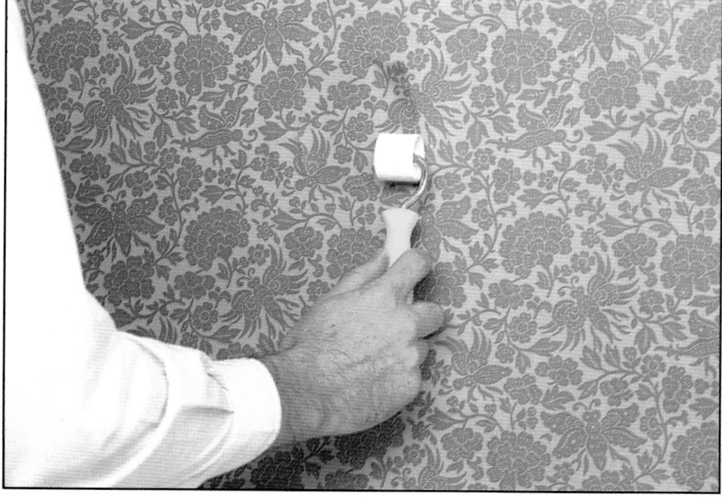

4 Paste the back of the patch and place it over the damaged area, aligning the pattern carefully. 'Iron' it into place with the aid of a seam roller.

CURING A DRY BLISTER

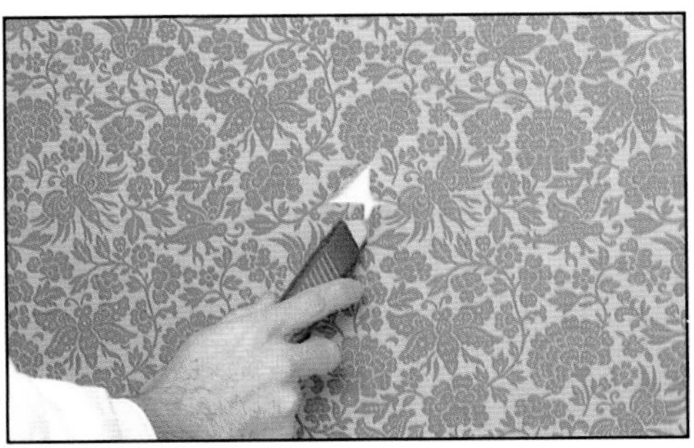

1 If a dry blister appears after wallpapering, use a sharp utility knife to make 2 cuts through the blister at right-angles.

2 Peel back the triangular tongues formed and apply a little paste to the wall surface and to the back of the tongues. Leave to soak for a few minutes.

3 Press the triangles back into place and run a seam roller along the cuts to bond the paper firmly to the wall and leave an almost invisible repair.

STICKING DRY SEAMS

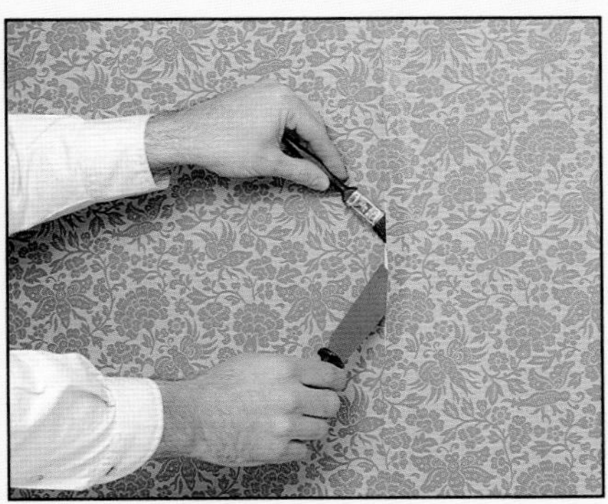

If a seam has failed to stick flat, lift it with a filling knife (putty knife) and use a slip of abrasive paper to sand off the dried paste behind it. Use the filling knife to hold the edge of the wall covering away from the wall, and brush a little paste on to the back of the paper and also on to the wall surface. Leave to soak. Press the seam down flat with a seam roller, then use a sponge or damp cloth to remove any paste that has oozed on to the face of the wall covering before it dries.

PATCHING A CARPET

1 First remove as much of the dirt as you can by vacuuming, placing the nozzle down over the dirt rather than sweeping it back and forth to avoid rubbing in the mark.

2 If the mark is only fairly light, try carefully trimming back the carpet pile, using a razor blade.

3 If the mark is ingrained, lift the carpet and place a piece of hardboard on top of the underlay, beneath the damage. Cut a matching piece of carpet, slightly larger than the damaged area, and place over the damaged area with the pile running the same way. Cut right through both carpets, then replace the old patch with the new.

REPLACING TRIM MOULDINGS

Trim mouldings are both practical and decorative. They are used as skirtings (baseboards) to protect wall surfaces at floor level from accidental damage, and around door and window openings as architraves (trims) to frame the opening and disguise the joint between the frame and the wall surface. Both can be plain or ornate, and can be painted, stained or varnished. They may need replacing if they are damaged or simply look unfashionable.

Skirtings are often fixed directly to masonry walls with large cut nails in older homes, or with masonry nails in more recent ones. Alternatively, they may be nailed to rough timber fixing blocks or grounds (furrings) which are themselves nailed to the masonry. Boards fixed to blocks are much easier to remove than those nailed directly to the wall, as both cut and masonry nails can have a ferocious grip. In the latter situation it is often easier to punch the nails through the boards and into the walls than to try to prise them out. Boards on wood-framed walls are simply nailed to the frame, and so are easy and quick to remove.

Architraves are pinned (tacked) in place to the edges of the door or window frame. It is an easy job to prise the trims away using a bolster (stonecutter's) chisel, without causing undue damage to the frame or the surrounding wall surface.

Replacing Architraves (Trims)

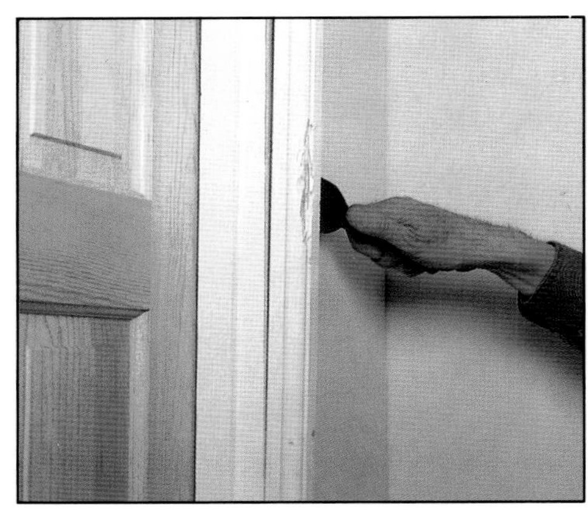

1 Prise off the old mouldings. They should come away easily. If necessary, lever against a small wooden block to avoid damaging the surface of the wall.

2 Hold an upright against the frame so that you can mark the inside of the mitre joint on it. Repeat for the other upright.

3 Cut the end of the moulding, using a mitre block or box. Alternatively, mark the line across the moulding with a protractor or combination square.

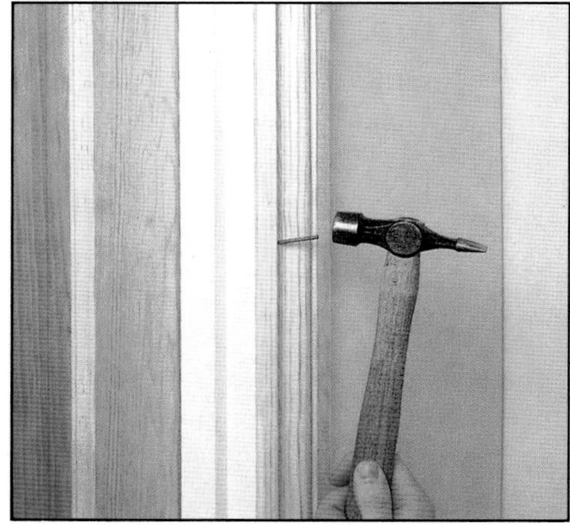

4 Fix the uprights to the frame by driving in nails at 30 cm/12 in intervals. Recess the heads with a nail punch and fill the holes later.

5 Hold the top piece above the uprights to mark the position for the mitre cut at each end. Make the cuts as before and test the piece for fit.

6 Nail the top piece to the frame, checking that the mitre joints are accurately aligned. Finally, drive a nail through each corner to secure the joint.

Replacing Skirtings (Baseboards)

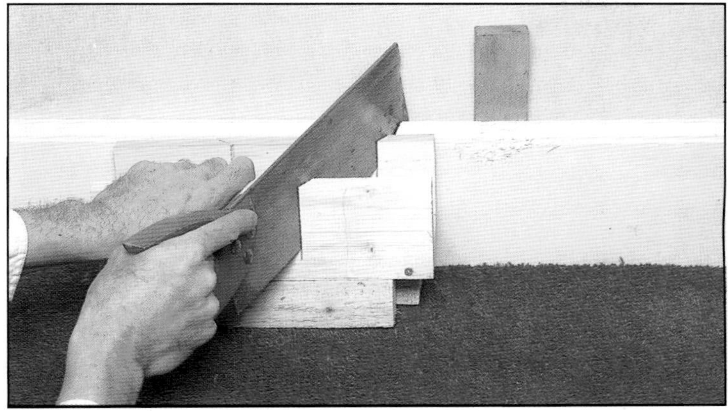

1 To replace a small area of damaged board, prise it away from the wall slightly, wedge it and use a tenon saw and mitre box to cut out a section.

2 Nail small support blocks behind the cut ends of the board, using masonry nails on solid walls, and then nail the cut ends to the support blocks.

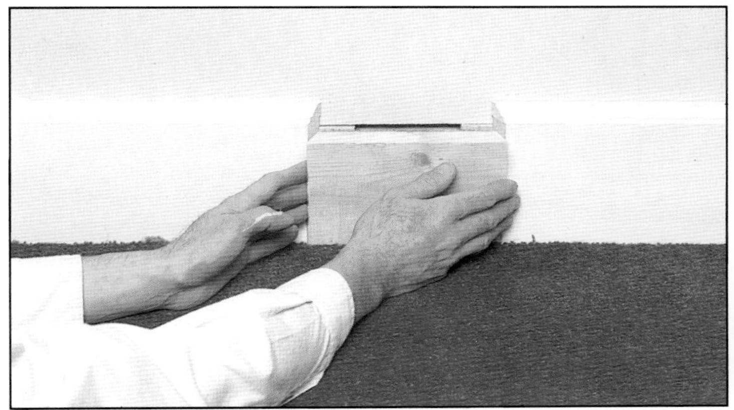

3 Cut a piece of replacement board to fit, with its ends mitred to match the cut-out section. Use plain wood if you are unable to match the skirting profile.

4 Nail the replacement board to the support blocks. If you are using plain wood, pin (tack) on decorative mouldings to build up a close match to the existing board.

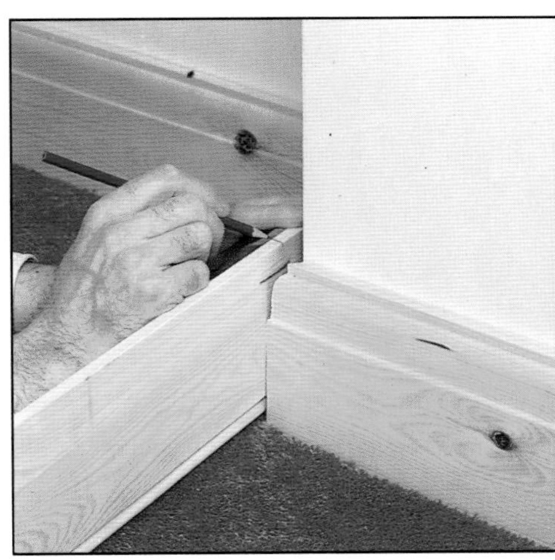

5 When replacing whole lengths, use mitre joints at external corners. Fix the first length, then mark the inside of the mitre on the back of the next board.

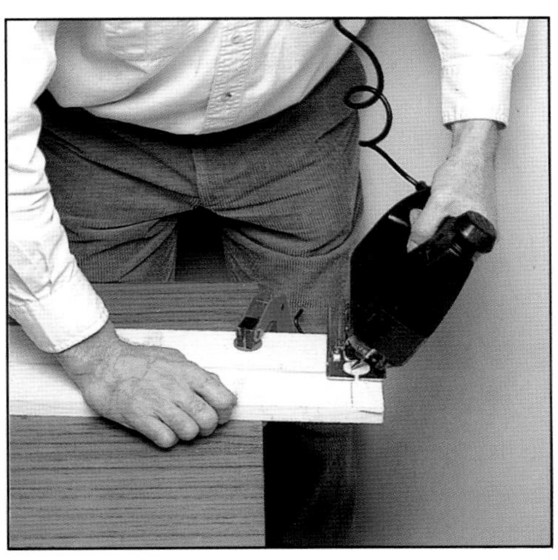

6 Cut the mitre joints with a power jigsaw (saber saw) with an adjustable sole plate. Set the cutting angle to just under 45° to ensure that the joint will fit well.

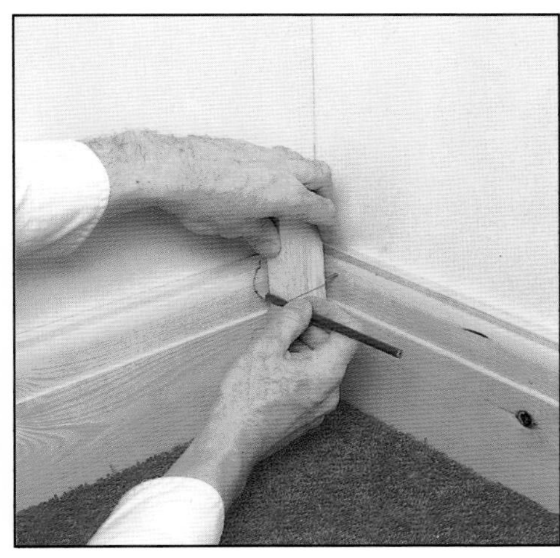

7 At internal corners, fit the first length right into the corner. Scribe its profile on to the second board, cut this with a coping saw and then fit it.

CURING DOOR PROBLEMS

A well-fitted door should have a long and trouble-free life. If it does start to misbehave, the problem is likely to be the door binding against its frame and, in extreme cases, failing to shut properly. There are 3 possible causes: a build-up of paint on the door and frame surfaces after years of re-painting, expansion due to atmospheric conditions – the door sticks in damp weather as moisture causes it to swell slightly, but shrinks and closes freely in dry weather; and hinge faults caused either by wear and tear or bad fitting.

Where a paint build-up is to blame, the remedy is quite simple: strip off the old paint from the door edge back to bare wood, and re-paint from scratch.

If atmospheric conditions are to blame, the solution is to plane down the door edges slightly to increase the clearance between door and frame. You will have to take the door off its hinges to do this unless it is only the leading edge that is binding.

Hinge faults that can cause binding include hinge screws standing proud or working loose, and hinge recesses being cut too deep or too shallow. In each case the cure is relatively simple; the biggest problem is often trying to undo the old hinge screws, especially if they have become encrusted with paint over the years. Clean out the slots in the screw heads thoroughly before trying to remove the screws; paint remover is useful for this. Then position the screwdriver in the slot and give the handle a sharp blow with a hammer in order to help free the grip of the threads in the wood.

1 If the hinge screws show signs of pulling out, remove them, drill out the screw holes and hammer in glued dowels. Then drill new pilot holes.

2 If the door is striking the frame because it has expanded over time, close it and mark a pencil line on the door face against the edge of the frame.

5 If the door binds on the hinge side of the frame, the hinge recesses may be too deep. Remove the hinge and pin some packing into the recess.

6 Drill fresh pilot holes for the screws through the packing piece, and drive the fixing screws back into place. Make sure that their heads fit in the countersinks.

3 Take the door off its hinges, remove the handles and the latch mechanism, and plane down the leading edge of the door until the pencil line has disappeared.

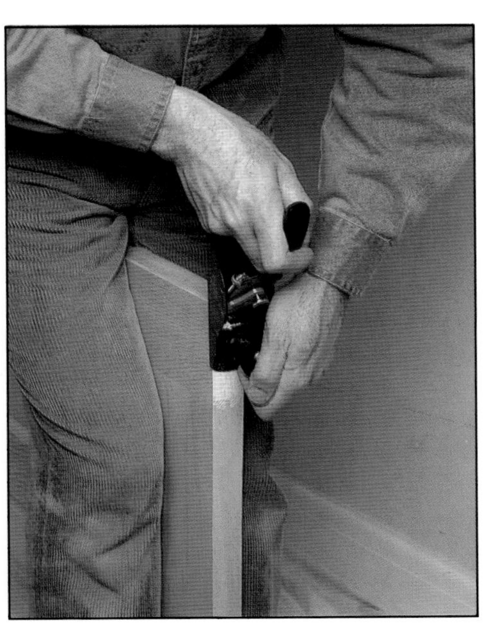

4 If the door is binding either at the top or bottom, take this opportunity to plane off a little wood there too. Plane inwards from the corners to avoid causing splits.

7 Alternatively, re-locate the hinges in a new position. Chisel out the new recesses and re-fit the hinges.

8 If the hinge recesses are too shallow, the hinge leaves will bind and prevent the door from closing. Remove the hinges and chisel out the recesses slightly.

CURING WINDOW PROBLEMS

By far the most common window problem is a cracked or broken pane, caused by a flying object or by the window being allowed to slam. Make a temporary repair to cracked glass with a clear waterproof repair tape – not household adhesive tape – but aim to replace the pane at the earliest opportunity. If the glass is broken, lift out all the loose pieces for safety's sake and make a temporary repair by fixing heavy-duty polythene (polyethylene) sheeting or a piece of board over the opening to keep out the cold.

When measuring up for the replacement glass, measure all four sides in case the rebate in the frame is not perfectly square, and use the smaller of each pair of figures. Subtract 3 mm/ ⅛ in from each one to allow for clearance all around, and note which way the pattern ran if the glass was obscured rather than clear. Take a piece of patterned glass with you when buying a replacement, so as to be sure of getting the correct type.

The other problems that windows suffer from are similar to those affecting doors – paint build-up, expansion and warping. They may also pull out of square if the frame corner joints start to open up, causing the casement to bind in its frame and possibly also cracking the glass. The trouble can be cured by strengthening the frame corners with small L-shaped metal repair plates; cut shallow recesses for them and disguise their presence with filler (spackle) and a coat of paint.

TIP

Always dispose of broken glass safely, by wrapping it in newspaper and then packing it in a box so that it cannot injure anyone.

REPLACING BROKEN GLASS

1 When a window breaks, remove all the loose glass immediately for safety's sake. Wear stout gloves to protect your hands and dispose of the glass safely.

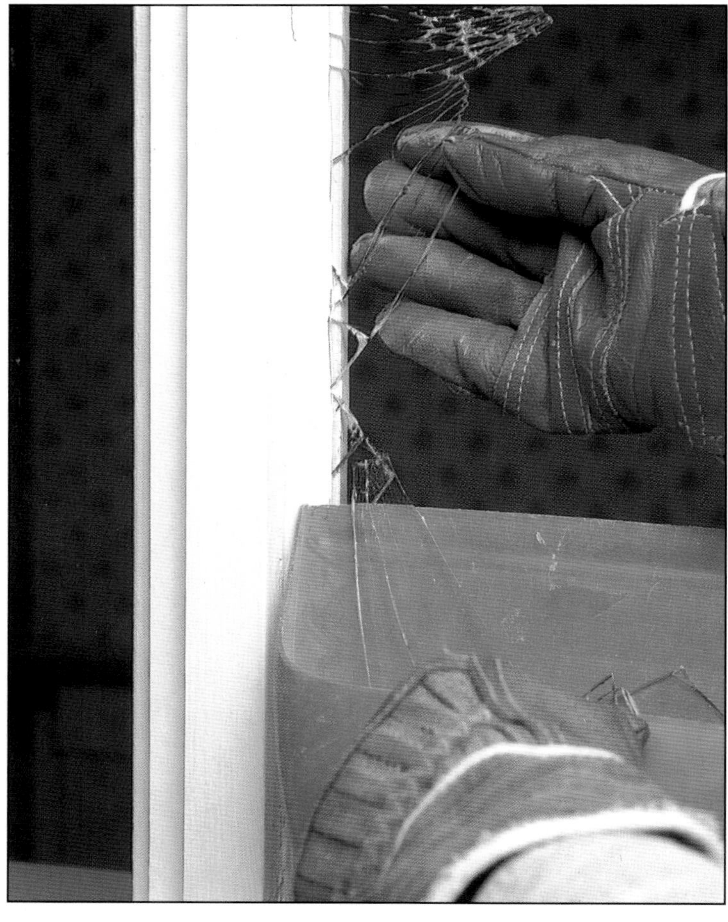

2 Use an old chisel or a glazier's knife to remove all the old putty from the rebate in the frame. Take care not to cut into the wood while doing this.

3 Use a pair of pincers or pliers to pull out the old glazing sprigs all around the frame. Metal frames have glazing clips; save these and re-use them.

4 Knead some putty with your hands to warm and soften it, then press it into the rebate by extruding it between your thumb and forefinger.

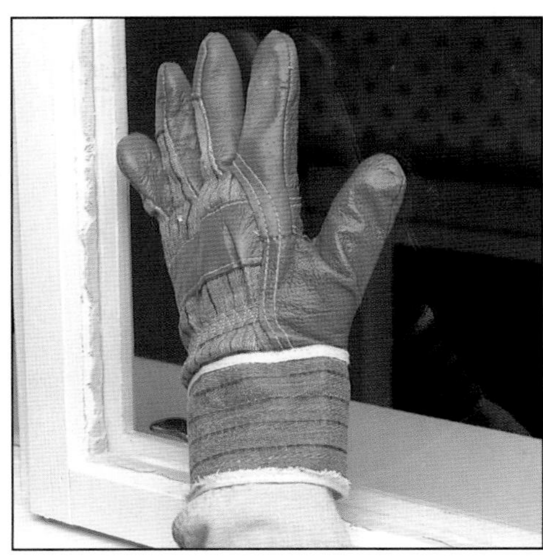

5 Set the replacement pane in position against the bedding putty with equal clearance all around, and press it into place around the edges to compress the putty.

6 Secure the pane in the rebate by tapping in glazing sprigs at roughly 30 cm/12 in intervals. Replace clips in their locating holes in metal frames.

7 Repeat step 4 to extrude a bead of facing putty all around the pane, then neaten it to a 45° bevel by drawing the blade of a putty knife along it.

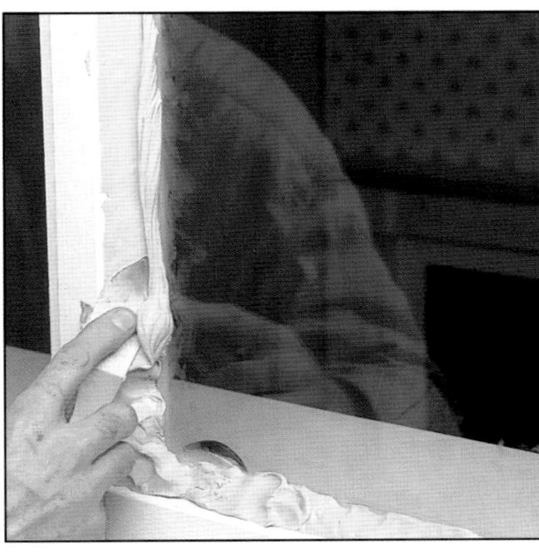

8 Trim off excess putty from the outside and inside of the pane and leave it to harden for about 14 days before painting over it to disguise and seal the joints.

Curing a Binding Casement

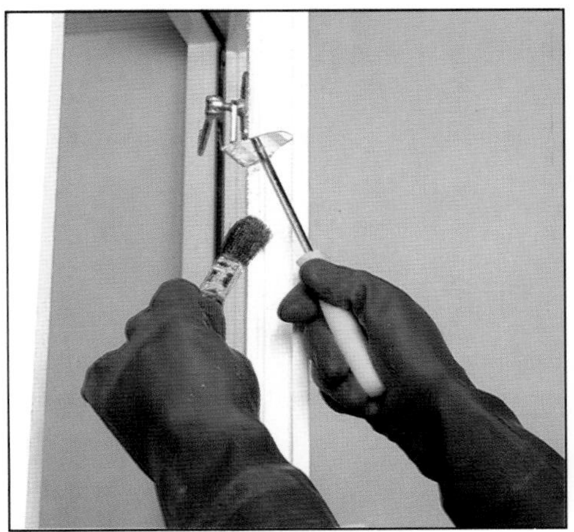

1 If a build-up of paint is causing the edge of the casement to bind against the frame, strip it back. Use chemical strippers for this, as heat may crack the glass.

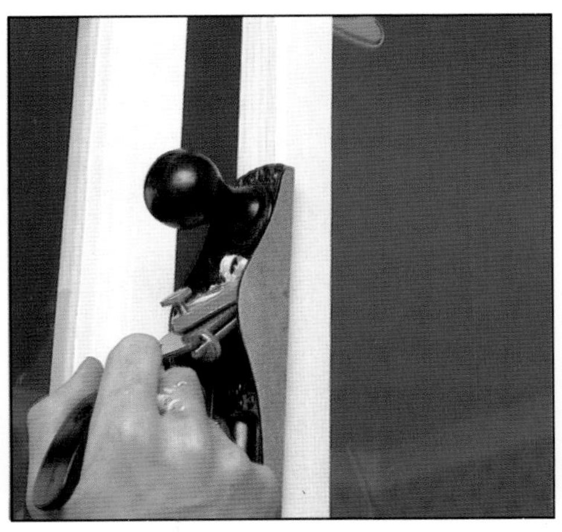

2 If the frame has swollen because of moisture penetration, plane a little wood off the leading edge. Prime and paint it immediately to keep the wood dry.

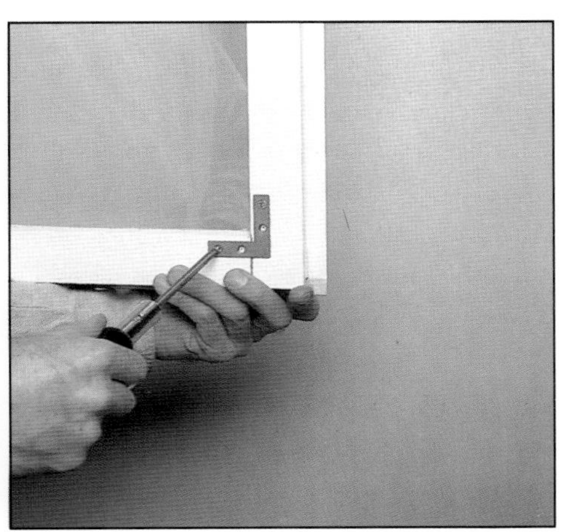

3 If the corner joints of a casement show signs of opening up and the frame is pulling out of square, screw on small L-shaped metal repair plates.

PATCHING WALL AND CEILING DAMAGE

Plasterboard (gypsum board) is an immensely versatile material for lining walls and ceilings, as it provides a smooth surface for any finish and also has useful sound-deadening and fireproofing properties. The one thing it does not do very well is to resist impacts, and resulting holes cannot simply be patched with filler (spackle) because the board's strength will have been lost at the point of damage. The solution is either to strengthen the board or to replace a section altogether.

Very small holes can be disguised with self-adhesive scrim tape and cellulose filler, but holes more than about 5 cm/2 in across need a more substantial repair. Use an offcut of plasterboard and cut a piece slightly narrower than the hole width and twice as long as its height to use as a patch. Pierce a hole in it, thread through a piece of string, tie one end to a nail and pull this against the face of the patch. Then butter some plaster or filler on to the other face of the patch and push it into the hole, keeping hold of the string with the other hand. Position the patch against the inner face of the plasterboard, pulling on the string to help the filler stick it in place. When it has stuck fast, fill the hole and cut off the string.

For larger holes – a foot through the ceiling, for example – in plasterboard and (in older properties) lath-and-plaster surfaces, the only solution is to cut out the damaged piece and nail on a new section in its place. You will need to fix supports around the edges of the opening where you have cut out the damaged section. Fill the cut edges, apply joint tape to hide them and then skim over the patch with a little plaster to complete the repair.

PATCHING A SMALL HOLE IN PLASTERBOARD (GYPSUM BOARD)

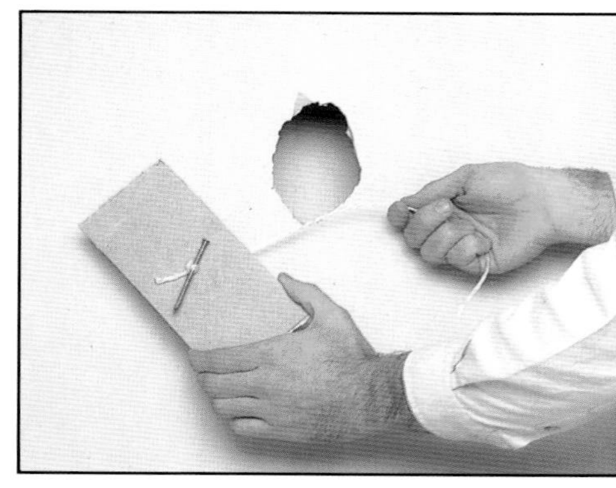

1 Cut a plasterboard patch slightly longer and narrower than the hole, and thread a length of string with a nail tied on through a hole in its centre.

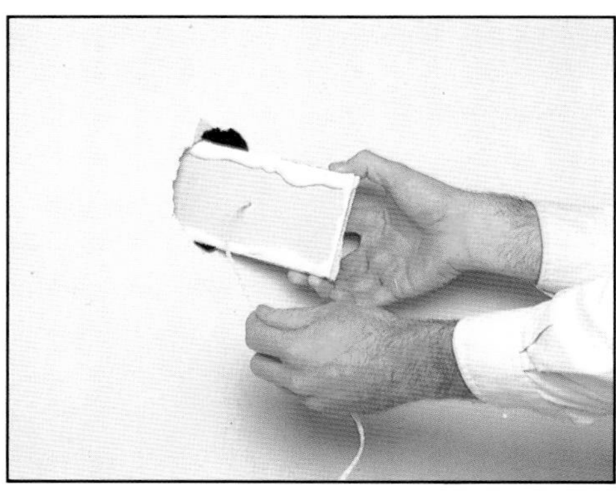

2 Butter some plaster or filler (spackle) on to the edges of the patch and feed it end-on into the hole, keeping hold of the string with the other hand.

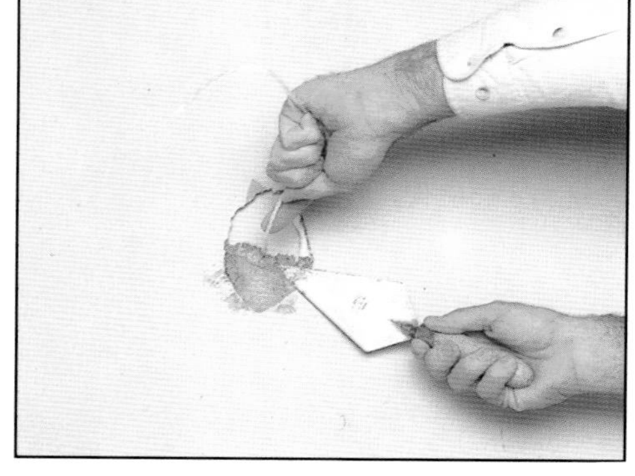

3 Pull the string to hold the patch against the rear face of the board, then fill the recess with either plaster or filler and cut off the string.

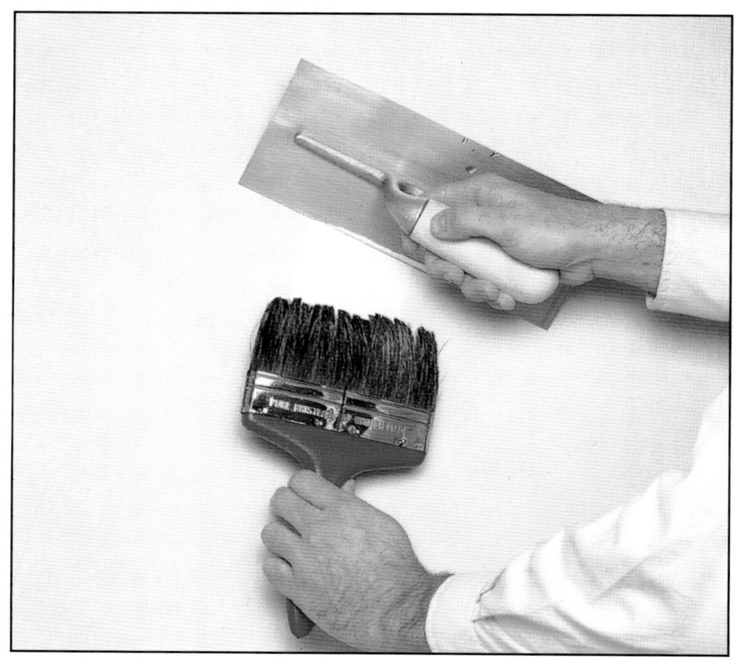

4 Complete the repair by applying a skim coat of plaster over the patch. Flick water on to the plaster with a brush and polish it smooth with a steel float.

Patching a Larger Hole in Plasterboard (Gypsum Board)

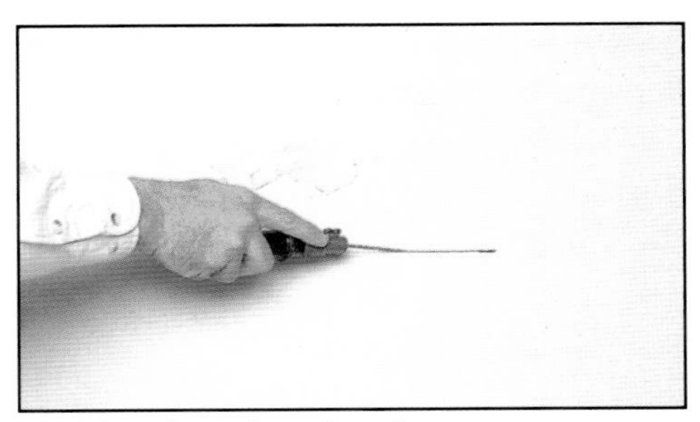

1 If the plasterboard surface is more extensively damaged, cut through it with a sharp knife back to the adjacent wall studs or ceiling joists.

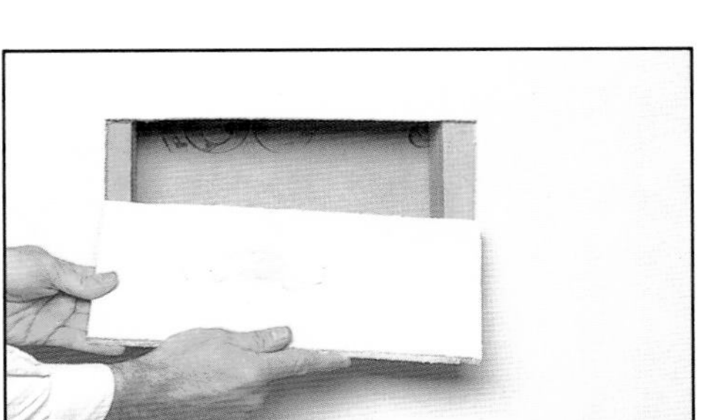

2 Cut across to the stud or joist centres, then make 2 vertical cuts down the centre of the stud or joist to free the damaged panel and remove it.

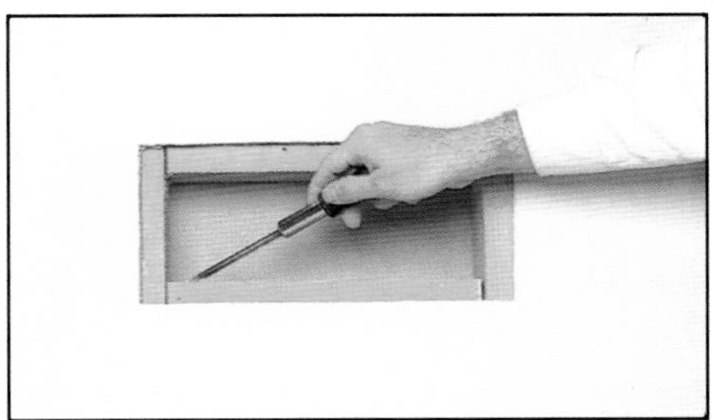

3 Cut 2 strips of wood to fit between the studs/joists, and screw or nail them into place so that they will support the edges of the main board and the patch.

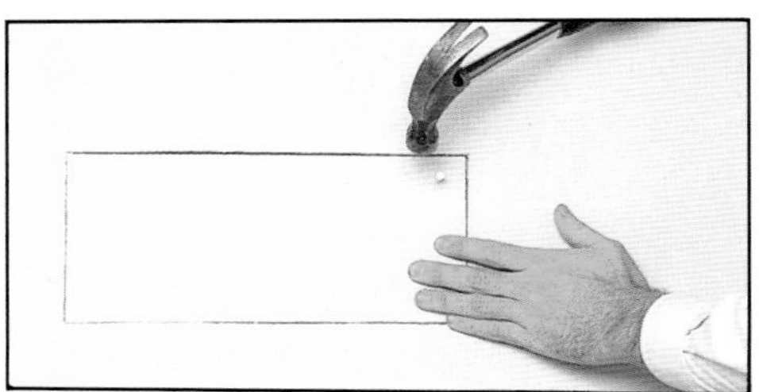

4 Cut a plasterboard patch to match the section removed, and nail it into place. Fill and tape the joints and skim plaster over the repair, then polish with a steel float.

Repairing a Lath-and-Plaster Surface

1 If the wood laths are split or broken, pull them away from the surface. Remove any loose sections of plaster from around the site of the damage.

2 Continue cutting back the old plaster and the laths behind it to expose the studs or ceiling joists at each side of the hole. Square off the edges.

3 Cut a plasterboard patch to fit the hole, and nail it in place. Add two support strips as described for patching plasterboard if the panel is large.

4 Complete the repair by plastering over the patch after filling and taping the cut edges all around. Then polish the repair with a steel float.

REPAIRING A FLOOR

Floorboards suffer more from being lifted for access to pipes and cables beneath them than they do from everyday wear and tear. If the floor has nothing worse than the occasional creak, the trouble can generally be cured by lifting floor coverings and then nailing – or better still, screwing – the offending board down again. With a chipboard (particle board) floor, make sure that the boards are nailed to every joist they cross, not just at the edges; if they are not, the boards can bow upwards and will then bang against the joists when walked on.

Before lifting a section of floor to gain access to services below it, look first of all to see whether someone has already cut an access panel. If they have not, it will be necessary to create one. Locate the joist position closest to where access is needed – the positions of the flooring nail will reveal its whereabouts. Then drill a starter hole and use a power jigsaw (saber saw) to make a 45° cut next to the joist. Prise up the cut end and wedge a strip of wood underneath it, then saw through the board over the centre of the next joist to free the section. To replace it, nail one end to the joist and either skew nail (toe nail) the other angled end to its neighbour or nail a support block to the side of the joist and nail or screw the board end to that.

With a concrete floor, the only repair that is likely to be needed is the filling of cracks or small potholes that may be revealed when an old floor covering is lifted. Cut back any loose edges, brush away loose material and fill the cracks with a fine mortar mix. If the floor surface is sound but uneven or out of level, lay a self-smoothing compound over it.

Creating an Access Panel

1 Start by locating an adjacent joist. Drill a starter hole for the saw blade. Cut through the board at 45° next to the joist with a power jigsaw (saber saw).

2 Use a bolster (stonecutter's chisel) or a similar broad-bladed levering tool to prise up the cut end of the board and release its fixing nails.

3 Slide a length of scrap wood under the raised end of the board to hold it clear of the floor, and saw through the board above the centre of the next joist.

4 To replace the panel, simply lay it back in position. Nail the square-cut end to its joist and skew nail (toe nail) the angled end to the neighbouring board.

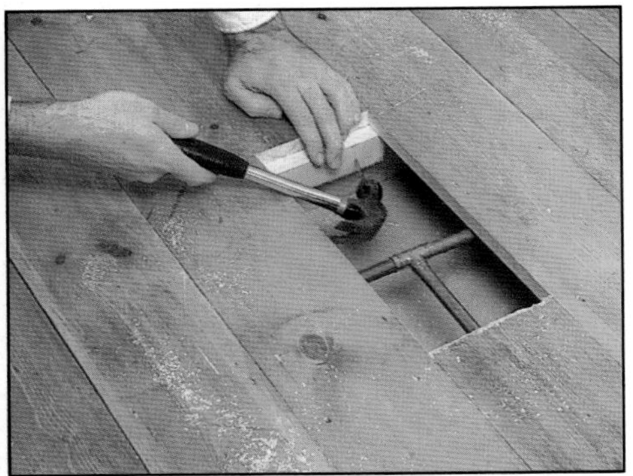

5 An alternative way of supporting the cut ends of an access panel is to nail small wood blocks to each side of the adjacent joists.

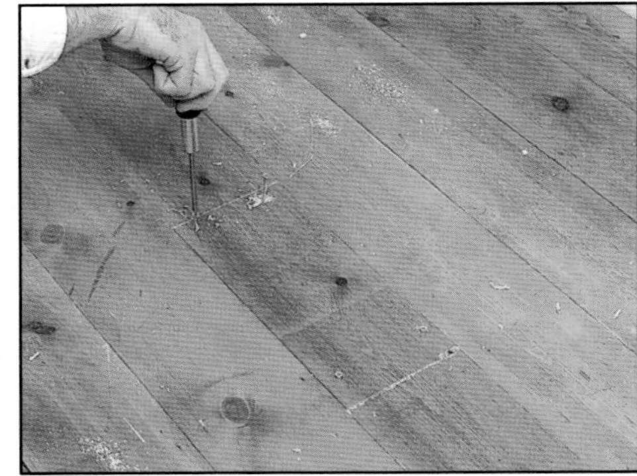

6 You can also screw down the panel on to the wooden blocks. This will allow easy access without damaging the panel.

Repairing a Concrete Floor

1 If you discover cracks in a concrete floor after lifting old floor coverings, use a cold (box) chisel and club (spalling) hammer to undercut the edges of the crack.

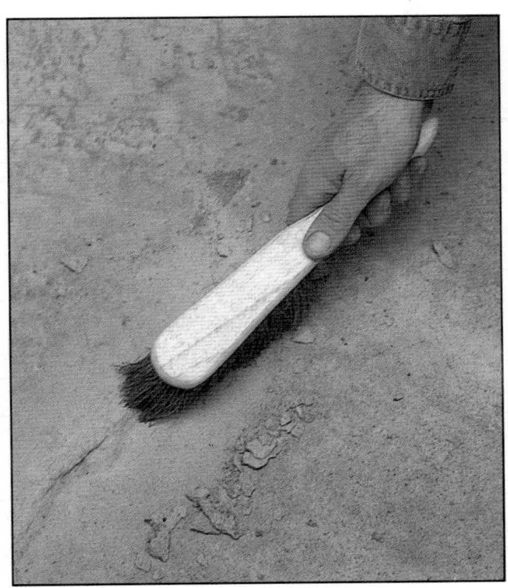

2 Brush away all loose material from the crack and use a vacuum cleaner to pick up the dust.

3 Dilute some PVA building (white general-purpose) adhesive, and brush it along the surface of the crack to help the repair mortar to bond to it securely.

4 Mix up some quick-setting repair mortar and trowel it into the crack, levelling it flush with the surrounding concrete. Leave it to harden.

5 If the floor has noticeable potholes in its surface, pack the hole with some small pieces of stone or other non-compressible filler.

6 Patch the pothole with quick-setting mortar, using the edge of a steel float to remove excess mortar so that the patch is flush with its surroundings.

Insulation and Ventilation

SAVING ENERGY IN THE HOME

Insulation means saving energy, and that is becoming more and more essential on every level, from the personal to the global. People are increasingly conscious of the importance of environmental issues. One of the greatest contributions that any one household can make is to cut down on the unnecessary wastage of fossil fuels, and so to reduce the amount of carbon dioxide released into the atmosphere by burning them. This means making more efficient use of energy, and insulation has a big part to play in this. It saves money, too.

Insulation is a means of reducing heat transfer from a warm area to a cold one, and substantially reduces heat loss. In temperate countries, the external air temperature is below what most people regard as a comfortable level for much of the year, so heating is needed for fairly long periods and heat is constantly lost to the outside.

All materials conduct heat to a greater or lesser extent. Wood is a good insulator, brick an average one and glass is downright poor, as anyone who has sat next to a window on a cold winter's day will testify.

Except in countries which have very cold winters, proper insulation of homes has until recently been a very low priority, both for housebuilders – who will not pay for something that provides only a hidden benefit unless they have to – and for the legislators who frame the regulations and codes with which builders must comply. At last, however, the tide is turning, and current building rules call for much higher standards of insulation than ever before. They have also recognized that over-insulation can cause condensation, both inside the rooms and within the building's structure.

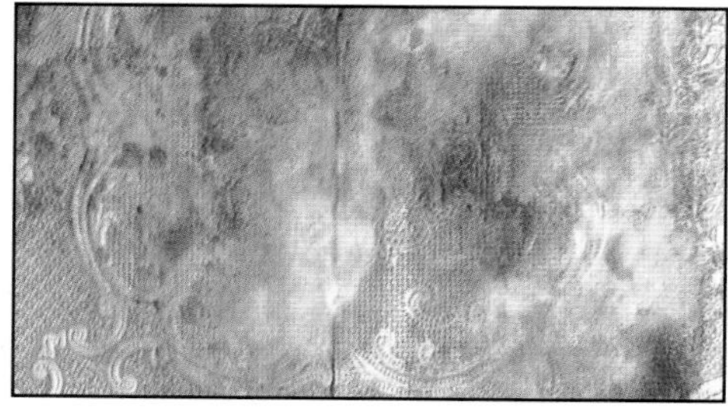

ABOVE Poor insulation, inadequate ventilation and poor heating levels can, in extreme cases, lead to patches of mould occurring around windows and inside fitted cupboards (closets).

SOURCES OF MOISTURE

People themselves are a major source of the moisture in the air inside a building. Breath is moist and sweat evaporates; one person gives off 250 ml/½ pint of water during 8 hours of sleep: 3 times that during the day.

Domestic activities create even more moisture. Cooking, washing up, a hot bath or shower, washing and drying clothes and so on can create as much as a further 10 to 12 litres/3 gallons of water a day, and every litre of fuel burnt in a flueless oil or paraffin heater gives off roughly another litre of water vapour. The air in the house is expected to soak up all this extra moisture invisibly, but it may not be able to manage unaided. However, a combination of improved insulation and controlled ventilation will go a long way towards eliminating the problem of condensation.

This will not help people living in older properties, many of which were built with no thought to their insulation performance at all. Over the years, various attempts will have been made to insulate houses like these, but what was deemed adequate 20 years ago will be well below par for today.

Condensation

Condensation is a big problem in many homes. It can lead to serious health problems and can also cause damage to the structure of the home.

The air always contains a certain amount of moisture – a lot on a humid summer's day, less on a clear winter one. When the air at a particular temperature cannot hold any more moisture, it is said to have reached saturation point, described as a relative humidity of 100 per cent.

Air at saturation point is the key to the problem. If that saturated air is cooled – for example, by coming into contact with a surface such as a window pane on a chilly day – it can no longer hold so much vapour. The excess moisture vapour in the air condenses into droplets of water, and these are deposited on the cold surface – first as a fine film that mists up the glass but then, as more moisture is deposited, the droplets combine to form rivulets that run down the surface to create pools of water on the window sill. This can ruin decorations and cause window sills and frames to rot and rust; it can also cause 2 further problems, both of which are potentially more serious.

ABOVE Constant condensation ruins paintwork and will eventually cause wooden window frames and sills to rot.

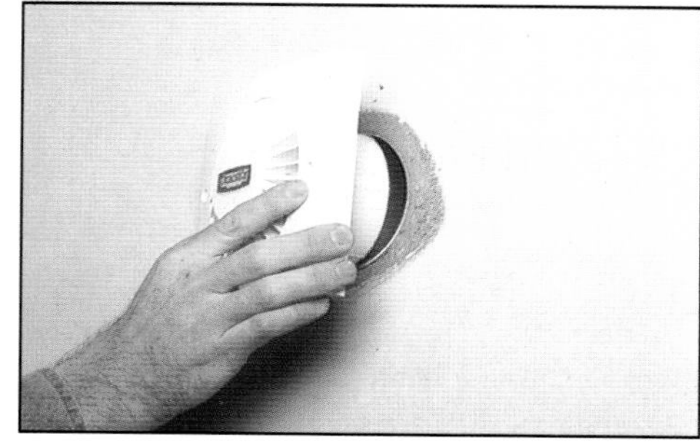

ABOVE Fit an extractor fan (exhaust fan) to control ventilation in a steamy room such as a kitchen or bathroom. The type linked to a humidity detector activates automatically.

ABOVE Fit a special brush draught excluder over a letter-box opening, and also to the bottoms of doors to minimize heat loss.

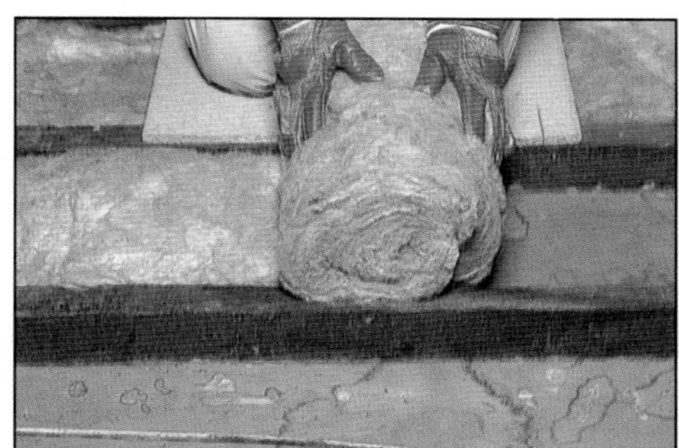

ABOVE If the roof of your house is pitched (sloping), lay blanket insulation over the loft (attic) floor to prevent heat loss.

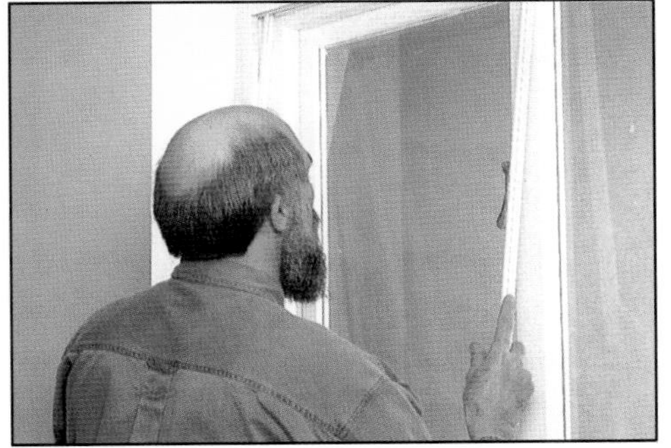

ABOVE Glass is an extremely poor insulator. Secondary glazing, known as double glazing, can cut down on heat loss, provided that the inner panes are well-sealed to their tracks.

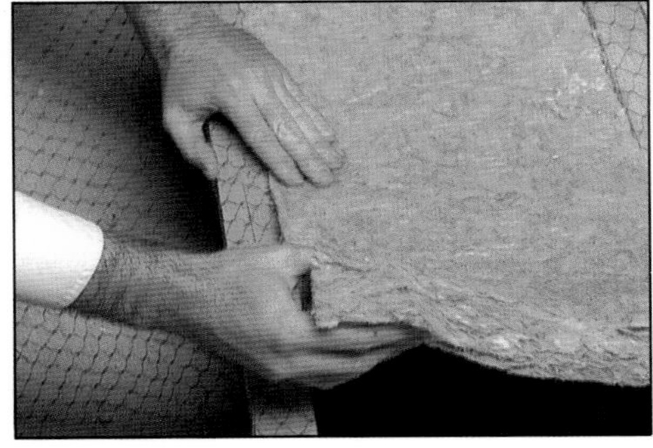

ABOVE With a suspended floor, you can lift the floorboards and suspend blanket insulation on netting stapled to the joists. Lay a vapour barrier, such as heavy plastic sheeting, on top.

The first is mould. Apart from moisture vapour, the air also contains millions of tiny spores which float around looking for somewhere to live and multiply. The one thing they need is a damp surface. The result is the patches of black, brown or dark green mould seen especially around windows, in fitted cupboards (closets) and in the upper corners of those rooms that have poor insulation and ventilation and inadequate heating.

The second problem is interstitial condensation. If the materials used to build walls, roofs and other parts of a building allow water vapour to penetrate, condensation can actually occur inside the structure. If moisture cannot evaporate to the outside the affected part of the structure remains damp; this can then encourage rot to grow on wood, and may also result in frost damage to masonry in cold weather, caused by the water expanding as it freezes. What is more, a damp wall has a lower resistance to the passage of heat than a dry one, and therefore becomes colder and encourages yet more condensation.

Ventilation

Always be aware that, no matter how well the home has been insulated, it is vital to ensure that it is well-ventilated too and that air can circulate freely to prevent the problems of condensation. When insulating your home it is essential to make allowances for air circulation by installing, for example, an extra air-brick, an extractor fan (exhaust fan) or window vents in a bathroom or kitchen, and even a cooker hood. Simply opening a window while cooking to allow steam out can make a difference. Fuel-burning appliances such as paraffin heaters, gas cookers, central-heating boilers and fires also require ventilation to work efficiently and to dispel potentially dangerous fumes.

QUICK WAYS TO INSULATE

Once icy winds begin to whistle around your home in the winter, you will soon find out where the chill gusts blow in and where all the expensive heat escapes. The following steps will all contribute to keeping your home warmer and energy-efficient.

- Sash windows are notorious for draughts, and their sliding action calls for special weatherproofing. A brush seal (with soft bristles) against inside sliding faces and a V-strip seal where sashes close against the top and bottom of the frame are best.
- An outside door is prone to swelling in cold, wet conditions. Seal it with a flexible PVC (vinyl) or brush strip pinned to the outer face.
- Keyholes can let in cold air, so fit coverplates on the outside.
- Fill gaps around overflow and waste pipes that pass through holes in exterior walls with an exterior-grade filler (spackle), mortar or an expanding foam filler.
- Fill any gaps in windows that remain closed throughout the winter with a flexible, clear sealant. Apply it with a mastic gun and, when you wish to open the windows again, simply peel off the sealant and discard.
- A porch built over a front or back door acts as an insulating barrier by preventing cold air from entering the house and keeping warm air in. It will also keep wet boots and coats from dripping over floors.
- In addition to traditional sausage-shaped door draught excluders, door curtains are a very effective way of reducing heat loss, and can also add a decorative finish to rooms.
- Insulate the wall immediately behind a radiator by simply placing tin foil behind it to reflect the heat back into the room again.
- Fix temporary 'double glazing' by sticking clear cellophone to the window frame with double-sided tape.
- Cling film (plastic wrap) can also serve as temporary double glazing. Stretch it over the window and make it taut with gentle heat blown from a hairdryer.

INSULATING A ROOF, FLOOR AND PIPEWORK

In a building with a pitched (sloping) roof, where the loft (attic) space is used only for storage, it is usual to insulate the loft floor, using either blankets of glass fibre or mineral wool (this is sold by the roll and is fireproof and resistant to damp or vermin attack); or else loose-fill material (vermiculite, a lightweight expanded mineral, is the most widely used).

Blanket materials are generally easier to handle than loose-fill types. The rolls are generally 60 cm/24 in wide to match standard joist spacing, and common thicknesses are 10 cm/4 in and 15 cm/6 in. Choose the latter unless there is already some thin loft insulation, and ensure that it is laid with eaves baffles to allow adequate ventilation of the loft. It is essential to wear protective clothing when handling glass-fibre insulation.

Loose-fill materials need laying to a greater depth – usually at least an extra 2.5 cm/1 in. With few ceiling joists being deeper than about 15 cm/6 in, there is nothing to contain the insulation and allow for maintenance access unless strips of wood are fixed along the top edge of every joist.

When the loft floor is completely insulated, remember to insulate any water tanks and pipework within the loft, as they will now be at the risk of freezing. For this reason, do not lay insulation under water tanks.

WALL INSULATION

Up to one-quarter of a home's heat loss can occur through the walls. The space between cavity walls can be filled with a variety of insulating materials, including polystyrene (styrofoam) pellets and expanding foam. These have to be pumped through holes drilled in the external wall, so you will need to call in a professional to undertake this job.

LAYING ROOF INSULATION

1 Clear all stored items from the loft (attic) area, then put down a sturdy kneeling board and vacuum up the dust and debris. Always put on gloves and a face-mask and wear long sleeves to handle the insulation. Unroll it between the joists, leaving the eaves clear for ventilation.

2 Butt-join the ends of successive lengths of blanket. To cut the material to length, either use long-bladed scissors or simply tear it.

3 While working across the loft, make sure that any electrical cables are lifted clear of the insulation so they cannot overheat.

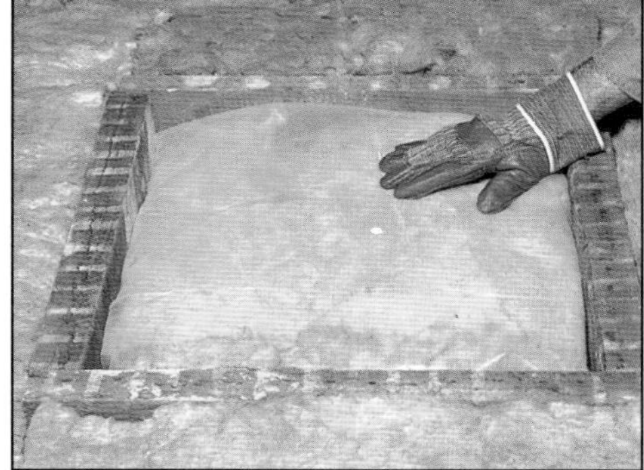

4 Insulate the upper surface of the loft hatch by wrapping a piece of blanket in plastic sheeting and then stapling this to the hatch door.

Insulating a Wooden Floor

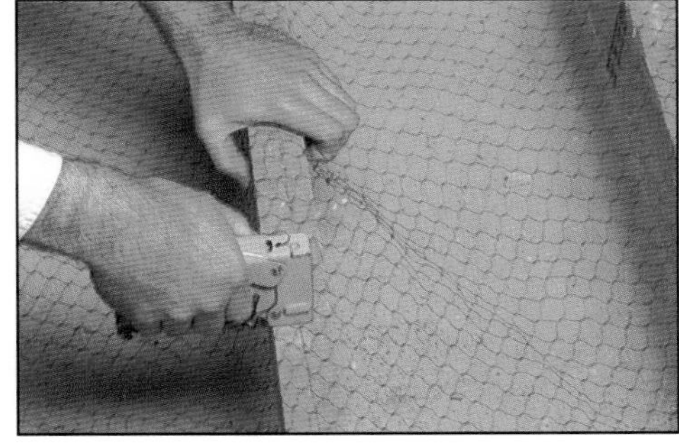

1 To insulate beneath a wooden floor, lift all the floorboards. Drape lengths of garden netting loosely over the joists and staple them in place.

2 Lay loft-insulation blanket or wall-insulation batts in the 'hammocks' between the joists. If the netting sags, pull it up a little and staple it again.

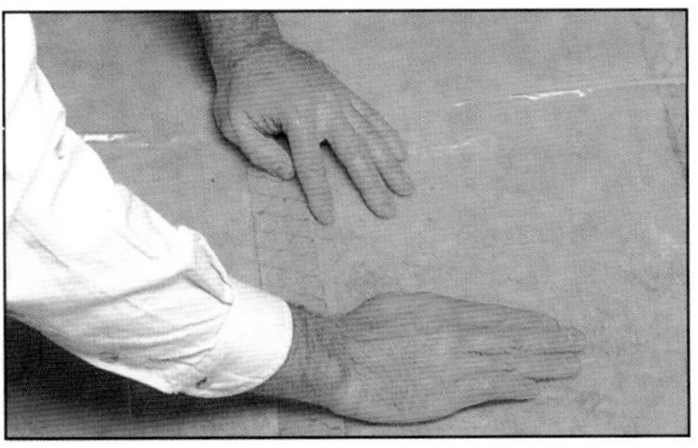

3 To prevent moisture from the house condensing within the insulation, cover it with a vapour barrier of heavy-duty polythene (polyethylene) sheeting.

4 Re-lay the floorboards by nailing them to the joists. Take this opportunity to close up any gaps in the joints between the boards for a neat finish.

Insulating Pipework

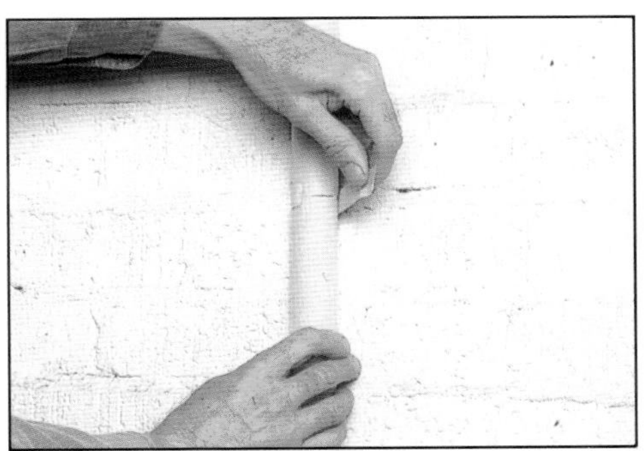

1 The quickest and easiest way of insulating pipework is to slip on lengths of foam pipe insulation, which are slit lengthwise.

2 To make neat joins in the insulation at corners, cut the ends at 45°, using a mitre box and a carving knife or hacksaw blade. Tape the corner joint.

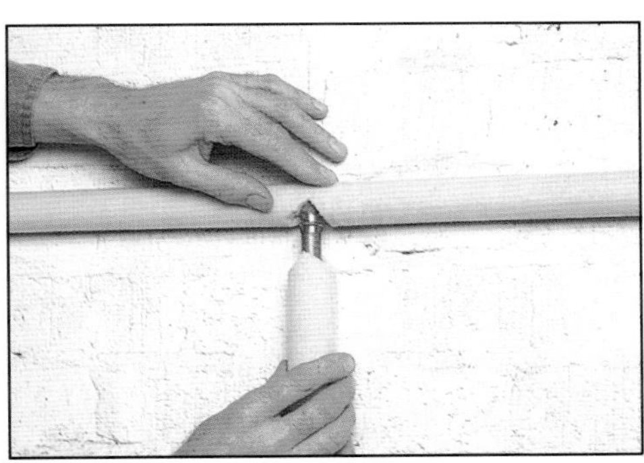

3 Make a V-shaped cut-out in the insulation at tee joints, then cut an arrow shape on the end of the insulation that will cover the branch pipe.

4 As with butt and corner joints, use PVC (vinyl) tape to secure the sections of insulation together and to prevent them from slipping out of position.

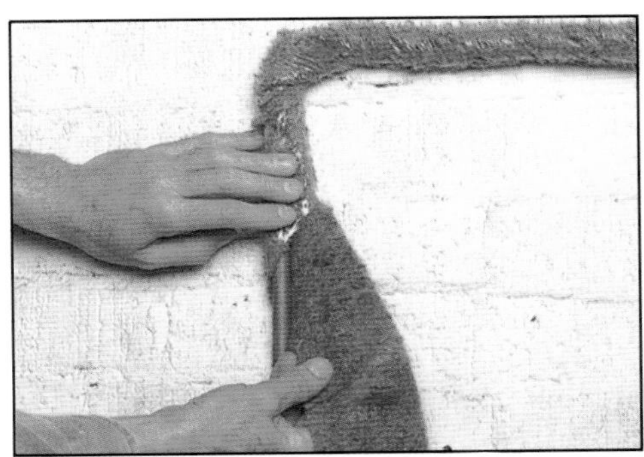

5 Pipe bandage can be used instead of foam insulation. Wrap it around the pipe in a spiral, with the turns just overlapping.

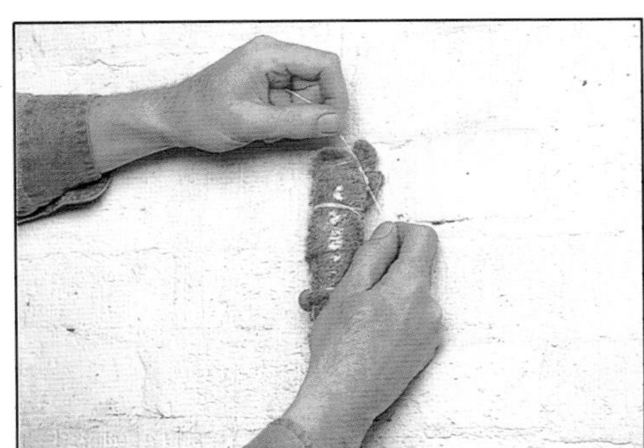

6 Tie the insulation bandage in place at the end of each length, or where the pipe passes through a wall. Simply tear the material to length as necessary.

Cleaning and Home Hints

Most of us can only relax once the house looks spotless and the chores are all finished, but this can be a never-ending task if not organized properly and carried out in the most efficient way. Make sure that you have time to relax, enjoy your family and entertain friends by following the time-saving guides for cleaning and good housekeeping given here.

CLEANING THE HOME

With so many objects around the home and numerous cleaning products from which to choose, it can be difficult to match object with product. Simple solutions are often the best, and, if you are unsure of how to tackle the cleaning of a specific item or the removal of a difficult stain without causing more damage, the following reference pages could save you a great deal of time, effort and money.

Antiques

Cleaning antiques must be done with the greatest of care – even damaging the patina can drastically reduce the value of an antique object.
Furniture: a damp, soft cloth with a little liquid soap should be sufficient to remove grubby marks from furniture. Wipe with a clean, damp cloth and use natural beeswax to polish, then buff softly to a shine.
Pictures: dust the frames of pictures with a feather duster, or use a soft make-up brush on elaborate gilded frames. You can clean old, but not particularly valuable, paintings with a special picture cleaner (available from artists' suppliers) – always follow the manufacturer's instructions. If you do not wish to clean a painting yourself, take it to a qualified restorer.

Appliances

Wipe the door fronts and sides of appliances with a cloth dipped in hot water and detergent, and wrung out until it is just damp. Move appliances easily to clean underneath and behind them by rubbing a little liquid soap in front of their feet before pulling.

Baths

Acrylic: never use scourers on acrylic or glass-fibre baths – a sponge and a gentle spray cleaner should be all that are required. Rinse thoroughly.
Enamelled: avoid using acid-based cleaners on enamelled baths as they will gradually etch into the surface. Use a cellulose sponge and liquid detergent to clean off tidemarks. Turpentine or white spirit (paint thinner) rubbed on with a soft cloth will remove stubborn marks. Use a limescale remover around the bases of the taps (faucets) to break down hard-water deposits.

Blinds and shades

Remove roller-type blinds and shades from their fixings and unroll them before washing with hot water and detergent. Use a soft brush on stubborn marks, if necessary. Rinse well with clean water, and leave to dry thoroughly before replacing.

Clean slatted blinds with a special U-shaped duster brush, or wear cotton gloves to grip and wipe along each slat. Always work from the top to the bottom to avoid dust settling on the cleaned slats beneath.

CLEANING ESSENTIALS

Keep the following items to hand.
- Dusting cloths made from discarded cotton T-shirts or clothes.
- Cleaning and polishing cloths in thick, absorbent knitted cotton and lint-free fabrics.
- Household gloves to protect your hands from chemicals, thin disposable gloves for delicate cleaning jobs and cotton gloves for dusting.
- A dustpan and 2 brushes – a hard brush for carpets and a soft brush for sweeping up dust from hard floors.
- A mop and bucket.
- A long-handled broom.
- Wire-wool and lightweight scouring pads, old toothbrushes and a nailbrush for reaching awkward areas.
- Cleaning products: spray cleaners for bathroom and kitchen surfaces that do not require rinsing; heavy cleaning liquids to remove grease and burned-on foods; cream cleaners with a light scouring action; bleach.

ABOVE A lemon dipped in salt is an effective brass cleaner, but rinse thoroughly after use.

Brass and copper

Wash lacquered brass in warm, soapy water, then rinse it and buff dry. Unlacquered brass should be cleaned with a proprietary brand of brass and copper polish – use an old toothbrush to reach fine detailing. A cut lemon dipped in salt is effective on very dirty areas – always wash the brass afterwards in hot, soapy water. Try a silicone car wax (marble-polishing powder) to maintain the shiny finish on brass.

Bronze

The characteristic patina on bronze should not be cleaned and scrubbed away. Remove surface marks with pure turpentine applied with a soft cloth. Alternatively, wash in warm, soapy water and buff up with a soft cloth.

Cane furniture

Most cane and wicker furniture has a lacquered finish, and only requires occasional buffing with a soft cloth and furniture polish. Clean ground-in dirt

on cane furniture with fine steel wool dipped in a washing-soda solution (a handful of soda to a bucket of warm water), or use a soft brush and warm, soapy water. Place old newspapers under the piece to be cleaned to catch drips. Wipe over with a clean, damp cloth and allow the cane to dry away from direct heat.

Carpets

Before shampooing a carpet, vacuum it thoroughly to remove grit, dust and crumbs. Move the furniture out of the room or stack it at one end. Choose a day when you can open the windows to let the carpets dry naturally. Use a special carpet shampoo and follow the manufacturer's instructions. If you do not have an electrical carpet cleaner of your own, you will be able to hire (rent) one fairly cheaply from DIY stores and some electrical suppliers.

Always check first that the colour will not run by rubbing an unobtrusive area with shampoo solution.

Start at the corner of the room furthest from the door and work back across the room to avoid treading on the damp areas. Cover an area of approximately 1 sq m/1 sq yd at a time, drawing the brush head of the cleaner towards you in strips across the area until no more water is drawn back into the head. Allow the carpet to dry thoroughly before replacing furniture.

Ceilings

Cigarette smoke and cooking can make ceilings dirty over time. Cover the furniture and carpet with old sheets or decorator's cloths (drop cloths) and brush away any loose cobwebs or dust first. Dip a clean floor mop (preferably one with a foam head) in warm water mixed with a little detergent. Squeeze out as much excess water as possible before working your way across the ceiling in a back-and-forth movement. Change the water as soon as it begins to look murky. Finish with clean water and leave to dry. Never allow water near light fittings (fixtures) or switches – use a damp cloth instead.

ABOVE Use a make-up brush and soapy water to clean delicate china ornaments.

Chimneys

It is usually best to call in a professional to clean the flue and chimney, but you can hire (rent) or buy chimney rods if you prefer to do the job yourself. Before starting, ensure that all the furniture and carpets are covered and that the windows and doors in the room are shut. Have a vacuum cleaner ready and old newspapers laid around the fireplace. Wear old clothes, shoes, rubber gloves and a protective face-mask. Follow the directions given with the rods, and, as the soot starts to drop, be ready to vacuum it up quickly. When leaving the room, remove your shoes to avoid the risk of treading soot into other rooms. Remove and wash the brush head on the vacuum cleaner.

China

Immerse china ornaments in warm, soapy water, and use an old shaving or make-up brush to work into awkward crevices. Rinse well and dry with a soft cloth. Clean china candlesticks that are covered in wax by immersing them in hot water to melt the wax, then clean them in soapy water.

To clean china plant pots with water marks, place them in a bowl and apply neat limescale remover to the marks. Leave for half an hour or until the limescale dissolves, then rinse and dry.

Chopping boards

After use, place chopping boards in the sink and carefully pour boiling water over them. Use a scrubbing brush, disinfectant and soapy water to clean it thoroughly. Rinse and allow to dry naturally. Do not soak wooden boards as they may warp. You should replace a chopping board that is heavily worn, as cuts and cracks can allow harmful bacteria to multiply.

Computers

Always unplug a computer before cleaning it. Vacuum regularly using the soft-brush attachment, and turn the keyboard over and tap it lightly to dislodge any crumbs or dust. Use a cotton bud (swab) dipped in neat methylated spirits (denatured alcohol) to clean individual keys. Finally, wiping a little dilute fabric conditioner over the computer with a damp cloth will help to reduce the static.

Cookers

Before cleaning, always switch off the power supply to an electric cooker. A self-cleaning oven can use up a lot of power when burning off food residues; it helps to line the bottom of the oven with heavy-duty tin foil which you can throw away once dirty. A watery paste of bicarbonate of soda and water,

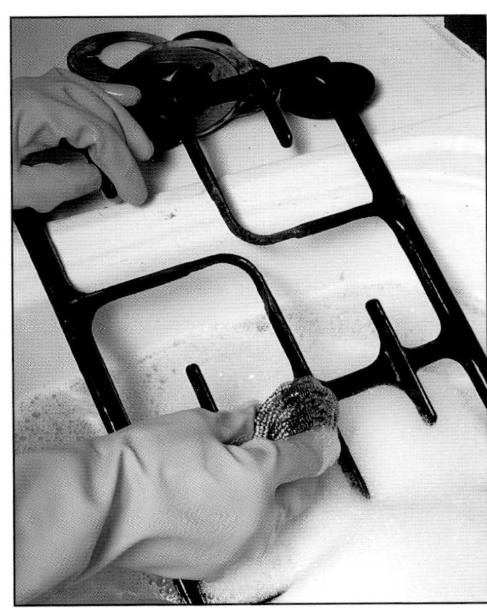

ABOVE Allow hob (burner) covers to soak before cleaning.

CLEANING THE HOME (continued)

allowed to dry on the oven floor, will absorb grease spatters and is easy to wipe out after cooking.

You can deal with a heavily soiled oven easily with proprietary brands of oven cleaners. Many contain sodium hydroxide which can cause serious burns, so follow the manufacturer's instructions carefully, wear protective gloves and goggles, and ensure that the kitchen is well-ventilated.

Always give the hob (burners) a quick wipe over after every use, in order to prevent foods from solidifying on the surfaces. Remove burned-on foods with an abrasive cream cleaner, or with a scourer and hot water with a few drops of ammonia added. Remove the ring trims and wipe underneath them. Do not wipe over a ceramic glass hob with a dishcloth, as food particles will cause staining once the heat is switched on. Instead, use the manufacturer's recommended cleaner. Be sure to clean up any acidic spillages such as fruit, vinegar, or sauces and sugar from the hob immediately, as they will pit the surface, otherwise leave the cleaning until the cooker has cooled.

Cooking pans

Aluminium: clean using a paste made from equal parts of baking powder, cream of tartar, washing powder and vinegar. Use a cellulose scourer to bring the surface to a shine, then rinse thoroughly. Leave the juice of a lemon diluted in 0.75 l/1 pint of water in pans overnight to remove water marks.
Enamelled: do not use scourers on vitreous-enamelled pans. Remove stains by soaking in a weak solution of bleach, and scrub dirt around handles with an old toothbrush and detergent.

Crystal stemware

High temperatures in a dishwasher will gradually weaken lead crystal, so wash this carefully in hand-hot water using a mild liquid detergent. Use a soft

ABOVE **A handful of rice and a warm detergent solution will clean marks from inside decanters or narrow-necked vases.**

dishcloth to wipe rims, but do not try to force it into narrow-necked vases or decanters. Crevices in cut crystal can be cleaned with an old toothbrush and soapy water. Rinse thoroughly and allow to dry before polishing with a glass cloth. Clean the inside of a decanter by swishing around a handful of rice grains mixed with some detergent and warm water. Dilute limescale remover will also tackle the white film found in vases.

Curtains and drapes

Close the curtains or drapes to spread out the gathers, then vacuum from the top down to the bottom. Gathered valances and pelmets should also be vacuumed regularly. When removing curtains and valances for cleaning, make sure that you know which side each should hang from by marking the linings with a small letter 'L' in waterproof ink at the top left and 'R' at the top right. Remove the hooks and keep them in a safe place. Flatten out the heading tapes for even cleaning.

Curtain tracks and poles

Dust and grime can settle on tracks and poles, preventing the smooth opening of curtains, so dust regularly with a soft cloth and wipe clean with a damp cloth and a few drops of liquid detergent. Wipe with clean water and allow to dry. Rub silicone wipes along the surfaces of tracks and poles for smooth, gliding curtains.

Cutlery (Flatware)

Wash, rinse and dry cutlery (flatware) as soon as possible after using it in order to prevent food from becoming dried on, or salt and acidic foods from staining the finish. Only place dishwasher-proof cutlery in the dishwasher; silver, bronze and bone-handled cutlery should always be washed by hand. Never leave bone-handled cutlery to soak, as this will cause the handles to work loose over time. Buff cutlery with a soft, clean cloth before putting away.

If you have several items of silver or silver-plated cutlery to clean, line the bottom of a plastic bowl with tin foil and place the cutlery on top. Add a handful of washing soda and cover with boiling water. The electrochemical reaction will remove the tarnish. Rinse and dry the cutlery before storing away.

Double glazing

Wear stout gloves before removing secondary double glazing for cleaning. Chamois leathers give professional results, but avoid using them with detergents. Use a solution of methylated spirits (denatured alcohol) or white-wine vinegar in tepid water. Particularly dirty windows can be cleaned using a solution of 120 ml/4 fl oz/½ cup each of ammonia and white-wine vinegar mixed into a bucket of water. Scrunched-up newspapers are also excellent for adding a gleam to windows – dip them in the solution and use instead of a chamois leather.

ABOVE Water and vinegar rubbed on to window panes with an old newspaper will really make them sparkle.

Drains

Fish out any debris caught in the cover of a drain and place it in a plastic bag before throwing away. Regularly rinse down drains with a household bleach or disinfectant. If fat has solidified around the drain, pour some neat ammonia on to it and leave for a couple of minutes, then carefully pour boiling water down it to flush.

Extractor fans

Switch off an electric extractor fan before removing the cover to clean the vents. Wipe the plastic cover with a cloth dipped in warm, soapy water.

Unscrew a non-electric, plastic window fan from its mountings and soak in warm, soapy water to remove dust and grit. Rinse and allow to dry.

Fireplaces

Brick: cleaning out a fire grate can create a lot of dust, so damp down the ashes first using either a plant spray gun or some used, damp coffee grounds. Rub soot deposits on brick fire backs and surrounds with a wire brush. Use neat malt vinegar to scrub the bricks and rinse with clean water.
Cast-iron: when cool, dampen the ashes and vacuum away dust and soot from the hearth and surround. Use a grate blackener or high-temperature stove paint to burnish and protect the metal. Do not wipe a tiled surround while it is hot, as water can cause the surface of the tiles to craze.
Stone: scrub a stone fireplace with a solution of 1 part bleach to 8 parts tepid water. Rinse with clean water and pat dry with absorbent cloths. Once dry, apply a clear brick and stone sealant for protection from further staining.

Floors

Brick and stone: sweep and wash with warm water and a mild detergent. Red brick can be brightened and polished with 'Cardinal Red' brick polish (all-purpose powdered cleanser).
Floorboards: vacuum out dirt from the gaps between floorboards before cleaning or polishing. Wipe over unvarnished boards with a damp cloth and leave them to dry before polishing with a wax floor polish. Buff varnished boards with a non-slip polish.
Lineoleum: start by removing obvious marks by scrubbing with a gentle cellulose scourer and soap. An abrasive cream cleaner applied with a cloth will also work well. Use a damp mop and soapy water to clean the linoleum thoroughly, then rinse.
Marble: avoid using any abrasive cleaner or applicator on marble. Mop the floor with warm water and a mild detergent, using a blunt knife to lift any stuck-on dirt. The surface can be polished with a silicone wax.
Slate: wash regularly with soap and detergent and rinse thoroughly. Restore the shine of slate by wiping a little milk over the surface.
Vinyl: grimy vinyl will clean up more easily if you mop a proprietary brand of floor cleaner over the floor and allow it to soak for 10 minutes before cleaning.

ABOVE Dirt and grit can soon make a window extractor work less efficiently.

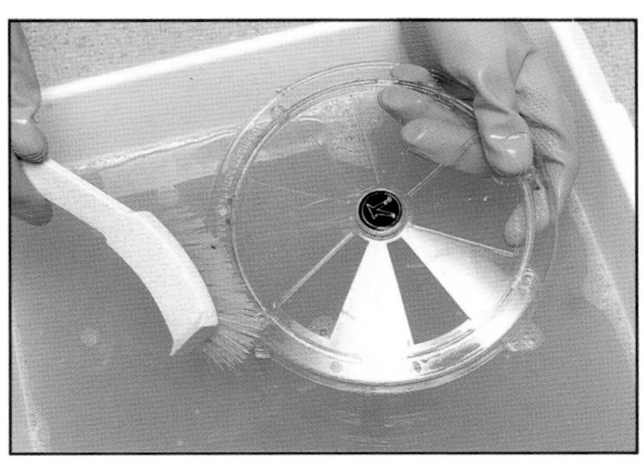

ABOVE Remove the extractor and allow to soak in a detergent solution to release the dirt gently then use a soft brush to clean the grooves.

FLOOR-CLEANING TIPS

- Remove a build-up of solvent-based polish by using medium-grade wire wool and white spirit (paint thinner). Use an ordinary floor cleaner with a little ammonia added to remove emulsion polish, then mop over.
- Always sweep or vacuum the floor before cleaning.
- Remove thick grime under a cooker by first softening the patch using a sponge dipped in hot water. Leave for 5 minutes, then use an old wallpaper-stripping blade wrapped in a cloth to prise off the grime.

CLEANING THE HOME (continued)

Freezers

A freezer needs to be de-frosted regularly. Start by removing all the food, packing it tightly in cold boxes or cardboard boxes lined with a thick layer of newspaper. Turn off the freezer and take out all the trays to be washed. Use a plastic spatula to prise off loose pieces of ice in the freezer, but do not hack at them as you may damage the freezer lining irreparably. Use a toothbrush dipped in warm, soapy water to reach into the seals, then rinse and wipe dry. If the ice is thick, direct the warm heat from a hairdryer on to it to speed the melting, keeping a plastic bowl to hand to catch the water. Wipe the inside of the freezer with a clean cloth, replace the shelves and re-pack the food.

Furniture

For home-made furniture cleaner, mix 2 parts white-wine vinegar, 2 parts turpentine and 2 parts paraffin with 1 part methylated spirits (paint thinner) in an old jar. Apply the solution to furniture with an old cloth and polish off straight away.

ABOVE Carefully lift all the items from a display cabinet so that you can give it a thorough clean before replacing the ornaments.

Some polishes clean and shine at the same time, and are most suited to varnished finishes. With old or valuable items, it is best to wipe them over with a barely damp cloth dipped in lukewarm water and a mild detergent to remove sticky marks, before polishing with a proprietary wax polish.

French polish: wipe off greasy and sticky marks with a damp cloth and wipe dry immediately.

Oiled wood: clean with a cloth moistened with turpentine.

Painted finishes: clean painted pieces of furniture with a soft cloth wrung out in warm, soapy water. Use clean water to wipe off any residue and leave to dry away from direct heat.

Varnished and sealed woods: treat as for painted finishes.

Waxed wood: wipe with a cloth wrung out in warm, soapy water. Wash down any heavily marked pieces and rub particularly bad patches with a cellulose sponge scourer. Remember always to follow the wood grain. Rinse and wipe with clean, absorbent cloths to remove all traces of water.

Glass

Add a water softener when washing everyday glass in a dishwasher. Clean delicate and cut glass by hand.

Grout

Revive the grouting between tiles using a little bicarbonate of soda (baking soda) mixed to a paste with bleach. Apply the paste with a toothbrush and leave for a few minutes. Rinse well and dry with a soft cloth. Scrape out heavy soap deposits with a blunt knife to aid the action of the paste.

REMOVING DENTS

Remove dents in wood furniture by placing a thick, damp cloth over the area, then placing the tip of a hot iron immediately over the dent. The steam will penetrate and swell the compacted wood, which can then be re-polished afterwards.

ABOVE Kitchen grease builds up quickly. Scrape it from the grouting around tiles using a blunt knife.

ABOVE Once washed and buffed, the tiles are as good as new.

Headboards

Iron: wipe over the bars and finials using a cloth wrung out in warm water and detergent. Wipe over with clean water and polish with a soft cloth.

Upholstered: use a proprietary brand of dry-clean foam, following the manufacturer's instructions.

Wood: wipe in the direction of the grain with warm water and detergent, or use a combined cleaner/polish spray.

Irons

Clean the casing when the iron is cool. The sole plate is best cleaned while hot. Use a proprietary brand of iron cleaner or bicarbonate of soda (baking soda), rubbed over with a damp cloth. Or rub the iron over a damp towel.

Jewellery

Wrap delicate filigree jewellery in fine cotton muslin (cheesecloth) and dip it into a proprietary brand of jewellery-cleaning solution. Otherwise, warm water with a few drops of ammonia, applied with a soft make-up brush, will remove dirt.

Most gemstones are fairly resilient but their settings may be delicate, so treat these with care. Use an old toothbrush and a liquid jewellery cleaner to reach behind the settings, or dip them in the solution. Rinse and dry with a soft cloth.

Lampshades

Brush or vacuum off dust, then 'spot clean' using dry-clean foam. Use the soft-brush attachment of the vacuum cleaner for pleated shades.

ABOVE Use a duster with an extending handle to reach high lampshades and cobwebs.

Lightbulbs

First switch off the electricity. If the light has been turned on, allow the bulb to cool before removing it. Wear cotton gloves to remove. A cotton bud (swab) dipped in methylated spirits (denatured alcohol) will remove fly marks. Remove a fluorescent tube from its fixing and wipe along the length using a cloth wrung out in soapy water and detergent. A cloth dipped in white spirit (paint thinner) will remove a greasy film on the tube. Dry thoroughly.

Marble

Avoid scratching the surface of marble with abrasive scourers, as this can lead to ingrained staining. Remove stains by dabbing neat lemon juice or white-wine vinegar on the mark. This will also etch the surface, so be sure to wash off the lemon juice or vinegar after a couple of minutes. 15 ml/1 tbsp of Borax mixed with 0.75 l/1 pt of water will also clean a marble surface, but always rinse before buffing dry with a soft cloth.

Mats and rugs

Clean bath mats in the washing machine and hang them up to dry. Vacuum other mats and rugs regularly to remove grit and dirt that can damage the pile. Take them outside occasionally, throw over the washing line or a garden seat and beat with a broom. Turn the rug every fortnight to ensure that all areas receive even wear. Valuable rugs should be cleaned professionally, otherwise clean as described for carpets.

Mattresses

Clean marks on mattresses using a special 'dry-clean' foam (available from department stores and supermarkets). Follow the manufacturer's instructions on the aerosol. Do not use water and detergent to clean a mattress, as it will only spread the mark.

Microwave ovens

Keep cleaning to a minimum by covering foods to prevent spatters from baking hard on the walls of the oven. Turn off the power at the wall before cleaning a microwave oven. Wipe it over with a damp cloth wrung out in warm, soapy water and detergent. A bowl of water brought to the boil inside the microwave will soften any tough pieces. Wipe the inside of the oven occasionally with a special disinfectant that will not taint foods. Leave the door ajar so that the oven can dry naturally.

Mirrors and mirror tiles

A soft cloth moistened with methylated spirits (denatured alcohol) will remove most marks from a mirror – even hairspray. Prevent a mirror from misting over in a steamy bathroom by rubbing a little washing-up liquid over it and polishing with a clean cloth.

ABOVE Wipe a little washing-up liquid over a bathroom mirror to prevent misting.

Patio furniture

At the end of the summer, clean and cover all patio furniture before the icy weather sets in.

Wrought-iron furniture: wash this down with a solution of warm water and detergent to remove tree sap and bird droppings. Allow to dry and either polish with a silicone wax or touch up chipped paintwork with a rust-inhibiting paint to prevent it from deteriorating over the winter.

Wood: wipe over wooden furniture and apply a good wax to unsealed wood, or varnish any areas that look worn.

Plastic and plastic-coated wire furniture: clean this with a window and conservatory cleaner, or wash it down with a solution of warm water and detergent. Rinse and dry. Do not use abrasives on the furniture – remove any scuffs using a cloth moistened with methylated spirits (denatured alcohol).

Pewter

Clean old or valuable pewter gently in a solution of warm water and washing-up liquid, then rinse and buff with a soft cloth. Clean new pewter with a non-abrasive metal polish.

CLEANING THE HOME (continued)

Refrigerators
You should sort out the fridge regularly and throw away any old and out-of-date foods. Pack all other items in a cold box. Switch off the power and remove all shelves and trays. Wash these in warm water and detergent, rinse and leave to dry. Wipe the inside of the refrigerator with a damp cloth wrung out in a solution of warm water and detergent, then rinse and dry. Use a nailbrush dipped in warm, soapy water to reach into the grooves of the seal, then rinse and dry. Replace the shelves and food only when the refrigerator is completely dry.

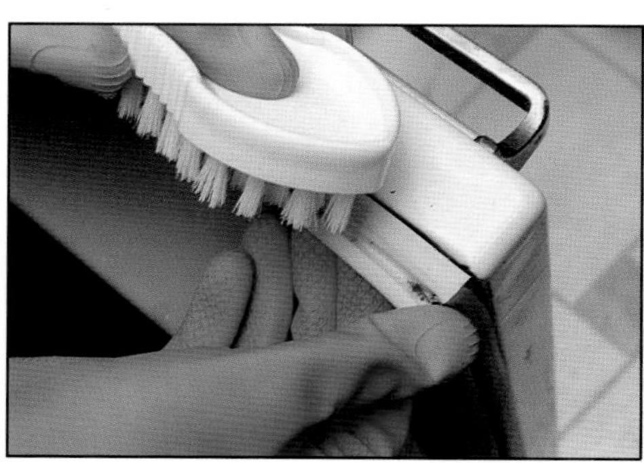

ABOVE A nail- or washing brush is excellent for cleaning out the seals on a refrigerator.

REFRIGERATOR SEALS

Rubber refrigerator seals need to be in good condition. Check that the seals on your fridge are in good working order by closing the door on a sheet of paper. If you can pull it out easily, either the seal needs replacing or the hinges need adjusting.

Shower curtain
Put a nylon shower curtain in with the normal wash when putting a load through the machine – the biological action of the detergent will remove soap build-up and mould spots. For other finishes, wash by hand in a solution of warm water and detergent, then rinse and allow to drip dry.

Shower head
Remove the shower head and immerse it in a dish of limescale remover or white-wine vinegar to clear deposits. An old toothbrush will clear blocked holes and debris from behind the plate.

Silver
Use a soft cloth and a non-abrasive cleaner – silver is a soft metal and easily damaged, and silver plate can be worn away to expose the base metal by constant cleaning. Embossed, engraved or raised decoration can accumulate dirt and polish. A badger-bristle shaving brush or soft artist's paintbrush dipped in polish is useful for reaching difficult areas. See cutlery (flatware) for cleaning silver cutlery.

Sinks
Tip a little neat disinfectant down the outlet and overflow once a week and leave overnight to work.
Vitreous-enamel: remove discolouration sing a weak solution of beach. Clean regularly with a liquid detergent to remove grease.
Stainless-steel: wipe a damp cloth dipped in a little limescale remover to clean white patches from a sink, drainer and taps (faucets). Rub with bicarbonate of soda (baking soda) mixed with a little water to make the sink gleam. Tough marks can be removed with a cellulose scourer and cleaning cream. Rinse and wipe dry.

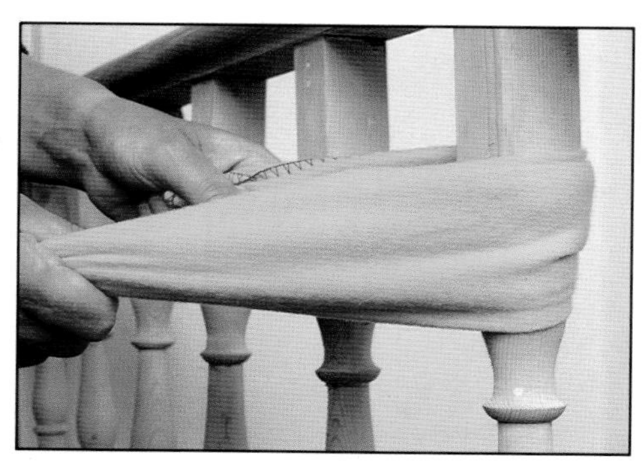

ABOVE Wrap a duster around the spindles and bannisters on a staircase to dust and polish.

SILVER TIPS

- Check with an expert before attempting to clean a valuable silver antique in case you damage it.
- Store silver in a dry place, wrapped in sheets of black or acid-free tissue to prevent tarnishing.
- Silver-cleaning fluids will stain a stainless-steel sink or cutlery. If contact occurs, wash immediately with water.

Taps (Faucets)
Wash taps (faucets) using a bathroom cream cleaner, then rinse and buff with a soft cloth. Remove dirt at the bases and behind the taps by brushing with an old toothbrush dipped in cleaner, and break down limescale deposits around the spouts of taps by filling a small plastic bag with dissolved water softener. Tie the bag around the spout so that it sits in the water solution. Leave overnight, then remove the bag and brush away any remaining scale.

ABOVE An old toothbrush is excellent for cleaning behind taps (faucets).

Telephones
Wipe over telephones regularly using a damp cloth and soapy water. Do not allow any water near the dialling keys or handset. Wipe the handset using some cotton wool (absorbent cotton) dipped in a dilute solution of disinfectant. A cotton bud (swab) dipped in methylated spirits (paint thinner) will clean the dialling pad.

Televisions
Switch off the power at the wall and pull the television forward slightly to vacuum all the surfaces. Wipe over the screen with a few drops of glass cleaner on a soft cloth and polish off immediately. Anti-static wipes are useful for reducing a build-up of dust.

Tiles
Ceramic floor tiles: sweep the floor thoroughly, then wash the tiles with a mop and warm, soapy water. Rinse but do not polish. Clean the grout between the tiles with a scrubbing brush dipped in soapy water.
Ceramic wall tiles: remove soap deposits with a liquid bathroom cleaner and a cellulose scourer. Dirty grout around the tiles is usually more of a problem when soap and limescale build up in the ridges. In this case, use a blunt knife to work your way gently along the grout to remove the worst of the grime. Finish with a nailbrush dipped in an abrasive cream cleaner, rinse well and wipe with a soft cloth.

Toilets
A quick 'flush and brush' in the morning and a little bleach or disinfectant at night should keep most toilets sparkling. Use a limescale remover on water marks and leave it to work for a little while before flushing it away. Wipe the seat regularly with disinfectant and use an old toothbrush to clean around the seat hinges.

Vases
Cracks in china vases can discolour after a time. Apply a little dilute bleach on a cotton bud (swab) to the crack and leave it to work for 10–15 minutes before rinsing and drying. Remove water marks with limescale remover. Clean the inside of a narrow-necked glass vase by swishing a mixture of rice, warm water and detergent around.

Upholstery
Remove pet hairs and fluff with a length of sticky tape wrapped around your hand.

Fabric: vacuum fabric-covered upholstery thoroughly, then clean off spots and marks before cleaning the whole piece of furniture. Use a foam upholstery shampoo and follow the manufacturer's instructions very carefully. Always test a small patch on a hidden area first to see if the dyes are fast. If not, call in professional cleaners.

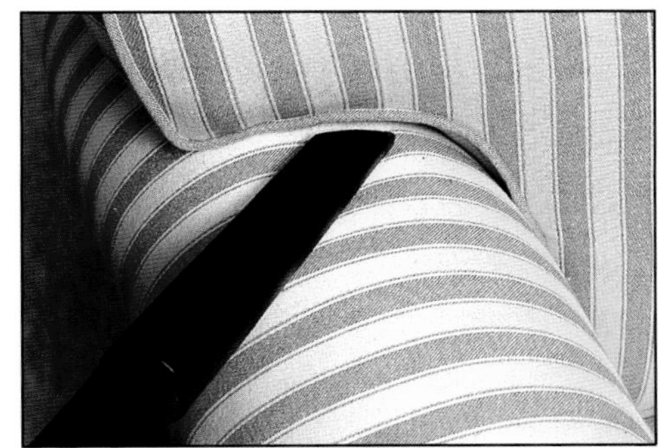

ABOVE Regularly vacuum upholstery to keep it looking fresh.

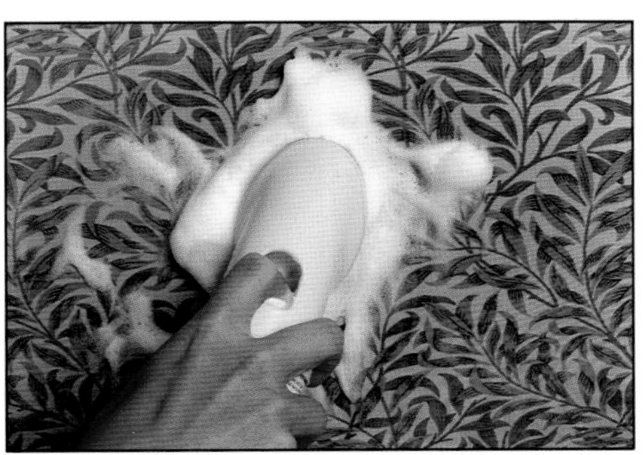

ABOVE 'Spot-clean' dirty marks on a sofa and chairs with a dry-foam cleaner.

To clean loose covers, remove them and follow the directions on the care-guide label inside. If there are no instructions, clean the covers on a low-temperature programme and dry them away from any direct source of heat.
Leather: before cleaning, check whether the leather is washable by putting a small drop of water on an unobtrusive area. If it remains on the surface you can clean it, if it sinks in and darkens the leather you must only dust and give it an occasional wipe with a damp cloth. Soap flakes dissolved in warm water will clean washable leather. Do not overwet the upholstery. Keep leather supple by 'feeding' it regularly with a leather cream.

Wall coverings
Read the care label supplied with a roll of wallpaper and follow its cleaning instructions. If the label is lost, try a small test patch (behind the door is a good place) and sponge the wallpaper with a little warm water and liquid detergent. If the colour does not smudge and the surface does not blister, continue around the room, working from the bottom of the walls to the top. Rinse with clean water by starting from the top of the walls and working to the bottom to prevent streaks appearing.

Remove grease splashes by covering the patch with a paper towel and then a warm iron. The warmth will draw the grease into the paper.

Walls
On painted walls, clean obvious marks first by gently rubbing with a damp cloth and a cream cleaner. Use warm, soapy water and work from the bottom of the walls to the top. Change the water regularly in order to prevent streaks from appearing. Use a long-handled sponge-head mop to reach and clean the tops of walls. Rinse from the top to the bottom, and finish by cleaning the skirtings (baseboards).

Window frames
Use a fungicidal wash to deal with mildew and follow the manufacturer's instructions for cleaning.
Painted and varnished: these should only require an occasional wipe over with a damp cloth wrung out in soapy water. Use a combined cleaner/polish spray to bring them to a shine.
Aluminium: Rub with a paste of Borax and water. Rinse and buff dry.

CLEANING LEATHER UPHOLSTERY

Try a suede-and-leather shoe cleaner for small areas. A water-repellent suede-and-leather shoe spray can protect the leather – always test a small area first in a hidden place.

CURING HOUSEHOLD SMELLS

Household smells can usually be remedied by removing the source, by cleaning the offending item or by disguising the unpalatable smell with a more pleasant one.

The kitchen

Old or rotting vegetables can be surprisingly pungent. To avoid this, keep vegetables in a cool, dark place and preferably in a paper bag.

A refrigerator can harbour a variety of smells which can emanate from strong cheese, spicy food or mouldy left-overs. Check the contents regularly and throw out any that have passed their 'best-before' date. Clean the fridge, including the shelves and seals, at least once a month.

To minimize cooking smells, close the doors to other rooms in the house when cooking and open the kitchen windows to allow steam and smells to escape. Buy an extractor fan or switch on the cooker hood, and leave them running for a time after you have finished cooking. Wipe over surfaces with a cloth wrung out in hot water to which lemon juice and detergent have been added. Wipe over chopping boards with half a cut lemon to leave them fresh. Lemon juice and water boiled in a microwave oven will also help to deodorize the interior.

ABOVE A halved lemon rubbed over a wooden chopping board will remove unpleasant odours.

To counteract odorous kitchen sinks, pour a little neat bleach down the plughole and outlet every few days, leave overnight and then rinse thoroughly.

ABOVE Keep drains fresh by pouring disinfectant down the sink outlet every day, followed by plenty of hot water.

The bathroom

Regular cleaning should keep the bathroom smelling fresh, but, on the odd occasion when this is not the case, light a scented candle or simply a match to clear the air. Protect the carpet around the toilet with a mat, and wash this regularly. Keep a disinfectant block looped inside the rim of the toilet.

Water trapped behind bath seals or tiles can smell, and condensation will eventually make the room damp and musty. Ensure the bathroom is well-ventilated, and, if necessary, add air vents or an extractor fan as well.

Pour disinfectant down the waste outlets in baths, bidets and basins to keep them fresh. If they do smell, they may be blocked and should be dealt with promptly.

The living room

Cigarette smoke can be neutralized by waving a dish towel dampened in water and vinegar around the room.

Try to prevent pets from lying on furniture, as their hair and body oils can leave an unpleasant odour. If they do, cover chairs and sofas with throw-over cloths that you can wash regularly. Place dishes of pot pourri in the room to disguise stale smells.

The bedrooms

Remove stale odours in a bedroom by opening the windows and spraying the room with an air freshener. Sprinkle the mattress with Borax and leave it for a few hours before vacuuming. Always air the bed, before making, and keep the room well-ventilated.

Outdoors

Cats who love to spray near doorways can be discouraged by rubbing the doorsteps with either menthol oil or orange peel.

POT-POURRI INGREDIENTS

Many fragrant ingredients can be used for making pot pourri. These include: dried rosemary, lavender and bay leaves, dried ground orris-root powder, dried rosemary leaves, a selection of essential oils, ground cinnamon, dried chillies and cinnamon sticks, whole cloves, a blend of dried flowers, and limes and lemons. The finely grated dried peel of citrus fruit can be added. Fresh flower petals smell sweet for a few days (shown here).

VACUUMING

The vacuum cleaner that you use is purely a matter of personal choice, but there are 5 main types from which to select, as described below. If you are buying a new cleaner, the layout of your home, the number of stairs, accessibility and so on, will probably determine your choice.

Cylinder

This type of vacuum cleaner is useful for cleaning curtains, drapes, rugs and floor coverings. Look for a compact but powerful suction rating (usually around 1000 watts). The flexible hose is useful for vacuuming stairs and narrow, awkward-to-reach areas such as under beds and pieces of furniture. The only disadvantage is that a cylinder cleaner has a tendency to tip over on uneven surfaces, or to knock into furniture when dragged behind you.

Upright

Look for beater bars that are good on fitted carpets and for removing embedded dirt and pet hairs. An upright cleaner is difficult to use on stairs and, unless it is used with attachments, may not lie flat enough to reach under furniture.

Wet-and-dry

This tends to be heavier and bulkier than a cylinder model, as it is designed to roll along – even when filled with water. It will also require more storage space. Most models vacuum, shampoo and suck up water. The hoses tend to be wider than average, which means that they can cope with bulky debris.

Cordless

This is best used for lightweight cleaning jobs, as its suction is not very strong. It can reach awkward areas and is useful for areas in which there are no sockets (receptacles), but it will only work for up to 15 minutes before it needs re-charging.

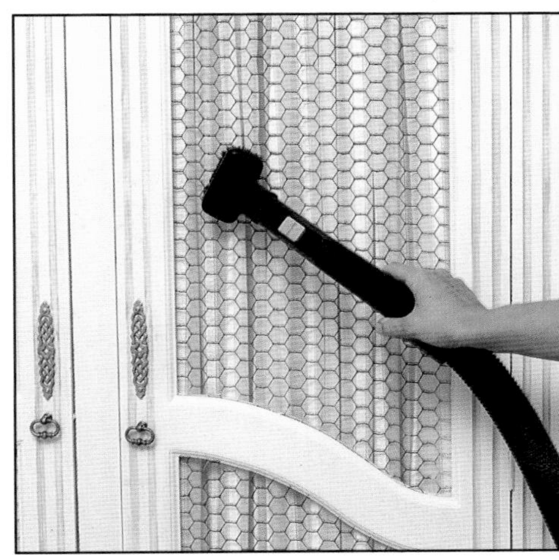

ABOVE For textured wall coverings or decorative finishes use a brush attachment.

ABOVE Use a crevice nozzle for fine gathers on curtains (drapes) and valances.

Built-in central system

With this cleaning system, outlets in each room enable a light hose to be attached. When switched on, the dirt is carried to the outlet and then carried through hidden suction pipes to a central bin. The system is quiet to use and easy to operate but is also expensive to install, so it is not recommended if you move house regularly.

VACUUMING TIPS

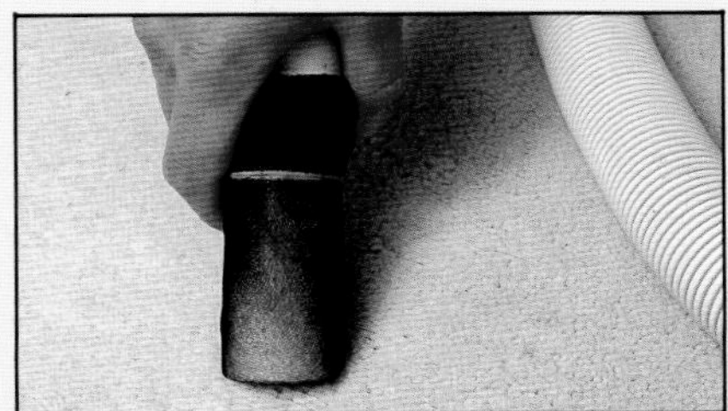

- If you drop a fine screw or even a contact lens, locate it with a vacuum nozzle covered with a piece cut from stockings (pantyhose) secured with an elastic band. Anything that the vacuum sucks up will be held against the stocking until you remove it.
- Use the flat, rectangular floor and carpet nozzle of a vacuum cleaner for cleaning carpets and hard floors.
- The narrow, angled crevice nozzle also works well on stairs, curtains and drapes, and will remove dust from around the buttoning on mattresses and along skirtings (baseboards). Use it to clean refrigerator grilles.
- The more powerful 'wet-and-dry' cleaners can unblock a drain by sucking up the blockage. You can also use them to suck out leaves from drain covers.
- Check the bag and empty it if necessary, and clean the filter before you put the vacuum cleaner away so that it works efficiently every time.
- If you run out of disposable dust bags, cut neatly along the base of the old one and shake out the contents. Fold the cut end over twice and staple securely before re-using.
- If you vacuum hard floors regularly, you will find that dirt is easier to remove, as it will not have time to build up into a sticky layer of grime.
- Fine ash from fires tends to blow about very easily. Wait until it is cold before vacuuming away, and clean the nozzle afterwards.
- Never attempt to suck up water or spills with an ordinary vacuum cleaner – the results of doing so could literally be electrifying.

DUSTING AND POLISHING

No matter how frequently you clean your home, dust will form and re-form continually, settling on every surface. Dust consists of many elements including tiny particles of fabric, dead skin cells, pollen and microscopic dust mites which can cause allergic reaction. Keeping a home well-dusted not only helps to reduce this risk but can also help appliances to work much more efficiently. A coating of dust on freezer and refrigerator coils prevents heat from being expelled, resulting in the appliance working harder to keep the temperature low.

Polishing is also an important part of keeping a home looking its best. The polishing of any surface – whether French-polished furniture or brass door knobs – needs to be done carefully, or the results can ruin its finish. The polishing of everyday items is less specialized and time-consuming, but needs to be done on a regular basis. Keeping all surfaces smooth and shiny will help to make the removal of dust and dirt easier, and will prevent stains from penetrating.

ABOVE Remove dust from artificial or dried-flower arrangements by blowing it away with a hairdryer.

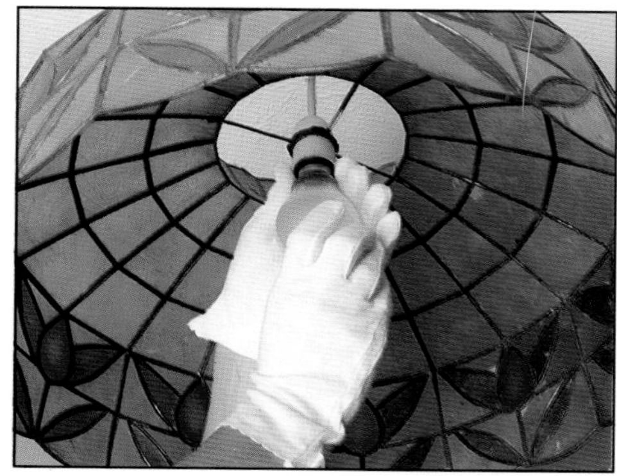

ABOVE Dust lightbulbs wearing a pair of cotton gloves.

ABOVE Clean Venetian blinds (shades) by wiping along the slats wearing cotton gloves.

Dusting equipment

A traditional feather duster is very gentle and can be used to flick the dust off every item in the house, as it is unlikely to damage even the most delicate piece. It will collect very little dust, however, so most of it tends to fall on the surfaces beneath, which in turn will need to be dusted or vacuumed. Replace feather dusters every couple of years, as they tend to shed their feathers.

A 'static wand' (static duster) is also very useful. Look for the nylon-fluff type with the extendable handle – this will reach into the corners of ceilings and on to light shades.

The most effective types of dusting cloths are the traditional soft-cotton ones, or home-made ones made from old T-shirts. Keep a pile of these to hand, and wash them after each use. A tiny amount of water sprayed on before use will prevent the dust from floating off the surface of the duster.

Frequent vacuuming is particularly recommended for homes in which dust mites cause allergic reaction, but remember to replace the dust bags regularly and to use them in conjunction with an insecticidal spray specifically designed to eradicate dust mites. Vacuuming is also a particularly effective way of removing dust that has settled on the mesh or grilles on electrical equipment.

EFFECTIVE DUSTING

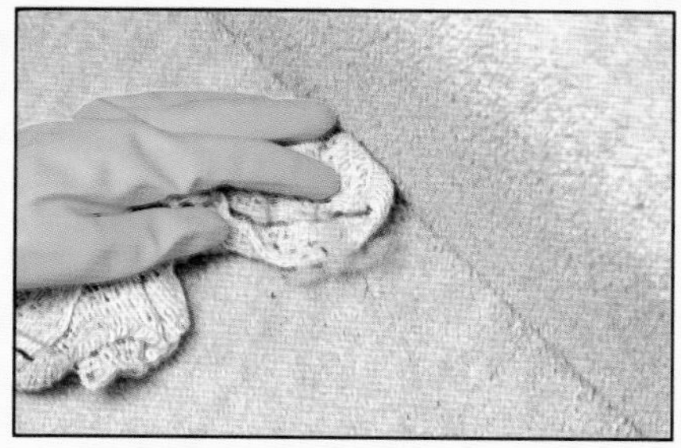

- Wipe hard-to-reach crevices on stair carpets with a damp cloth.
- As dust will float downwards to settle on the surfaces beneath, always dust from the top of a room down.
- Reduce the amount of dust attracted to the surface of a television, hi-fi (stereo) system, or glass-topped tables that are prone to static electricity by wiping them with a cloth wrung out in a solution mixed with 15 ml/1 tbsp liquid fabric conditioner and 150 ml/¼ pt/⅔ cup warm water.
- Shake duvets, pillows, small rugs and loose cushions outdoors to freshen them and remove dust where it can blow away in the breeze.
- Do not forget to dust the panels and mouldings on traditional doors, or the top edges, as dust will dull the paintwork over time.
- A baby's bottle-brush works wonders on louvre doors and between and behind radiators.

Polishing wood

Polishing wood will help to nourish it, but do not use liquid or spray polishes containing silicone or acrylic resin on antique wood, as they will seal the surface. Genuine beeswax is the best type of polish to use, and will have been responsible for helping old furniture to maintain its sheen over the years. Most wooden furniture tends to be varnished, lacquered or waxed. Oiled wood has a soft, low sheen and should not be polished. Instead, use a proprietary wood oil applied sparingly with a soft cloth. Rub this in the direction of the grain and gently buff to a lustre using a clean, soft cloth.

If you wish, save money by making your own furniture polish. Combine 30 ml/2 tbsp each of water and turpentine with 450 ml/¾ pt/2 cups of boiled linseed oil and mix together thoroughly. This polish requires a lot of buffing but will give a rich, deep shine to wood.

ABOVE Apply polish to furniture and buff in the direction of the wood grain using a clean, soft cloth or duster.

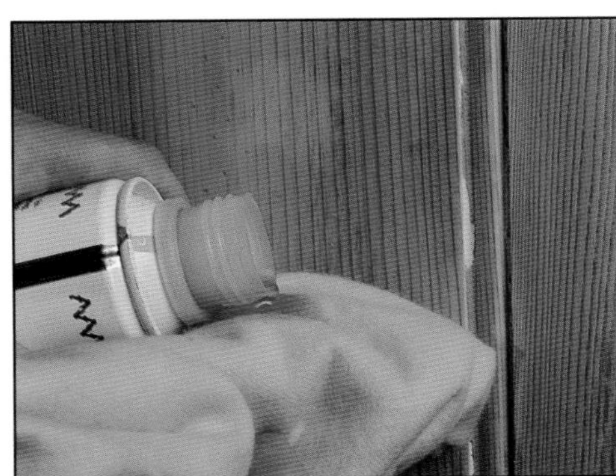

ABOVE Oiled wood only requires re-oiling once or twice a year to maintain its looks.

WOOD-POLISHING TIPS

- Always wipe a wood surface with a damp, lint-free cloth first to remove dust and grime, or the polishing action will simply grind them in.
- Select a polish that is recommended for the type of wood or finish required.
- Colours added to some waxes will help to disguise fine scratches and blemishes at the same time as polishing the surface.
- Heat and damp will damage polish. If it has done so, remove the flaking layer using the finest-grade of steel wool dipped in a little turpentine. Wipe it off immediately and re-polish to blend in.
- Apply floor polish sparingly, as too much will be difficult to shine and will cause dust to stick as it settles. Use only one type of floor polish, as different makes can react with one another resulting in a patchy, tacky finish.

Polishing metal

Aluminium: place lemon rind, apple peelings, rhubarb or any other acidic food in aluminium cooking pans, then top up with water and simmer for 5 minutes. Rinse in clean water and buff to a shine. Alternatively, rub on a paste of Borax and water, rinse and buff with a soft cloth.

Brass and copper: wash lacquered items before polishing, and then buff using a soft cloth. Polish unlacquered pieces with a tarnish-inhibiting brass-and-copper polish. To clean a heavily tarnished item, rub a wedge of lemon that has been dipped in salt over it. Rinse thoroughly, dry and polish.

Soak items that have a build-up of verdigris in a strong washing-soda solution, and brush the affected areas with an old toothbrush. Rinse and buff with a soft cloth.

Chrome: this can be polished by applying bicarbonate of soda (baking soda) on a damp cloth and rubbing to a bright shine.

Make your own chrome polish by mixing together 2 parts paraffin with 1 part methylated spirits (denatured alcohol). Apply to the item using a damp cloth, then buff with a soft cloth. A piece of scrunched-up tin foil rubbed on chrome will also polish it to a shine.

Bronze: apply a little brown shoe polish or a coloured-wax polish to bronze, then buff with a soft cloth.

Pewter: avoid abrasive cleaners on pewter – use all-purpose metal-polish wadding instead. An application of clear-wax polish will inhibit tarnishing.

Silver: use impregnated polishing mitts for large items, and dip smaller items in a dish of silver dip. Rinse silver in warm water containing a little washing-up liquid, then rinse again in clear water before buffing to a shine.

ABOVE Polish silver with soft wadding impregnated with a non-abrasive polish.

Polishing lead crystal and glass

Polish lead crystal and glass by hand using a soft, lint-free cloth. Hold the cloth in one hand and rotate the item against it until it sparkles. A little methylated spirits (denatured alcohol) or white-wine vinegar added to the final rinsing water will make lead crystal or glass ornaments gleam.

Polish glass window panes to a shine using a mixture of equal parts of paraffin, water and methylated spirits.

Polishing ceramic tiles

Do not use polish on ceramic floor or wall tiles. Simply clean them with a damp cloth and cream cleaner, rinse and leave to dry. Use a soft cloth to buff the tiles to a shine. Multi-purpose bathroom spray foams are quick to use and will also leave tiles sparkling.

WASHING AND DRYING

Start by finding the international textile-care label, which is usually sewn to an inside seam of a garment. Check the symbols against the chart shown opposite and follow them closely. If the garment does not have detailed instructions, establish what type of fabric it is made from and then follow the directions given below.

Fabric-cleaning guide

Acetate: dry clean unless the label says 'hand-washable'. In this case, pre-treat stains with a pre-wash stain remover, and wash using a mild liquid detergent and warm water. Rinse and dry away from direct heat.

Acrylic: acrylic garments are best cleaned inside-out. Pre-treat stains, then either hand wash in a mild liquid detergent and warm water or in a machine on the low-temperature 'synthetics' cycle. Dry flat.

Cotton: this is strong and can be washed at higher temperatures than synthetics. Iron when still slightly damp, using a hot iron on a 'steam' setting or spray starch for the best results. White cotton can be brightened by soaking in a mild bleach solution, but you must rinse it thoroughly.

Linen: linen can be dry cleaned, machine washed or hand-laundered. Iron on a hot setting while still damp. White linen can be bleached by soaking briefly in a mild bleach solution, then rinsing thoroughly.

Lycra/Spandex: use warm water and a mild detergent for hand washing or set the machine to the low-temperature 'synthetics' cycle. Avoid washing white Lycra with coloured garments and never use bleach, as this will perish the fibres. Drip dry or place in a tumble drier on a low setting. Iron while damp on a low setting.

Nylon: delicates are best washed by hand or in a protective mesh bag in a washing machine. In a machine, use the 'synthetics' cycle and a biological detergent. Let the garments drip dry, or tumble dry on a low setting. Brighten nylon net curtains by washing in a proprietary nylon-whitener. For best results, rinse the nets first to remove loose dirt and dust, then wash following the manufacturer's instructions.

Polyester: hand or machine wash polyester garments in warm water or on a warm setting, and tumble dry on a low setting. Iron on a moderate setting with a water-spray mist.

Silk: dyes used to colour silk can run, so dry clean if in doubt. Otherwise, hand wash items separately in warm, soapy water. Gently squeeze out excess moisture but do not wring. Dry away from direct heat and iron while damp.

Wool: this must never be washed in hot water as it will shrink, so either dry clean or wash carefully by hand.

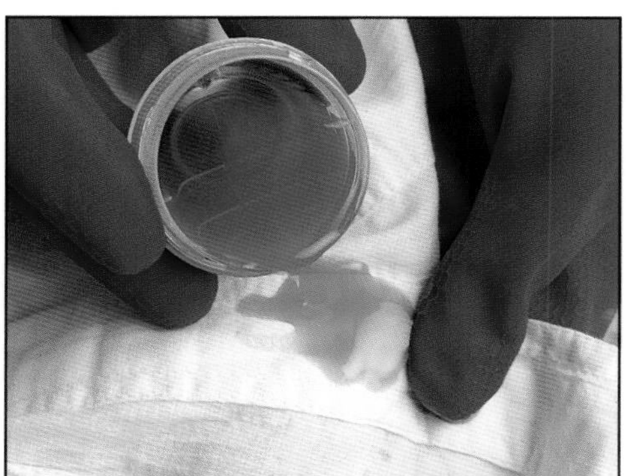

ABOVE Apply a neat biological detergent to marks on garments before placing them in a washing machine.

Washing awkward or delicate items

You can wash large, bulky items such as curtains, drapes, blankets and quilts by hand in a bath or a large sink if the label says that they are washable.

Lingerie is best washed by hand, but you can wash several pairs of tights or stockings (pantyhose) in the washing machine by placing them in a pillow case tied at the open end.

Trainers and soft toys made with synthetic fabrics can be machine washed if the label recommends it.

WASHING GUIDELINES

- Follow the cleaning guidelines on the international care-guide label inside the garment (see symbol chart).
- Sort washing into 'Whites' and 'Coloureds', and wash each bundle separately to avoid problems with colours running.
- Always check that pockets of garments are empty before putting the garments in a washing machine.
- Treat heavy soiling with neat liquid detergent before washing.
- Select the correct machine programme for the type of wash required.
- Only use the recommended dose of detergent for each wash.
- Rinse garments thoroughly after hand washing.
- Regularly remove fluff and debris from both washing-machine and tumble-drier filters.
- Secure zips (zippers) and fastenings before washing to prevent them from snagging other garments.

Drying garments

There are 3 basic methods to use for removing the moisture from washed clothes. The first is spin drying, which is usually combined with the wash cycle on washing machines. 'Spin-only' programmes are useful for items that have been hand washed.

Tumble drying uses a lot of electricity, so remove as much water as possible from the items first. It is vital to choose the correct setting on a tumble drier for the type of fabric, as excessive heat can damage fibres causing them to shrink, crease or melt. If in doubt, always refer to the instruction manual.

Line drying is the most natural and economic way of drying clothes. You can stretch an indoor clothes' line across the laundry room or, if space is limited, across the bath.

Drying different items

Sweaters: a synthetic or wool sweater can be dried successfully from a clothes' line by threading a pair of old tights (pantyhose) through the armholes and pegging them at the wrist and neck holes to support the garment. Dry delicate sweaters or shawls flat over a rack suspended over a bath or sink.

T-shirts: the cotton knit of T-shirts will tend to pull in different directions, so either peg from the bottom or place on a hanger to dry.

Trousers: hang trousers from the turn-ups or hems on the inside legs, or drape over trouser hangers before hanging on the line.

Pleated skirts: clip pleats together with clothes pegs (pins).

LEFT Prevent clothes-peg (-pin) marks from spoiling a sweater by running a pair of tights (pantyhose) through the cuffs and neck to hang the sweater from a washing line to dry.

Shirts: hang shirts from 2 hangers with the hooks facing so that they will not be blown off a washing line.

INTERNATIONAL WASHING, DRYING AND IRONING SYMBOLS

COTTON WASHES

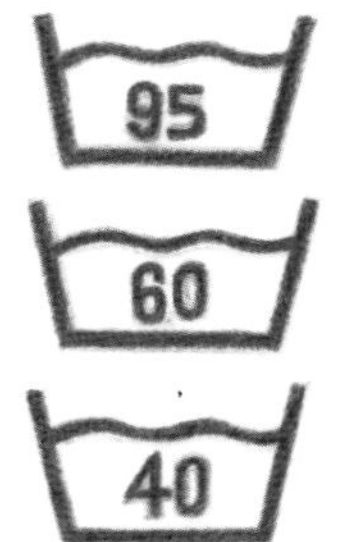

Items will withstand a normal, full wash cycle at the temperature advised

SYNTHETIC WASHES

Items, such as blends and synthetics, will withstand a medium wash cycle at advised temperature

WOOL WASH

Items, wool blends and machine-washable wools, will withstand a minimum wash cycle at this temperature

HAND WASH ONLY

Items must not be machine-washed

TUMBLE DRYING

Items can be tumble-dried

Items can be tumble-dried using a high heat setting

Items can only be tumble-dried using a low heat setting

BLEACHING

Items can be treated with chlorine bleach

IRONING

Items, such as cotton and linen, can be ironed on a hot setting

Items, such as polyester mixtures and wool, can be ironed on a warm setting

Items, such as acrylic, nylon and polyester, can be ironed on a cool setting

DRY CLEANING

Items can be dry cleaned

ABOVE Dry delicate sweaters or other wool garments flat on a rack suspended over a bath to catch the drips.

DRYING TIPS

- Do not leave damp garments in a washing machine or drier as they will soon start to smell musty and will have to be rinsed again to freshen them up.
- Do not leave a tumble drier running for longer than required, as this wastes electricity, as well as 'setting' creases.
- Overloading a tumble drier will lead to patchy drying. Leave a gap at the top of the drum to allow the clothes to move about freely.
- The action of tumble drying can cause static to build up, so use a fabric conditioner with each wash.
- Remove fluff from the tumble-drier filter after each use, or it will reduce the amount of water vapour that can escape in subsequent cycles.

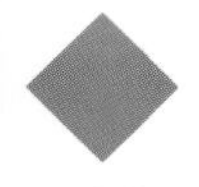

IRONING

Freshly ironed shirts, blouses and bed linen look good and feel even better. The difference between pressing and ironing is that, to press fabrics, the iron is lifted and lowered lightly on to the fabric, whereas to iron fabrics, the iron should be glided smoothly up and down. Delicate fabrics, jersey, wool and pleated fabrics should be pressed, and bed linens, cotton, polyester and silk can be ironed.

Before ironing any fabric, check the care-label guide and then set the iron temperature accordingly.

Avoiding shiny patches

Iron acrylic or fabrics with a slightly raised nap on the reverse side, or press them using a pressing cloth – a clean dish towel placed over the fabric is ideal. Avoid shine appearing on bulky patches such as thick seams or zip (zipper) fastenings by pressing over a cloth. If it is too late and the fabric is already shiny, wring out the pressing cloth in clean water, place it over the area and steam press it. Use a soft brush to raise a flattened nap.

Ironing bulky fabrics

Always iron bulky fabrics, such as denim and canvas, inside-out, particularly if the fabric is dark, in order to avoid fabric shine on thick seams.

Large items

Fold sheets, duvet covers and table cloths first and then place them on the ironing board before ironing each folded section – rather like ironing the pages of a book. Obtain crease-free curtains and drapes by ironing them from top to bottom with a chair placed behind the ironing board to prevent the fabric from dropping on to the floor.

Silk

Ensure that the fabric is damp, then iron the reverse of the garment using a pressing cloth to prevent the iron from making shiny patches. Place embroidered silk face-down on to a white towel, then press it on the reverse side. This will make the embroidery stand out attractively.

ABOVE Keep ironing to a minimum by hanging up or folding clothes as soon as they come out of the tumble drier.

Pleats

Lay out very fine pleats in sections no more than 15 cm/6 in wide and press them carefully to secure. Allow to cool before repeating with the next section. Press wide pleats individually.

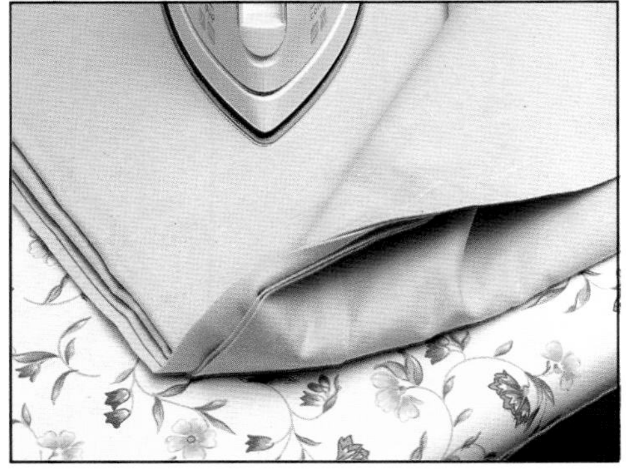

ABOVE Fold a sheet into manageable sections, and then iron them flat one by one.

IRONING TIPS

- Cover metal, mother-of-pearl or plastic buttons with a spoon to prevent heat from the iron damaging them.
- Clean an iron while it is still hot. Rub it on an old piece of towel to remove stickiness, then dip a damp rag in bicarbonate of soda (baking soda) or a proprietary sole-plate cleaner. Wipe with a clean, damp cloth.
- If you are away on business or holiday and cannot borrow an iron, hang creased clothes in a steamy bathroom or sprinkle water over them and blow air from a hairdryer to help the creases to drop out.
- Padded hangers will prevent 'shoulder marks' from appearing on delicate fabrics.

GOOD HOUSEKEEPING

With an average of 2 out of every 3 women working outside the home, research shows that, despite the advent of the 'new man', most housework is still done by women. How you tackle the household chores will depend a great deal on your lifestyle. If you have children, keeping the house in order can sometimes seem an impossible task, so perhaps now is the time to become organized and make sure that everyone helps to get the chores done.

Begin by organizing a rota, so that everyone knows what they are expected to do, and make sure that they stick to it by putting up a star every time a job is completed. Try using incentives to get the jobs done rather than punishment if they are not – extra pocket money or a treat means that everyone ends up happy. Encourage young children to tidy up their toys and pull their quilts down to air the beds in the morning, or ask them to help you make your bed so that they learn how it is done properly at the same time. Laying the table and wiping down low cupboard doors are also easy tasks for them to do. Older children can help with dusting, cleaning or washing up. Do not differentiate between boys' and girls' jobs, as everyone needs to know how to clean, tidy and wash up.

Keep the mop and cleaning materials together so that no one will have an excuse to say that they could not find the right things. A plastic bucket with dusters, rags and polish is useful – check it regularly and replace contents as containers become empty.

Ask the family to fill in a 'Weekly Planner' or to tell you what they are doing, where and when. Keep the planner pinned to the wall where you can see it easily – you will find it invaluable when you need to check that children are safe or whether you will be free to take them to and collect them from an after-school activity. Keep a note of the telephone numbers of their friends to check that children are safe if they do not get home on time.

A year planner takes up wall space, but is useful for jotting down important dates for the family such as birthdays, anniversaries and holidays. A wipeable planner is useful where dates are regularly changed.

When you sit down together in the evening, ask the members of the family whether there are any items of shopping that need to be bought the following day, or appointments for the dentist or doctor to be made. Put letters to be posted near the door so that they will not be forgotten when you leave the house. Keep a working list of jobs that need doing and cross them out as soon as you have dealt with them.

Prevent panics in the morning when clothes cannot be found or homework has not been finished by checking the night before. Even if there is a good programme on the television, the ironing can still be done, shoes polished and clothes mended while it is on. An extra washbasin or shower installed in a bedroom can also help to relieve the morning rush and inevitable queues for the bathroom.

Keep a small notebook and pencil with you at all times so that a job you have overlooked, or a telephone call you must remember to make, is noted down and not forgotten again. If you wake in the night and remember a string of things that you have forgotten to do during the day, a piece of paper and a pencil next to the bed will get them written down for the morning.

Put telephone messages or reminders in one place where everyone is likely to look. Papers with a tacky strip on one side are ideal for sticking on doors at eye-level where they will not be overlooked, or next to the item that needs dealing with.

ORGANIZED FILING

Keep a general file with receipts for goods that are under guarantee, and instruction manuals for all electrical appliances in case you need to refer to them. Keep another file containing all important documents such as birth certificates, driving licences, passports, insurance documents and even your Will in a safe place so that you can find it quickly if necessary.

LEFT Even young children can help with the housework: ask them to tidy up their toys and to pull their quilts down to air their own beds in the morning.

EVERYDAY CHORES

Busy lifestyles can leave little time for all the essential household chores. Fortunately, however, there are plenty of shortcuts that still give good results.

The kitchen

Do not waste time scrubbing out the burned-on mess in saucepans. Fill non-stick and enamelled pans with water, add a handful of washing soda and leave it to soak overnight. Use a biological detergent and water in aluminium pans, as washing soda reacts with the aluminium to create toxic fumes.

Clean a very dirty kitchen floor by swishing it first with a solution of hot water and detergent. Leave for 10 minutes before washing and rinsing.

If you do not own a self-cleaning oven, wipe a fairly strong solution of bicarbonate of soda (baking soda) and water over the walls, door and shelves. Set the oven to a low heat for 30 minutes, then leave it to cool. Clean with hot water and detergent, and then give the oven a final wipe over with a weak solution of bicarbonate of soda and water – this will make it much easier to clean the next time.

LEFT Use hot water to rinse suds from plates, glasses and cutlery (flatware) to help them to dry quickly by themselves.

Wash plates and cutlery (flatware) quickly after using them to prevent food from drying on and becoming difficult to shift. Rinse off suds with hot water so that the heat will dry the cutlery and plates as they drain.

Rinse the sink with a little liquid fabric detergent after washing up to remove stains and grease.

Strips of paper placed on the tops of cupboards (closets) will absorb the grease and dust that inevitably accumulate in the kitchen. Simply throw the paper away when it becomes dirty and replace with more paper to save time on cleaning.

The bathroom

The following tips take no time at all to carry out every day, and will cut down the time and effort needed for an 'all-over' bathroom clean.

At night, squirt a little toilet cleaner around the bowl so that a quick brush in the morning keeps it sparkling. As the bath water is emptying, add a few drops of liquid detergent to the water – this will remove any scum from the water as it drains away.

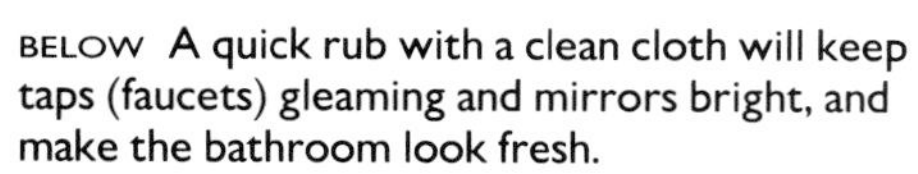

BELOW A quick rub with a clean cloth will keep taps (faucets) gleaming and mirrors bright, and make the bathroom look fresh.

Keep a clean cloth under the washbasin to wipe over the taps (faucets) and mirror as they become dirty. Wipe the washbasin, too, after the morning rush ready for the evening.

ABOVE Add a little liquid detergent to the bath water as it drains away to remove any scum. A dash of disinfectant down the plughole every now and then will keep it fresh.

The living room

Wipe a little white spirit (paint thinner) mixed with water over furniture to give it an instant gleam. Open windows to freshen the room, and shake cushions or rugs out of the windows in order to minimize the amount of dust in the house. A quick vacuum will pick up stray crumbs, ash from ashtrays and dust from every nook and cranny. Just 5 minutes a day should keep the cleaning well in hand.

Try sprinkling the carpet with herbs or lavender and leaving for an hour before vacuuming if the room smells stale. A vacuum cleaner can be used to remove dust from a multitude of surfaces, but empty the bag straight into the dustbin (trash can) to prevent dust from blowing back into the house.

The bedrooms

When you get up, roll back the bedding and allow the beds to air while you have breakfast. Air pillows, too, and check them regularly to pull out any protruding feathers or to even out lumps and bumps. If a pillow is limp and saggy and flops when placed over

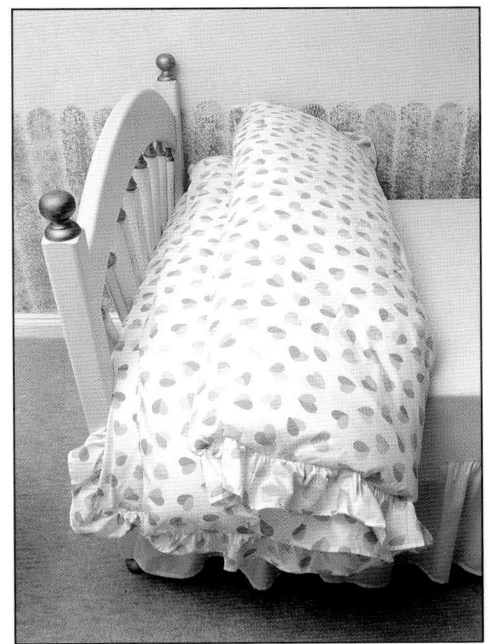

ABOVE After getting up in the morning, turn down the bedding for a while to allow the bed to air before re-making it.

your arm, you need to replace it. Once beds have aired, you can make them.

There is nothing quite like the feel of a bed newly made up in the traditional way with sheets and blankets, and the technique actually becomes very quick and easy with practice. Many people now prefer duvets, however.

Getting a duvet into its cover can be done simply by pushing a corner of the duvet into place. Use 1 or 2 clothes pegs (pins) to hold it in position. Do the same with the other corner, then just shake the duvet down into the clean cover before removing the pegs.

Finally, having made the bed, quickly flick a duster over the furniture, curtains or drapes and shelves, then leave for the dust to settle before vacuuming it all up.

Traditional Bed-Making

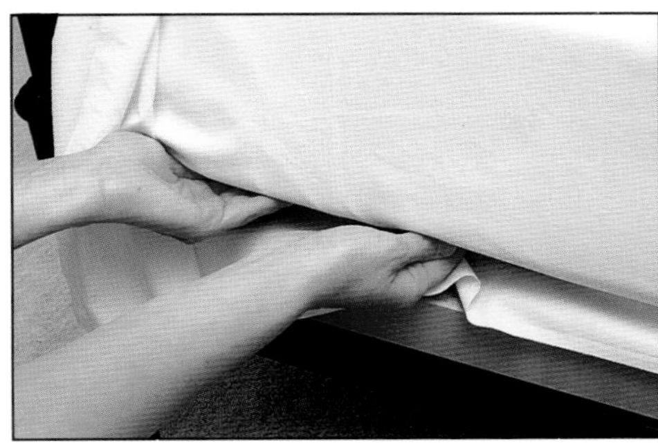

1 Start with the bottom sheet. Tuck in the sheet along the edges and just at the base of the mattress, starting at the head end and working towards the base.

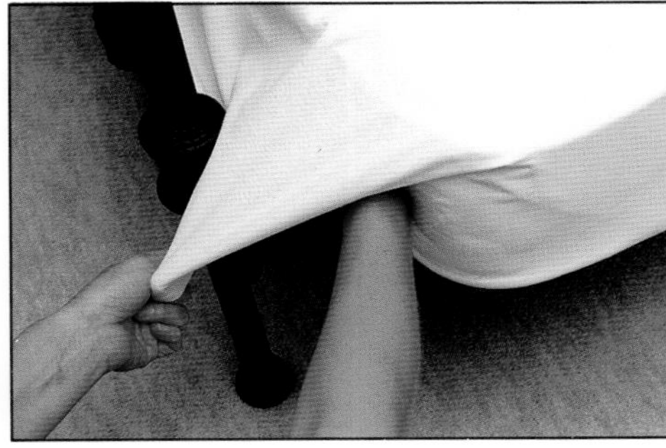

2 Pull the bottom of the sheet taut and fold it in an 'envelope' over the tucked-in corners to make a neat fold.

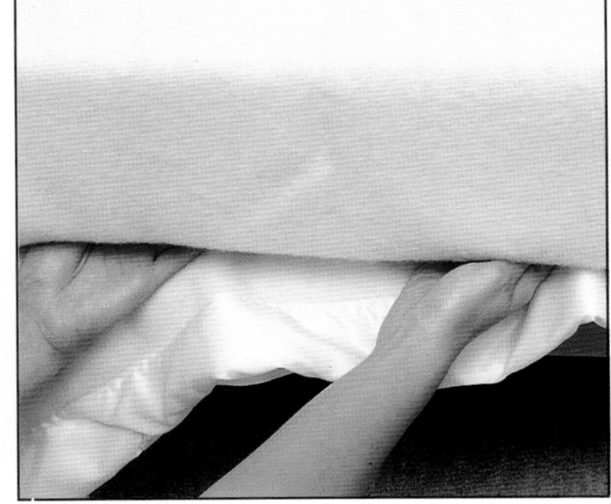

3 Centre the top sheet on the bed with the wide or embroidered hem at the top so that it almost touches the headboard. Lay the blankets on top of the sheet, and tuck both blankets and sheet under the mattress in one go. Make an 'envelope' at the corners as with the bottom sheet, ensuring that the corners are pulled taut.

4 Place the bed cover over the bed, turn the top sheet and blanket over it and replace the pillows.

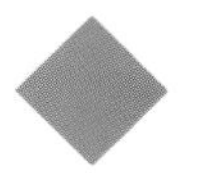

REMOVING STAINS

Stains that are not treated at an early stage run the risk of 'setting' and becoming permanent. Take immediate action to stop a stain from spreading or sinking deeper into the fibres by blotting up the excess with a clean cloth, absorbent tissues or salt.

Stains generally fall into 4 simple categories:

- Stains that can be removed with normal washing, such as water-based paints and milk.
- Those that can be removed by bleaching or a combination of a hot wash and detergent – for example, tea, fruit juice or non-permanent ink.
- Those requiring a pre-wash treatment and/or soak before washing, such as grass stains or blood.
- Those requiring special treatments before cleaning, such as gloss paint.

Sometimes a combination of these treatments will be necessary to remove a stain completely, but remember never to mix more than one chemical at a time, as toxic fumes can be given off. Always bear in mind the key factor of speed, as stains that have been left too long or have become set by heat can be virtually impossible to remove, and none of the treatments will be likely to succeed without damaging the item they are on.

On garments, even if a care label says that the fabric is colourfast, always check this by carrying out a 'test run' on a hidden part such as a seam, hem or inside the waistband. Hold a clean, white cloth behind the fabric and dab on the cleaning fluid (whether water, detergent or solvent). If colour seeps on to the cloth, the garment should be professionally cleaned.

Carpets and upholstery can be more of a problem, so a sample test is important. Specific carpet and upholstery foams and dry-cleaning fluids are available, but, unless you are confident that you can deal with a stain successfully yourself, it is advisable to call in professional cleaners.

If you are in the middle of a party and someone spills a drink over the carpet, there is no need to panic. Act quickly by blotting up the liquid, then tackle it more thoroughly once the guests have left – or, easier still, remove the carpets before they arrive.

STAIN REMOVAL KIT

Keep a stock of as many of the following items as possible, so that you will be prepared to deal with any stain or spillage as soon as it occurs. Refer to the following pages as to which product to use for each type of stain.

Talcum powder: use this to blot up grease or oil as soon as it is spilled.
A blunt knife: this is useful for scraping off matter such as jam or egg.
Clean white cloths: keep these at hand to soak up spills or to apply cleaner. A small, natural sea sponge, cotton wool (absorbent cotton) and white paper towels will also be very useful.
Detergents: spray pre-wash liquid, a detergent soap bar and liquid biological detergent are all good stain removers.
Methylated spirits (denatured alcohol): helpful for removing grass stains on colourfast fabrics.
Glycerine: this should be diluted with an equal amount of water to soften dried-in stains. Leave it for up to an hour before washing the garment.
Acetone or nail-polish remover: good for dealing with nail-varnish stains, but do not use on acetate fabrics.
Hydrogen peroxide: test fabrics for colourfastness before using. Buy the 20-volume strength and mix 1 part to 9 parts water for soaking dried-in stains before washing.
Dry-cleaning fluid or white spirit (paint thinner): pre-test fabrics for colourfastness and use neat, dabbed on grease or fresh paint stains (not to be used on acetates).
White-wine vinegar: vinegar helps to neutralize odours as well as removing pet stains and perspiration marks on garments.
Borax: this is a mild alkali and will work to neutralize acid stains such as wine, fruit juice and coffee.

LEFT The key factor to removing stains is speed: quickly blot up the excess with a clean cloth or tissues. Soaking or a pre-wash treatment before washing will dissolve many stains, but some need special treatment.

Bleaches

There are 2 types of bleach – chlorine bleach and oxygen bleach. Chlorine bleach deodorizes, accelerates the action of detergents, kills germs and generally cleans. It is not suitable for coloured clothes, silk, wool, mohair, leather or Lycra, and should never be poured directly on to clothes. Oxygen bleach is 'colour-safe' and, although it brightens colours and keeps whites white, it is unlikely to make greying nylon whiter. It can be used on coloured fabrics and unbleachable whites (such as silk and wool).

Specific stain removal

When a stain only covers a small area on a garment, you should apply the cleaning solution only to that area, and prevent it from spreading to other areas of the fabric. Place an absorbent cloth or towel underneath the area that is to be cleaned. If the stain is on a trouser leg or sleeve, slide the cloth or towel down the middle to prevent the cleaning solution and stain from working through to the other side.

When a small stain requires saturating in cleaning solution, hold the cloth by the stained area, then twist the unstained area before dipping in the fabric. This will prevent the solution from spreading. If the stain requires soaking for a long period, wrap the unstained parts of the garment in a plastic bag and lie them slightly higher than the stained area, or the solution will spread along the fibres.

Check on the following list to find the stain closest to the one that you need to treat, then follow the instructions given. Once the stain has been removed, wash the item as usual.

Adhesives

Cyanoacrylate or 'super glues' should be treated immediately with a little lighter fuel dabbed on before they set. Very hot or boiling water can be effective, but is only recommended for use on cotton or linen. Other glues can be removed with amyl acetate, which is available from chemists (drugstores).

Ballpoint pen

Use a proprietary cleaner or dab with nail-polish remover or surgical spirit (rubbing alcohol).

ABOVE Surgical spirit (rubbing alcohol) or nail-polish remover will lift ballpoint-pen and ink stains.

Beer or lager

Apply a little dilute glycerine, then follow by treating with a pre-wash laundry aid. Alternatively, a brief soak in a mild white-wine vinegar/water solution should be sufficient.

BELOW Pick off cold candle wax using your fingers or a blunt knife, depending on the surface. Place blotting paper or paper towels over the top of the wax (or on either side if it is a garment) before ironing with a warm iron.

Blood

Rinse off under cold running water, then soak the garment in a solution of biological washing liquid and tepid water. Soak white garments in a mild ammonia/water solution, then wash.

Burns

Scorch marks can sometimes be rubbed off with a blunt knife. Treat fine fabrics with a little dilute glycerine and wash as usual. Treat more stubborn marks with a hydrogen-peroxide solution of 1 part to 9 parts water.

Butter and margarine

Scrape off as much of the grease as possible, then apply a biological liquid to the patch. Wash in as high a temperature as the fabric will stand.

Candle wax

Gently pick or scrape off the cooled wax using a blunt knife. Place blotting paper or paper towels above and beneath the mark, then iron over the top paper, replacing it as soon as it becomes saturated with wax. Repeat until no more wax comes off. Coloured wax may leave a deeper mark: treat with methylated spirits (denatured alcohol) before washing.

Car oil

Dab the mark with a proprietary grease solvent, or treat with a pre-wash aid.

REMOVING STAINS (Continued)

Chewing gum
Chill the garment in the refrigerator, then pick off the solid matter. Dab with methylated spirits (denatured alcohol) or dry-cleaning fluid.

Chocolate
Apply neat biological washing liquid to the stain. Sponge the area with warm water, then wash as usual.

Coffee
Wash immediately under cold running water, then soak in a strong detergent solution. Treat stubborn marks with a dilute hydrogen-peroxide solution (1 part hydrogen peroxide to 9 parts water) before washing.

Crayon
Dab the affected area with white spirit (paint thinner). Use a heavy-duty detergent containing oxygen bleach for the remainder.

Discoloration and dyes
Use a glycerine solution to soak the area, or a dilute solution of household bleach and water on white fabrics only. Alternatively, wash in a heavy-duty detergent containing oxygen bleach.

Egg
Scrape off the excess using a blunt knife, then apply a neat biological washing liquid to the stain. Old stains can be removed by soaking in a solution of 1 part hydrogen peroxide to 9 parts water before washing as usual.

Fats, grease and cooking oils
Dampen the fabric with water and apply a heavy-duty liquid detergent to the stain. Wash immediately in the hottest water the fabric will stand.

Fruit and fruit juice
Sprinkle Borax over the stain to absorb the moisture and neutralize the acid. Rinse in cold water, then wash in a solution of hot water and detergent. Treat stubborn marks with a solution of dilute household bleach and water (1 part bleach to 4 parts water).

Grass stains
Dab these with methylated spirits (denatured alcohol) (not to be used on acetate or tri-acetate fabrics), then rinse and wash.

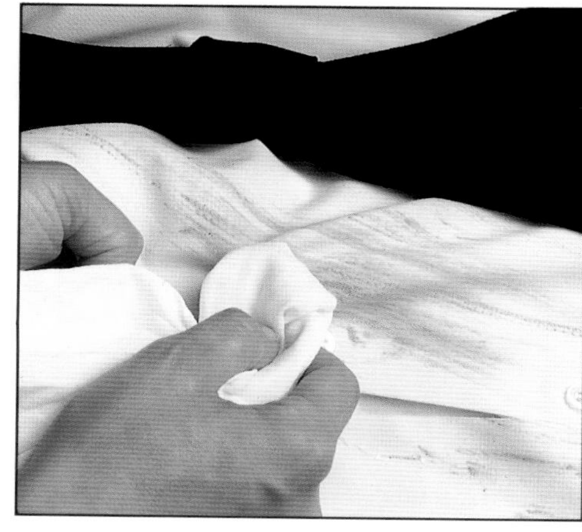

ABOVE Grass stains on school shirts and gym clothes can be removed with methylated spirits (denatured alcohol) before washing.

Heat rings
Rub along the grain of the wood with a soft cloth dipped in turpentine. Alternatively, metal polish rubbed over the marks should remove them. Wipe over with a clean, damp cloth before re-polishing.

ABOVE Remove heat rings on furniture with a little metal polish rubbed over the affected area before re-polishing.

Inks
Dab unknown inks with nail-varnish remover. Cover blue and black fountain-pen inks with salt and lemon juice, and leave them overnight. Finally, rinse and wash with a biological liquid detergent.

Jam
Scrape off the excess using a blunt knife, and dab with a pre-wash laundry aid. Wash as usual.

Tomato ketchup (catsup)
Scrape off the excess, then hold the garment under cold running water. Dab the area with a little neat biological washing liquid or a detergent soap bar, then wash as usual. Treat deep stains with a solution of 1 part hydrogen peroxide to 9 parts water.

Lipstick
Dab first with white spirit (paint thinner), then apply a liquid detergent straight on to the mark and work it into the fibres. Wash in water as hot as the fabric will stand.

ABOVE With a lipstick stain, scrape off as much of the excess as possible. Apply a strong detergent solution, and work from the outside in.

Milk
Rinse under cold running water, then wash using a biological detergent.

Mud
Scrape off the excess using a blunt knife, then apply neat biological washing liquid or soap before washing as usual.

Nail varnish
Dab with nail-varnish remover or acetone before washing as usual. Non-colourfast fabrics should be dry cleaned professionally.

Perfume
Rinse in cold water before washing, or, if the perfume stains, dab the area with white spirit (paint thinner) and wash using a biological detergent.

Perspiration
Dab with a solution of 1 part white-wine vinegar to 10 parts water, or treat the affected area with a biological pre-wash detergent, then wash as usual. White cotton and linen can be treated with a dilute household-bleach solution, and silk, wool and synthetics with a hydrogen-peroxide solution (see **Tomato ketchup** for proportions).

Plasticine and moulding paste
Scrape off the excess matter using a blunt knife, then dab the area with white spirit (paint thinner) or lighter fuel. Wash using a heavy-duty detergent containing oxygen bleach.

Shoe polish
Scrape off any surface polish, then dab the area either with a grease solvent or methylated spirits (denatured alcohol). Soak in a strong detergent solution, then wash.

Tar and beach oil
Scrape off the excess using a blunt knife, and soften the remaining deposit with butter, turpentine or lighter fuel. Wipe away with a clean cloth, then rub the spot with neat liquid detergent before washing.

ABOVE Tar and beach oil can be softened prior to washing by applying butter or turpentine.

Urine
Soak in a gentle solution of cold water and ammonia. Alternatively, soak for a short time with biological washing liquid before washing in the hottest water that the fabric will stand.

ABOVE Urine stains can be soaked in a mild solution of cold water and ammonia. Or soak in biological washing powder before a hot wash.

Vomit
Scrape off the excess or blot it with old cloths. Scrub with a solution of tepid water and a biological detergent to which a little white-wine vinegar and disinfectant have been added. Rinse and repeat if necessary before washing.

Wine
For red wine, cover the stain with salt, then scrape up the saturated salt/wine mixture before blotting with clean, absorbent cloths. Apply cold water to the affected area. Always work from the outside in, to prevent the stain from spreading. Blot again and clean in the usual manner. For white wine, blot up as much as possible with a dry cloth. Treat with cold water before washing.

ABOVE Tip salt over red wine to soak it up as soon as it has been spilled.

STAIN-REMOVAL TIPS

- Always follow the manufacturer's directions before using any stain-removing product.
- Never mix chemicals – if you do, the resulting fumes could be lethal. Never smoke or have an exposed flame near cleaning fluids, as many are highly flammable. Keep the room well-ventilated while working with them in order to avoid inhaling fumes. Wear household gloves when using solvent and bleach cleaners.
- Expensive carpets and upholstery should always be treated with a water and stain repellent. This will help accidental spills to bead up on the surface and not penetrate the fibres.

SEWING AND MENDING

Even if you have little or no needlework knowledge, the following guidelines will help you to deal quickly with minor repair jobs and simple alterations. Always keep a basic sewing kit in the house, containing the following items: a packet of assorted needles; a needle threader; a tape measure; a box of dressmaking pins; a pair of small, sharp scissors; white polyester thread; black polyester thread; invisible thread (transparent nylon monofilament to match all colours); assorted white and black buttons; iron-on invisible mending tape (for hems and turn-ups); and iron-on patches for lightweight fabrics. A kit consisting of these basic items should be sufficient for most minor repairs and sewing tasks.

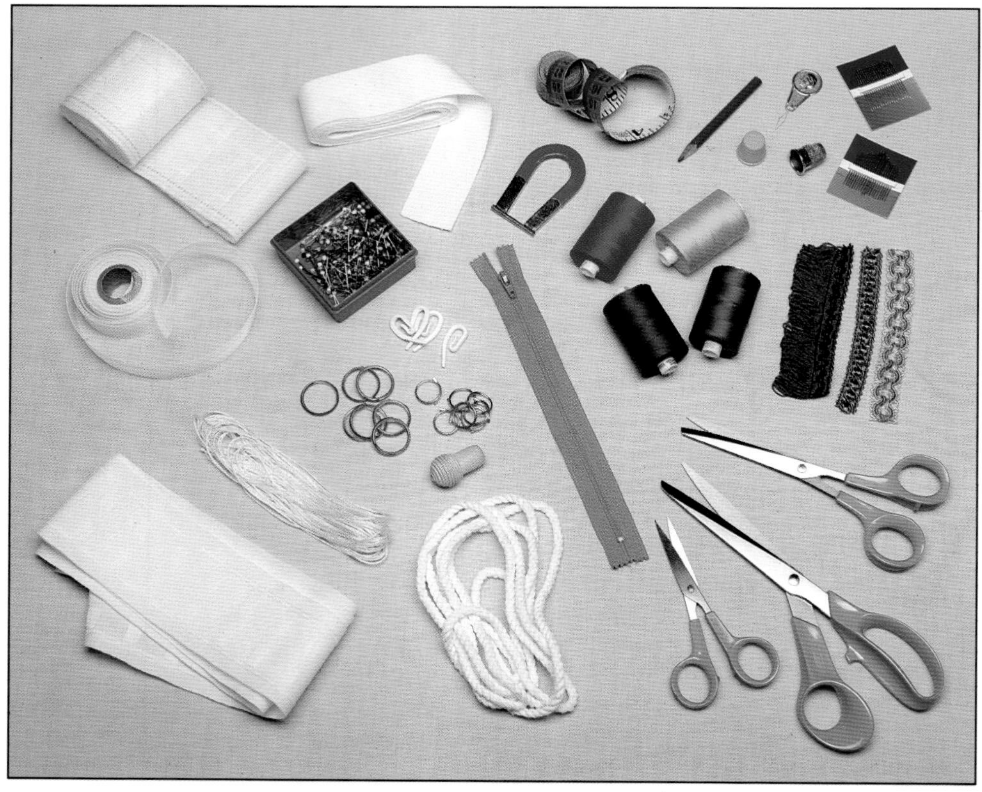

ABOVE A basic sewing and mending kit should contain scissors, various coloured threads, spare zips (zippers), pins and needles, a tape measure, a thimble and iron-on invisible mending tape.

Sewing on buttons

Buttons need to be sewn to fabric with small lengths of thread remaining underneath the buttons, making them flexible but strong. If they are too tightly sewn, the buttons will not have sufficient space to lie flat against the buttonholes, resulting in the fabric being pulled.

Remove an old or broken button by sliding the teeth of a comb around the base threads, then cutting through with a razor blade. To sew on a replacement button, cut a length of thread approximately 50 cm/20 in long. Thread a needle and pull half the thread through, let the other piece hang down, then grip both ends together and tie a knot about 20 mm/¾ in from the cut ends. This will give you a strong doubled thread of a manageable length for sewing. If you try to work with a longer thread, in an attempt to avoid re-threading for sewing on several buttons, you may find it a false economy, as the thread will twist and tangle very easily, forcing you to cut the thread and begin again.

Starting on the underside of the fabric, push the needle up and through one hole in the button, and back through the opposite hole. A matchstick (wooden match) placed between the button and fabric will ensure that you leave enough thread to give flexibility. After going in and out of the hole 6 to 8 times, remove the matchstick and wind the thread around the stitches a few times. Push the needle through to the underside of the fabric and secure with a few more stitches before cutting off the thread end close to the fabric.

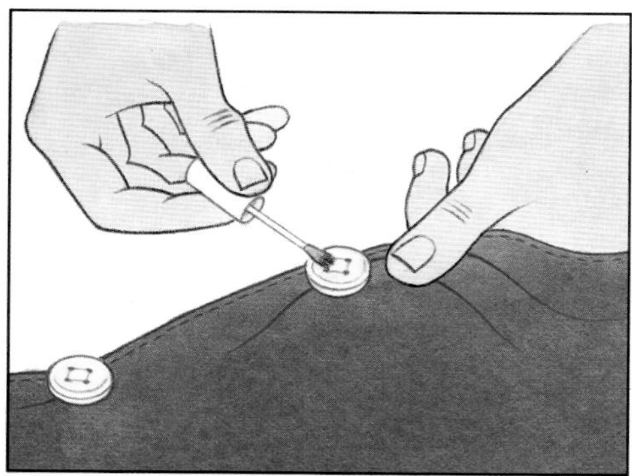

LEFT A little clear nail varnish dabbed on the threads after sewing on a button will help it stay on securely.

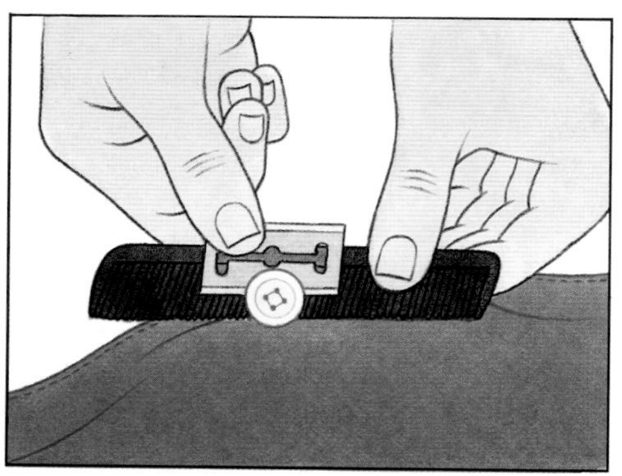

ABOVE Protect garments when removing buttons by sliding a comb under the button.

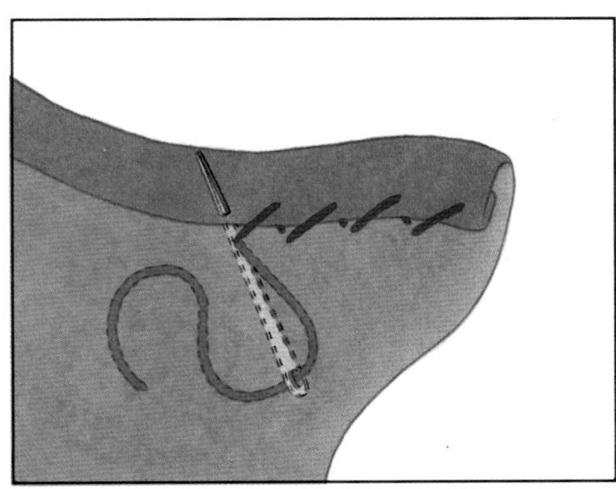

ABOVE To stitch a hem, run large stitches on the inside of the garment, catching a single thread on the outside of the garment each time.

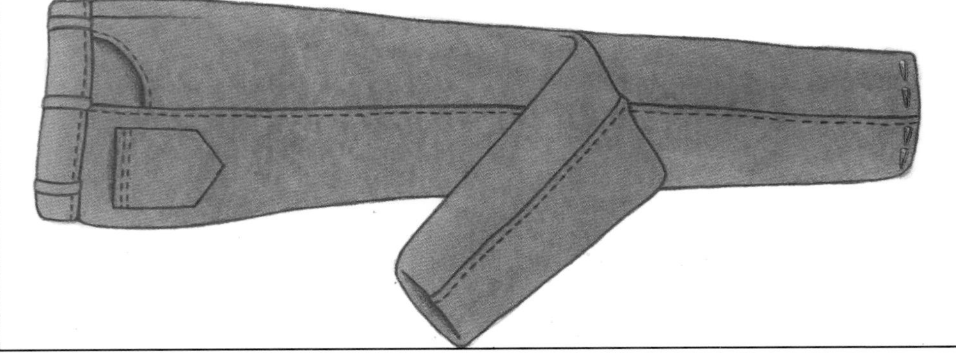

ABOVE When turning up trousers, lay them flat on a table to check that both hems are even and the same length. But first check that the length is right by asking the person who is going to wear the trousers to try them on.

Turning up hems and trousers

Ask the person who is going to wear the garment to put it on to make accurate alterations. If it is your own garment, use a tape measure or use existing hemlines or trouser lengths as a guide.

If the existing hem is straight, cut the fabric to a point approximately 5 cm/ 2 in below the length at which you wish the hem to be. Turn the garment inside-out, turn up the raw edge by about 20 mm/¾ in, pinning it all round as you go, and press it with an iron. Remove the pins and turn up the remaining 3 cm/1¼ in, then pin and press again. Stitch the hem securely by running large stitches on the inside of the garment and catching just a single strand of fibre each time on the outside of the garment.

Mending a zip (zipper)

A zip (zipper) that has become stuck can be loosened with a little liquid soap rubbed on to the teeth. Fabric that has been caught needs to be gently wriggled and prised free. If the zip head comes right off the top or bottom, cut off the lowest few teeth and push it back on. Oversew the patch where you have cut off the teeth in order to prevent the zip from coming off again.

Mending a tear

Rips in bed linen or garments can be invisibly mended by 'patching' the reverse with an iron-on adhesive patch – follow the manufacturer's instructions for use. Prevent further stress from pulling the area by running stitches around the edge of the tear.

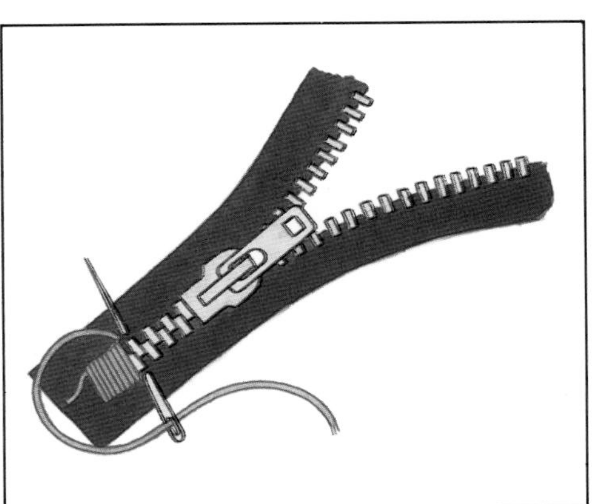

ABOVE Use strong cotton to stitch over the base of a weak zip (zipper).

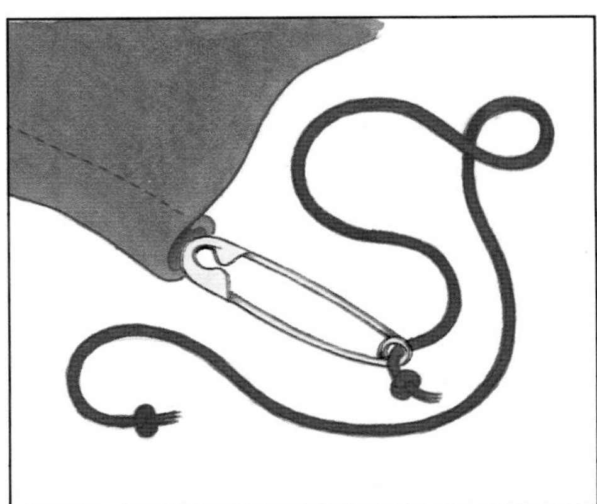

ABOVE Attach a safety pin to the end of a drawstring to make threading easier.

MENDING TIPS

- When a hem drops and cannot be mended immediately, use a length of sticky tape to make a temporary invisible mend.
- Stop runs in stockings and tights (pantyhose) by dabbing on a little clear nail varnish at the top and bottom of the run.
- Dab a little nail varnish on to the threads holding metal buttons in place to prevent them from wearing away.
- If you find it difficult to pass a piece of thread through the eye of a needle, wipe a little soap on it to keep the ends from splitting.
- As soon as you notice that a button is coming loose, tie a knot in the unravelling thread until you find time to mend it properly.
- A quick alternative to sewing a hem is iron-on invisible mending tape, which creates a long-lasting and invisible repair.

GOING ON HOLIDAY AND MOVING HOME

Taking a holiday is all about relaxing, not about worrying that you have left the oven on, the door open or have forgotten to take out insurance cover.

Moving home, on the other hand, is considered to be one of the most stressful and exhausting experiences that we have to face. You can, however, make it less of an ordeal by ensuring that you are well-prepared before the day itself, to minimize the risk of anything going wrong.

Holiday preparations

Whether you will be travelling by air, sea or car, choose the best luggage that you can afford, as cheap suitcases will soon weaken. Tie round a coloured tape or buy straps with your name woven on them to help you to identify your luggage quickly at an airport. Never write your name and home address on luggage labels where they can easily be seen – anyone dishonest will instantly know where their next 'job' is to be.

Several weeks before you are due to travel, check that all passports are up to date and will not expire while you are away. You will also need to find out well in advance whether you need visas for the countries to which you will be travelling, and, if so, to organize them with the relevant authorities, which can take some time.

Take out holiday insurance and make sure that, in the event of having to cancel at the last moment, you will be given a refund. Holidays in which sports are involved may require additional cover. Always check that, in the case of an accident, you will be flown back home for long or specialist treatment. Check with your doctor whether any vaccinations or a course of tablets are required for the country or countries that you will be visiting.

Order some currency and arrange traveller's cheques for the remainder of the money – this is both safer in case of loss or theft, and more convenient.

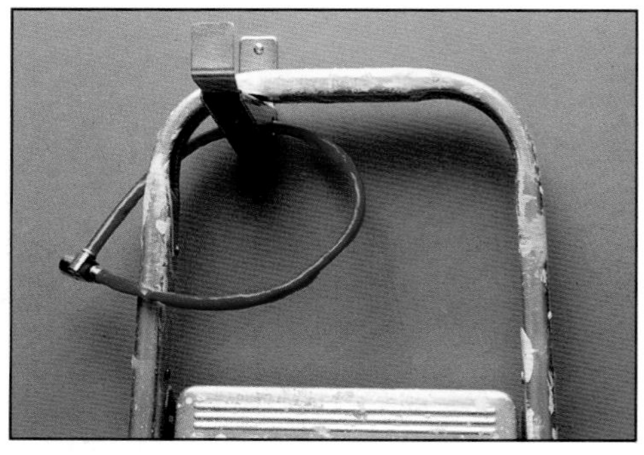

ABOVE Lock ladders to a garage or shed wall so that would-be burglars cannot use them to gain entry to your home.

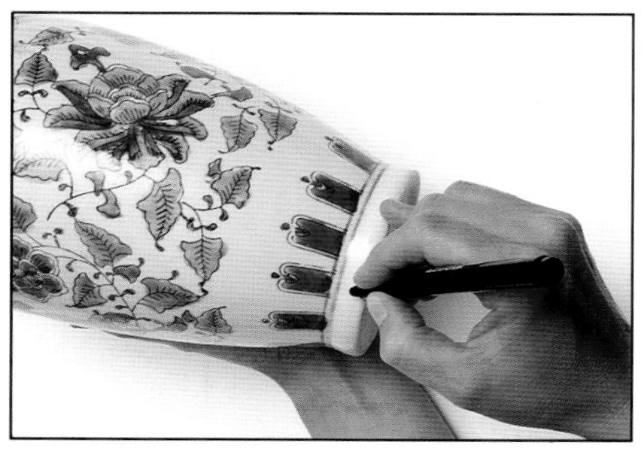

ABOVE Mark all your valuables with an engraver and stencil or ultra-violet pen so that, in the event of a burglary while you are on holiday, the items can be identified should they be recovered. Many stolen items such as hi-fi (stereo) equipment are found by the police, but cannot be returned because of lack of identification.

Home security

Giving a little thought to security before you go on holiday will greatly reduce the chances of a burglary while you are away. Some of these suggestions may seem obvious, but it is surprising how often they are forgotten.

Ask a neighbour to call in every day to remove flyers and letters from the mat, as a pile of these is a good indication that you are away. Cancel milk and paper deliveries, as these can alert any passer by to the fact that no one is at home, if they are stacked up on the doorstep. Keeping houseplants watered is also a good way of ensuring that the house looks occupied.

Fit door and window locks if you have not already done so (this may be a requirement of your insurance policy in any case, so you must do this or your policy could be invalidated in the event of a burglary). Padlock ladders to a wall and lock up the garden shed if you have one so that tools cannot be used by burglars to gain entry. Buy timeswitches to operate the television and some lights to give the impression that people are in the house.

Leaving washing up on the drainer and a couple of magazines scattered around will also make it look as if the house is occupied.

Travelling with children

Stop boredom from setting in by taking a selection of games and toys with you. Guessing games and stories also help to pass the time enjoyably. Acupressure wristbands and travel-sickness tablets are useful for long journeys. Another remedy is to eat crystallized (preserved) ginger, which prevents nausea.

TRAVEL KIT

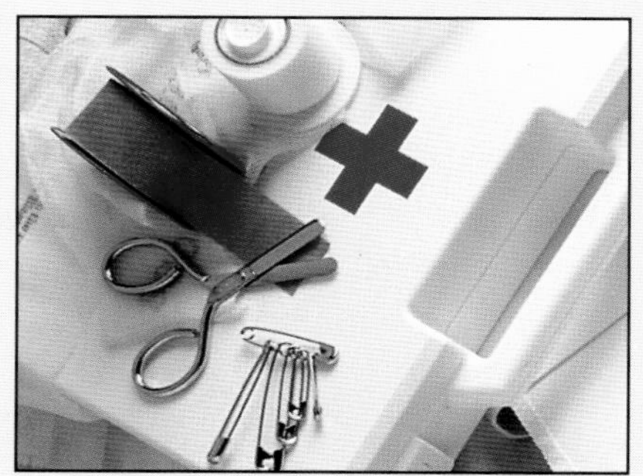

This should include the following:

- Sun-screen lotion.
- After-sun lotion.
- Insect repellent.
- Antiseptic wipes.
- Sticking plasters and bandages.
- Upset-stomach tablets or medicine.
- Tweezers.
- Thermometer.
- Paracetamol or other pain-relief tablets for adults and children.
- Rehydration packs for diarrhoea.

BEFORE MOVING

- Buy a pack of change-of-address cards, or fill one out and photocopy it to save time writing out dozens. Ensure that your insurance company, bank, credit card issuer, pension company, and all the other businesses you deal with know of your move.
- Arrange building and contents insurance at the new house to start from the day you move in.
- Cancel regular deliveries of groceries or newspapers.
- Arrange by telephone, and confirm in writing, transfers of the electricity, gas, water and telephone accounts. Before leaving, read the meters.
- Make arrangements for the gas, electricity and water to be switched on at the new house.

House-moving preparations
If you intend to use a professional removal company, contact 2 or 3 different removal companies as soon as you know that the move is on and ask them to visit and quote for the job. Ask neighbours or friends for their recommendations, too, as they may be able to offer useful advice on local companies. Firms which are reluctant to visit may be best avoided, as a guessed estimate may cause problems on the day if they do not know, for instance, that there will be a spiral staircase, low doors or an attic or loft stashed with boxes to cope with.

When the removal men arrive, point out anything that may make parking near the house a problem, and remember to tell them if they are likely to encounter difficulties at the new address. Show items requiring careful handling such as antiques, computer or hi-fi (stereo) equipment, as well as anything that has to be dismantled before it can be moved such as large wardrobes (closets). Giving all this information at the start will make the removal company's quotation as accurate as possible and prevent a nasty surprise when the bill arrives.

Removal insurance
Always read the small print on the documentation and check that the house contents will be insured for the duration of the move. Many removal firms' contracts state that you must let them know within 10 days of the move if anything is damaged or missing. Be sure to open every box and inspect the contents thoroughly as soon as you arrive, even if they remain otherwise untouched for weeks afterwards. Most firms will pack and unpack the contents themselves, but may give a discount if you do it yourself. This could affect the insurance cover, however, so check this before you decide.

Check your own house-contents insurance, as it is likely that the insurance will not cover items lost or damaged during a move. If necessary, ask the company to extend the cover.

Hiring (renting) a van
Doing the move yourself is cheaper, but driving a large van packed with furniture can be an alarming experience if you are unused to it. Unless you are fit and reasonably strong and can spare the time, it can in fact end up being a false economy. Hiring (renting) a van and driver could be a happy medium – check whether you will be charged extra for mileage, or whether the price quoted is inclusive.

BELOW Wrap plates individually and pack them vertically to minimize the risk of breakages.

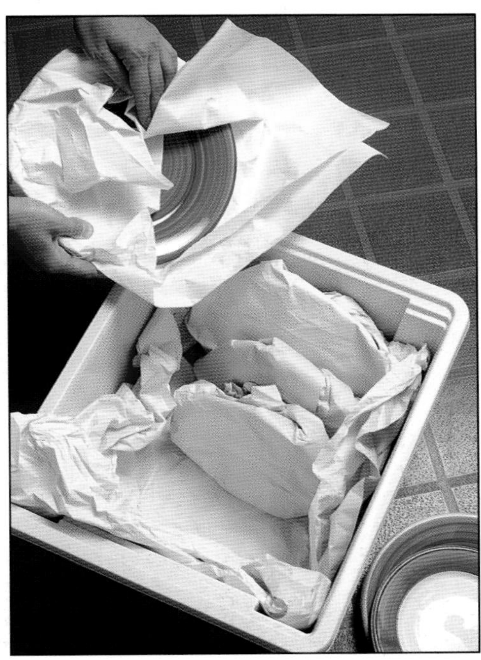

Packing
Begin packing a few weeks ahead of the move. Start with items in the attic or loft that you rarely use – this is also a good time to throw out items that you no longer need. Additional, purely decorative items and ornaments can also be wrapped up at this early stage.

Collect boxes from the supermarket and save newspapers for packing items. Buy bubble wrap (padded plastic wrapping, available from stationers) to protect delicate or easily marked items. Use large but manageable boxes, and mark each lid with a bold pen to show which room it belongs in at the new house. Alternatively, place a colour-coded label on the box, for example blue for the bathroom, yellow for the kitchen, green for the living room, and so on. When you arrive at the new house, stick matching labels on the relevant door to each room so that the removal company knows exactly where everything needs to go. When labelling boxes, give details of the contents (e.g., kitchen pans and crockery; food processor and attachments) so that you do not spend frustrating time trying to find one item.

Line boxes containing china with a thick layer of bubble wrap or with scrunched-up paper to protect the contents. Wrap plates in paper or bubble wrap and stack them vertically in the boxes. In the event of the box being knocked or dropped, the plates will be less likely to crack if the weight is not resting on those at the bottom.

Leave soap, toilet paper, hand towels and tea- and coffee-making items (including cups and the kettle) until last, then pack them in a brightly coloured plastic box so that you can see it easily the instant you arrive. Pack tools, lightbulbs, extension cables, spare fuses and screws in another brightly coloured box so that rooms can be lit and quick repairs undertaken.

CONSERVATION AND RECYCLING

We all know of the need to reduce the level of environmental pollution. No matter how insignificant a small action may seem – such as placing a jar in a recycling bin, switching off a light when it is not needed or mending a dripping tap (faucet) – if everyone made an effort, the waste of vital resources could be drastically reduced.

Everyday recycling

Buy re-fill containers to fill up bottles and minimize the number of unwanted plastic containers ending up on landfill sites. Separate your household waste into groups: vegetable waste which can be composted in the garden; items that you can take to a local recycling centre such as paper, card (cardboard) and newspaper, metal drinks and food cans and tin foil, glass jars and bottles; and finally any waste which cannot be recycled and needs to go in the dustbin (trash can).

Re-use old envelopes and cut up old letters and scrap paper for writing lists and messages. Keep old margarine tubs to store nails, screws and small fittings, and use jars or bottles to keep scraps of ribbon, string and elastic together – the latter containers are especially convenient as they enable you to see at a glance the contents inside.

ABOVE Keep a large bag in which to place recyclable waste such as cans, jars and bottles until you can take them to the recycling centre.

Home ideas

It takes the energy of 1 gallon/4.5 litres of petrol (gasoline) to make just 30 house bricks. Use reclaimed bricks when building to help save the earth's resources and to give a traditional weathered look to houses, gardens and patios at the same time. The use of reclaimed architectural materials such as floorboards, baths and windows looks good and rarely costs more than the modern equivalent.

ABOVE Using architectural salvage not only recycles unwanted items, but also adds character to a home.

When buying woods, choose only those that you are satisfied come from sustainable sources. Avoid hardwoods cut from tropical rainforests, including teak and mahogany – the de-forestation caused by the removal of such woods results in rare species being forced into extinction, and massive forest fires which contribute to global warming. There are plenty of sustainable alternatives, with pine, beech and rubberwood being among the best. These woods can be stained, waxed or varnished to darken them or even painted to achieve a range of attractive effects. To save on new paper, buy toilet paper and kitchen paper (paper towels) that contains a high percentage of recycled material, and look for 'non-chlorine-bleached' labels as the use of bleach increases pollution.

Avoid buying aerosols that contain CFCs (chlorofluorocarbons). These destroy the ozone layer, resulting in dangerous ultra-violet radiation from the sun penetrating to the earth. Foam-blown plastics (used for food cartons), air conditioners and some refrigerators also release CFCs into the atmosphere, so bear this in mind when buying. There are so many excellent alternatives to all these products that there is no excuse for buying them.

You can also greatly reduce your consumption of fuel by insulating your home properly. Good insulation saves money on heating bills as well as reducing the amount of pollution, so it is a good idea for both reasons. The burning of fossil fuels also creates 'acid rain' which kills forests and eats away at buildings that form our architectural heritage, and should be reduced as much as possible.

Electrical appliances

When replacing an appliance such as a refrigerator, freezer, cooker or washing machine, look for the models that are energy-efficient and have 'economy' programmes. Take your old fridge or freezer for recycling, and to a place where harmful CFCs can be recycled or disposed of safely. For economic running, place the refrigerator and freezer on an outside wall and well away from the cooker or a hot dishwasher. De-frosting the freezer regularly will prevent thick layers of ice from building up, which in turn prevent the freezer from functioning correctly and cause it to use more electricity to maintain a low temperature.

Try to cook in batches when using the oven, by making several dishes at one time and using all the oven-shelf space. A microwave oven cooks quickly and consumes far less energy than a conventional oven. It is ideal for re-heating foods which tend to dry up under a grill (broiler) or in an oven.

If you plan to install a gas central-heating system, choose one of the latest energy-efficient condensing boilers, as it will save both on fuel bills and on unwanted carbon-dioxide emissions.

Only operate a dishwasher when you have a full load, and use the 'economy' setting for normal soiling.

Heat and light

Avoid wasting heat by fitting thermostatic radiator valves to each radiator, so that you can control the temperature of each room to suit your needs. Shelves above radiators help to deflect heat back into the room, as well as creating valuable storage space. Turning down the central-heating thermostat by just a degree or so and reducing the length of time that your central heating is switched on makes little difference to comfort levels, but saves a considerable amount of energy during the course of a year.

Line curtains or drapes with special insulating fabric to help keep the heat in a room. Blinds (shades) also act as simple heat barriers, so close them at night for additional insulation. Block gaps under doors and prevent draughts by using 'sausage' draught excluders.

To save on the cost of lighting, switch to low-energy lightbulbs. Although these are more expensive than ordinary bulbs, they last up to 6 times longer and use approximately 75 per cent less energy. Try also to get into the habit of switching off lights as you leave a room. Fitting 2-way switches in the hallway and on the landing will ensure that you have good lighting while going up and down stairs, but can also switch off the lights when they are not required.

ABOVE Fit thermostatic radiator valves to each radiator to avoid wasting heat. They mean that you can control the temperature of each room separately.

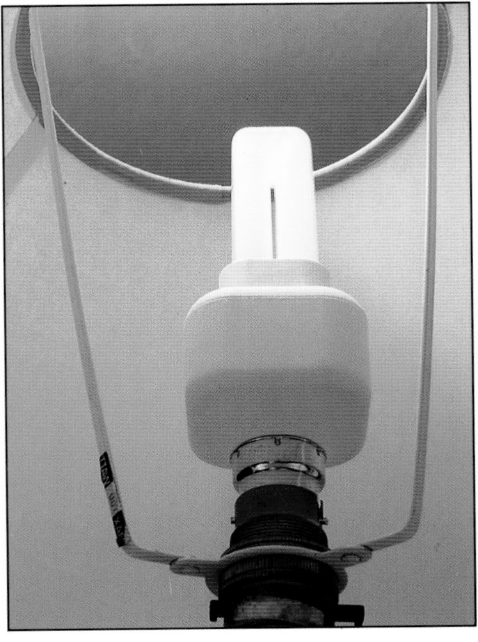

ABOVE Low-energy lightbulbs cut down on the amount of electricity required to use them, ultimately reducing the carbon dioxide released into the atmosphere from power stations.

ENERGY-SAVING TIPS

• Taking a shower instead of a bath uses up to 60 per cent less water and the energy required to heat it.

• Use stacking saucepans rather than individual ones, so that you can cook several different items over a single ring (burner).

• When boiling a kettle for just one mug of tea, fill the mug with water and then tip this into the kettle so that you do not heat up unwanted water.

Home Cooking

From a tasty breakfast to an indulgent Sunday lunch, there is nothing more appealing than a home-cooked meal. Here you'll find tips on how to prepare everything from the perfect boiled egg to a succulent pot-roast, plus how to make modern favourites like pizzas, stir-fries and curries. And why not develop your creative skills by discovering the pleaures of baking your own bread, and decorating cakes for friends and family.

ROASTING MEAT

The dry heat of oven roasting is best suited to tender cuts of meat. If they do not have a natural marbling of fat, bard them by covering with strips of bacon to prevent the meat from drying out. Alternatively, marinate the meat or baste it frequently with the roasting juices during cooking.

Meat should be at room temperature for roasting. Roast on a rack in a tin (pan) as, without a rack, the base of the joint will stew and not become crisp. There are 2 methods of roasting meat: searing the joint at a high temperature and then reducing the heat for the rest of the cooking time; or roasting at a constant temperature throughout. Both methods produce good results – it is prolonged cooking, not the method, that affects juiciness and shrinkage – so use whichever method you prefer.

SUGGESTED ROASTING TIMES

Using the second roasting method, in a 180°C/350°F/Gas 4 oven, approximate timings in minutes per 450g/1lb are as follows:

Beef, rare, 20 + 20 extra*
medium, 25 + 25 extra
well done, 30 + 30 extra
Veal, 25 + 25 extra
Lamb, 25 + 25 extra
Pork, 35 + 35 extra
(*Prime cuts such as rib of beef and tenderloin need less time.)

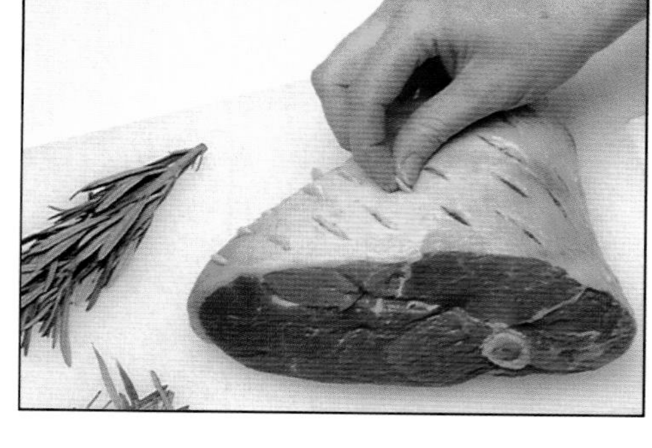

1 According to the recipe, rub the joint with oil or butter and season. If you wish, for extra flavour, make little slits in the meat all over the surface, using the tip of a sharp knife. Insert flavourings such as herbs, slivers of garlic, olive slices, shards of fresh ginger and so on.

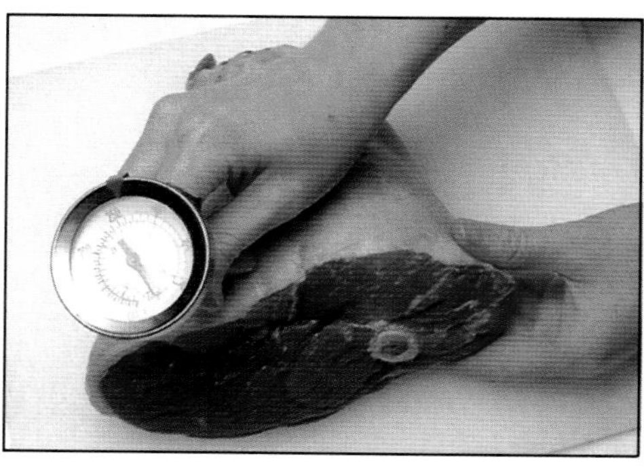

2 Insert a meat thermometer into the thickest part, not touching a bone. (An instant-read thermometer is sometimes inserted towards the end of roasting.) Roast for the suggested time (see below left), basting if necessary.

3 Transfer the cooked meat to a carving board. Leave it to 'rest' for 10–15 minutes before carving so that the flesh can re-absorb the juices. During this time, make gravy with the roasting juices, if you like.

ROAST LEG OF LAMB

Trim a 2.25–2.7kg/5–6lb leg of lamb, removing almost all the fat. Cut 2–3 garlic cloves into very thin slices. Pull the leaves from 3 sprigs of fresh rosemary. Insert the garlic slices and rosemary leaves into slits in the lamb. Rub the lamb with olive oil and season with salt and pepper. Roast until cooked to your taste. *Serves 8.*

MEAT-THERMOMETER READINGS

Beef		**Lamb**	
rare	52–54°C/125–130°F	rare	54–57°C/130–135°F
medium-rare	57°C/135°F	medium	60–63°C/140–145°F
medium	60–63°C/140–145°F	well-done	71°C/160°F
well-done	71°C/160°F		
		Pork	
Veal		medium	66°C/150°F
well-done	71°C/160°F	well-done	71–74°C/160–165°F

Boned Pork Loin with Apple-cream Sauce

Serves 6

1 × 1.35 kg/3 lb boned pork loin, rolled and tied

15 ml/1 tbsp fresh thyme leaves or 5 ml/1 tsp dried thyme

salt and pepper

fresh thyme sprigs, watercress and sliced apples, to garnish

For the sauce

20 g/⅔ oz/1½ tbsp butter

1 onion, chopped

2 apples, peeled, cored and chopped

150 ml/¼ pint/⅔ cup whipping or double (heavy) cream

7.5 ml/1½ tsp Dijon mustard

15 ml/1 tbsp creamed horseradish

1 Preheat a 190°C/375°F/Gas 5 oven.

2 Untie the pork loin. Trim off the skin and most of the fat. Lay the pork out flat, outer-side down. Sprinkle it with the thyme, salt and pepper and press into the meat.

3 Roll up the loin again and tie it into a neat shape with string.

4 Put the pork loin on a rack in a small roasting tin (pan). Roast for 1¼–1½ hours or until well-cooked.

5 Meanwhile, for the sauce, melt the butter in a saucepan and add the onion and apples. Cook over a low heat for 20–25 minutes, stirring occasionally, until very soft.

6 Allow the apple mixture to cool slightly, then transfer it to a food processor. Add the cream, mustard and horseradish. Blend until smooth. Season with salt and pepper. Return the sauce to the pan and re-heat just before serving.

7 When the pork is cooked, remove it from the oven to rest for about 10 minutes before carving. Garnish with thyme, watercress and apples.

COOK'S TIP

A boned joint will take longer to cook than the same-weight joint with bone. This is because the bone conducts heat more readily than the flesh.

PAN-FRYING, SAUTÉING AND STIR-FRYING MEAT

Tender cuts of meat, such as steaks and chops, slices of calf's liver and hamburgers, are ideal for cooking quickly in a heavy frying pan. Before pan-frying and sautéing, trim excess fat from steaks, chops, escalopes, etc., then dry them very thoroughly with paper towels. For cooking, choose a fat that can be heated to a high temperature. If using butter, an equal amount of vegetable oil will help prevent burning, or you could use clarified butter if you prefer (see page 154).

After pan-frying or sautéing, you can make a simple yet delicious sauce in the pan; the same method is ideal for making gravy to accompany roast meats. It is also a good way to maximize flavour in stews and casseroles. Before de-glazing, remove the meat and keep it warm. Pour or spoon off all the fat from the pan, unless a recipe calls for shallots, garlic, etc., to be softened. In that case, leave 5–10 ml/1–2 tsp of fat and cook the vegetables in it.

For stir-frying, a wok is excellent because its high sides let you stir and toss the ingredients briskly so that they cook quickly and evenly. Use long cooking chopsticks or a wooden spatula to keep the ingredients moving.

PAN-FRYING OR SAUTÉING MEAT

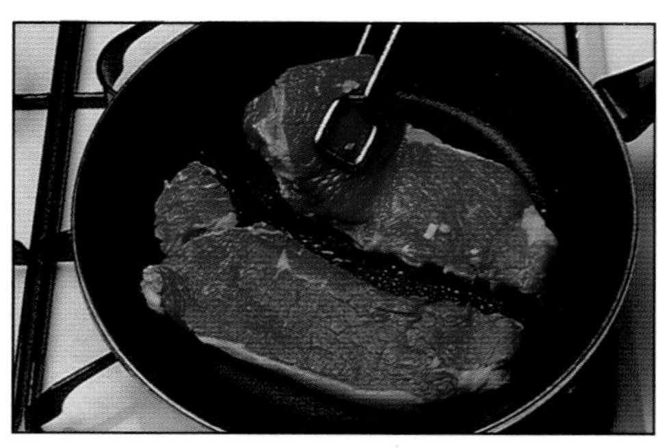

1 Heat the fat in the pan over a high heat until very hot but not browning. Put in the meat, in one layer. Do not crowd the pan.

2 Fry until browned on both sides and done to your taste. If pan-frying pork or veal chops, reduce the heat to moderate once they are in the pan.

PAN-FRIED TERIYAKI STEAK

Combine 45 ml/3 tbsp vegetable oil, 15 ml/1 tbsp each soy sauce, honey, red-wine vinegar and finely chopped onion, 1 crushed garlic clove and 2.5 ml/½ tsp ground ginger in a plastic bag. Add 4 rump or sirloin steaks and turn to coat well. Put the bag in a dish and marinate for 2 hours. Drain the steaks and pat dry, then pan-fry until cooked to your taste. The steaks can also be grilled (broiled). *Serves 4.*

CUTS FOR PAN-FRYING

Beef: fillet steak (tournedos), sirloin steak (porterhouse), rump steak, T-bone steak, hamburgers.
Lamb: cutlets, noisettes (boned cutlets), loin chops, chump chops, leg steaks, fillet.
Pork: loin chops, spare-rib chops, cubes or slices of fillet (tenderloin).

CUTS FOR STIR-FRYING

Beef: strips of rump and other steaks.
Lamb: strips of shoulder fillet, leg.
Pork: cubes of fillet (tenderloin).

DE-GLAZING FOR A PAN SAUCE

1 Pour in the liquid called for in the recipe (wine, stock, vinegar, etc.). Bring to a boil, stirring well to scrape up the browned bits from the bottom of the pan and dissolve them in the liquid.

2 Boil over a high heat for 1–2 minutes or until the liquid is almost syrupy. If the recipe instructs, enrich the sauce with cream or butter. Season to taste with salt and pepper and serve.

TESTING STEAK

A reliable way to test steak is by pressing it with your finger. When raw, it is soft and can be squashed. When cooked rare, it will be only slightly springy. When medium-cooked, it will offer more resistance and drops of red juice will appear on the surface. When well-done, it will be firm to the touch.

STIR-FRIED BEEF WITH MANGE-TOUT (SNOW PEAS)

Cut 450 g/1 lb lean, boneless, tender beef into very thin strips. Combine 45 ml/3 tbsp soy sauce, 30 ml/2 tbsp dry sherry, 15 ml/1 tbsp brown sugar and 2.5 ml/½ tsp cornflour (cornstarch) in a bowl. Heat 15 ml/1 tbsp vegetable oil in the hot wok. Add 15 ml/1 tbsp each finely chopped fresh ginger and garlic and stir-fry for 30 seconds. Add the beef and stir-fry for 2 minutes or until well browned. Add 225 g/8 oz mange-tout (snow peas); stir-fry for 3 minutes. Stir the soy sauce mixture until smooth, then add to the wok. Bring to a boil, stirring and tossing, and simmer just until it is thickened and smooth. Serve immediately, accompanied by freshly boiled rice. *Serves 4.*

STIR-FRYING MEAT

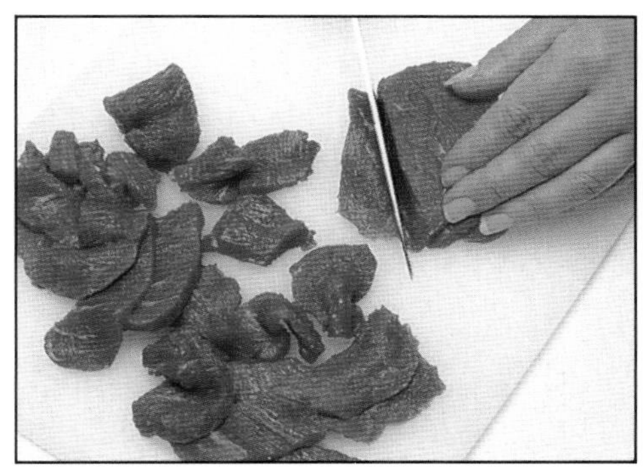

1 Prepare all the stir-fry ingredients in uniformly sized pieces, following recipe instructions if you wish.

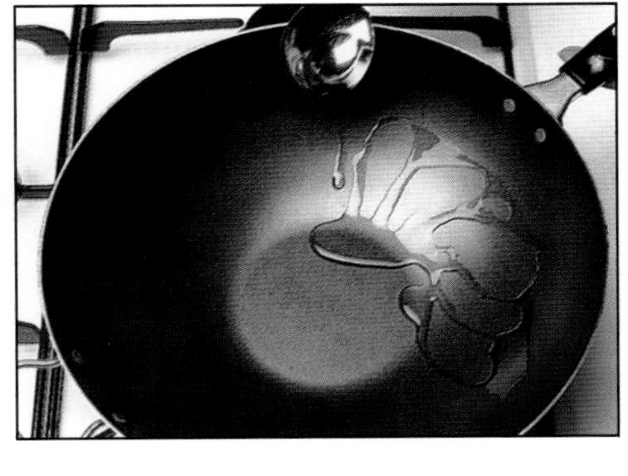

2 Heat a wok or large, deep frying pan over a moderately high heat. Dribble in the oil down the sides.

3 When the oil is hot (a piece of vegetable should sizzle on contact), add the ingredients in the order specified in the recipe. (Those that take longer to cook should be added first.) Do not add too much to the wok at a time, or the ingredients will start to produce steam rather than frying properly.

4 Fry, stirring and tossing constantly with chopsticks or a spatula, until the ingredients are just cooked: vegetables should be crisp-tender and meat and poultry tender and juicy.

5 Push the ingredients to the side of the wok or remove them. Pour liquid or sauce as specified in the recipe into the bottom. Cook and stir, then mix in the ingredients from the side of the wok. Serve immediately.

ROASTING POULTRY

Where would family gatherings be without the time-honoured roast bird? Beyond the favourite chicken, all types of poultry can be roasted – from small poussins to large turkeys – although older, tougher birds are better pot-roasted (see opposite page).

PROTECT AND FLAVOUR

Before roasting, loosen the skin on the breast by gently easing it away from the flesh with your fingers. Press in softened butter – mixed with herbs or garlic for extra flavour – and smooth back the skin.

POUSSINS WALDORF

Preheat a 180°C/350°F/Gas 4 oven. For the stuffing, melt 30 g/1 oz/2 tbsp butter and fry 1 finely chopped onion until soft. Tip into a bowl and add 300 g/10 oz/2¼ cups cooked rice, 2 finely chopped celery stalks, 2 cored and finely diced red apples, 55 g/2 oz/½ cup chopped walnuts, 75 ml/5 tbsp cream sherry or apple juice and 30 ml/2 tbsp lemon juice. Season and mix well.

Divide the stuffing among 6 poussins, each weighing about 575 g/1¼ lb, stuffing the body cavities. Truss and arrange in a roasting tin (pan). Sprinkle with salt and pepper and drizzle over 55 g/2 oz/4 tbsp melted butter. Roast for 1¼–1½ hours. Untruss before serving.

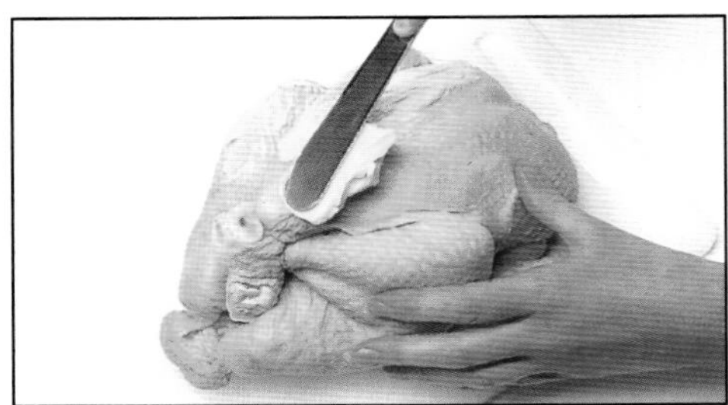

1 Wipe the bird inside and out, using damp paper towels. Stuff the bird if you wish and truss it. Spread the breast of a chicken with butter or oil; bard (cover with strips of bacon) a lean game bird; prick the skin of a duck or goose.

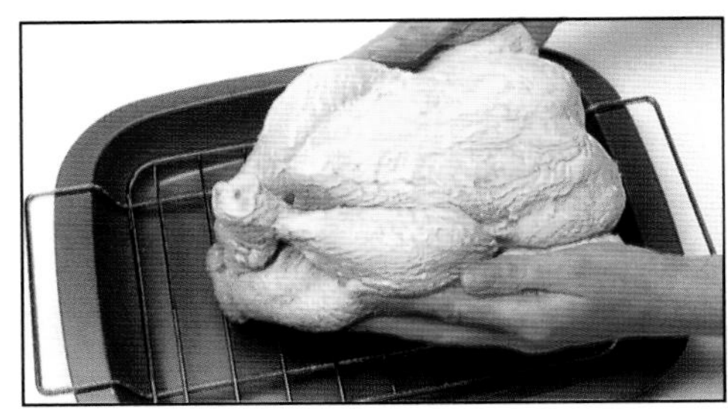

2 Set the bird breast-up on a rack in a small roasting tin (pan) or shallow baking dish. If you are roasting a game bird which has very little fat, set the bird in the tin breast-down.

3 Roast the bird, basting it every 10 minutes after the first ½ hour with the accumulated juices and fat in the tin. If the skin is browning too quickly, cover the bird loosely with tin foil.

4 Transfer the bird to a carving board and leave to rest for at least 15 minutes before serving. During that time, make a simple sauce or gravy with the juices in the tin if you wish.

ROASTING TIMES FOR POULTRY

Note: Cooking times given here are for unstuffed birds. For stuffed birds, add 20 minutes to the total roasting time.

Bird	Weight	Time
Poussin	450–700 g/1–1½ lb	1–1¼ hours at 180°C/350°F/Gas 4
Chicken	1.12–1.35 kg/2½–3 lb	1–1¼ hours at 190°C/375°F/Gas 5
	1.5–1.8 kg/3½–4 lb	1¼–1¾ hours at 190°C/375°F/Gas 5
	2–2.25 kg/4½–5 lb	1½–2 hours at 190°C/375°F/Gas 5
	2.25–2.7 kg/5–6 lb	1¾–2½ hours at 190°C/375°F/Gas 5
Capon	2.25–3 kg/5–7 lb	1¾–2 hours at 170°C/325°F/Gas 3
Duck	1.35–2.25 kg/3–5 lb	1¾–2¼ hours at 200°C/400°F/Gas 6
Goose	3.6–4.5 kg/8–10 lb	2½–3 hours at 180°C/350°F/Gas 4
	4.5–5.4 kg/10–12 lb	3–3½ hours at 180°C/350°F/Gas 4
Turkey (whole bird)	2.7–3.6 kg/6–8 lb	3–3½ hours at 170°C/325°F/Gas 3
	3.6–5.4 kg/8–12 lb	3–4 hours at 170°C/325°F/Gas 3
	5.4–7.2 kg/12–16 lb	4–5 hours at 170°C/325°F/Gas 3
Turkey (whole breast)	1.8–2.7 kg/4–6 lb	1½–2¼ hours at 170°C/325°F/Gas 3
	2.7–3.6 kg/6–8 lb	2¼–3¼ hours at 170°C/325°F/Gas 3

Pot-roast Chicken with Sausage Stuffing

Serves 6

2 × 1.12 kg/2½ lb chickens

30 ml/2 tbsp vegetable oil

360 ml/12 fl oz chicken stock, or half wine and half stock

1 bay leaf

For the stuffing

450 g/1 lb pork sausagemeat (ground sausage)

1 small onion, chopped

1–2 garlic cloves, finely chopped

5 ml/1 tsp hot paprika

2.5 ml/½ tsp hot pepper flakes (optional)

2.5 ml/½ tsp dried thyme

1.25 ml/¼ tsp ground allspice

45 g/1½ oz/¾ cup coarse breadcrumbs

1 egg, beaten to mix

salt and pepper

1 Preheat a 180°C/350°F/Gas 4 oven.

2 For the stuffing, put the sausagemeat (ground sausage), onion and garlic in a frying pan and fry over a moderate heat until the meat is lightly browned and crumbly, stirring and turning so that it cooks evenly. Remove from the heat and mix in the remaining ingredients with salt and pepper to taste.

3 Divide the stuffing between the chickens, packing it into the body cavities (or, if you prefer, stuff the neck end and bake the left-over stuffing separately). Truss the birds.

4 Heat the oil in a flameproof casserole just big enough to hold the chickens. Brown the birds all over.

Variation

For Pot-roast Guinea Fowl, substitute 2 guinea fowl for the chickens.

5 Add the stock and bay leaf and season. Cover and bring to a boil, then transfer to the oven. Pot-roast for 1¼ hours or until the birds are cooked (the juices will run clear).

6 Untruss the chickens and spoon the stuffing on to a serving platter. Arrange the birds and serve with the strained cooking liquid.

JOINTING POULTRY

Although chickens and other poultry are sold already jointed into halves, quarters, breasts, thighs and drumsticks, sometimes it makes sense to buy a whole bird and to do the job yourself. That way you can prepare either 4 larger pieces or 8 smaller ones, depending on the recipe, and you can cut the pieces so that the backbone and other bony bits (which you can save for stock) are not included. In addition, a whole bird is cheaper to buy than pieces. A sharp knife and sturdy kitchen scissors or poultry shears make the job of jointing poultry very easy.

SAFE HANDLING OF RAW POULTRY

Raw poultry may harbour potentially harmful organisms, such as salmonella bacteria, so it is vital to take care in its preparation. Always wash your hands, the chopping board and all cutting tools in hot soapy water before and after handling the poultry. It is a good idea to use a chopping board that can be washed at high temperature in a dishwasher and, if possible, to keep the chopping board just for the preparation of raw poultry. Thaw frozen poultry thoroughly in a refrigerator – never at room temperature, as this can breed salmonella – before cooking.

1 Using a sharp knife, cut through the skin on 1 side of the body down to the point at which the thigh joins the body. Holding the leg between your thumb and fingers, bend it out away from the body and twist it to break the ball-and-socket joint.

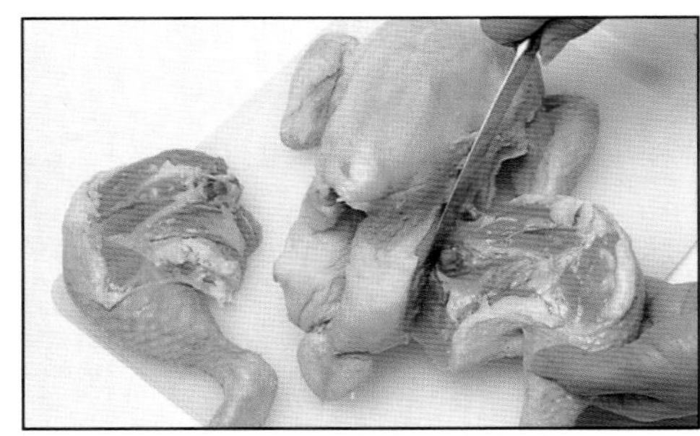

2 Hold the leg out away from the body and cut through the ball-and-socket joint, taking the 'oyster meat' from the backbone with the leg. Repeat the procedure on the other side.

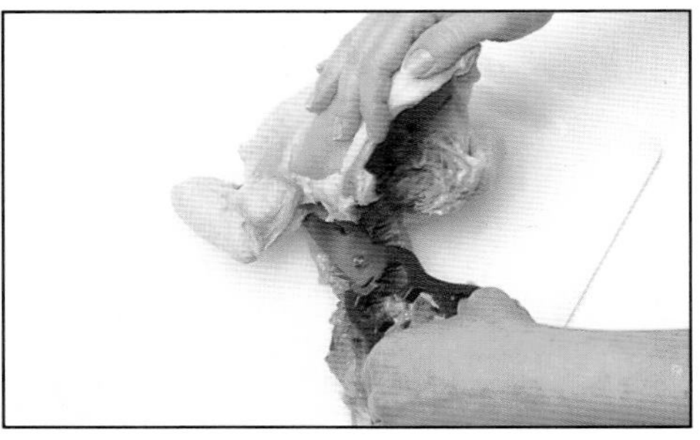

3 To separate the breast from the back, cut through the flap of skin just below the rib cage, cutting towards the neck. Pull the breast and back apart and then cut through the joints that connect them on each side. Reserve the back for making stock.

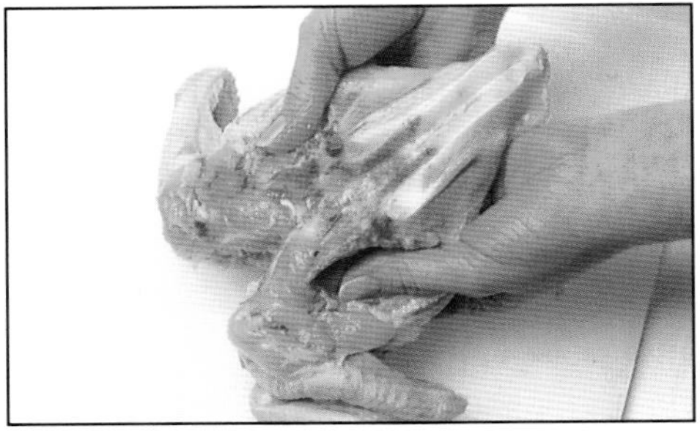

4 Turn the whole breast over, so that it is skin-side down. Take one side of the breast in each hand and bend it back firmly so that the breastbone pops free. Loosen the bone on both sides with your fingers and, with the help of the knife, remove it.

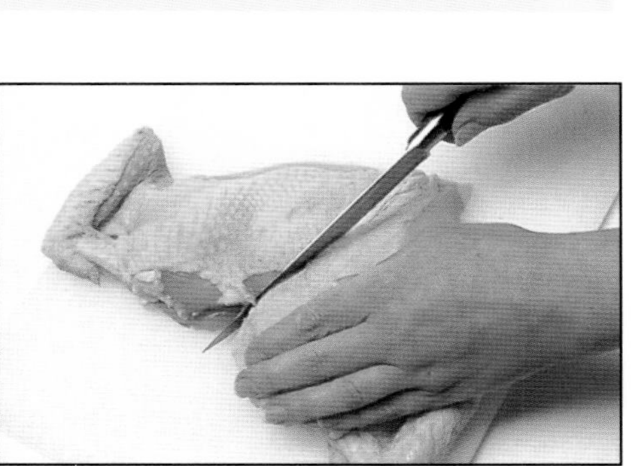

5 Cut the breast in half lengthwise, cutting through the wishbone. You will now have 2 breasts with wings attached and 2 leg portions.

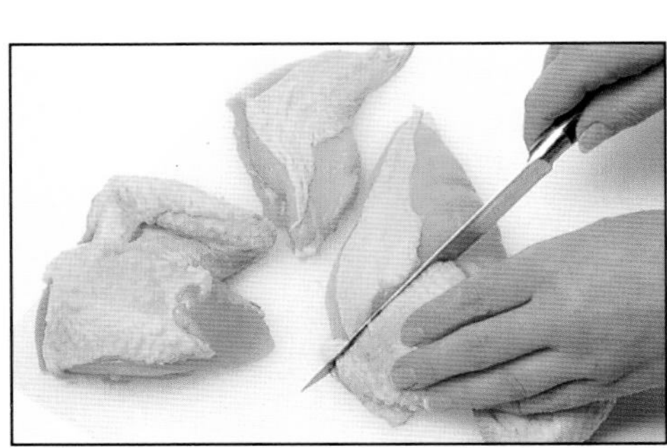

6 For 8 pieces, cut each breast in half at an angle so that some breast meat is included with a wing portion. Trim off any protruding bones.

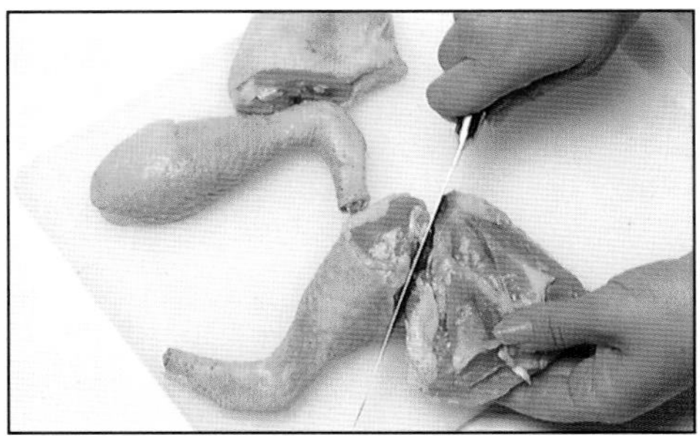

7 Finally, cut each leg portion through the ball-and-socket joint to separate the thigh and drumstick.

SIMPLE CHICKEN CURRY

SERVES 4

30 ml/2 tbsp vegetable oil

1 onion, chopped

1 green or red pepper, seeded and diced

1 garlic clove, finely chopped

20 ml/1 ½ tbsp curry powder

2.5 ml/½ tsp dried thyme

450 g/1 lb tomatoes, skinned, seeded and chopped, or canned chopped tomatoes

30 ml/2 tbsp lemon juice

120 ml/4 fl oz/½ cup water

55 g/2 oz/⅓ cup currants or raisins

salt and pepper

1 × 1.5 kg/3½ lb chicken, cut into 8 pieces and the pieces skinned

boiled rice, to serve

1 Preheat a 180°C/350°F/Gas 4 oven.

2 Heat the oil in a wide, deep frying pan that has an ovenproof handle, or in a flameproof casserole. Add the onion, diced pepper and garlic. Cook, stirring occasionally, until the vegetables are soft but not browned.

3 Stir in the curry powder and dried thyme, then add the tomatoes, lemon juice and water. Gradually bring the sauce to a boil, stirring frequently. Stir in the currants or raisins. Season to taste with salt and pepper.

4 Arrange the chicken pieces in a single layer in the pan or casserole. Turn to coat them with the sauce. Cover the pan and transfer to the oven for 40 minutes or until the chicken is tender. Turn halfway through cooking.

5 Remove the chicken and sauce to a warmed serving platter. Serve with freshly boiled rice.

VARIATION

For Curried Chicken Casserole, omit the diced pepper and cook 20 ml/ 1½ tbsp finely chopped fresh ginger and 1 green chilli, seeded and finely chopped, with the onion and garlic in a flameproof casserole. In step 3, stir in the curry powder with 450 ml/¾ pint/ ⅞ cup plain yogurt; omit the tomatoes, lemon juice and water. Add the chicken pieces, cover tightly and cook in a 170°C/325°F/Gas 3 oven for between 1–1¼ hours.

SAUTÉING AND FRYING POULTRY

A sauté combines frying and braising, producing particularly succulent results. It is a method suitable for pieces of poultry as well as for small whole birds such as quails and poussins. Be sure to dry the poultry thoroughly with paper towels before cooking to ensure that it browns quickly and evenly.

Fried chicken is justifiably popular – crisp and brown on the outside and tender and juicy within. It is a quick and easy cooking method that can also be applied to pieces of rabbit and hare, and small turkey joints. Dry the pieces thoroughly with paper towels before frying. If they are at all wet, they will not brown properly. If the recipe directs, lightly coat the pieces with egg and crumbs or with a batter.

COUNTRY-CHICKEN SAUTÉ

Cook 175 g/6 oz chopped bacon in 10 ml/2 tsp oil over a moderately high heat until lightly coloured. Remove and reserve. Dredge a 1.5 kg/3½ lb chicken, cut into 8 pieces, in seasoned flour. Fry in the bacon fat until evenly browned. Add 45 ml/3 tbsp dry white wine and 240 ml/8 fl oz/1 cup poultry stock. Bring to a boil and add 225 g/8 oz quartered mushrooms sautéed in 15 g/½ oz/1 tbsp butter and the reserved bacon. Cover and cook over low heat for 20–25 minutes, or until the chicken is tender. *Serves 4.*

MAKING POULTRY SAUTÉS

1 Heat a little oil, a mixture of oil and butter, or clarified butter (see page 154) in a heavy frying pan or sauté pan.

2 Add the poultry and fry it over a moderately high heat until it is golden brown, turning to colour evenly.

3 Add any liquid and flavourings called for in the recipe. Bring to a boil, cover and reduce the heat. Cook gently until the pieces or birds are done, turning once or twice.

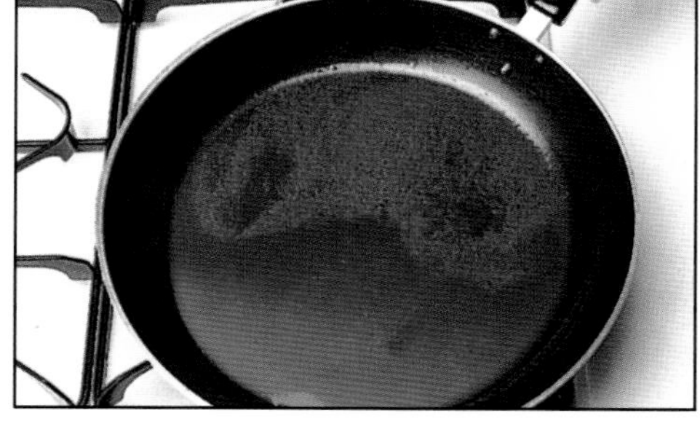

4 If the recipe instructs, remove the poultry from the pan while finishing the sauce. This can be as simple as boiling the cooking juices to reduce them, or adding cream for a richer result.

THICKENING COOKING JUICES

1 Thicken with equal weights of butter and flour mashed together, called 'beurre manié'. Use 30 g/1 oz/2 tbsp of this paste to 240 ml/8 fl oz/1 cup liquid. Whisk small pieces gradually into the boiling sauce until smooth and silky.

2 Another method of thickening cooking juices is to add 10 ml/2 tsp cornflour (cornstarch) blended with 15 ml/1 tbsp water to 240 ml/8 fl oz/1 cup liquid. Boil for 2–3 minutes, whisking constantly, until the sauce is syrupy.

Pan-frying Poultry

1 Heat oil, a mixture of oil and butter, or clarified butter (see page 154) in a large, heavy-based frying pan over a moderate heat. When the oil is very hot, put in the poultry pieces, skin-side down. Do not crowd them or they will not brown; cook in batches if necessary.

2 Fry until deep golden brown all over, turning the pieces so that they colour evenly. Fry until all the pieces are thoroughly cooked. Remove pieces of breast before drumsticks and thighs (dark meat takes longer to cook than white meat). Drain on paper towels.

Deep-frying Poultry

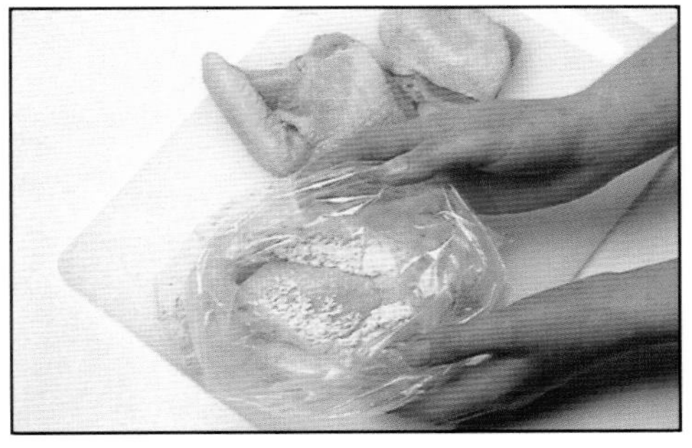

1 Dip the pieces into a mixture of milk and beaten egg, then coat lightly with seasoned flour; leave to 'set' for 20 minutes before frying. Alternatively, coat with a batter before frying.

2 Half-fill a deep pan with vegetable oil. Heat it to 185°C/365°F. You can test the temperature with a cube of bread: if it takes 50 seconds to brown, the oil is at the correct temperature.

3 Using a fish slice (spatula) or tongs, lower the poultry pieces into the oil, a few at a time, without crowding them. Deep-fry until they are golden brown all over and cooked. Turn them so that they colour evenly.

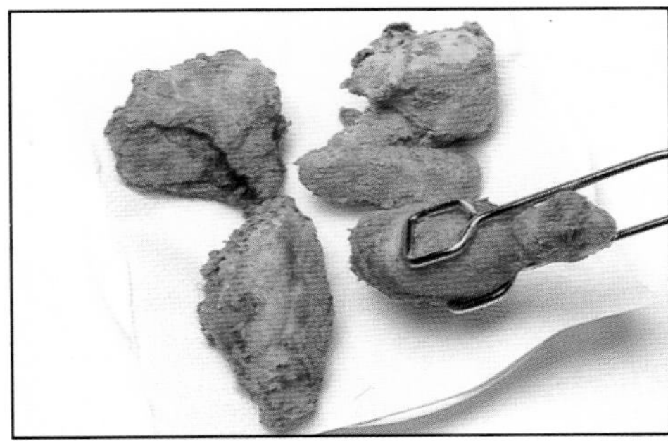

4 Drain on paper towels and serve hot. If you want to keep a batch of fried poultry hot while you fry the rest, put it into a low oven, but don't cover it or it will become soggy.

Succulent Fried Chicken

Mix 240 ml/8 fl oz/1 cup milk with 1 beaten egg in a shallow dish. On a sheet of greaseproof (waxed) paper, combine 145 g/5 oz/1¼ cups plain (all-purpose) flour, 5 ml/1 tsp paprika, and some salt and pepper. One at a time, dip 8 chicken pieces in the egg mixture and turn them to coat all over. Then dip in the seasoned flour and shake off any excess. Deep-fry for 25–30 minutes, turning the pieces so they brown and cook evenly. Drain on paper towels and serve very hot. *Serves 4.*

Grilling (Broiling) Poultry

If you prefer to cook poultry without using oil or butter, grilling (broiling) is a good alternative. Small birds can be 'spatchcocked' by removing the backbone, flattening out the bird and securing it with skewers. Cook whole birds or large pieces 10–15 cm (4–6 in) from the heat, or thinner pieces nearer the heat. If the poultry browns too quickly, turn the heat down slightly.

Fish and Seafood

PREPARING FISH FOR COOKING

Most fish have scales, and you should remove these before cooking unless you are going to fillet the fish or remove the skin before serving. Fish sold by fishmongers will normally be scaled as well as cleaned (eviscerated or gutted), but you can do this yourself, if necessary. Trimming the tail gives a whole fish a neat appearance.

Round fish and large flat fish such as halibut are often cut into steaks and cutlets for cooking. Steaks are cut from the tail end of the fish, while cutlets are cut from the centre. They are usually cut about 2.5–4cm/1–1½in thick.

Fillets are boneless pieces of fish, and for this reason are very popular. A sharp filleting knife, with its thin, flexible blade, is the tool to use for removing the fillets. Be sure to keep all the bones and trimmings for making stock. Round fish are easy to fillet and they produce a boneless piece from each side. Large flat fish are filleted slightly differently from round fish and yield 4 narrow fillets – 2 from each side.

Before cooking, dark or tough skin is usually removed from fish fillets. If you salt your fingers, you will get a better grip on the tail end so that you can hold the skin taut as you cut. If you are going to grill (broil) fish fillets, however, do not remove the skin as it will help to keep the shape.

All fish preparation is best done in or near the sink, with cool water running.

Preparing Whole Fish

1 **To scale**: Grasp the tail firmly and scrape off the scales using a special fish scaler or a knife, working from the tail towards the head. Rinse the fish well. Repeat on the other side.

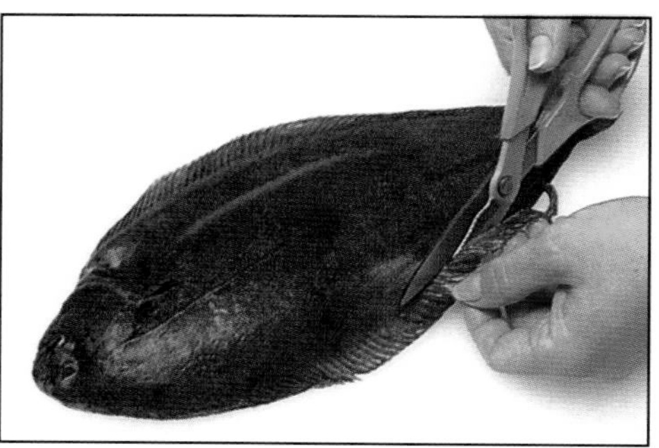

2 **To trim**: For flat fish to be cooked whole, use kitchen scissors to trim off the outer half of the small fin bones all round the fish.

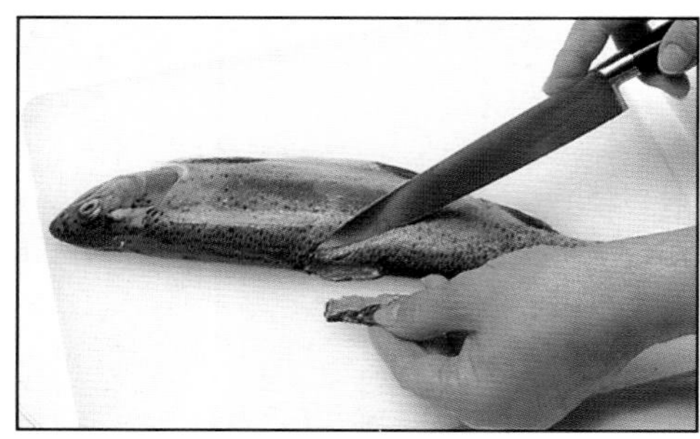

3 For round fish, cut the flesh on both sides of the anal and dorsal (back) fins and pull them out; the small bones attached will come out too. Trim off the other fins. If you intend to cook the fish whole, leave the fins on, or just trim them, because they will help to keep the shape of the fish.

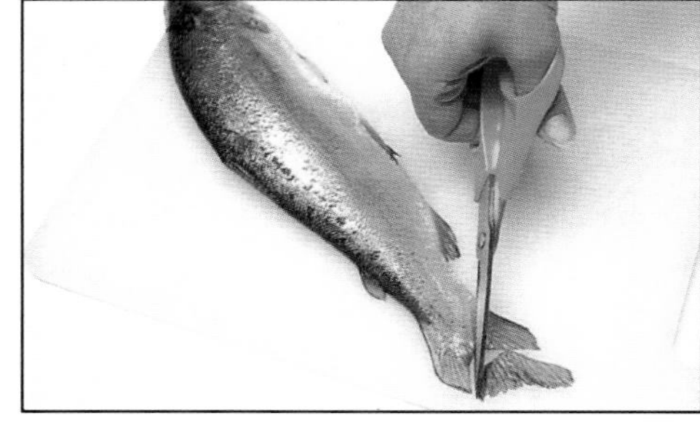

4 **To trim the tail**: If you are leaving the tail on, cut a neat V-shape in the centre with scissors. The fish is now ready for cooking.

Cutting Fish Steaks and Cutlets

1 Using a large, sharp knife, slice the fish across, at a right-angle to the backbone, into slices of the desired thickness.

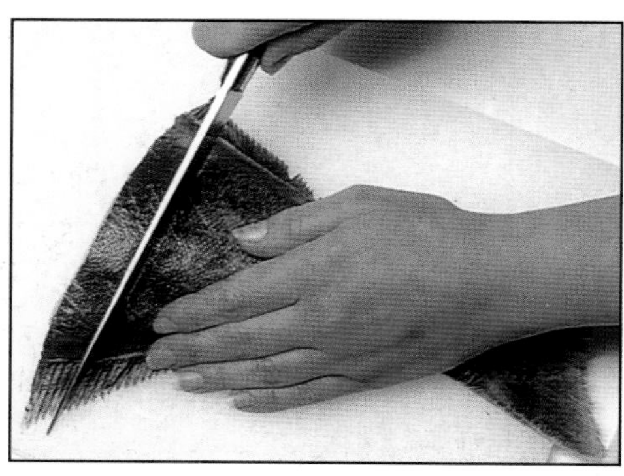

2 If necessary, cut through the backbone using kitchen scissors or a knife with a serrated blade.

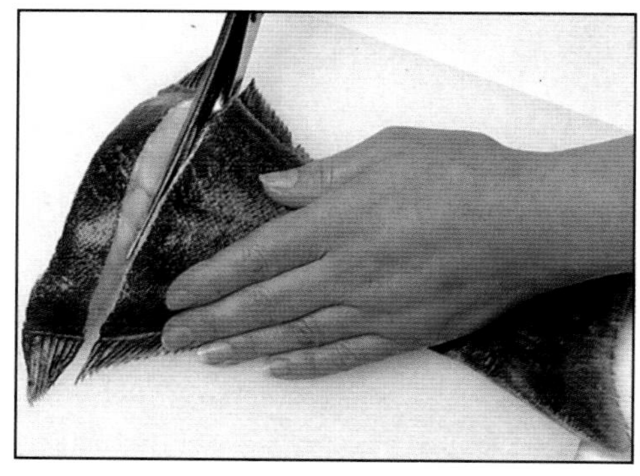

Cutting Fish Fillets

1 To fillet a round fish: Lay the fish flat, on its side. First cut off the head. Using the tip of a filleting knife, cut through the skin all along the length of the backbone.

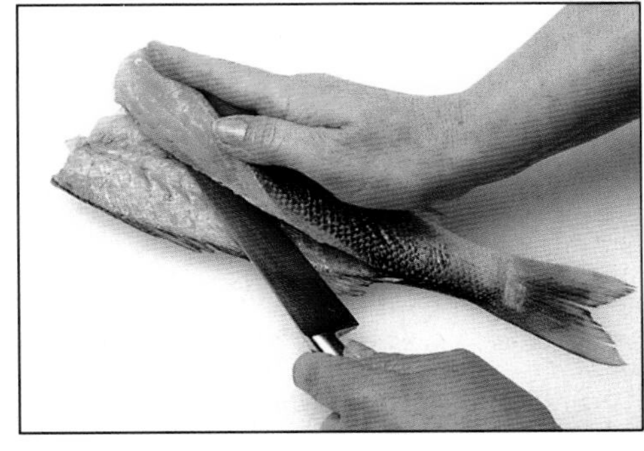

2 Working from head to tail and holding the knife almost parallel to the fish, use short strokes to cut 1 fillet off the rib bones. Follow the slit cut along the backbone. At the tail, cut across to release the fillet. Repeat on the other side to remove the second fillet.

Filleting Small Flat Fish

You can take 2 fillets from smaller flat fish (1 from each side). To do this, cut behind the head and down the sides of the fish as described for filleting flat fish, but do not make the central cut. Starting from the head end on one side and working down the fish, cut the flesh away from the rib bones until you reach the centre (the backbone). Rotate the fish and repeat on the other side to cut away the whole fillet. Turn the fish over and repeat.

3 Run your fingers over the flesh side of each fillet to locate any stray bones. Use a pair of tweezers to pull them out.

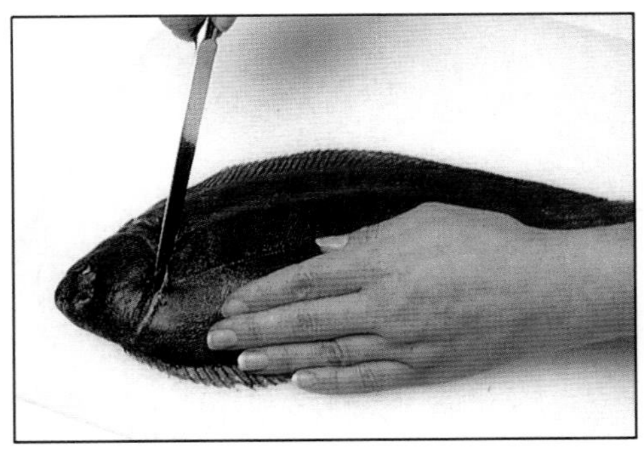

4 To fillet a flat fish: Lay the fish flat and make a curved cut behind the head, cutting down to but not through the backbone. Using the tip of the knife, slit the skin down both sides of the fish where the fin bones meet the rib bones, 'outlining' the fillets, and slit across the tail.

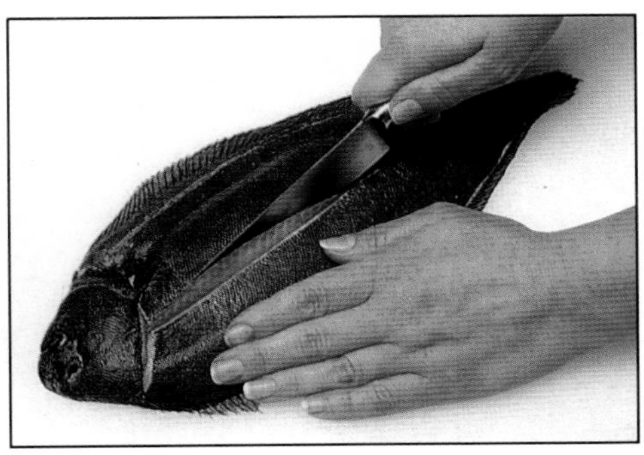

5 Slit straight down the centre line of the fish, from head to tail, cutting down to the backbone. Working from the centre at the head end, cut 1 fillet neatly away from the rib bones on 1 side. Hold the knife blade almost parallel to the fish as you do this and use short strokes.

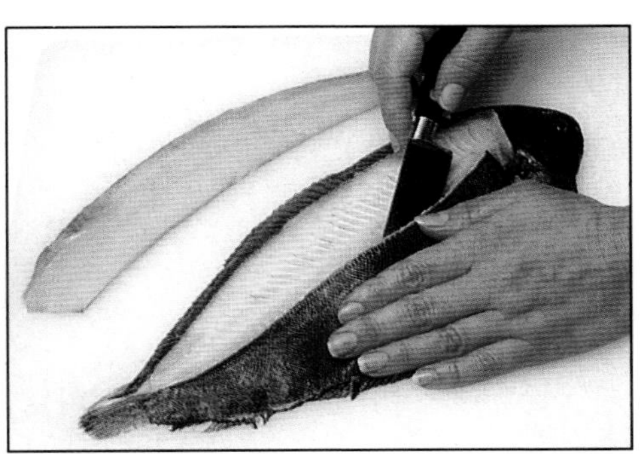

6 Rotate the fish and cut away the second fillet. Turn the fish over and repeat to remove the 2 fillets on the other side. Pull out any stray bones using a pair of tweezers.

Skinning Fish Fillets

1 Lay the fillet flat, skin-side down, with the tail end towards you. Make a small crosswise cut through the flesh down to the skin at the tail end.

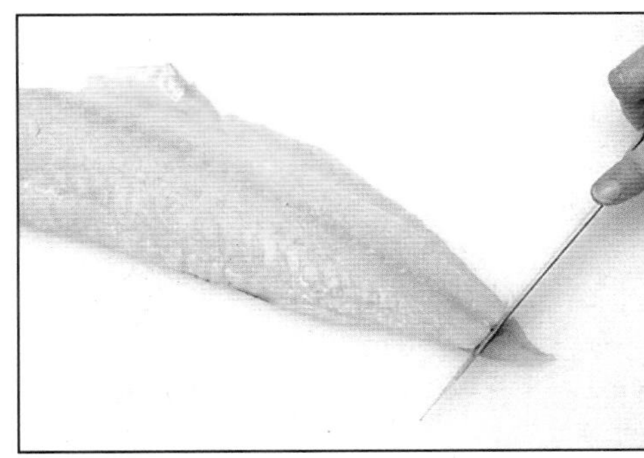

2 Grip the skin and insert the knife blade so that it is almost parallel to it, then cut away the fillet. Use a gentle sawing motion and make a continuous cut.

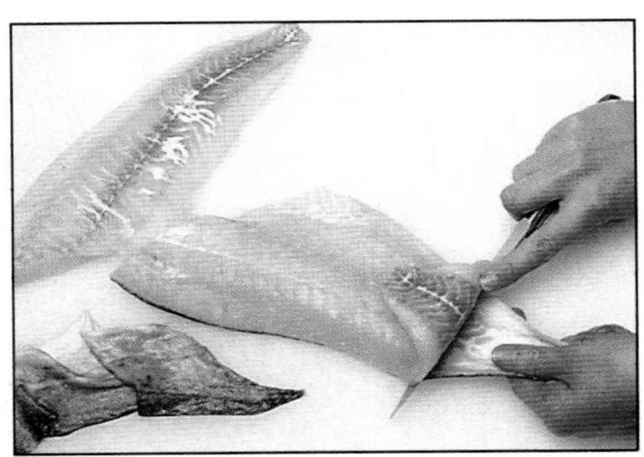

POACHING FISH

Whole fish, large and small, as well as fillets, cutlets and steaks, are excellent poached because the gentle cooking gives succulent results. Poached fish can be served hot or cold, with a wide variety of sauces. The poaching liquid may be used as the basis for the sauce.

POACHING CONTAINERS

A long, rectangular fish kettle with a perforated rack will enable you to lift the fish out of the liquid after cooking. You could also use a large wire rack set in a deep tin (pan).

1 **To oven-poach small whole fish, fillets, cutlets or steaks**: Place the fish in a buttered flameproof dish large enough to hold the pieces comfortably. Pour in enough liquid to come two-thirds of the way up the side of the fish.

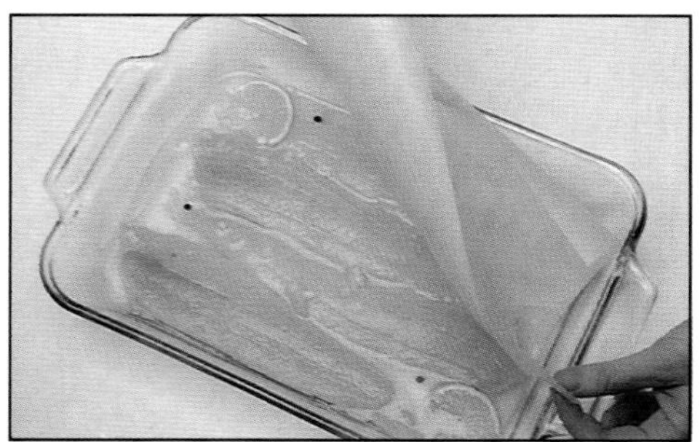

2 Add any flavourings called for in the recipe. Press a piece of buttered greaseproof (waxed) paper on top to keep in the moisture without sticking to the fish.

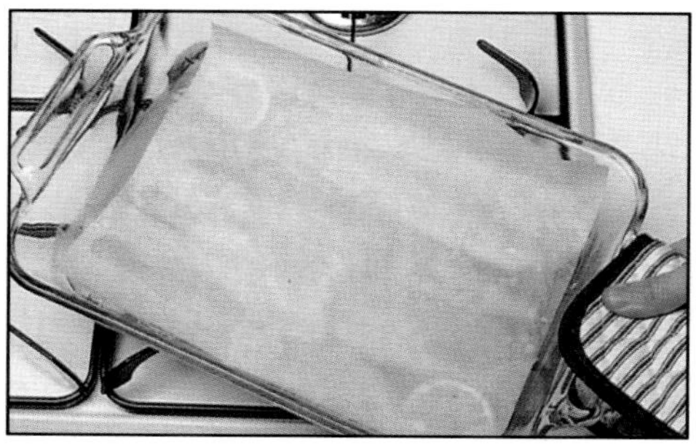

3 Set the dish over a moderate heat and bring the liquid just to a boil. Transfer the dish to a 180°C/350°F/ Gas 4 oven and poach until the fish is just cooked. To test this, make a small cut into the thickest part of the fish using the tip of a sharp knife: the flesh should be slightly translucent.

4 **To poach whole fish, fillets, cutlets or steaks on top of the stove**: Put large whole fish on the rack in a fish kettle, or set on muslin (cheesecloth) used like a hammock. Poach small whole fish, fillets, cutlets and steaks in a fish kettle on a rack, or set them directly in a wide saucepan or frying pan.

5 Prepare the poaching liquid (salted water, milk, wine or stock) in the fish kettle or in a large casserole, or in a wide saucepan or frying pan for fillets, cutlets and steaks. Set the rack in the kettle, or the muslin hammock in the casserole. Add more liquid, if necessary, so that it covers the fish.

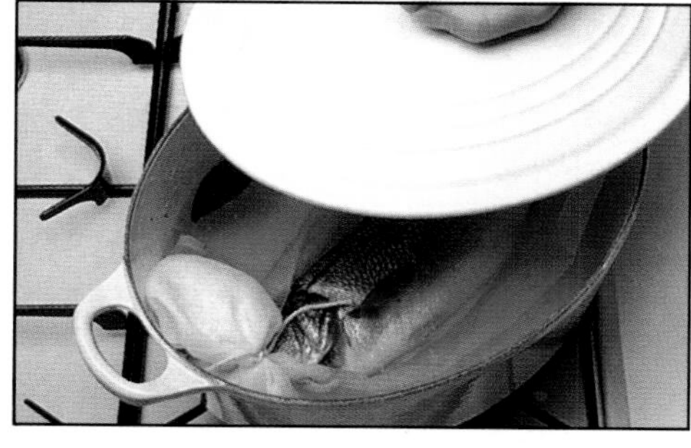

6 Cover the kettle or casserole and bring the liquid just to a boil. Reduce the heat and simmer very gently until the fish is cooked.

POACHED SOLE FILLETS

Oven-poach 8 skinless sole fillets, about 700 g/1½ lb, each 1.5 cm/½ in thick. Use 300 ml/½ pint/1¼ cups dry white wine or fish stock with 4–6 chopped spring onions (scallions), 4–6 lemon slices and a few allspice berries for flavouring. Simmer for 3–5 minutes, then remove the fish. Boil the cooking liquid until reduced to 60 ml/ 4 tbsp, then strain it. Season with salt and pepper. *Serves 4.*

BAKED FISH STUFFED WITH CRAB

SERVES 4

4 streaky (lean) bacon rashers
30 g/1 oz/2 tbsp butter
55 g/2 oz spring onions (scallions), chopped
1 large celery stalk, diced
grated zest of 1 large lemon
15 ml/1 tbsp chopped fresh parsley
30 g/1 oz/½ cup crumbs made from day-old French or Italian bread
salt and pepper
170–225 g/6–8 oz white crabmeat
1 egg, beaten to mix
4 whole fish such as trout or red snapper, 340–450 g/¾–1 lb each, scaled if necessary, gutted and boned for stuffing

1 Preheat a 190°C/375°F/Gas 5 oven.

2 Fry the bacon rashers in the butter in a frying pan until crisp. Drain on paper towels. Chop the bacon.

3 Pour off all but 15 ml/1 tbsp of the fat from the frying pan into a small bowl and reserve. Brush a little reserved fat over the bottom of a baking dish or roasting tin (pan) that is large enough to accommodate the fish comfortably, then set aside.

4 Heat the fat still in the frying pan and cook the spring onions (scallions) and celery, stirring occasionally, for 5–7 minutes or until soft.

5 Mix together the vegetables, lemon zest, parsley, breadcrumbs, salt and pepper. Fold in the crabmeat and bacon. Bind with the egg.

6 Open up each fish like a book, skin-side down. Spread the stuffing over one half. Pack it down firmly, then fold over the fish and press down gently. Close the opening with cocktail sticks (toothpicks), if you wish.

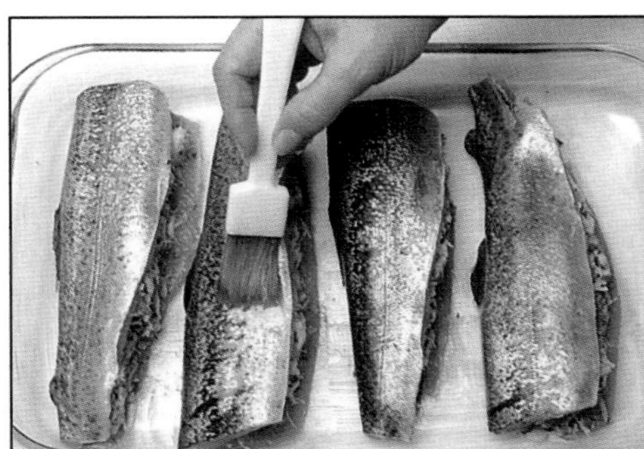

7 Set the fish in the prepared baking dish or roasting tin. Brush the tops of the fish with a little of the reserved fat. Bake for about 25–30 minutes or until the fish is cooked.

8 Using a fish slice (slotted spoon), carefully transfer the fish to warmed serving plates and serve immediately.

PREPARING PRAWNS (SHRIMP)

Prawns (shrimp) can be cooked in their shells, and are often presented in this way as an appetizer or garnish for a salad. More often, however, they are peeled first (the shells can be used to make an aromatic stock). The black intestinal vein that runs down the back is removed from large prawns mainly because of its appearance, although the vein may also contain grit which makes it unpleasant to eat.

Prawns in shells are sold with their heads still on. These are easily pulled away from the bodies, and can be used to enhance the flavour of stock made with the discarded shells.

1 Holding the prawn (shrimp) firmly in 1 hand, pull off the legs with the fingers of your other hand. Pull off the head above the legs.

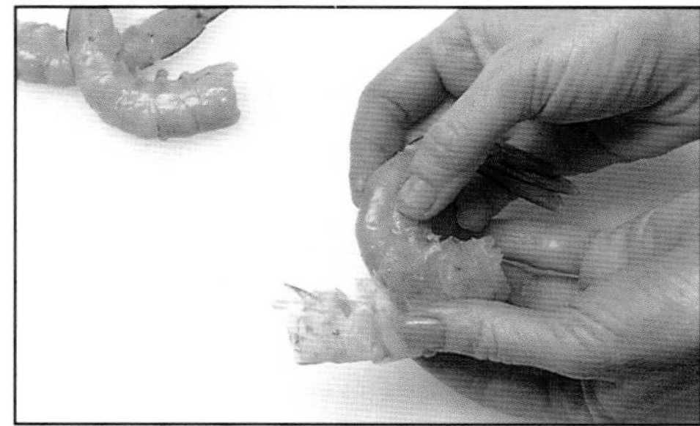

2 Peel the shell away from the body. When you reach the tail, hold the body and pull away the tail; the shell will come off with it. Alternatively, you can leave the tail on the prawn and just remove the body shell.

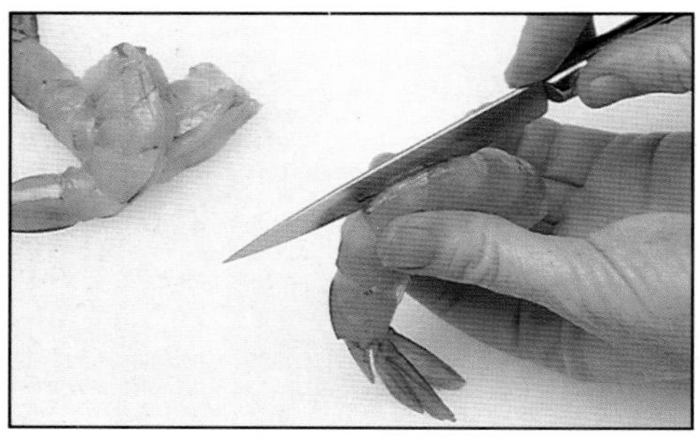

3 Make a shallow cut down the centre of the curved back of the prawn. Pull out the black vein, using a cocktail stick (toothpick) or your fingers.

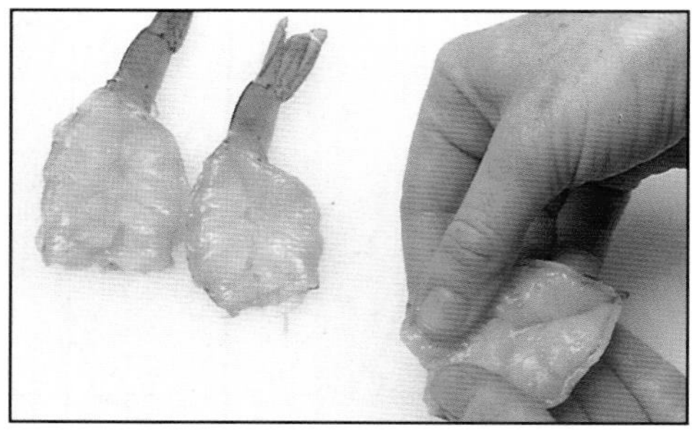

4 **To butterfly prawns**: Cut along the de-veining slit to split open the prawn, without cutting all the way through. Open up the prawn flat.

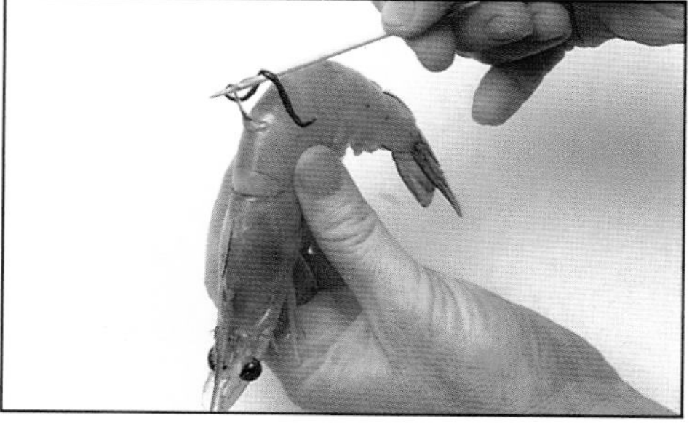

5 **To de-vein prawns in the shell**: Insert a cocktail stick crosswise in several places along the back where the shell overlaps, and lift out the vein.

SPICY BUTTERFLIED TIGER PRAWNS (SHRIMP)

SERVES 4–6

90 ml/6 tbsp olive oil
75 ml/5 tbsp orange juice
60 ml/4 tbsp lime juice
1 large garlic clove, finely chopped
5 ml/1 tsp allspice berries, crushed
1.25 ml/¼ tsp hot chilli flakes
salt and pepper
900 g/2 lb raw tiger or king prawns (shrimp), peeled, de-veined and butterflied
lime wedges, to serve

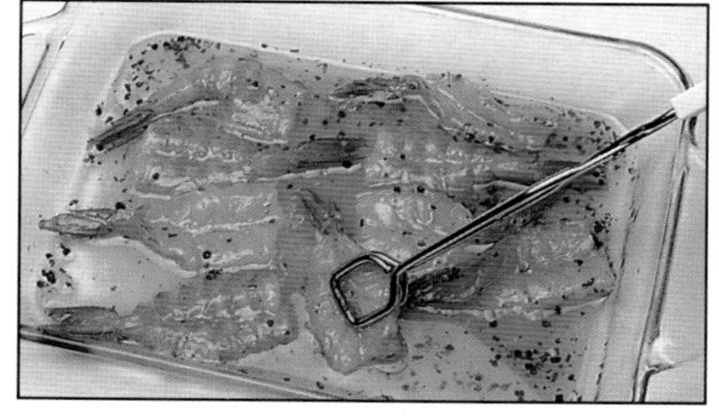

1 Combine the oil, fruit juices, garlic, allspice, chilli flakes and seasoning in a large, shallow baking dish. Add the prawns (shrimp) and turn to coat completely with the spiced oil.

2 Cover the dish and leave to marinate for 1 hour at room temperature, or for at least 2 hours in the refrigerator.

3 Preheat a grill (broiler).

4 Spread out the prawns in one layer in the baking dish, arranging them cut-side up as much as possible. Grill (broil) about 10 cm/4 in from the heat for 6–8 minutes or until the flesh becomes opaque. There is no need to turn them.

5 Serve hot, with lime wedges.

Scallops Wrapped in Parma Ham (Prosciutto)

Serves 4

24 medium-sized scallops, without corals (roes), prepared for cooking

lemon juice

8–12 slices of Parma ham (prosciutto), cut lengthwise into 2 or 3 strips

olive oil

freshly ground black pepper

red-pepper strips and basil sprigs, to serve

1 Preheat a grill (broiler) or prepare a charcoal fire.

2 Sprinkle the scallops with lemon juice. Wrap a thin strip of Parma ham (prosciutto) around each scallop. Thread on to 8 skewers.

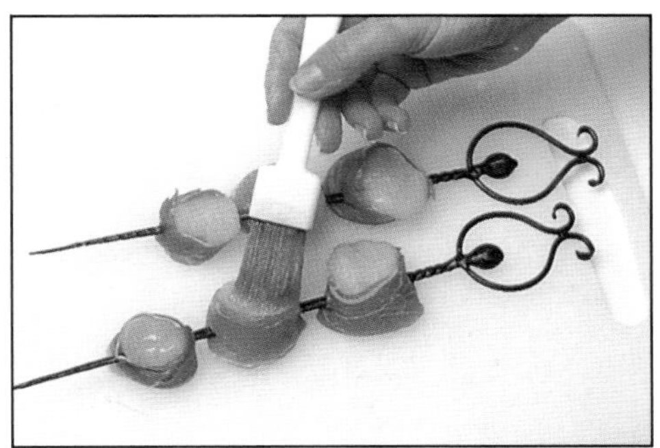

3 Brush with oil. Arrange on a baking sheet if grilling (broiling). Grill about 10 cm/4 in from the heat, or cook over charcoal, for 3–5 minutes on each side or until the scallops are opaque.

4 Set 2 skewers on each plate. Sprinkle the scallops with freshly ground black pepper and serve garnished with red-pepper strips and sprigs of fresh basil.

PREPARING SCALLOPS

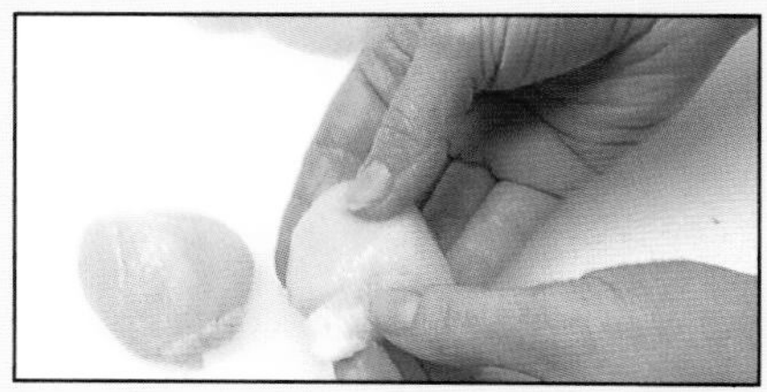

If the scallops are still in their shells, use a short, sturdy knife to pry them open. Discard the membrane and dark organs. Set the red-orange corals (roes) aside. Pull off and discard the small piece of gristle from the side of the white meat. Rinse well.

BELOW LEFT Spicy Butterflied Tiger Prawns (Shrimp); BELOW Scallops Wrapped in Parma Ham (Prosciutto).

PREPARING AND COOKING VEGETABLES

To enjoy their full flavour, fresh vegetables are often best prepared and served in simple ways. These guidelines for vegetable preparation and cooking will help you to make the most of seasonal bounty.

Serving ideas include suggested amounts of raw prepared vegetable to serve per person. Season all dishes according to taste.

ROOTS AND BULBS

Carrots

Preparation: If carrots are young, just trim the ends and scrub well; peel larger carrots. Leave whole or cut as specified in the recipe.

Cooking: *To boil*, drop into boiling salted water and simmer until just tender: 8–10 minutes for whole baby carrots, 10–20 minutes for larger whole carrots, 4–10 minutes for sliced or grated carrots. *To steam*, cook whole baby carrots, covered, over boiling water for about 10 minutes. *To braise*, cook whole baby carrots or thinly sliced carrots with 45 ml/3 tbsp stock or water and 30 g/1 oz/2 tbsp butter per 450 g/1 lb, tightly covered, for about 5 minutes. Boil, uncovered, to evaporate excess liquid before serving.

Serving ideas (115 g/4 oz each)

- Dress hot carrots with butter and chopped fresh herbs.
- Add a little sugar or honey and a squeeze of lemon or orange juice when braising; or try spices such as nutmeg, ginger or curry powder.
- Serve raw carrot sticks with a dip.

Parsnips

Preparation: Trim and peel. Leave small parsnips whole; cut up large ones.

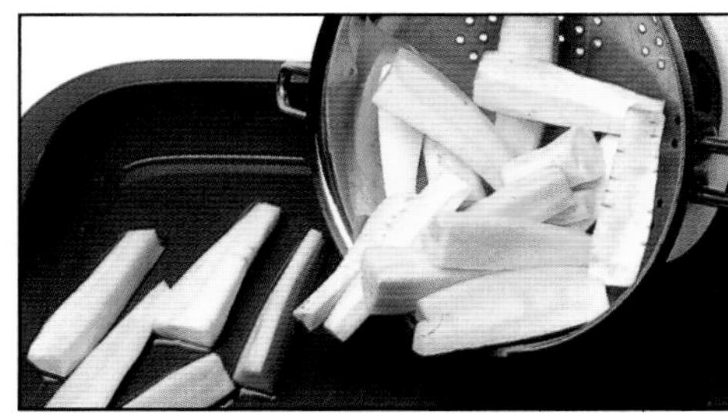

Cooking: *To roast*, blanch in boiling salted water, then put in a roasting tin (pan) with butter or oil and cook in a 200°C/400°F/Gas 6 oven for about 40 minutes. Baste occasionally. *To boil*, simmer in salted water for 5–10 minutes. *To fry*, blanch in boiling water for 1–2 minutes and drain. Fry in butter for 10–12 minutes.

Serving ideas (145 g/5 oz each)

- Sauté sliced parsnips with sliced carrots; sprinkle with chopped herbs.
- Bake 600 g/1¼ lb parsnips with 150 ml/¼ pint/⅔ cup orange juice and 45 g/1½ oz/3 tbsp butter, covered, in a 180°C/350°F/Gas 4 oven for 1 hour.

Swede (Rutabaga)

Preparation: Peel, removing all tough skin and roots. Cut as recipe specifies.

Cooking: *To boil*, simmer chunks or slices in salted water for 15 minutes or until tender. *To braise*, cook with 30 g/1 oz/2 tbsp butter and 75 ml/5 tbsp stock or water per 450 g/1 lb, covered, for 5–7 minutes. *To roast*, put chunks around meat and coat with fat. Roast at 200°C/400°F/Gas 6 for 45 minutes.

Serving ideas (145 g/5 oz each)

- Braise 600 g/1¼ lb grated swede (rutabaga) seasoned with 15 ml/1 tbsp brown sugar and 5 ml/1 tsp soy sauce.
- Mash 600 g/1¼ lb boiled swede; beat in 2 eggs, 60 ml/4 tbsp cream, 30 ml/2 tbsp flour and 1.25 ml/¼ tsp nutmeg. Bake in a buttered dish in a 180°C/350°F/Gas 4 oven for 30 minutes.

Potatoes

Preparation: If the potato skins will be eaten, scrub them well. Otherwise, peel potatoes.

Cooking: *To bake*, prick skins and bake in a 200°C/400°F/Gas 6 oven: 1–1½ hours or 30–40 minutes for sweet potatoes. *To boil*, put into cold salted water, bring to a boil, and simmer for 10–20 minutes. *To roast*, blanch for 1–2 minutes and drain. Put around meat in a roasting tin (pan) and roast for 1–1½ hours. *To sauté*, boil until partly cooked, then fry slices in butter until crisp. *To deep-fry* (chips), cut into sticks, soak in cold water for 30 minutes and drain. Fry in oil heated to 190°C/375°F until beginning to colour: 3–7 minutes. Drain, then fry again for 3 minutes until golden.

Serving ideas (170 g/6 oz each)

- Dress boiled new potatoes with butter and chopped parsley and mint.
- Mash boiled or baked sweet potatoes. Add butter to taste, orange juice to moisten and ground cinnamon.

Onions

Preparation: Peel off the papery skin, then slice, chop, etc. as the recipe specifies. For spring onions (scallions), trim the root end and cut off any wilted or discoloured green leaves. Cut as specified, using just the white bulbs or both white and green parts.

Cooking: *To fry*, cook chopped or sliced onions, uncovered, in butter and/or oil over moderate heat, stirring occasionally, for about 5 minutes or until soft and translucent. If directed, continue cooking until the onions are golden brown. *To slow-cook*, cook sliced or chopped onions, covered, in butter and/or oil over low heat, stirring occasionally, for about 30 minutes or until very soft and golden. *To boil* small onions, drop into a pan of boiling salted water and simmer for about 15–20 minutes or until tender.

Serving ideas

- Top hamburgers or steaks with slow-cooked sliced onions.
- Combine 450 g/1 lb boiled button (pearl) onions with 45 g/1½ oz/3 tbsp butter and 70 g/2½ oz/5 tbsp soft light brown sugar; cook over a low heat, stirring, for about 10 minutes or until the sugar has caramelized.
- Trim all but 5 cm/2 in of green from spring onions (scallions). Stir-fry in hot oil and sprinkle with soy sauce.
- Use thin slices of sweet red onions raw in salads.

Leeks

Preparation: Trim the root end and the dark green leaves, leaving just the pale green and white. (Save the dark green leaves for the stockpot.) Unless you are going to cook the leeks whole, slit them open lengthwise, to the centre. Put them in cold water and soak for about 20 minutes, then drain well. If slicing or chopping leeks, do this before rinsing them thoroughly under cold water.

Cooking: *To braise,* cook with 30 g/1 oz/2 tbsp butter and 75 ml/5 tbsp stock or water per 450 g/1 lb, tightly covered, until just tender. *To boil*, drop into boiling salted water or stock and simmer for 10–15 minutes or until tender. *To steam*, cook in a covered steamer over boiling water, allowing approximately 5–7 minutes for sliced or whole baby leeks.

Serving ideas (170 g/6 oz each)

- Boil whole leeks, then cool slightly. Marinate in a vinaigrette dressing; serve the leeks cool, not cold.
- Toss hot sliced leeks with butter and fresh herbs such as sage, tarragon, thyme or parsley.

FRUITING VEGETABLES

Aubergines (Eggplant)

Preparation: Trim off the stalk end. Leave whole or cut according to the recipe instructions.

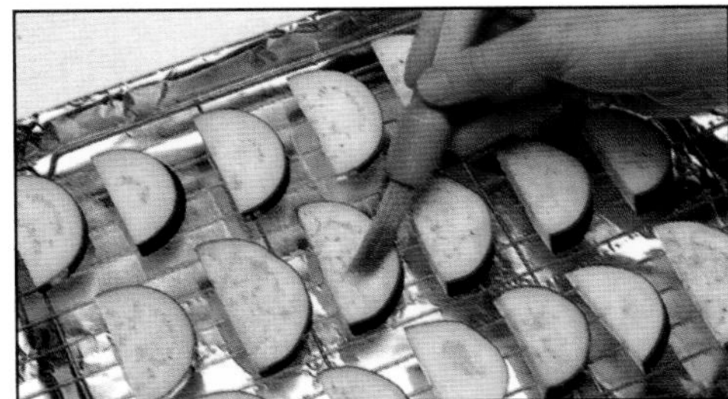

Cooking: *To grill (broil)*, brush cut surfaces with oil. Grill, 7.5–10 cm/3–4 in from the heat, for 10 minutes or until tender and well-browned; turn once and brush with oil. *To fry*, coat slices or thick sticks with flour if recipe specifies, then fry in hot oil or butter for 5 minutes on each side or until golden. *To braise*, brown slices or wedges in a little hot oil, add 60 ml/4 tbsp stock or water per 450 g/1 lb, cover and cook for 12 minutes or until tender. *To bake*, prick whole aubergines all over with a fork. Bake in a 200°C/400°F/Gas 6 oven for about 20 minutes or until soft.

Serving ideas (145 g/5 oz each)

- Baste grilled aubergines (broiled eggplant) with garlic- and herb-flavoured olive oil.
- When braising aubergines, after browning add skinned, seeded and chopped tomatoes and basil.

Courgettes (Zucchini)

Preparation: Trim the ends from courgettes (zucchini). Cut as specified.

Cooking: *To fry*, cook sliced courgettes in butter or oil for 5–10 minutes or until tender and golden brown. *To boil*, drop into boiling salted water and simmer until tender: 10–12 minutes for whole courgettes, 3–8 minutes for slices. *To steam*, cook in a covered steamer over boiling water until tender. *To braise*, cook sliced courgettes in a covered pan, with 30 g/1 oz/2 tbsp butter and 75 ml/5 tbsp stock or water per 450 g/1 lb, for 4–5 minutes or until tender.

Serving ideas (115–145 g/4–5 oz each)

- Sauté sliced courgettes (zucchini) with finely chopped garlic and chopped fresh parsley and oregano.
- Cut small courgettes in half lengthwise and spread the cut surfaces with wholegrain mustard. Grill (broil) 10 cm/4 in from the heat for about 5 minutes or until tender but still firm.

PREPARING AND COOKING VEGETABLES (continued)

LEAFY, GREEN AND OTHER VEGETABLES

Spinach

Preparation: Spinach can hide a lot of grit, so it needs careful rinsing. Immerse in cold water, swish round and soak for 3–4 minutes. Lift out the spinach and immerse in fresh cold water, repeat, then drain. Pull off tough stalks.

Cooking: *To steam-boil*, put into a large pan with no extra water. Cook for 5–7 minutes, stirring occasionally to help evaporate the liquid. Drain well and press the spinach between two plates or squeeze it in your fist. *To braise*, cook, covered, with a large knob of butter until wilted. Uncover and boil to evaporate excess liquid. *To stir-fry*, cook small or shredded leaves in hot oil for 3–5 minutes or until wilted.

Serving ideas (145–175 g/5–6 oz each)

- Add 30–45 ml/3–4 tbsp double (heavy) or whipping cream and mix a generous pinch of grated nutmeg into braised spinach.
- Steam-boil spinach leaves; chop finely after draining. Fry in olive oil with chopped garlic, stirring, until the garlic just starts to turn golden.
- Combine equal parts of chopped cooked spinach and cooked rice with butter and seasoning to taste.

Green beans

Preparation: Top and tail using scissors or a knife. For older beans with strings, snap off the ends, pulling the strings from the sides as you do so. Cut large beans diagonally or into slivers.

Cooking: *To boil*, drop into boiling salted water and simmer until just tender but still crisp and bright green: 3–15 minutes, according to size. *To steam*, cook in a covered steamer over boiling water until tender. *To braise*, cook tightly covered, with about 75 ml/5 tbsp stock or water and 30 g/1 oz/2 tbsp butter per 450 g/1 lb, until tender. *To stir-fry*, blanch in boiling water for 2 minutes; drain, refresh and dry. Stir-fry in hot oil for 2–3 minutes.

Serving ideas (115 g/4 oz each)

- Dress boiled or steamed beans with melted butter, chopped herbs and a squeeze of lemon juice.
- Add 90 ml/6 tbsp cream to 450 g/1 lb braised beans. Cook uncovered, stirring, until the liquid has reduced and the beans are glazed.

Peas

Preparation: If green peas are in the pod, split the pods open and pop out the peas. Top and tail mange-tout (snow peas) and sugar-snap peas, and pull any tough strings from the sides.

Cooking: *To steam*, cook in a covered steamer over boiling water until tender. *To boil*, drop into boiling salted water and simmer until tender: 5–10 minutes for peas, 1–2 minutes for mange-tout. *To braise*, cook covered, with 30 g/1 oz/2 tbsp butter and 60 ml/4 tbsp stock or water per 450 g/1 lb, until tender: 5–10 minutes for green peas, 2 minutes for mange-tout and sugar-snap peas.

Serving ideas (115 g/4 oz each)

- Add sliced spring onions (scallions), shredded lettuce and a little sugar when braising green peas.
- Stir-fry mange-tout (snow peas) with sliced onions and mushrooms.
- Add 60 ml/4 tbsp whipping cream to 450 g/1 lb braised sugar-snap peas and cook uncovered, stirring, until almost all the liquid has evaporated.

Broccoli

Preparation: Trim off the end of the stalk. According to recipe instructions, leave the head whole or cut off the florets, taking a little stalk with each one. Cut the remainder of the peeled stalk across into thin slices.

Cooking: *To steam*, cook in a covered steamer over boiling water until tender. *To boil*, drop into boiling salted water and simmer until just tender: 7–12 minutes for whole, 4–6 minutes for florets and stalks. *To braise*, cook covered, with 75 ml/5 tbsp stock or water and 30 g/1 oz/2 tbsp butter per 450 g/1 lb, until tender.

Serving ideas (145 g/5 oz each)

- Toss hot broccoli with butter mixed with chopped fresh herbs.
- Cover hot broccoli with a cheese

sauce, sprinkle with grated Parmesan and brown under a grill (broiler).

- Blanch small broccoli florets for 1 minute; drain and refresh. Serve cold dressed with vinaigrette and sprinkled with toasted nuts.

Cauliflower

Preparation: Cut away the large green leaves. Trim the stalk level with the head. Cut out the core. Leave the head whole, or break into florets before or after cooking.

Cooking: *To steam*, cook florets in a covered steamer over boiling water for 12–15 minutes. *To steam-boil*, place core-down in a pan with 2.5 cm/1 in boiling salted water and a bay leaf. Cover and cook until just tender: 15–30 minutes for whole heads, 5–9 minutes for florets. Drain well. *To braise*, cook florets covered, with 30 g/1 oz/2 tbsp butter and 75 ml/5 tbsp stock or water per 450 g/1 lb, for 5–7 minutes.

Serving ideas (145 g/5 oz each)

- Dress hot cauliflower with butter; sprinkle with chopped fresh chives, toasted flaked almonds or chopped pecan nuts, or paprika.
- Coat florets in egg and crumbs, then deep-fry and serve with mayonnaise flavoured with garlic or a little Worcestershire sauce and a dash of Tabasco sauce.

Cabbage

Preparation: Discard any wilted or discoloured outer leaves. Cut the heads into small wedges or halve long, loose heads. Cut out the stalk from the wedges before cooking, or quarter heads and shred them. Leave loose heads whole and cut across the leaves to shred.

Cooking: *To braise*, quickly blanch chopped or shredded green, Savoy or red cabbage. (There is no need to blanch Chinese leaves.) Cook tightly covered, with about 75 ml/5 tbsp stock or water and 30 g/1 oz/2 tbsp butter per 450 g/1 lb, allowing 3–4 minutes for green, Savoy and Chinese leaves and 30 minutes for red cabbage (use more liquid). *To boil*, drop into boiling salted water and simmer until just tender: 6–8 minutes for wedges and 3–5 minutes for shredded green, Savoy or Chinese leaves. *To steam*, cook in a covered steamer over boiling water until tender.

Serving ideas (115 g/4 oz each)

- Blanch larger outer leaves of green or Savoy cabbage, then roll them up around a minced-meat stuffing and simmer in a rich tomato sauce.
- Add sliced apples, cooked diced bacon and spices (cinnamon, nutmeg) when braising red cabbage.
- Use shredded Chinese leaves raw in tossed salads.

Brussels sprouts

Preparation: Remove any discoloured leaves. Cut an 'X' in the base of the stalk so that it will cook in the same time as the rest.

Cooking: To *braise*, put in a pan, with 75 ml/5 tbsp stock or water and 30 g/1 oz/2 tbsp butter per 450 g/1 lb. Cover tightly for cooking. *To boil*, drop into boiling salted water and simmer for 7–10 minutes or until just tender but not soft. *To steam*, cook in a covered steamer over boiling water for about 10–12 minutes.

Serving ideas (115–145 g/4–5 oz each)

- Toss with butter and orange zest and serve immediately.
- Toss with toasted nuts, braised or poached chestnuts or some canned water chestnuts.
- Shred and blanch for 2–3 minutes; drain and refresh in cold water. Add chopped onion and celery and toss with a vinaigrette dressing.
- Cut the heads in half lengthwise and blanch in boiling water for about 2–3 minutes, then drain and refresh in cold water. Stir-fry in hot oil with a little finely chopped ginger and garlic for about 2–3 minutes or until tender and lightly browned.

CAULIFLOWER CHEESE

Cut a large cauliflower into florets and steam until just tender. Spread in a buttered gratin dish and scatter over 85 g/3 oz sliced, fried mushrooms. Pour 600 ml/1 pint cheese sauce (see page 168) evenly over the top and sprinkle with a mixture of grated Cheddar and fine breadcrumbs. Brown quickly under a hot grill (broiler). *Serves 4.*

PREPARING ASPARAGUS

When asparagus is young and tender, you need do nothing more than trim off the ends of the stalks before cooking. However, larger spears, with stalk ends that are tough and woody, require some further preparation.

COOKING UPRIGHT

Asparagus spears can be cooked loose and flat in simmering water (as described below) or they can be tied into bundles and cooked standing upright in a tall pot. With the latter method, the tips are kept above the water so they cook gently in the steam.

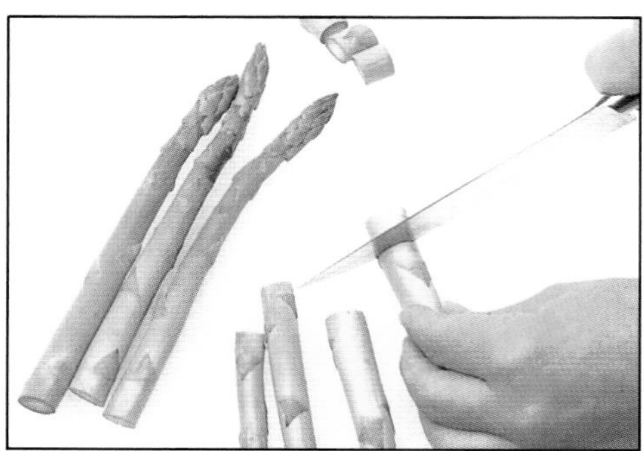

1 Cut off the tough, woody ends. Cut the spears so that they are all roughly the same length.

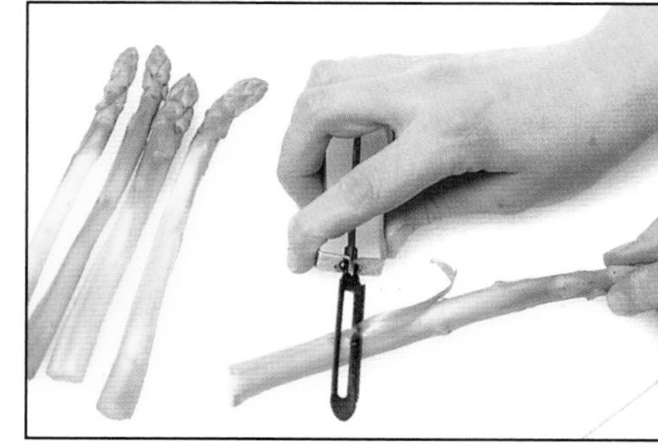

2 If you like, remove the skin. To do this, hold a spear just below the tip. Using a vegetable peeler, shave off the skin, working lengthwise to the end of the stalk. Roll the spear so that you can remove the skin from all sides.

ASPARAGUS WITH HAM

SERVES 4

700–900 g/1 ½–2 lb medium-sized asparagus spears, prepared for cooking

180 ml/6 fl oz/¾ cup clarified butter (see below right)

10 ml/2 tsp lemon juice

30 ml/2 tbsp chopped spring onions (scallions)

15 ml/1 tbsp chopped parsley

salt and pepper

4 slices Parma ham (prosciutto)

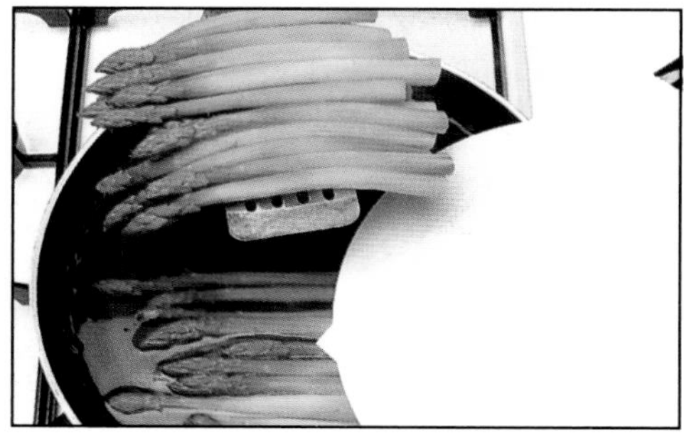

1 Half-fill a frying pan with salted water. Bring to a boil. Simmer asparagus spears for 4–5 minutes or until they are just tender. (Pierce the stalk to test.) Remove and drain well.

2 Combine the butter, lemon juice, spring onions (scallions) and parsley in a small saucepan. Season with salt and pepper to taste. Gently heat the mixture until it is lukewarm.

3 Divide the asparagus among 4 warm plates. Drape a slice of ham over each portion. Spoon over the herb butter and serve.

CLARIFIED BUTTER

Put the butter in a heavy saucepan over a low heat. Melt gently. Skim off all the froth from the surface. You will then see a clear yellow layer on top of a milky layer. Carefully pour the clear fat into a bowl. Discard the milky residue.

SKINNING AND SEEDING TOMATOES

Some tomatoes have fairly tough skins and seeds. During cooking, these can become separated from the flesh and can spoil both the appearance and the texture of a dish. In addition, some people find tomato skins indigestible, so it is often desirable to remove them for that reason. In these cases, unless you are intending to sieve a soup, sauce or other dish before serving it, it is best to skin and seed the tomatoes before using them in a recipe.

If the tomatoes have tender skins and they will be eaten raw, or only briefly cooked, removing the peel is less essential. However, many people prefer to skin tomatoes for eating raw as well.

1 **To skin tomatoes**: Cut a small cross in the skin at the base of each tomato. Immerse, 3 or 4 at a time, in boiling water. Once the cut skin begins to roll back, in about 10 seconds, lift the tomatoes out and immerse in iced water. Drain and peel.

2 **To seed tomatoes**: Cut out the core, then cut each tomato in half across (around the 'equator'). Gently squeeze each half in turn and shake the seeds and juice into a bowl. Scrape out any remaining seeds, using a dessertspoon or table knife.

SPICY-TOMATO BARBECUE SAUCE

SERVES 6

30 ml/2 tbsp vegetable oil
1 onion, finely chopped
1 garlic clove, finely chopped
300 ml/½ pint/1¼ cups passata (sieved tomatoes)
225 g/8 oz tomatoes, skinned, seeded and chopped
120 ml/4 fl oz/½ cup cider vinegar
15 ml/1 tbsp Worcestershire sauce
70 g/2½ oz/5 tbsp soft light brown sugar
10 ml/2 tsp chilli powder, or to taste
1 bay leaf
few drops of mesquite liquid smoke flavouring (optional)
salt and pepper

1 Heat the oil in a saucepan, add the onion and cook until soft, stirring occasionally. Stir in the garlic and cook for 30 seconds. Add the passata (sieved tomatoes), tomatoes, vinegar, Worcestershire sauce, brown sugar, chilli powder, bay leaf and liquid smoke, if using. Season to taste.

2 Bring to a boil, reduce the heat, and simmer for 15 minutes, stirring from time to time. Taste and adjust the seasoning, if necessary.

3 Use as a basting sauce for grilled (broiled) or barbecued hamburgers, chicken, spare-ribs and steak. Serve extra sauce to accompany the food.

PREPARING SALAD GREENS

Crisp, fresh green and variegated leaves are very appetizing, as well as being healthy. Use them as the background for a vegetable, fish, meat or fruit salad or make the leaves the focus.

It is vital that you rinse all salad leaves thoroughly with cold water to remove any grit or insects, as well as residues of sprays. Just as important is to dry the salad leaves well so that the dressing will not be diluted.

Lettuce

The four main types are: crisphead, with solid heads of tightly packed, crisp leaves (iceberg); butterhead, with looser heads of soft-textured leaves (round, 'quattro stagioni'); Cos and romaine (Boston), with elongated heads of crisp leaves; and looseleaf, with leaves that do not form a compact head ('feuilles de chêne', 'lollo rosso').

Preparation: Discard wilted or damaged leaves. Twist or cut out the central core. Rinse the leaves thoroughly in cold water and soak briefly to draw out any grit. Drain and blot or spin dry.

Chicory and Endive

These have an appealing bitterness. 'Frisée' or curly endive has fine, frilly green leaves with a coarse texture. Escarole has broader, fleshier leaves with a firm texture. The slim leaves of chicory are white with greenish tips. Radicchio is red Italian chicory.

Preparation: Core the base of chicory. Discard wilted or damaged leaves. Rinse thoroughly and dry the leaves.

Lamb's Lettuce

Also known as corn salad or 'mâche', this salad green has a pleasantly firm, chewy texture and mild flavour.

Preparation: Remove any wilted or damaged leaves. Trim roots. Rinse well, as the leaves can be sandy.

RINSING AND CRISPING SALAD GREENS

Put the leaves in cold water and swirl them round to wash off any dirt or insects. Leave to settle for 1–2 minutes. Lift the leaves out of the water on to a tea (dish) towel and pat dry. Wrap loosely in a clean tea towel and put in a plastic bag. Refrigerate for 1 hour.

Rocket (Arugula)

This member of the mustard family has a pungent peppery, nutty taste. The deep green leaves have a texture similar to that of spinach.

Preparation: Discard any wilted or damaged leaves. Pull off the roots. Rinse thoroughly and dry on paper towels – a salad spinner could bruise the tender leaves.

Watercress

Another member of the mustard family, the round dark green leaves have a wonderful peppery flavour that will enliven any salad.

Preparation: Discard any discoloured, wilted or damaged leaves and snap off thick stalks. Rinse well and spin dry, or dry on paper towels.

Green Salad with Oranges and Avocado

Serves 4

1 round lettuce
1 small bunch of watercress
a few leaves of frisée lettuce
1 small bunch of rocket (arugula)
1 red onion, thinly sliced into rings
2 seedless oranges, peeled and segmented
1 ripe avocado, peeled, stoned (pitted) and cubed
55 g/2 oz/½ cup walnut pieces, toasted

For the dressing

90 ml/6 tbsp olive oil
15 ml/1 tbsp walnut oil
45 ml/3 tbsp lemon juice
30 ml/2 tbsp orange juice
5 ml/1 tsp grated orange zest
5 ml/1 tsp Dijon mustard
pinch of caster (superfine) sugar
salt and pepper

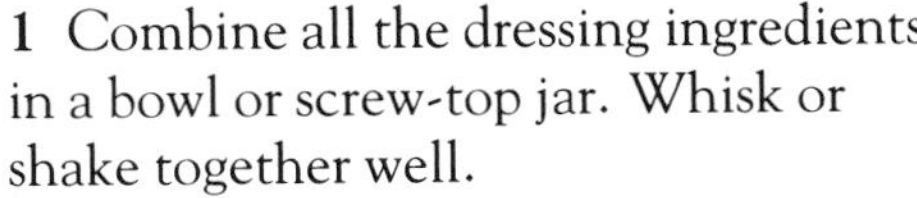

1 Combine all the dressing ingredients in a bowl or screw-top jar. Whisk or shake together well.

2 Put the rinsed and crisped salad greens in a bowl and add the onion, orange segments and avocado.

3 Add the dressing and toss the salad to combine well. Scatter the walnuts on top and serve immediately.

VARIATION

For Green Salad with Tuna and Peppers, omit the oranges and walnut pieces. Add 1 × 200 g/7 oz can drained, flaked tuna and 1 roasted red pepper, peeled and sliced.

PREPARING FRESH FRUIT

Fresh fruit presented in unusual ways can make a table look very attractive, and will be a real talking point at a party. The ideas shown here take very little time to carry out.

Pineapples, for example, can be prepared in many decorative ways in addition to rings, spears and cubes.

Melons make attractive containers for salads, both sweet and savoury. Small melons can be used for individual servings, while large watermelons will hold salads to serve a crowd. Special tools, including melon cutters and melon-ball scoops, make decorative preparation easier.

Sorbets and fruit ices are most refreshing desserts. A fruit ice is made by freezing a sweetened fruit purée, whereas a sorbet is made from fruit juice or purée mixed with a sugar syrup. In addition, there are sorbets based on wine or liqueur. The Italian 'granita' uses the same mixture as a sorbet, but it is stirred during freezing to give it its characteristic coarse texture.

WATERMELON BASKET

Cut a watermelon basket as directed on the right, but leave a strip for the 'handle'. Scoop out the flesh using a melon-ball scoop and nick out the pips. Mix the melon balls with balls of charentais and honeydew melon, blueberries and strawberries. Pile the fruit into the basket.

MAKING PINEAPPLE BOATS

1 Trim off any browned ends from the green leaves of the crown. Trim the stalk end if necessary. Using a long, sharp knife, cut the pineapple in half lengthwise, through the crown. Cut a thin slice from the base of each half so that it has a flat, stable surface and will not rock about.

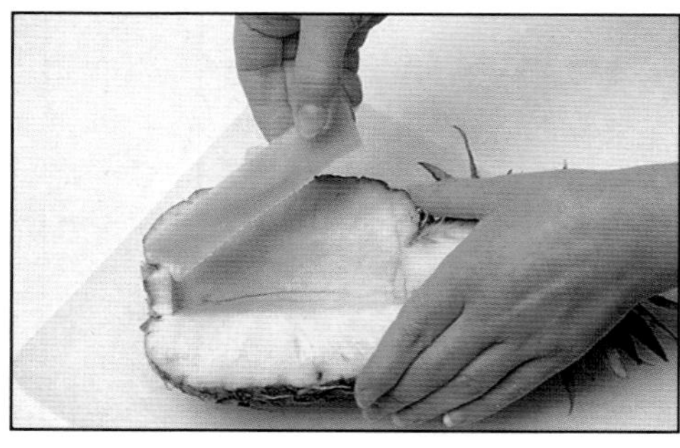

2 Using a small, sharp knife, cut straight across the top and bottom of the central core in each half, then cut lengthwise at a slant on either side of the core. Remove the core.

3 Using a curved, serrated grapefruit knife, cut out the flesh from each half. The boats are now ready for filling with a salad, a dessert, or with ice cream, fruit ice or sorbet.

PREPARING MELON

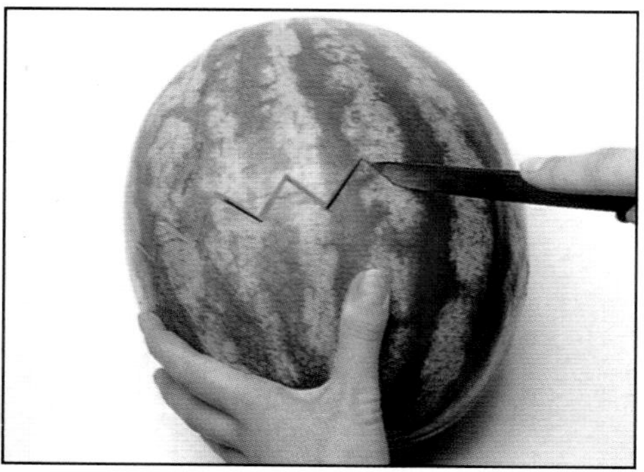

1 Cut a line around the circumference of the melon and insert a sharp knife on the line at an angle. Make a cut 1.5–5 cm/½–2 in long, according to the size of the melon, right into the centre. Insert the knife again at the top of the angled cut, and cut back to the line at a right-angle, forming a V-shape.

2 Continue in this way all round the melon, then lift the 2 halves apart. Remove the seeds and scoop out the flesh.

Making a Fruit Ice

1 Prepare the fruit, removing peel, stones (pits), hulls, stalks, etc. Purée the fruit with sugar and liquid in a blender or food processor until very smooth. Be sure that the sugar has dissolved completely.

2 Add additional flavourings as directed in the recipe (alcohol or herbs, for example). If using berries with seeds (raspberries, blackberries, etc.), press the purée through a fine-mesh nylon sieve. Chill the purée well. Transfer to an ice-cream machine and freeze following the maker's instructions.

Making a Sorbet

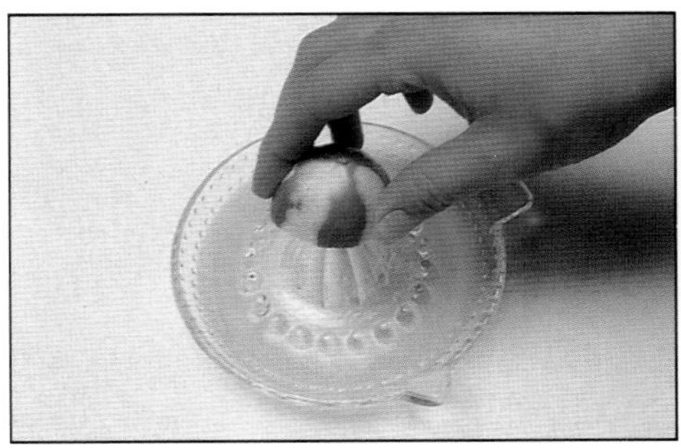

1 If you are using citrus fruit, peel off strips of zest. Squeeze the juice from the fruit. Alternatively, purée fruit in a blender or food processor (cooking it first if necessary).

2 Put the strips of zest (or other flavouring such as a vanilla pod or spices) in a saucepan with sugar and water and bring to a boil, stirring to dissolve the sugar. Leave to cool.

3 Stir in the fruit juice or purée. Strain the mixture into a bowl, if necessary, and chill well. Transfer the mixture to an ice-cream machine and freeze following the maker's instructions.

Still-Freezing Fruit Ice

If you do not have an ice-cream machine, you can 'still-freeze' the fruit ice or sorbet in the freezer. Pour it into a metal tin (pan) or tray, cover and freeze until set round the edge. Turn it into a bowl and break it into small pieces. Beat with an electric mixer or in a food processor until slushy. Return to the tin and freeze again until set round the edge. Repeat the beating twice more, then freeze until firm.

Strawberry Ice

Purée 500 g/1 lb 2 oz strawberries with 100 g/3½ oz caster (superfine) sugar and 120 ml/4 fl oz/½ cup orange juice. Be sure the sugar has dissolved completely. Add 15 ml/1 tbsp lemon juice. Taste the mixture and add more sugar or orange or lemon juice if required. (The mixture should be highly flavoured.) Chill well, then transfer to an ice-cream machine and freeze until firm. *Makes about 600 ml/1 pint.*

Variations

- Use raspberries or blackberries instead of strawberries, or, as another idea, 700 g/1½ lb peeled and sliced peaches or nectarines.
- Add 15–30 ml/1–2 tbsp of fruit liqueur (to match the fruit used).

BOILING, POACHING AND SCRAMBLING EGGS

The derisive expression, 'can't boil an egg', indicates the importance of this basic cooking skill, although, to be accurate, eggs are in fact simmered rather than boiled.

For many people, a boiled egg with toast is an everyday breakfast. But the soft-boiled egg and its cousin the coddled egg have many delicious applications. If you are going to peel them for serving, cook them for the longest time suggested below. The salt in the cooking water aids in peeling. Hard-boiled eggs can be used to make classic salads and sandwich fillings, as well as cold first course and buffet dishes and hot main dishes.

The perfect poached egg has a neat oval shape, a tender white and a soft yolk. It is unbeatable on a slice of hot buttered toast, or it can be partnered with vegetables (artichoke hearts, asparagus), seafood (crab, smoked salmon) or meat (ham, bacon, steak) and dressed with a rich sauce. Use the freshest eggs possible because they will be the easiest to poach.

Tender, creamy scrambled eggs are perfect for breakfast or brunch, but you can also add flavourings for a more unusual snack or supper dish.

IDEAS FOR SOFT-BOILED AND CODDLED EGGS

- For *Caviar-crowned Eggs*: cut the top 20mm/¾in from each egg, in its shell. Put a spoonful of soured (sour) cream on top, followed by a little caviar, for an exotic taste.
- For *Smoked-salmon Eggs*: prepare as above and top each egg with a spoonful each of soured cream and diced smoked salmon.
- Put a hot peeled egg in the centre of a bowl of cream-of-spinach or watercress soup to give it extra richness and flavour.

BOILING EGGS

1 **To hard-boil eggs**: Bring a pan of well-salted water to a boil. Using a slotted spoon, lower each egg into the water. Reduce the heat so that the water is just simmering. Cook for 10 minutes. Immediately plunge the eggs into a bowl of iced water to cool.

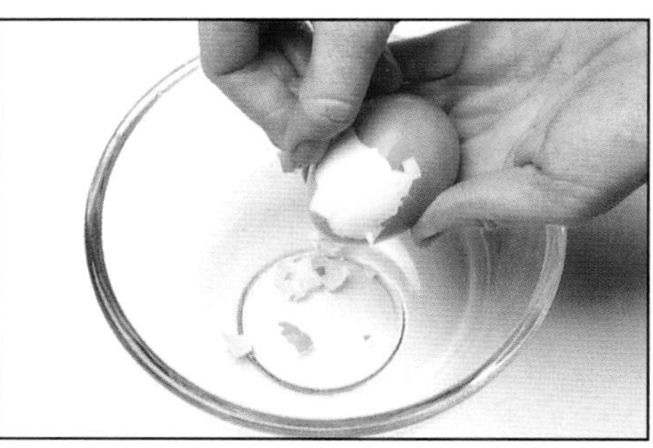

2 When the eggs are cool enough to handle, peel them. If you do not intend to use them immediately, keep the peeled eggs in a bowl of cold, salted water. Alternatively, store the eggs, still in their shells, in the refrigerator; they will keep for up to a week.

3 **To coddle eggs**: Lower them into a pan of boiling salted water. Cover the pan and remove it from the heat. Leave for 6–8 minutes or until the eggs are done to your taste. Lift out each egg, place in an egg cup and cut off the top of the shell for serving. Alternatively, to peel, plunge the eggs into a bowl of cold water. When they are cool enough to handle, peel carefully.

4 **To soft-boil eggs**: Bring a pan of well-salted water to a boil. Using a slotted spoon, lower in each egg. Reduce the heat so that the water just simmers. Cook for 3–5 minutes or until the eggs are done to your taste (depending on how firm you like the white; the yolk will be runny).

EGG MAYONNAISE

Chop several hard-boiled eggs. Mix with chopped spring onions (scallions) and chopped parsley to taste. Bind with mayonnaise. Season with mustard.

HARD-BOILED-EGG TIPS

- Always cool hard-boiled eggs in iced water. The abrupt temperature change helps to prevent a grey layer from forming round the yolk.
- To peel hard-boiled eggs, tap them on a hard surface to crack the shell. Peel under cold running water.

EGG, POTATO AND BEAN SALAD

Bring a pot of salted water to a boil. Add 450 g/1 lb small, unpeeled new potatoes. Bring back to a boil and simmer for 10 minutes. Add 225 g/8 oz green beans and simmer for 4–5 minutes or until the potatoes and beans are just tender. Drain well in a colander and refresh under cold running water. Turn the vegetables into a large bowl. Sprinkle 60 ml/4 tbsp olive oil and 30 ml/2 tbsp balsamic vinegar over them. Season with salt and pepper to taste and toss well. Scatter 2 grated hard-boiled eggs and 45 ml/3 tbsp coarsely shredded mixed fresh mint and basil over the top. Serve the salad warm or at room temperature. *Serves 4–6.*

POACHING EGGS

1 Bring a large, deep pan of water to a gentle boil. Break each egg and slip into the water. Reduce the heat to low so that the water just simmers. Poach for 3–4 minutes or until the eggs are cooked to your liking.

2 Using a slotted spoon, lift out each egg and press it gently; the white should feel just firm to the touch but the yolk should still be soft.

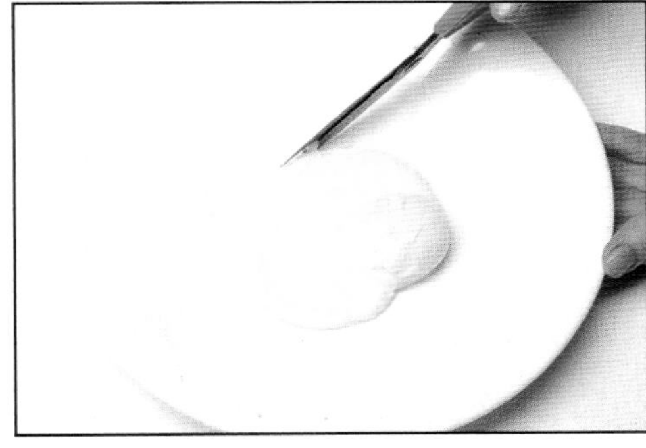

3 If there are any strings of cooked egg white, trim them off with a knife or kitchen scissors. Drain briefly on paper towels. Serve immediately, if wished, or warm the eggs in a bowl of hot water for serving. If the eggs will be served cold, immerse them in a bowl of iced water until ready to serve. Drain and gently blot dry before serving.

THE CLOTTING FACTOR

If your eggs are not really fresh, adding white-wine vinegar to the poaching water will help the egg white to coagulate, although it will flavour the egg slightly. Use 30 ml/2 tbsp vinegar to 1 litre/2 pints water.

SCRAMBLING EGGS

1 Put the eggs in a bowl and add a little salt and pepper. Beat the eggs with a fork until they are well blended. Melt butter in a frying pan over a moderately low heat (there should be enough to cover the bottom of the pan fairly generously). Pour in the beaten eggs.

2 Cook, scraping up and turning the eggs over, for 3–5 minutes or until they are softly set and still moist. The eggs will continue to cook after being removed from the heat, so undercook them slightly even if you prefer a firmer end result.

IDEAS FOR ENLIVENING SCRAMBLED EGGS

- Add chopped fresh herbs (chives, tarragon) to the eggs.
- Cook diced vegetables (onions, mushrooms, peppers) or ham in butter before adding the eggs.
- Stir in a little grated cheese or bits of full-fat soft cheese just before the eggs are ready.
- Fold some peeled, cooked prawns (shrimp) into scrambled eggs.

MAKING ROLLED OMELETTES AND SOUFFLÉS

The versatile rolled or folded omelette can be served plain or filled with a range of ingredients. There are also flat omelettes and soufflé omelettes. At its simplest, an omelette is made with 2 or 3 eggs, 5–10 ml/1–2 tsp water, and salt and pepper.

Despite their reputation as tricky, soufflés are not difficult to make. The base for a soufflé is simply a thick sauce (sweet or savoury) or a purée. Into this, stiffly whisked egg whites are folded, and the whole is baked until it has risen and is lightly set. Proper preparation of the dish, enabling the soufflé to 'climb' up the sides, will encourage good rising. Generously butter or oil the dish, including the top edge. If the recipe specifies, coat the bottom and sides with a thin layer of fine crumbs, sugar, etc., before adding the mixture. Serve the soufflé as soon as it is cooked.

IDEAS FOR OMELETTES

- Add 15 ml/1 tbsp chopped fresh herbs (a mixture of parsley, chives and tarragon, for example) to the beaten-egg mixture.
- Scatter 30–45 ml/2–3 tbsp grated cheese (Gruyère, Cheddar) over the omelette before folding it.
- Sauté skinned, seeded and chopped tomatoes in butter for 1–2 minutes. Season and stir in a little chopped fresh basil. Use to fill the omelette.
- Fill the omelette with strips of cooked ham or Parma ham (prosciutto), roasted vegetables, sautéed sliced mushrooms, sautéed potatoes, buttered asparagus tips or slow-cooked onions.
- Warm left-over pasta (buttered or in sauce); if the shape is long, such as spaghetti, cut it into short pieces. If using buttered pasta, add strips of canned pimiento, sliced black olives, capers, etc. Use to fill the omelette, fold and sprinkle with a little grated Parmesan or other cheese.

MAKING A ROLLED OMELETTE

1 Break the eggs into a bowl, and add the water and some salt and pepper. Beat with a fork until just blended but not frothy.

2 In a 20 cm/8 in omelette or frying pan, melt 30 ml/2 tbsp butter over a moderate heat. Rotate the pan to coat the bottom and sides with butter.

3 When the butter is foaming and just beginning to turn golden, pour in the egg mixture. Tilt and rotate the pan to spread the eggs in an even layer over the bottom.

4 Cook for 5–10 seconds or until the omelette starts to set. Using a palette knife (spatula), lift the cooked base and tilt the pan so that the uncooked egg mixture runs underneath. Continue in this way until most of the omelette is set but the top is still creamy.

5 Using the palette knife, loosen the edge of the omelette on one side and tilt the pan so that one-third of the omelette folds over on to itself.

6 Continue loosening the omelette from its folded edge, holding the pan over a warmed plate. As the omelette slides out, use the edge of the pan to guide it so that the omelette folds over again on itself into thirds.

Making a Soufflé

1 Separate the eggs, taking care that there is no trace of egg yolk in the whites. (It is best to separate 1 egg at a time and to check each white before adding to the rest.)

2 For a savoury soufflé, make a thick white sauce. Beat in the yolks and the soufflé flavouring. For a sweet soufflé, make a thick custard using the yolks; mix in the flavouring.

3 In a large, scrupulously clean bowl, whisk the egg whites until they hold stiff peaks. (Any grease on the bowl or beaters will prevent maximum volume.) If not using a copper bowl, add a pinch of cream of tartar once the whites are frothy. For a sweet soufflé, add sugar once the whites hold soft peaks (the tips flop over), then continue whisking.

4 Add one-quarter of the egg whites to the sauce base. Using a large metal spoon or a rubber spatula, stir in the whites to lighten the base. Add the remaining whites and fold them in as lightly as possible by cutting down with the spatula to the bottom of the bowl and then turning over the mixture.

5 Spoon the mixture into the prepared dish. Bake in a preheated oven until the soufflé has risen about 5 cm/2 in above the rim of the dish and is lightly browned. Serve the soufflé immediately because it will only hold its puff for a few minutes, once out of the oven, before it begins to deflate.

Separating Eggs

It is easier to separate the yolks and whites if eggs are cold, so take the eggs straight from the refrigerator. Tap the egg once or twice against the rim of a small bowl to crack the shell. Break open the shell and hold half in each hand. Carefully transfer the unbroken yolk from one half shell to the other several times, letting the egg white dribble into the bowl. Put the yolk in a second bowl.

Cheese Soufflé

Butter a 1.5 litre/2½ pint soufflé dish and coat it with a layer of breadcrumbs. Make 300 ml/½ pint/1¼ cups thick white sauce (see page 168). Add 4 egg yolks and 115 g/4 oz grated cheese such as Gruyère, mature (sharp) Cheddar, blue, or a mixture of Parmesan and Gruyère. If you like, season the mixture with 10 ml/2 tsp Dijon mustard. Whisk 6 egg whites until stiff, then fold into the sauce base. Bake in a 200°C/400°F/Gas 6 oven for about 20–25 minutes until well-risen and golden brown on the top. Never open the oven door while a soufflé is cooking, as this will cause it to sink dramatically. *Serves 4.*

MAKING BATTER AND PANCAKES (CRÊPES)

Batter consists mainly of flour, eggs and liquid. It may be thick in consistency – for making fritters or coating food to be fried – or thin and pourable, for Yorkshire pudding, or other batter puddings, and pancakes. For a very light result, you can separate the eggs, whisk the whites and fold them in.

Thin, lacy pancakes, or crêpes, are wonderfully versatile. They can be served very simply with just lemon juice and sugar, or turned into more elaborate dishes: folded and warmed in a sauce, rolled round a savoury or sweet filling, or layered with a filling.

PORK AND APPLE BATTER PUDDINGS

Make the batter with 115 g/4 oz/1 cup plain (all-purpose) flour, a pinch of salt, 1 egg and 300 ml/½ pint/1¼ cups mixed milk and water. Mix together 450 g/1 lb pork sausagemeat (ground sausage), 115 g/4 oz/¾ cup finely chopped or coarsely grated cooking apple, 1 small grated onion, 15 ml/1 tbsp chopped fresh parsley, and salt and pepper. Form into 16 balls. Oil 4 600 ml/½ pint baking dishes and heat in a 220°C/425°F/Gas 7 oven. Divide the balls among the dishes and bake for 10 minutes. Pour over the batter and bake for 35–40 minutes or until risen and golden. Serve hot. *Serves 4.*

MAKING BATTER

1 Sift plain (all-purpose) flour into a bowl with other dry ingredients such as sugar, baking powder or bicarbonate of soda (baking soda), salt, ground spices, etc., as directed in the recipe.

2 Make a well in the centre of the dry ingredients and add the eggs or egg yolks and some of the liquid.

3 Using a wooden spoon, beat the eggs and liquid in the well just to mix them.

4 Gradually draw in some of the flour from the sides, stirring vigorously.

5 When the mixture is smooth, stir in the remaining liquid. Stir just until the ingredients are combined – the trick is not to overmix.

6 If the recipe specifies, whisk egg whites to a soft peak and fold them into the batter (made with yolks). Do this just before using the batter.

Making Pancakes (Crêpes)

Makes about 12

170 g/6 oz/1½ cups plain (all-purpose) flour

10 ml/2 tsp caster (superfine) sugar (for sweet pancakes)

2 size 3 (medium) eggs

450 ml/¾ pint/scant 2 cups milk

about 30 g/1 oz/2 tbsp melted butter

1 Make the pancake batter and leave to stand for 20 minutes. Heat a 20 cm/8 in pancake (crêpe) or frying pan over a moderate heat. The pan is ready when a few drops of water sprinkled on the surface jump and sizzle immediately. Grease the pan lightly with a little melted butter. Pour 45–60 ml/3–4 tbsp batter into the pan. Quickly tilt and rotate the pan so that the batter spreads out to cover the bottom thinly and evenly; pour out any excess batter.

2 Cook for 30–45 seconds or until the pancake is set and small holes have appeared. If the cooking seems to be taking too long, increase the heat slightly. Lift the edge of the pancake, using a palette knife (spatula); the base of the pancake should be lightly brown. Shake the pan vigorously back and forth to loosen the pancake completely, then turn or flip it over. Cook the other side for about 30 seconds. Serve or leave to cool.

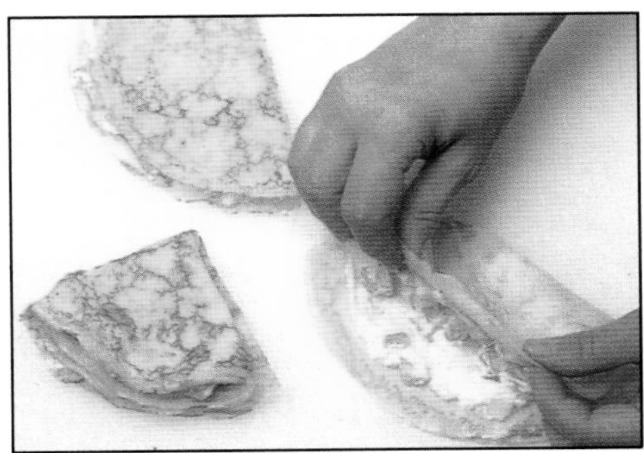

3 **To fill pancakes**: For folded pancakes, spread 45–60 ml/3–4 tbsp of filling evenly over each pancake. Fold in half then in half again, into quarters. For rolled pancakes, put 45–60 ml/3–4 tbsp of filling near one edge of each pancake and roll up from that side. For pancake parcels, spoon 45–60 ml/3–4 tbsp of filling into the centre of each pancake. Fold in two opposite sides, over the filling, then fold in the other two sides. Turn the parcel over for serving. Filled pancakes are usually baked before serving, to re-heat them.

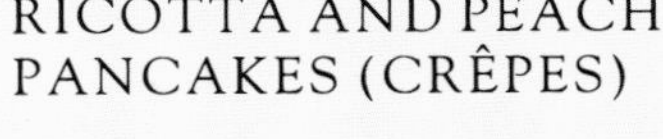

RICOTTA AND PEACH PANCAKES (CRÊPES)

Combine 450 g/1 lb ricotta cheese, 30 g/1 oz/4 tbsp icing (confectioners') sugar, 5 ml/1 tsp vanilla essence (extract) and 30 ml/2 tbsp brandy in a bowl. Mix well. Add 4 large, ripe peaches, peeled and diced, and fold in gently. Divide the ricotta and peach mixture among 12 pancakes (crêpes) and spread it evenly over them. Fold each pancake in half and then in half again, into quarters. Arrange the pancakes in a buttered large oval baking dish, slightly overlapping them. Brush with 30 g/1 oz/2 tbsp melted butter and sprinkle generously with icing sugar. Bake in a 190°C/375°F/Gas 5 oven for about 10 minutes. Serve hot. *Serves* 6.

PANCAKE- (CRÊPE-) MAKING TIPS

- Pancake (crêpe) batter should be the consistency of whipping cream. If the batter is at all lumpy, strain it. If it does not flow smoothly to make a thin pancake, add a little more liquid.
- Like most batters, pancake batter can be made in a blender or food processor. Leave to stand before using.
- Your first pancake may well be unsuccessful because it will test the consistency of the batter and the temperature of the pan, both of which may need adjusting.
- If more convenient, pancakes can be made ahead of time. Cool, then stack them, interleaved with greaseproof (waxed) paper, and wrap in tin foil. They can be refrigerated for up to 3 days or frozen for 1 month.
- A pancake pan has a flat bottom and straight sides; these give the pancake a well-defined edge.

MAKING STOCKS

A good home-made poultry stock is invaluable. It is simple to make, and you can store it in the freezer for up to 6 months. Add the giblets if available, but not the livers, as these make stock bitter. Fish stock is very quick to make. Ask your fishmonger for heads, bones and trimmings from white fish. The most delicious meat soups, stews, casseroles, gravies and sauces rely on a good home-made meat stock for success. Once made, you can keep meat stock in the refrigerator for 4–5 days, or freeze it for longer storage (up to 6 months). Vegetable stock is also easy to make. Refrigerate, covered, for up to 5 days, or freeze for up to 1 month.

MAKING POULTRY STOCK

MAKES ABOUT 2.5 LITRES/4 PINTS

1.12–1.35 kg/2 ½–3 lb poultry wings, backs and necks (chicken, turkey, etc.)

2 unpeeled onions, quartered

4 litres/6 ½ pints cold water

2 carrots, roughly chopped

2 celery stalks, with leaves if possible, roughly chopped

a small handful of fresh parsley

a few fresh thyme sprigs or 5 ml/1 tsp dried thyme

1 or 2 bay leaves

10 black peppercorns, lightly crushed

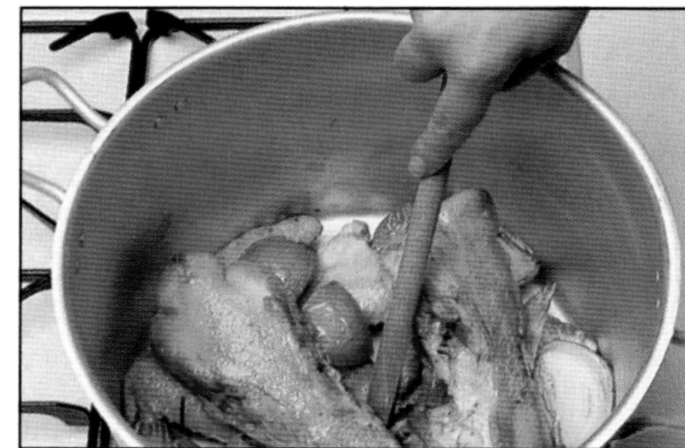

1 Combine the poultry wings, backs and necks and the onions in a stockpot. Cook over a moderate heat, stirring occasionally, until the poultry and onion pieces are lightly browned.

2 Add the water and stir well to mix in the sediment on the bottom of the pot. Bring to a boil and skim off the impurities as they rise to the surface.

3 Add the remaining ingredients. Partly cover the pot and gently simmer for 3 hours. Strain the stock into a bowl and leave to cool, then refrigerate.

4 When cold, remove the layer of fat that will have set on the surface.

MAKING FISH STOCK

MAKES ABOUT 1 LITRE/2 PINTS

700 g/1 ½ lb heads, bones and trimmings from white fish

1 onion, sliced

2 celery stalks with leaves, chopped

1 carrot, sliced

1 bay leaf

a few fresh parsley sprigs

6 black peppercorns

1.35 litres/2 ¼ pints water

150 ml/¼ pint/⅔ cup dry white wine

1 Rinse the fish heads, bones and trimmings well. Put in a stockpot with the vegetables, herbs, peppercorns, water and wine. Bring to a boil, skimming the surface frequently, then reduce the heat and simmer for about 25 minutes. Strain the stock, without pressing down on the ingredients in the sieve. If you do not intend to use the stock immediately, leave it to cool and then refrigerate. Use fish stock within 2 days, or freeze it for up to 3 months.

MAKING MEAT STOCK

MAKES ABOUT 2 LITRES/3½ PINTS

1.8 kg/4 lb beef bones, such as shin, leg, neck and clod, or veal or lamb bones, cut into 6 cm/2½ in pieces
2 unpeeled onions, quartered
2 carrots, roughly chopped
2 celery stalks, roughly chopped
2 tomatoes, coarsely chopped
4.5 litres/7½ pints cold water
a handful of parsley stalks
a few fresh thyme sprigs or 5 ml/1 tsp dried thyme
2 bay leaves
10 black peppercorns, lightly crushed

1 Preheat a 230°C/450°F/Gas 8 oven. Put the bones in a roasting tin (pan) or flameproof casserole and roast, turning occasionally, for 30 minutes or until they start to brown.

2 Add the onions, carrots, celery and tomatoes and baste with the fat in the tin. Roast for a further 20–30 minutes or until the bones are well-browned. Stir and baste occasionally.

3 Transfer the bones and vegetables to a stockpot. Spoon off the fat from the roasting tin. Add a little of the water to the roasting tin or casserole and bring to a boil on top of the stove, stirring well. Pour this liquid into the stockpot.

4 Add the remaining water. Bring to a boil, skimming to remove foam from the surface. Add the parsley, thyme, bay leaves and peppercorns. Cover and simmer for 4–6 hours, topping up with water from time to time.

5 Strain the stock through a sieve. Skim as much fat as possible from the surface. The best way to do this is to cool the stock and then refrigerate it; the fat will then rise to the top and set in a layer that you can remove easily.

MAKING VEGETABLE STOCK

MAKES ABOUT 2.5 LITRES/4 PINTS

2 large onions, coarsely chopped
2 leeks, sliced
3 garlic cloves, crushed
3 carrots, coarsely chopped
4 celery stalks, coarsely chopped
a large strip of lemon zest
a handful of parsley stalks (about 12)
a few fresh thyme sprigs
2 bay leaves
2.5 litres/4 pints water

1 Put the vegetables, lemon zest, herbs and water in a stockpot and bring to a boil. Skim off the foam that rises to the surface from time to time.

2 Reduce the heat and then simmer, uncovered, for 30 minutes. Strain the stock and leave it to cool.

MAKING SAUCES

Some chefs consider flour-thickened sauces old-fashioned and replace them with butter sauces, vegetable purées or reduced cream. A basic white sauce is, however, an essential ingredient in many dishes, and lends itself to many flavourings. The recipe given here makes a medium-thick sauce.

Tomato sauce is a very useful standby to have on hand in the refrigerator or freezer. When tomatoes are in season, make a large batch and freeze it. At other times of the year, use canned whole Italian plum tomatoes (drain, cut in half, scrape out the seeds and chop).

MAKING WHITE SAUCE

MAKES ABOUT 600 ML/1 PINT/ 2½ CUPS

45 g/1½ oz/3 tbsp butter

45 g/1½ oz/6 tbsp plain (all-purpose) flour

600 ml/1 pint/2½ cups milk

a good pinch of grated nutmeg

salt and pepper

SAUCE-MAKING TIP

A whisk will blend the mixture more thoroughly than a spoon and will help to prevent lumps from forming.

1 Melt the butter in a heavy saucepan over a low heat. Remove the pan from the heat and stir in the flour to make a smooth, soft paste (known as a 'roux').

2 Add about one-quarter of the milk and mix it in well, using a whisk. When smooth, mix in the remaining milk.

3 Set the pan over a moderately high heat and bring gradually to a boil, whisking constantly.

4 When the sauce bubbles and starts to thicken, reduce the heat to very low and simmer the sauce gently for 5–10 minutes, whisking well from time to time. Add the grated nutmeg and season the sauce to taste with salt and pepper. Serve the sauce hot.

WHITE-SAUCE VARIATIONS

- For *Thin White Sauce* to serve with meat or to use as a base for cream soups: use 30 g/1 oz/2 tbsp butter and 30 g/1 oz/ 4 tbsp plain (all-purpose) flour.
- For *Thick White Sauce* to use as a soufflé base: use 55 g/2 oz/4 tbsp butter and 55 g/2 oz/½ cup flour.
- For *Blond Sauce*: add the flour to the melted butter and cook, stirring constantly, for 1–2 minutes or until the roux is a pale beige colour. Heat the liquid and then add it to the roux, off the heat. Bring to a boil, whisking, and simmer for 3–5 minutes.
- For *Velouté Sauce*: cook the roux as for a blond sauce until it is lightly browned and smells nutty. Use hot chicken or fish stock, or a mixture of stock and wine, instead of milk.
- For *Béchamel Sauce*: heat the milk with a slice of onion, 1 bay leaf and a few black peppercorns. Remove from the heat, cover and infuse for 20 minutes. Strain before adding to the roux, made as for a blond sauce.
- For *Cream Sauce*: substitute cream for some of the milk.
- For *Cheese Sauce*: stir 115–225 g/ 4–8 oz grated cheese and 5–10 ml/ 1–2 tsp spicy brown mustard into white, blond or béchamel sauce; add a pinch of cayenne pepper instead of nutmeg. Use a flavourful cheese that melts easily.
- For *Mustard Sauce*: stir 15 ml/1 tbsp Dijon mustard and 2.5 ml/½ tsp sugar into white, blond or béchamel sauce.
- For *Mushroom Sauce*: cook 225 g/8 oz sliced mushrooms in about 20 g/⅔ oz/ 1½ tbsp butter until soft; continue cooking until the excess liquid has evaporated. Add to white, blond, béchamel, velouté or cream sauce.

Making Tomato Sauce

Makes about 600 ml/1 pint/ 2½ cups

30 g/1 oz/2 tbsp butter

900 g/2 lb tomatoes, skinned, seeded and finely chopped

1.25–2.5 ml/¼–½ tsp sugar

salt and pepper

PREPARATION TIP

Skin and seed tomatoes following the instructions on page 155.

1 Melt the butter in a heavy-based saucepan over a low heat. Add the tomatoes and stir to mix with the butter. Cover and cook for 5 minutes.

2 Uncover and stir in the sugar. Partly cover the pan and simmer gently, stirring occasionally, for 30 minutes or until the tomatoes have softened and the sauce is thick.

3 Season the sauce to taste with salt and pepper. Use immediately, or cool and then refrigerate or freeze.

EGGS BAKED IN TOMATO SAUCE

For each serving, put 20 ml/1½ tbsp of tomato sauce in a lightly buttered ramekin. Break an egg into the ramekin and sprinkle with pepper to taste and 15 ml/1 tbsp of freshly grated Parmesan or Cheddar cheese. Make as many servings as needed, then put the ramekins in a roasting tin (pan) and add cold water to come halfway up the sides. Bring to a boil on top of the stove, then transfer to a 200°C/400°F/ Gas 6 oven and bake for 5–7 minutes. Serve immediately.

TOMATO-SAUCE VARIATIONS

- For *Rich Tomato Sauce*: stir another 20 g/⅔ oz/1½ tbsp butter into the sauce before serving.
- For *Smooth Tomato Sauce*: purée the sauce in a blender or food processor to achieve a smooth texture.
- For *Tomato-garlic Sauce*: use 15 ml/ 1 tbsp olive oil instead of butter. In a separate small pan, cook 1–2 finely chopped garlic cloves in the olive oil for approximately 1 minute. Add the garlic to the tomato sauce for the last 5 minutes of cooking.
- For *Tomato-herb Sauce*: stir in about 60 ml/4 tbsp chopped fresh herbs (parsley, basil, chives, thyme, oregano, marjoram – either singly or in a mixture of 2 or 3 different herbs at the most) before serving.
- For *Italian Tomato Sauce*: finely chop 1 onion, 1 small carrot and 1 celery stalk. Cook gently in 30 ml/2 tbsp olive oil until soft. Add 1–2 finely chopped garlic cloves and cook for a further minute. Add the tomatoes with 1 bay leaf and 1 large sprig of fresh rosemary or 2.5 ml/½ tsp crumbled dried rosemary. Continue cooking as for ordinary tomato sauce. Discard the herbs before serving.
- For *Tomato-wine Sauce*: finely chop 3 shallots or ½ onion and cook in 30 g/1 oz/2 tbsp butter or 30 ml/2 tbsp olive oil until soft. Add 1 finely chopped garlic clove and cook for a further minute. Stir in 120 ml/4 fl oz/ ½ cup dry white wine, bring to a boil and boil until almost completely evaporated. Add the tomatoes and continue cooking as for tomato sauce. For a smooth sauce, purée in a blender or food processor.
- For *Tomato-mushroom Sauce*: fry 225 g/8 oz thinly sliced mushrooms in 30 g/1 oz/2 tbsp butter for about 5–7 minutes until they are soft and lightly browned. Add the tomatoes and cook as for the basic tomato sauce.

MAKING YEAST AND PIZZA DOUGH

Making bread is an extremely enjoyable culinary experience. With no other preparation do you have such 'hands-on' contact, and from the kneading to the shaping of the risen dough, you are working with a living organism, yeast, not a chemical raising agent. You can use either fresh or dried yeast, which is also available in an easy-blend variety.

Although you can buy pizza bases, it is very easy to make your own at home, and takes much less time than you would expect. The range of toppings for pizzas is virtually limitless.

EVERYDAY WHITE BREAD

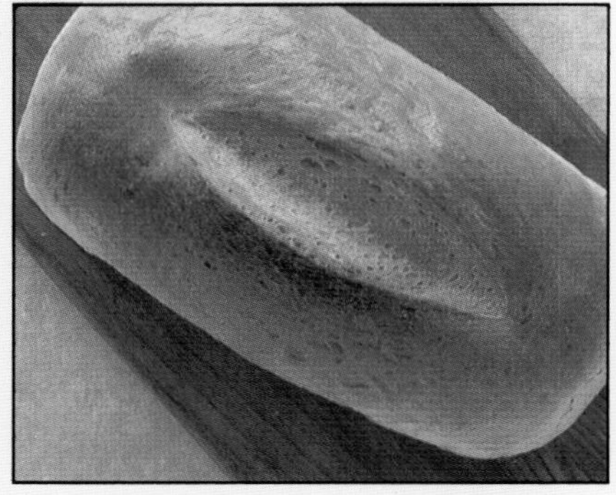

Sift 700 g/1½ lb strong plain (all-purpose) flour into a large bowl with 7.5 ml/1½ tsp salt and 15 ml/1 tbsp caster (superfine) sugar. Stir in 10 ml/2 tsp easy-blend dried yeast. Make a well in the centre and add 450 ml/¾ pint/scant 2 cups mixed warm water and milk and 30 g/1 oz/2 tbsp melted and cooled butter. Mix to a soft dough, adding more flour or liquid if necessary, then knead until smooth and elastic. Leave to rise until doubled in bulk. Knock back the dough to deflate. Divide it in half and shape each piece into a loaf, tucking the ends under. Put in 2 greased 21 × 11 cm/8½ × 4½ in loaf tins (pans). Leave in a warm place to rise for 30–45 minutes. Glaze the tops of the loaves with 1 egg beaten with 15 ml/1 tbsp milk. Bake in a 230°C/450°F/Gas 8 oven for 30–35 minutes. *Makes 2 loaves.*

MAKING YEAST DOUGH

1 If using ordinary dried yeast, put it in a bowl, add some of the warm liquid called for in the recipe and mix until dissolved. Add sugar if specified. Sift the flour into a warm bowl with other dry ingredients. Make a well and add the yeast plus any other liquid ingredients.

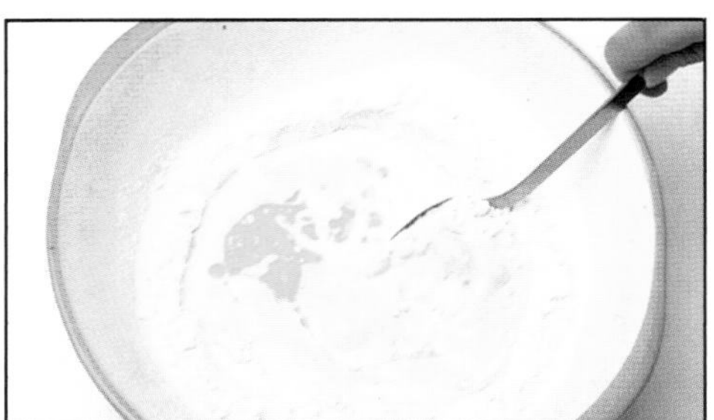

2 Using a spoon, gradually draw the flour into the liquids. Mix until all the flour is incorporated and the dough pulls away from the sides of the bowl. If the dough feels too soft and wet, work in a little more flour. If it fails to come together, add a little more liquid.

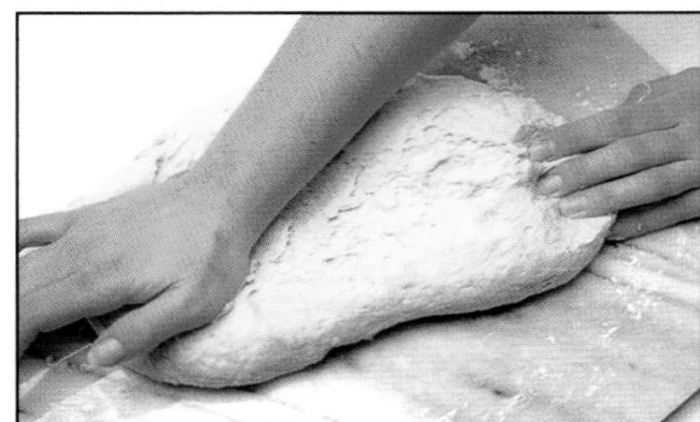

3 Turn the dough on to a floured surface. Fold the dough over towards you and then press it down away from you. Continue kneading until the dough looks satiny and feels elastic.

4 Put the dough in a lightly greased bowl and turn to grease all over. Cover with a towel or cling film (plastic wrap). Leave to rise in a warm place until doubled in bulk, 1–1½ hours.

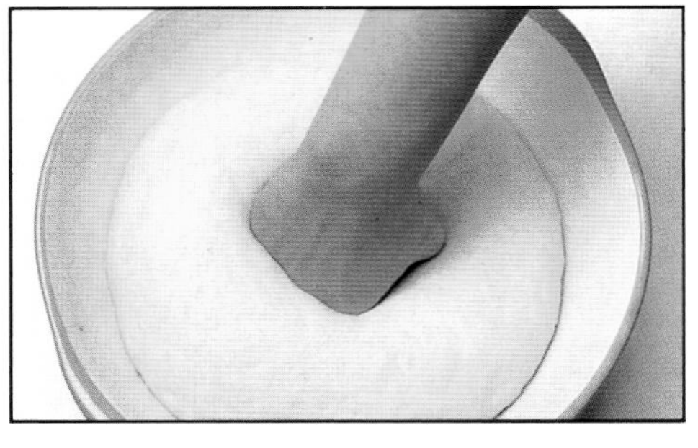

5 Gently punch the centre of the dough with your fist to deflate it and fold the edges to the centre. Turn the dough on to a lightly floured surface and knead it again for 2–3 minutes.

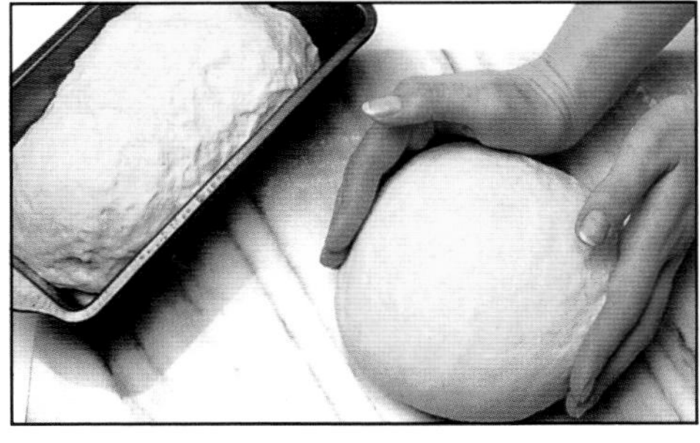

6 Put into prepared tins (pans) or on to baking sheets. Cover and leave for 1 hour. Bake until golden brown. To test, tip the loaf out of the tin and tap the base – it should sound hollow.

Making Pizza Dough

Makes a 35 cm/14 in pizza base
10 ml/2 tsp dried yeast
180 ml/6 fl oz/¾ cup warm water
315 g/11½ oz/scant 3 cups strong plain (all-purpose) flour
5 ml/1 tsp salt
20 ml/1½ tbsp olive oil

TOMATO AND MOZZARELLA PIZZA

Spread 300 ml/½ pint/1¼ cups tomato purée (paste) over the pizza base, not quite to the edges. Scatter 115 g/4 oz grated Mozzarella cheese evenly over the sauce (plus thinly sliced pepperoni or salami if liked). Sprinkle over freshly grated Parmesan cheese and then add a drizzle of olive oil. Bake in a 240°C/475°F/Gas 9 oven for 15–20 minutes.

FOOD-PROCESSOR PIZZA DOUGH

Combine the yeast, flour, salt, olive oil and half of the warm water in the processor container. Process briefly, then add the rest of the water. Work until the dough forms a ball. Process for 3–4 minutes to knead the dough, then knead it by hand for 2–3 minutes.

1 Put the yeast in a small bowl, add 60 ml/4 tbsp of the water and leave to soak for 1 minute. Whisk lightly with a fork until the yeast has dissolved.

2 Sift the flour and salt into a large, warm bowl. Make a well in the centre and add the yeast mixture, olive oil and remaining warm water.

3 Using your fingers, gradually draw the flour into the liquids. Continue mixing in this way until all the flour is incorporated and the dough will just hold together.

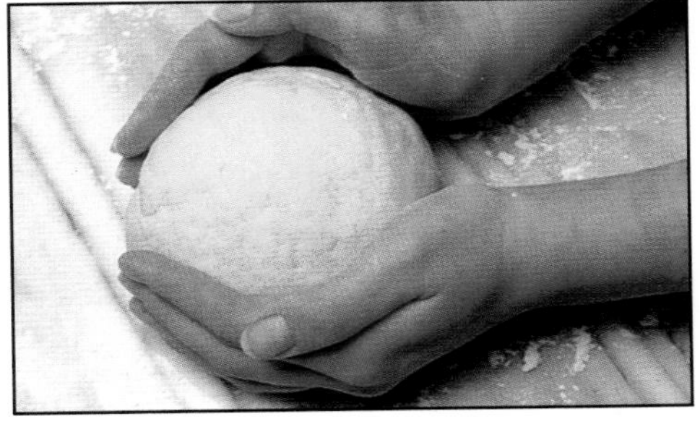

4 Turn the dough on to a lightly floured surface. Knead it until it is smooth and silky, about 5 minutes. Shape the dough into a ball. Put it in an oiled bowl and rotate to coat the surface evenly with oil.

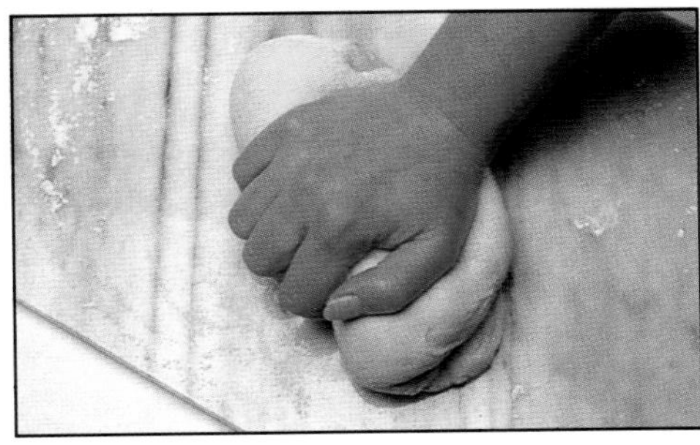

5 Cover the bowl with cling film (plastic wrap). Set aside in a warm place to rise for about 1 hour until doubled in bulk. Turn the dough on to the lightly floured surface again. Gently knock back to deflate it, then knead lightly until smooth.

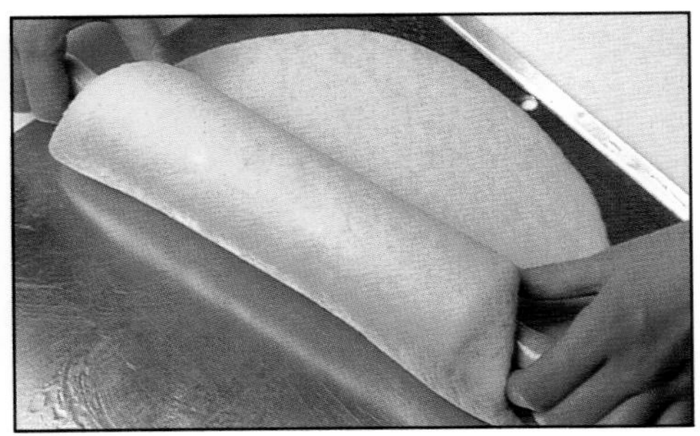

6 Roll out the dough into a round or square about 5 mm/¼ in thick. Transfer it to a lightly oiled metal pizza tin (pan) or baking sheet. Add the topping as specified in the recipe, then bake until the pizza crust is puffy and well browned at the edges. Serve hot.

Sesame-seed Bread

Makes 1 loaf

10ml/2 tsp active dry yeast
300ml/½ pint/1¼ cups lukewarm water
200g/7oz/1¾ cups plain (all-purpose) flour
200g/7oz/1¾ cups wholewheat flour
10ml/2 tsp salt
70g/2½oz/5 tbsp toasted sesame seeds
milk, for glazing
30ml/2 tbsp sesame seeds, for sprinkling

1 Combine the yeast and 75ml/5 tbsp of the water and then leave to dissolve. Mix the flours and salt in a large bowl. Make a well in the centre and pour in the yeast and water.

2 Using a wooden spoon, stir from the centre, incorporating flour with each turn, to obtain a rough dough.

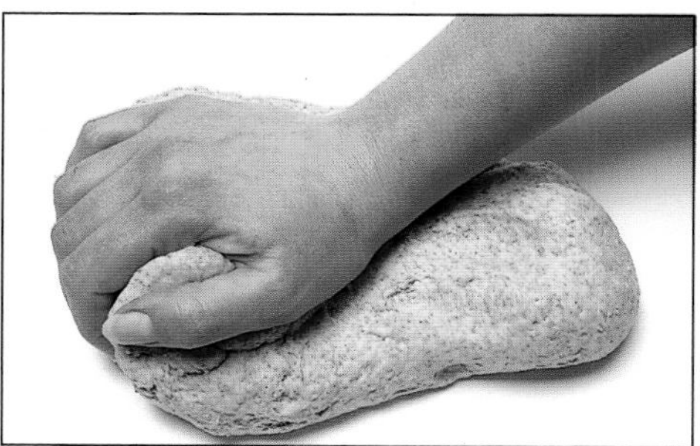

3 Transfer to a floured surface. To knead, push the dough away from you, then fold it towards you and push away again. Repeat until smooth and elastic, then return to the bowl and cover. Leave in a warm place until doubled in volume, 1½–2 hours.

4 Grease a 23cm/9in cake tin (pan). Punch down the dough and knead in the sesame seeds. Divide the dough into 16 balls and place in the tin. Cover with cling film (plastic wrap) and leave in a warm place until risen above the rim of the tin.

5 Preheat a 220°C/425°F/Gas 7 oven. Brush the loaf with milk and sprinkle with the sesame seeds. Bake for 15 minutes. Lower the heat to 190°C/375°F/Gas 5 and bake until the bottom sounds hollow when tapped, about 30 minutes more. Cool on a wire rack.

DRIED-FRUIT LOAF

MAKES 1 LOAF

450 g/1 lb mixed dried fruit, such as currants, raisins, and chopped ready-to-eat dried apricots and cherries

300 ml/½ pint/1¼ cups cold strong tea

200 g/7 oz/scant 1 cup dark brown sugar

grated rind and juice of 1 small orange

grated rind and juice of 1 lemon

1 egg, lightly beaten

200 g/7 oz/1¾ cups plain (all-purpose) flour

15 ml/1 tbsp baking powder

0.75 ml/⅛ tsp salt

1 In a bowl, mix the dried fruit with the tea and soak overnight.

2 Preheat a 180°C/350°F/Gas 4 oven. Line a 23 × 13 cm/9 × 5 in loaf tin (pan) with greaseproof (waxed) paper and grease the paper.

3 Strain the fruit, reserving the liquid. In a bowl, combine the sugar, orange and lemon rind, and fruit.

4 Pour the juice from the orange and lemon into a measuring jug (cup); if the quantity is less than 250 ml/8 fl oz/1 cup, top it up with the soaking liquid.

5 Stir the citrus juices and egg into the dried fruit mixture.

6 In another bowl, sift together the flour, baking powder and salt. Stir into the fruit mixture until blended.

7 Transfer to the prepared tin and bake until a skewer inserted in the centre comes out clean, about 1¼ hours. Leave the loaf to stand in the tin for about 10 minutes before turning out. Cool on a wire rack.

MAKING SHORTCRUST PASTRY

A meltingly short, crumbly pastry sets off any filling to perfection, whether sweet or savoury. The pastry dough can be made with half butter or margarine and half white vegetable fat, or with all one kind of fat, depending on your personal preference.

Baked-custard and cream fillings can make pastry soggy, so the cases for these flans and tarts are often given an initial baking before the filling is added and the final baking is done. The technique is also used for pastry cases that are to be filled with an uncooked or pre-cooked mixture. Such pre-baking is referred to as baking 'blind'. The purpose of using weights during the baking process is to prevent the bottom of the pastry case from rising too much and becoming distorted, thus losing its neat, flat shape.

For a 23 cm/9 in pastry case

225 g/8 oz/2 cups plain (all-purpose) flour

1.25 ml/¼ tsp salt

115 g/4 oz/½ cup fat, chilled and diced

approximately 45–60 ml/3–4 tbsp iced water

1 Sift the flour and salt into a bowl. Add the fat. Rub it into the flour with your fingertips until the mixture resembles coarse crumbs.

PASTRY-MAKING TIPS

- It helps if the fat is cold and firm, particularly if you are making the dough in a food processor. This is because cold fat has less chance of warming and softening too much when it is being rubbed into the flour, resulting in an oily pastry. Use block margarine rather than the soft type.
- When rubbing the fat into the flour, if it begins to soften and feel oily, put the bowl in the refrigerator to chill for 20–30 minutes. Then continue making the dough.
- Liquids used for making pastry should be ice-cold so that they will not soften or melt the fat.
- Take care when adding the water: start with the smaller amount (added all at once, not in a dribble), and add more only if the mixture will not come together into a dough. Too much water will result in tough pastry.
- When gathering the mixture together into a ball of dough, handle it as little as possible: overworked pastry will be tough.
- To avoid shrinkage, refrigerate the dough before rolling out and baking. This 'resting period' will allow any elasticity developed during the mixing process to relax.

2 Sprinkle 45 ml/3 tbsp water over the mixture. Using a fork, toss gently to mix and moisten it.

3 Press the dough into a ball. If it is still too dry to form a dough, add the remaining water.

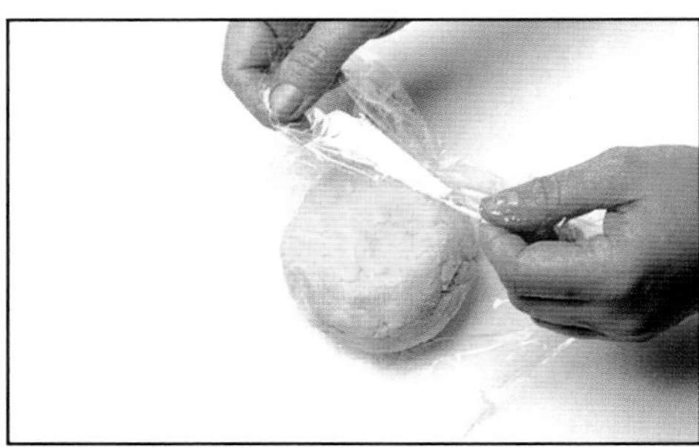

4 Wrap up the ball of dough with a piece of cling film (plastic wrap) or greaseproof (waxed) paper, or place it in a plastic bag. Refrigerate the dough for at least 30 minutes to allow the elasticity to relax.

5 **To make pastry in a food processor**: Combine the flour, salt and cubed fat in the work bowl. Process, turning the machine on and off, just until the mixture is crumbly. Add the iced water and process again briefly – just until the dough starts to pull away from the sides. Remove the dough and gather it into a ball. Wrap and refrigerate.

SHORTCRUST-PASTRY VARIATIONS

- For *Nut Shortcrust*: Add 30 g/1 oz/ 2 tbsp finely chopped walnuts or pecan nuts to the flour mixture.
- For *Rich Shortcrust*: Use 225 g/8 oz/ 2 cups flour and 170 g/6 oz/¾ cup fat (preferably all butter), plus 15 ml/1 tbsp caster (superfine) sugar if making a sweet pie. Bind with 1 egg yolk and 30–45 ml/2–3 tbsp water.
- For a *2-crust Pie*, increase the proportions by 50%, so the amounts needed for basic shortcrust pastry are: 340 g/12 oz/3 cups flour, 2.5 ml/½ tsp salt, 170 g/6 oz/¾ cup fat, 75–90 ml/ 5–6 tbsp water. For Nut Shortcrust, as above with 55 g/2 oz/4 tbsp nuts. For Rich Shortcrust, as above but using 260 g/9 oz/1¼ cups fat, 1 egg yolk and 60–75 ml/4–5 tbsp water.

ROLLING-OUT AND LINING TIPS

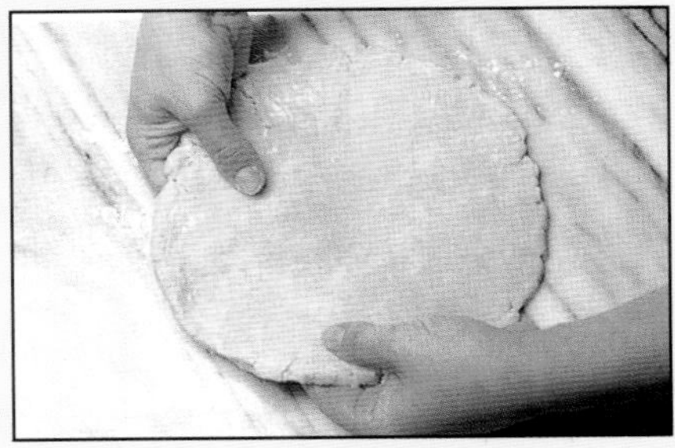

- Lift up the dough and give it a quarter turn from time to time during the rolling. This will prevent the dough from sticking, and will help to keep the thickness even.
- When rolling out and lining the pie or tart tin (pan), do not stretch the dough. It will only shrink back during baking, spoiling the shape.
- A pastry scraper will help to lift the dough from the work surface, to wrap it around the rolling pin.
- When finishing the edge, be sure to hook the dough over the rim all round or to press the dough firmly to the rim. This will prevent the dough from pulling away should it start to shrink.

BAKING BLIND

1 Set the pie or flan tin (pan), or flan ring, on a sheet of greaseproof (waxed) paper or tin foil. Draw or mark around its base. Cut out a circle about 7.5 cm/ 3 in larger all round than the drawn or marked one.

2 Roll out the pastry dough and use it to line the tin or ring set on a baking sheet. Using a fork, prick the bottom of the pastry case (pie crust) all over.

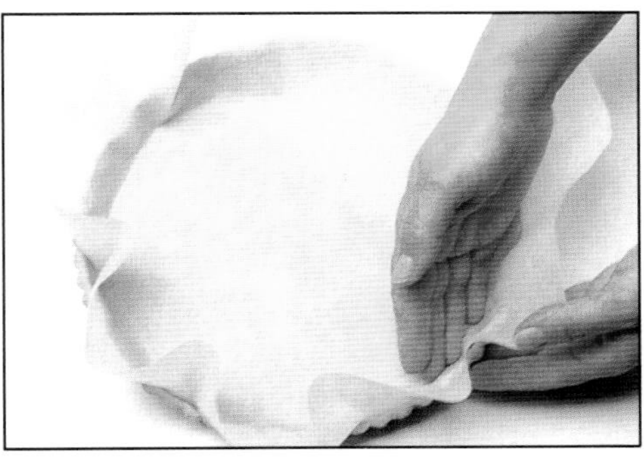

3 Lay the circle of greaseproof paper or foil in the bottom of the pastry case and press it smoothly over the base and up around the side.

4 Put enough dried beans or baking beans in the pastry case to cover the bottom thickly.

5 **For partially baked pastry**: Bake the case in a 200°C/400°F/Gas 6 oven for 15–20 minutes or until it is slightly dry and set. Remove the paper or foil and beans. The pastry is now ready to be filled and baked further.

6 **For fully baked pastry**: After baking for 15 minutes, remove the paper or foil and beans. Prick the bottom again with a fork. Return to the oven and bake for 5–10 minutes or until golden. Leave to cool before adding the filling.

USING SHORTCRUST PASTRY

Succulent layers of pastry enveloping a sweet filling – what could be nicer? Use the same method for making small pies, such as mince pies.

A neat pastry case that does not distort or shrink during baking is the desired result. The key to success is handling the dough gently. Remove the chilled dough from the refrigerator and allow it to soften slightly at room temperature. Unwrap and put it on the lightly floured surface to roll.

A woven pastry lattice also makes a very attractive finish for a pie. Prepare shortcrust for a 2-crust pie, then roll out half the pastry dough and line the pie tin (pan). Trim the dough to leave a 12 mm/½ in overhang all round. Put in the filling. Roll out the second piece of dough into a circle that is about 5 cm/2 in larger all round than the pie tin.

AMERICAN-STYLE APPLE PIE

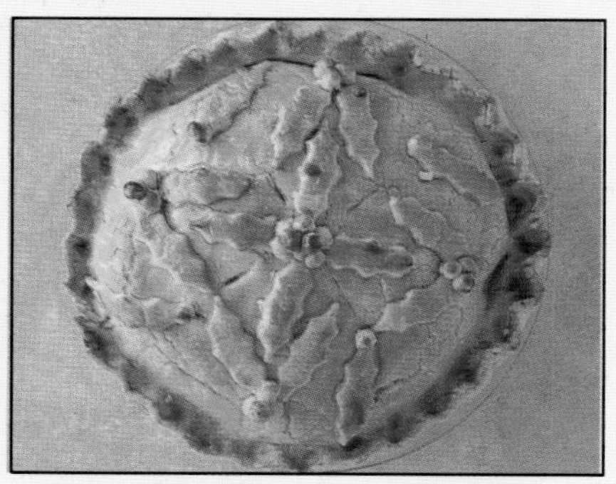

Combine 900 g/2 lb peeled, cored and thinly sliced green eating apples, 15 ml/1 tbsp plain (all-purpose) flour, 100 g/3½ oz/scant ½ cup caster (superfine) sugar and 3.75 ml/¾ tsp mixed spice (allspice). Toss to coat the fruit evenly with the sugar and flour. Use to fill the two-crust pie. Bake in a 190°C/375°F/Gas 5 oven for about 45 minutes or until the pastry is golden brown and the fruit is tender (test with a skewer through a slit in the top crust). Cool on a wire rack.

MAKING A 2-CRUST PIE

1 Roll out half the pastry dough on a floured surface and line a pie tin (pan) that is about 5 cm/2 in deep. Trim the dough even with the rim.

2 Put in the filling. Brush the edge of the pastry case evenly with water to moisten it.

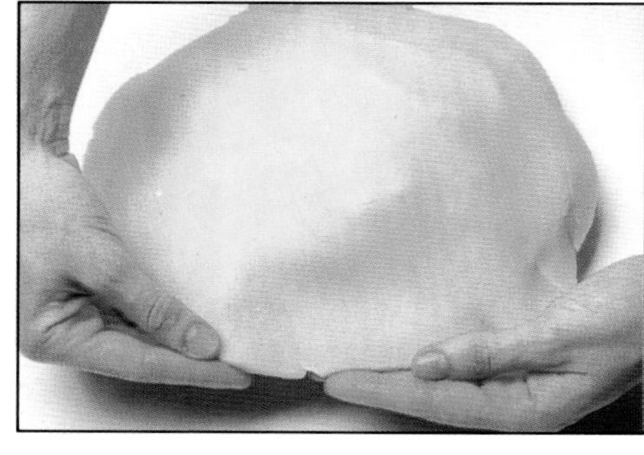

3 Roll out a second piece of dough to a circle 2.5 cm/1 in larger than the tin. Roll it up around the rolling pin and unroll over the pie. Press the edges together. Trim to leave a 12 mm/½ in overhang and cut steam vents.

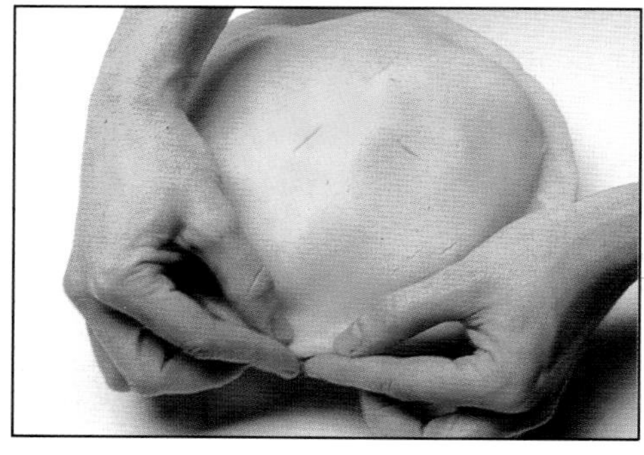

4 Fold the overhang of the lid under the edge of the case. Press the pastry together gently and evenly to seal. Finish the edge as wished.

5 Brush the top of the pie with milk or cream for a shiny finish, or brush with 1 egg yolk mixed with 5 ml/1 tsp water for a glazed golden-brown finish.

6 If you like, cut out decorative shapes from the trimmings. Moisten these with water and press them on to the top. Glaze the decorations before baking.

MAKING A LATTICE TOP

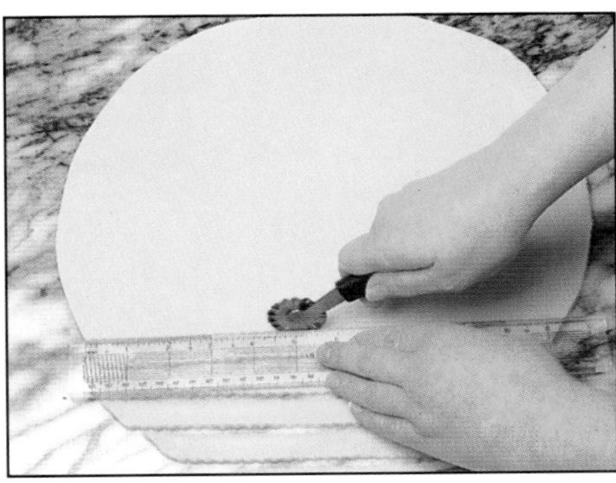

1 With the help of a ruler, cut neat, straight strips of dough, each about 12 mm/½ in wide, using a knife or fluted pastry wheel.

2 **For a square woven lattice**: Lay half the strips across the pie filling, keeping them neatly parallel and spacing them at equal intervals.

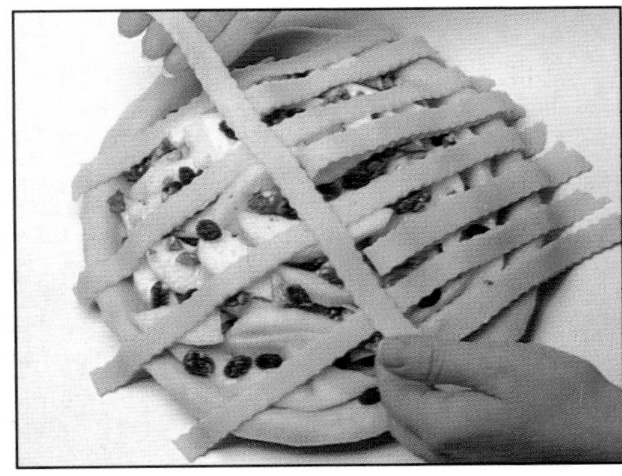

3 Fold back every other strip from the centre. Lay another strip across the centre, on the flat strips, at right-angles to them. Lay the folded strips flat again.

4 Fold back those strips that were not folded the first time. Lay another strip across those that are now lying flat, spacing this new strip an even distance from the centre strip.

5 Continue folding the strips in this way until you have completed half the lattice. Repeat the procedure to cover the other half of the pie.

6 Trim the ends of the strips even with the rim of the pie tin (pan). Moisten the edge of the pastry case with a little water and press the strips gently to it to seal. Finish the edge.

7 **For a diamond lattice**: Weave as above, laying the strips diagonally instead of at right-angles. Alternatively, lay half the strips over the filling and the remaining strips on top.

APRICOT LATTICE PIE

Toss together 1 kg/2¼ lb peeled, stoned (pitted) and thinly sliced apricots, 30 ml/2 tbsp plain (all-purpose) flour and 100 g/3½ oz/scant ½ cup sugar. Fill the pastry case and make a lattice top. Glaze with milk and bake in a 190°C/375°F/Gas 5 oven for about 45 minutes or until the pastry is golden and the filling is bubbling. Leave to cool completely on a wire rack.

COOK'S TIP

A simple cut-out lattice top can also make a pie look very attractive. To do this, roll out the dough for the top into a circle. Using a small pastry cutter, cut out shapes in a pattern, spacing them evenly and not too close together.

BASIC SPONGE RECIPES

The quick-mix sponge cake is a no-fuss, all-in-one cake, where the ingredients are quickly mixed together. The following quantities and instructions are for a deep 20cm/8in round cake tin (pan) or a 20cm/8in ring mould.

Swiss (jelly) rolls are traditionally made without fat, so they do not keep as long as most other cakes. However, they have a deliciously light texture and provide an ideal basis for all sorts of delicious fillings and tasty toppings.

MAKING A QUICK-MIX SPONGE CAKE

INGREDIENTS

115g/4oz/1 cup self-raising (-rising) flour
5ml/1 tsp baking powder
115g/4oz/½ cup soft margarine
115g/4oz/½ cup caster (superfine) sugar
2 size 3 (medium) eggs

1 Preheat a 160°C/325°F/Gas 3 oven. Grease the round cake tin (pan), line the base with greaseproof (waxed) paper and grease the paper, or grease and flour the ring mould.

2 Sift the flour and baking powder into a bowl. Add the margarine, sugar and both of the eggs.

3 Beat with a wooden spoon for 2–3 minutes. The mixture should be pale in colour and slightly glossy.

4 Spoon the mixture into the prepared tin or mould and bake for 20–30 minutes. To test if cooked, press the cake in the centre. If firm, it is done; if it is still soft, cook for a little longer. Alternatively, insert a skewer into the centre. If it comes out clean, the cake is ready. Turn out on to a wire rack, remove the paper and leave to cool.

STORING

The cake can be wrapped in cling film (plastic wrap) and stored in an airtight container for up to 2 days.

FLAVOURINGS

The following amounts are intended for use in a 2-egg cake, as for the recipe given here. Increase the amounts proportionally in order to make larger-sized cakes.

To make a chocolate cake: fold 15ml/1 tbsp cocoa powder blended with about 15ml/1 tbsp boiling water into the cake mixture.

For a citrus flavouring: fold 10ml/2 tsp finely grated lemon, orange or lime zest into the cake mixture. (You can add a little more than this if you wish, but too much will destroy the delicate 'tang'.)

Making a Swiss (Jelly) Roll

Ingredients

4 size 3 (medium) eggs, separated
115 g/4 oz/½ cup caster (superfine) sugar
115 g/4 oz/1 cup plain (all-purpose) flour
5 ml/1 tsp baking powder

1 Preheat a 180°C/350°F/Gas 4 oven. Grease a 33 × 23 cm/13 × 9 in Swiss-roll tin (jelly-roll pan), line with greaseproof (waxed) paper and grease the paper.

2 Whisk the egg whites in a clean, dry bowl until stiff. Beat in about 30 ml/2 tbsp of the sugar.

3 Place the egg yolks, remaining sugar and 15 ml/1 tbsp water in a bowl and beat for about 2 minutes until the mixture is pale and leaves a thick trail when you lift the beaters.

4 Using a large metal spoon, carefully fold the beaten egg yolks into the egg-white mixture.

5 Sift together the flour and baking powder. Using a large metal spoon, carefully fold the flour mixture into the egg mixture.

6 Pour the cake mixture into the prepared tin and then smooth the surface, being careful not to press out any air as you do so.

7 Bake in the centre of the oven for 12–15 minutes. To test if cooked, press lightly in the centre. If the cake springs back, it is done. It will also start to come away from the edges of the tin.

8 Turn out the cake on to a piece of greaseproof paper lightly sprinkled with caster (superfine) sugar. Peel off the lining paper and cut off any crisp edges of the cake. Spread with jam and roll up, using the greaseproof paper as a guide. Leave to cool on a wire rack.

VARIATION

Vary the flavour of a Swiss (jelly) roll by adding a little grated orange, lime or lemon zest to the basic mixture.

MAKING FRUIT CAKES

A rich fruit cake is the traditional choice for many special occasions such as weddings, Christmas, anniversaries and christenings. Make the cake a few weeks before icing, keep it wrapped and stored in an airtight container and it should mature beautifully. Because of all the rich ingredients that it contains, this fruit cake will keep moist and fresh for several months.

If you prefer a lighter fruit cake, you can make a less-rich version that is still ideal for marzipanning and covering with either sugarpaste or royal icing (see pages 186–9).

Making a Rich Fruit Cake

Makes a 23 cm/9 in round or a 20 cm/8 in square cake

450 g/1 lb/3 cups currants
300 g/11 oz/1¾ cups sultanas
175 g/6 oz/1 cup raisins
115 g/4 oz/½ cup glacé cherries, halved
115 g/4 oz/1 cup almonds, chopped
100 g/3½ oz/⅔ cup mixed (citrus) peel
grated rind of 2 lemons
45 ml/3 tbsp brandy
300 g/11 oz/2¾ cups plain (all-purpose) flour
7.5 ml/1½ tsp ground mixed spice (allspice)
5 ml/1 tsp ground nutmeg
75 g/3 oz/1 cup ground almonds
250 g/9 oz/scant 1¼ cups soft margarine or butter
275 g/10 oz/1⅓ cups soft brown sugar
20 ml/1½ tbsp black treacle or molasses
6 size 3 (medium) eggs

1 Preheat a 140°C/275°F/Gas 1 oven. Grease a deep cake tin (pan), line with a double thickness of greaseproof (waxed) paper and grease the paper.

2 Place all the ingredients in a large mixing bowl.

3 Stir to combine and then beat thoroughly with a wooden spoon for 3–6 minutes, until well-mixed.

4 Spoon the mixture into the tin and smooth the surface with the back of a wet metal spoon. Make an impression in the centre to help prevent doming.

5 Bake in the centre of the oven for 3¼–3¾ hours. Test the cake about 30 minutes before the end of the baking time. If it is browning too quickly, cover the top loosely with a piece of tin foil. To test if baked, press lightly in the centre. If the cake feels firm and when a skewer inserted in the centre comes out clean, it is done. Test again at short intervals if necessary.

6 Leave the cake to cool in the tin, then turn out when it is completely cool. The lining paper can be left on to help keep the cake moist.

Making a Light Fruit Cake

Makes a 23 cm/9 in round or a 20 cm/8 in square cake

275 g/10 oz/1⅓ cups soft margarine or butter

275 g/10 oz/1⅓ cups caster (superfine) sugar

grated rind of 1 orange

6 size 3 (medium) eggs, beaten

400 g/14 oz/3½ cups plain (all-purpose) flour

5 ml/1 tsp baking powder

12.5 ml/2½ tsp ground mixed spice (allspice)

225 g/8 oz/1½ cups currants

225 g/8 oz/1⅓ cups sultanas

225 g/8 oz/1⅓ cups raisins

75 g/3 oz/2l ready-to-eat dried apricots, chopped

150 g/5 oz/1 cup mixed (citrus) peel

1 Preheat a 150°C/300°F/Gas 2 oven. Grease a deep cake tin (pan), line the base and sides with a double thickness of greaseproof (waxed) paper and grease the paper.

2 Place all the ingredients in a large mixing bowl. Stir to combine, then beat thoroughly with a wooden spoon for 3–4 minutes, depending on the size of the cake, until well-mixed.

3 Spoon the mixture into the prepared cake tin and then smooth the surface with the back of a wet metal spoon. Make a slight impression in the centre in order to help prevent the cake from doming as it begins to rise during the cooking process.

4 Bake in the centre of the oven for 3¼–3¾ hours. Test the cake about 15 minutes before the end of the baking time. If it is browning too quickly, cover the top loosely with tin foil. To test if baked, press in the centre. If the cake feels firm, and when a skewer inserted in the centre comes out clean, it is done. Test again at intervals if necessary. Leave the cake to cool in the tin, then turn out. The lining paper can be left on to help keep the cake moist.

STORING

Wrapped and in an airtight container, a fruit cake will keep for several months.

MAKING BASIC ICINGS

The creamy, rich flavour and silky smoothness of butter icing are popular with both children and adults. The icing can be varied in colour and flavour and makes a decorative filling and coating for sponge cakes or Swiss (jelly) rolls. Simply swirled, or more elaborately piped, butter icing gives a delicious and attractive finish. The quantity given here makes enough to fill and coat the sides and top of a 20 cm/8 in round sponge cake.

Glacé icing can be made in just a few minutes and can be varied by adding a few drops of either food colouring or flavouring. The quantity specified in the recipe makes sufficient icing to cover the top and decorate a 20 cm/8 in round sponge cake.

Rich, delicious fudge frosting can transform a simple sponge cake. Spread the frosting smoothly over the cake, or swirl or pipe it – it is very versatile. The amount given in the recipe will fill and coat the top and sides of a 20 cm/8 in round sponge cake.

As shiny and smooth as silk, dark satin-chocolate icing can be poured over a sponge cake. A few fresh flowers, pieces of fresh fruit, simple chocolate shapes or white-chocolate piping add the finishing touch. The recipe given here makes sufficient to cover a 20 cm/8 in square or a 23 cm/9 in round cake.

Making Butter Icing

Makes 350 g/12 oz

75 g/3 oz/6 tbsp butter, softened, or soft margarine

225 g/8 oz/2 cups icing (confectioners') sugar, sifted

5 ml/1 tsp vanilla essence (extract)

10–15 ml/2–3 tsp milk

FLAVOURINGS

These amounts are for a single quantity of butter icing. Increase or decrease the amounts proportionally as needed.

Chocolate: blend 15 ml/1 tbsp cocoa powder with 15 ml/1 tbsp hot water. Cool before beating into the icing.

Coffee: blend 10 ml/2 tsp instant-coffee powder or granules with 15 ml/1 tbsp boiling water. Allow to cool before beating into the icing.

Lemon, orange or lime: substitute the vanilla essence (extract) and milk for lemon, orange or lime juice and 10 ml/2 tsp finely grated citrus zest. Omit the zest if using the icing for piping. Lightly colour with the appropriate shade of food colouring, if you wish.

1 Put the butter or margarine, icing (confectioners') sugar, vanilla essence (extract) and 5 ml/1 tsp milk in a bowl.

2 Beat with a wooden spoon, adding sufficient extra milk to give a light, smooth and fluffy consistency.

Making Glacé Icing

Makes 225 g/8 oz

225 g/8 oz/2 cups icing (confectioners') sugar

30–45 ml/2–3 tbsp warm water or fruit juice

food colouring (optional)

1 Sift the icing (confectioners') sugar into a large mixing bowl to eliminate any lumps.

2 Using a wooden spoon, gradually stir in enough water to make an icing with the consistency of thick cream. Beat until the icing is completely smooth. It should be thick enough to coat the back of the spoon. If it is too runny, beat in a little more sifted icing sugar to thicken it slightly.

3 To colour the icing, beat in a few drops of food colouring. Use the icing immediately for coating or piping, before it begins to set.

Making Fudge Frosting

Makes 350 g/12 oz

50 g/2 oz/2 squares plain chocolate

225 g/8 oz/2 cups icing (confectioners') sugar, sifted

50 g/2 oz/4 tbsp butter or margarine

45 ml/3 tbsp milk or single (light) cream

5 ml/1 tsp vanilla essence (extract)

1 Break or chop the chocolate into small pieces. Put the chocolate, icing (confectioners') sugar, butter or margarine, milk and vanilla essence (extract) in a saucepan. Stir over a very low heat until the chocolate and butter or margarine melt. Remove from the heat and stir until blended.

2 Beat the icing frequently as it cools until it thickens sufficiently to use for spreading or piping. Use immediately and work quickly once it has reached the correct consistency.

Making Satin-chocolate Icing

Makes 225 g/8 oz

175 g/6 oz/6 squares plain chocolate

150 ml/¼ pint/⅔ cup single (light) cream

2.5 ml/½ tsp instant-coffee powder

1 Break or chop the chocolate into small pieces. Put the chocolate, cream and coffee in a heavy-based saucepan. Place the cake on a wire rack.

2 Stir over a very low heat until the chocolate melts and the mixture is smooth and evenly blended.

3 Remove from the heat and pour the icing over the cake, letting it run down the sides to coat it completely. Spread the icing with a palette knife (spatula) as necessary, working quickly before the icing has time to thicken.

Decorating Ideas

Generous swirls of butter icing give a mouth-watering effect to a cake.

Drizzled or spread, glacé icing can quickly turn a plain cake into something special.

Thick, glossy swirls of fudge frosting almost make a decoration in themselves.

Satin-chocolate icing brings a real touch of sophistication to the most humble of cakes.

CAKES FOR A SPECIAL OCCASION

Both plain and flavoured sponge cakes can be decorated to produce beautiful cakes for a special occasion – or for when you simply feel like a treat.

The mouth-watering chocolate cake is very quick to make. The white-chocolate decorations make a lovely contrast against the rich, dark icing.

The light lemon quick-mix sponge cake would be ideal for celebrating Easter. It is decorated with lemon butter icing and marzipan flowers.

CHOCOLATE LEAVES

Choose freshly picked leaves with very well-defined veins, such as rose leaves. Holding on to the stem and using a small paintbrush, coat the underside of each leaf with melted chocolate (do not go over the edge or the leaf will be difficult to peel off). Leave to set, then carefully remove the leaf.

RICH CHOCOLATE CAKE

SERVES 8–10

175 g/6 oz/¾ cup butter, softened
115 g/4 oz/½ cup caster (superfine) sugar
250 g/9 oz/9 squares plain chocolate, melted
200 g/7 oz/2⅓ cups ground almonds
4 size 3 (medium) eggs, separated
115 g/4 oz/4 squares white chocolate, melted, to decorate

1 Preheat a 180°C/350°F/Gas 4 oven. Grease a deep 21 cm/8½ in springform cake tin (pan), line the base with greaseproof (waxed) paper and grease the paper.

2 Place 115 g/4 oz/½ cup of the butter and all of the sugar in a bowl and beat until fluffy. Add two-thirds of the plain chocolate, the almonds and the egg yolks and beat until blended.

3 Whisk the egg whites in another clean, dry bowl until stiff. Fold them into the chocolate mixture, then transfer to the prepared tin and smooth the surface. Bake for 50–55 minutes or until a skewer inserted into the centre of the cake comes out clean. Leave the cake in the tin for about 5 minutes, then turn out on to a wire rack, peel off the lining paper and leave to cool completely.

4 Place the remaining butter and remaining melted plain chocolate in a small saucepan. Heat very gently, stirring constantly, until melted together. Pour over the cake, allowing the topping to coat the sides of the cake too. Leave to set for at least 1 hour. To decorate, fill a small greaseproof-paper piping bag with about one-third of the melted white chocolate and snip the end. Drizzle around the top of the cake to make a double border. Use the remaining chocolate to make leaves. Leave to set completely.

EASTER SPONGE CAKE

SERVES 10–12

1½ × quantity lemon-flavoured Quick-Mix Sponge-Cake mix (see page 178)

2 × quantity lemon-flavoured Butter Icing (see page 182)

55 g/2 oz/½ cup flaked almonds, toasted

55 g/2 oz white marzipan (see page 186)

green, orange and yellow food colourings

1 Bake the sponge cake following the instructions on page 178, but dividing the mixture between 2 greased and lined 20 cm/8 in sandwich tins (shallow cake pans). When completely cool, sandwich the cakes together with one-quarter of the butter icing. Spread the side of the cake evenly with another one-quarter of icing.

2 Press the almonds on to the sides to cover them evenly. Spread the top of the cake evenly with another one-quarter of icing and finish with a palette knife (spatula) dipped in hot water, spreading backwards and forwards to give an even, lined effect.

3 Put the remaining icing into a nylon piping bag fitted with a medium-sized gâteau nozzle and then carefully pipe a scroll edging.

4 Colour the marzipan with the food colourings, and use flower cutters to make the cut-out marzipan flowers.

5 Arrange the marzipan flowers on the cake and leave the icing to set.

MAKING AND USING MARZIPAN AND SUGARPASTE ICING

Marzipan can be a decorative icing in its own right, or it can provide a smooth, moisture-proof undercoat for sugarpaste or royal icing. It can also be crimped, embossed, cut out and modelled into all kinds of shapes, and the white variety takes colour well. The recipe given here is sufficient to cover the top and sides of an 18 cm/7 in round or a 15 cm/6 in square cake.

Once you have applied the marzipan, leave it to dry for a day or two before icing the cake. If you do not wish to make your own marzipan, or if you have any concerns about using raw eggs in uncooked recipes, do buy ready-made marzipan. It is very good-quality, does not contain raw egg and is available in 2 colours, white and yellow.

Sugarpaste icing is pliable, easy to make and use, and can be coloured and moulded in the most imaginative fashion. It gives a softer look to a cake than royal icing (see overleaf), and requires only 1 rolled-out layer. Fruit cakes are usually covered with marzipan first, but this is not necessary with a sponge base. Add a little food colouring to tint if you wish. The recipe given here makes sufficient to cover the top and sides of an 18 cm/7 in round or a 15 cm/6 in square cake. Alternatively, shop-bought sugarpaste (also known as 'easy-roll icing') is very good-quality and handy to use.

MAKING MARZIPAN

Put 225 g/8 oz/2¼ cups ground almonds, 115 g/4 oz/1 cup sifted icing (confectioners') sugar and 115 g/4 oz/½ cup caster (superfine) sugar into a bowl and mix together. Add 5 ml/1 tsp lemon juice, 2 drops almond essence (extract) and enough beaten egg to mix to a soft but firm dough. Gather together with your fingers to form a ball. Knead the marzipan on a work surface lightly dusted with sifted icing sugar for several minutes until it is smooth. *Makes 450 g/1 lb.*

MAKING SUGARPASTE ICING

Put 1 size 3 (medium) egg white and 15 ml/1 tbsp warmed liquid glucose in a bowl. Stir with a wooden spoon to break up the egg white. Add 350 g/12 oz/3 cups sifted icing (confectioners') sugar and mix well with a palette knife (spatula), using a chopping action, until the icing begins to bind together. Knead the mixture with your fingers until it forms a ball. Knead the sugarpaste on a work surface dusted with sifted icing sugar until smooth, soft and pliable. If the icing is too soft, knead in a little more sifted icing sugar. *Makes 350 g/12 oz.*

MARZIPANNING AND COVERING A CAKE WITH SUGARPASTE ICING

1 Brush the cake with a little warmed and sieved apricot jam. Dust a work surface with icing (confectioners') sugar. Roll out the marzipan to a 5 mm/¼ in thickness and large enough to cover the top and sides of the cake, allowing about an extra 7.5 cm/3 in all round for trimming. Place the marzipan over a rolling pin and drape it over the cake to cover it evenly.

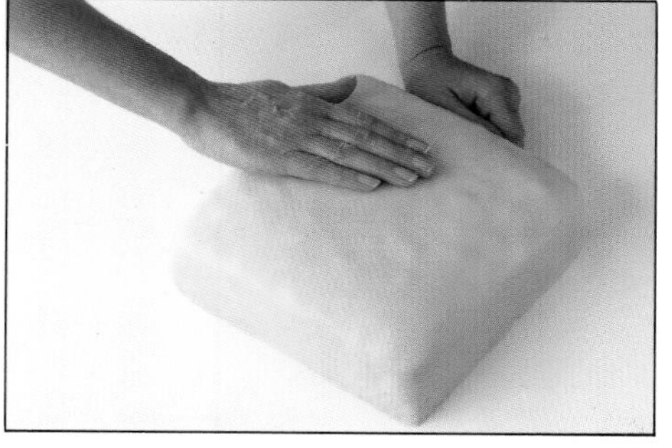

2 Ensure that there are no creases in the marzipan – all the excess should fall on to the work surface. Use the palms of your hands to smooth the sides, then trim the excess marzipan. Using your hands, work in a circular motion over the surface of the marzipan to give it a smooth finish. Lay a piece of greaseproof (waxed) paper over the top, then leave to dry before covering with icing.

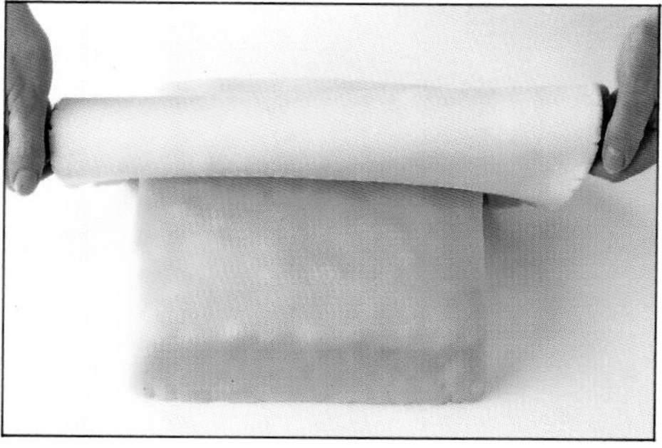

3 To cover with icing, brush a little water or sherry over the marzipanned surface to help the icing stick to the marzipan. Dust a work surface with icing (confectioners') sugar. Roll out the sugarpaste to a 5 mm/¼ in thickness and large enough to cover the top and sides of the cake, plus a little extra. Place the sugarpaste over a rolling pin and drape it over the cake.

MARZIPANNING A CAKE FOR ROYAL ICING

1 If the cake is not absolutely flat, fill any hollows or build up the top edge (if it is lower than the top of the cake) with a little marzipan. Brush the top of the cake with warmed and sieved apricot jam. Dust a work surface with icing (confectioners') sugar. Roll out about one-third of the marzipan to a round 5 mm/¼ in thickness and approximately 12 mm/½ in larger in size than the top of the cake.

2 Invert the top of the cake on to the marzipan. Trim the marzipan, then press it inwards so that it is flush with the edge of the cake. Carefully turn the cake the right way up and brush the sides with apricot jam. Knead the remaining marzipan and any trimmings to form a ball. For the sides of the cake, measure the circumference with a piece of string, and the height of the sides with another piece.

3 Roll out a strip of marzipan to the same thickness as the top, matching the length and width to the measured string. Hold the cake on its side and roll it along the marzipan strip, pressing the marzipan neatly into position. Trim if necessary. Smooth the joins together using a palette knife (spatula). Lay a piece of greaseproof (waxed) paper very loosely over the cake to protect the surface, then leave for at least 24 hours to dry before covering with icing. (It is important always to leave marzipan to dry out so that it will provide a good moisture-proof layer.)

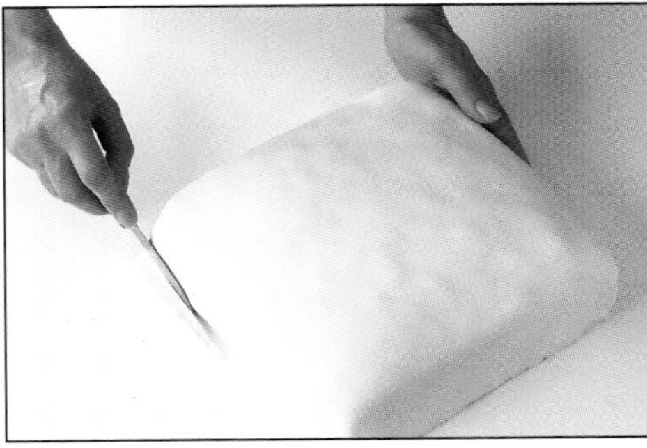

4 Dust your hands with a little cornflour (cornstarch). Smooth the top and sides of the cake with your hands, working from top to bottom, to eliminate any air bubbles. Using a sharp knife, trim off the excess sugarpaste, cutting flush with the base of the cake.

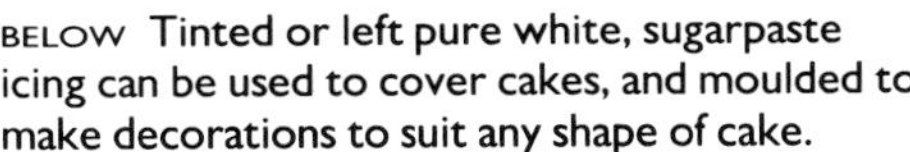

BELOW **Tinted or left pure white, sugarpaste icing can be used to cover cakes, and moulded to make decorations to suit any shape of cake.**

MAKING AND USING ROYAL ICING

Royal icing has gained a regal position in the world of icing. Any special-occasion cake that demands a classical, professional finish uses this smooth, satin-like icing. The following recipe makes sufficient to cover the top and sides of a 23 cm/9 in round or a 20 cm/8 in square cake.

The 'Noel' Christmas cake is a simple, traditional design with easy-to-pipe decorations. Green and red food colourings are added to the icing to create the holly and berries.

MAKING ROYAL ICING

Put 3 size 3 (medium) egg whites in a bowl and stir lightly with a wooden spoon to break them up. Add about 675 g/1½ lb/6 cups sifted icing (confectioners') sugar gradually in small quantities, beating well with a wooden spoon between each addition, to make a smooth, white, shiny icing with the consistency of very stiff meringue. It should be thin enough to spread, but thick enough to hold its shape. Beat in 7.5 ml/1½ tsp glycerine, a few drops of lemon juice and a little food colouring, if you wish. Cover the icing with damp cling film (plastic wrap) or a lid so that it does not dry out, and leave to stand for 1 hour. Stir before using to burst any air bubbles. Even when working with royal icing, always keep it covered so that it does not dry out. *Makes 675 g/1½ lb.*

COVERING A ROUND CAKE WITH ROYAL ICING

A cake that is to be coated with royal icing is always covered with marzipan first (see page 187). The marzipan should be applied 1–2 days before the royal icing so that it has time to dry, providing a firm surface.

1 To flat-ice a cake, first put about 30 ml/2 tbsp of icing in the centre of the marzipanned cake. Using a small palette knife (spatula), spread the icing over the top of the cake, working back and forth to eliminate any air bubbles, until the top of the cake is completely covered. Trim any icing that extends over the edge of the cake.

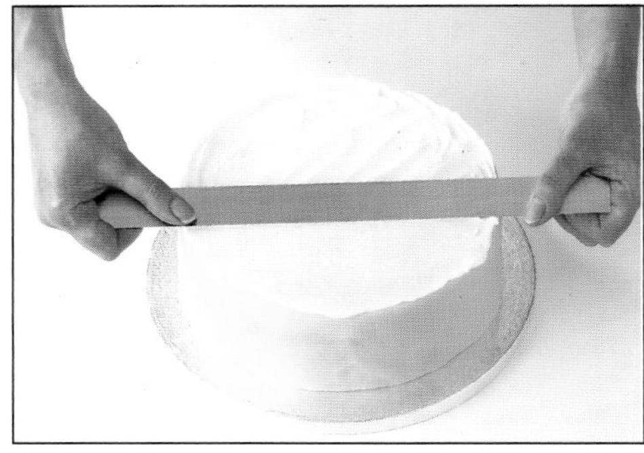

2 Position a straightedge on the top edge of the cake furthest away from you. Slowly and smoothly pull the straightedge across the surface of the icing in one movement, holding it at a slight angle. Trim any excess icing from the top edges of the cake to give a straight, neat edge. Leave the icing to dry for several hours, or overnight.

3 Place the cake on a turntable. To cover the sides, spread some icing on to the sides of the cake using a palette knife. Rock the knife back and forth as you spread the icing to eliminate air bubbles. Rotate the turntable as you work your way around the cake.

4 Hold a plain side-scraper against the side of the cake at an angle. Turn the turntable round in a continuous motion, while pulling the scraper smoothly in the opposite direction. When you have completed the turn, carefully lift the scraper to leave a neat join. Trim off any excess icing. Leave the cake to dry, uncovered, then apply 2 or 3 more coats of icing in the same way. For a really smooth final layer, use a slightly softer consistency of icing.

'NOEL' CHRISTMAS CAKE

SERVES 50

1 quantity Rich-Fruit-Cake mix (see page 180)

30 ml/2 tbsp apricot jam, warmed and sieved

800 g/1¾ lb white marzipan

1½ × quantity Royal Icing (see opposite)

44 large gold dragées

red and green food colourings

2½ m/2½ yds × 20 mm/¾ in wide gold ribbon

2½ m/2½ yds × 5 mm/¼ in wide red ribbon

1 Bake the cake following the instructions on page 180 and allow to cool. Brush with the apricot jam, cover with marzipan (see page 187) and place on a 25 cm/10 in silver cake board.

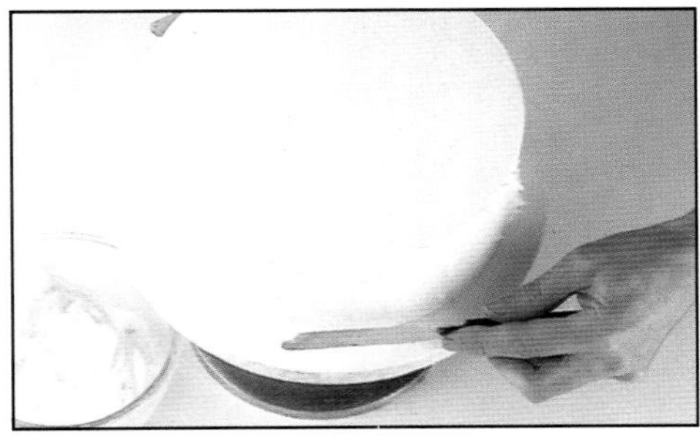

2 Flat-ice the top of the cake with 2 layers of royal icing and leave until dry. Keep any icing that is not in use covered to prevent it from drying out. Using a small palette knife (spatula), ice the sides of the cake with peaked icing, leaving a space around the centre of the side to fit the ribbon.

3 Put half of the remaining royal icing in a greaseproof- (waxed-) paper piping bag, fitted with a No. 0 plain writing nozzle, and pipe beads of icing around the top edge of the cake. Place a gold dragée on every other bead of icing.

4 Put the rest of the royal icing in another piping bag, fitted with a No. 1 plain writing nozzle. Write NOEL across the cake and then pipe holly leaves, stems and berries. Carefully fit the gold ribbon around the cake, pressing it into the icing. Fit the red ribbon over the top of the gold, and secure with a bead of icing. Tie a neat red bow and attach it to the front of the cake. Use the remaining ribbon around the cake board, securing with a pin.

5 Colour 30 ml/2 tbsp of the remaining royal icing bright green and 15 ml/1 tbsp bright red with food colouring. Put the red icing in a greaseproof-paper piping bag fitted with a No. 0 plain writing nozzle. Pipe NOEL in red over the white icing, pipe the holly berries, and pipe alternate dots around the edge of the cake. Wash the piping bag, put in the green icing and pipe the leaves.

CHILDREN'S NOVELTY CAKES

A brightly coloured cake in a familiar shape will be the centrepiece of any children's party. The cakes shown here are easy to make and taste delicious.

For the tree, choose whichever fruit you prefer. You could make the apples green instead of red, have a mixture of red and green apples, or make golden pears, all of which will contrast well with the green icing. The delightful beehive cake would be perfect for a spring or summer party outdoors.

POSITIONING TIP

To stand the tree up at a slight angle, cut out a 'template' of thick card (cardboard) from around the un-iced cake. Decorate the cake on the card and prop it up on a small block of wood. Alternatively, decorate the cake flat on a cake board.

APPLE-TREE CAKE

SERVES 10–12

1 quantity chocolate-flavour Quick-Mix Sponge-Cake mix (see page 178)

1 quantity chocolate-flavour Swiss- (Jelly-) Roll mix (see page 179), baked and rolled with ¼ quantity chocolate-flavour Butter Icing (see page 182)

¼ quantity chocolate-flavour Butter Icing

½ quantity Butter Icing, coloured green with food colouring

225 g/8 oz white marzipan

red food colouring

desiccated (shredded) coconut, coloured green with food colouring

tiny fresh flowers, to decorate (optional)

1 Preheat a 180°C/350°F/Gas 4 oven. Grease and flour a 450 g/1 lb fluted round cake tin (pan) or pudding basin. Spoon in the cake mixture and smooth the surface. Bake in the centre of the oven for 35–40 minutes or until a skewer inserted into the centre of the cake comes out clean. Leave in the tin for about 5 minutes, then turn out on to a wire rack and leave to cool.

2 Arrange the Swiss (jelly) roll on a card (cardboard) template (see above left) or cake board. Swirl the chocolate butter icing over the tree trunk. Use three-quarters of the green icing for the top of the tree, making it peak and swirl. Position on top of the tree trunk.

3 Colour about 25 g/1 oz of the marzipan green. Colour the remainder red, then roll it into cherry-size balls. Roll the green marzipan into tiny sausage shapes to make the stalks and leaves. Use a cocktail stick (toothpick) to make tiny holes in the tops of the apples, then insert the stalks and leaves. Twist a length of florist's tape around florist's wire, then cut it into 7.5 cm/3 in lengths. Press the lengths of wire through the apples, bending the ends so that the apples cannot fall off when hanging. Press the apples into the tree, reserving the extra apples to scatter around the bottom.

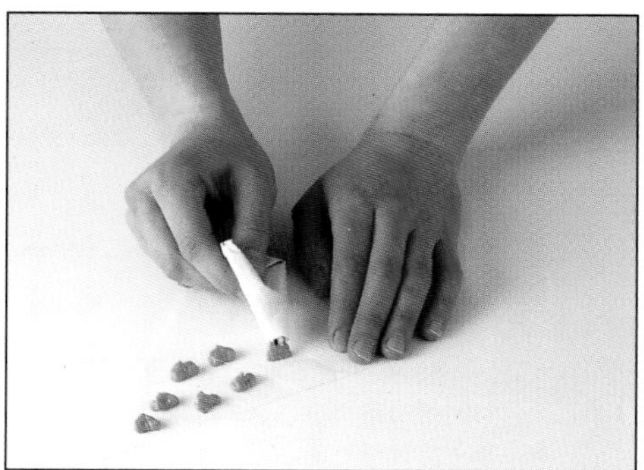

4 Use the remaining green icing to fill a greaseproof- (waxed-) paper piping bag. Practise piping the leaves on greaseproof paper before piping leaves all over the tree top. Scatter the green coconut around the base of the tree and pipe a few extra leaves. Add a few tiny fresh flowers, if you wish. Remove the wires from the cake before serving.

Beehive Cake

Serves 8–10

1 quantity Quick-Mix Sponge-Cake mix (see page 178)

900 g/2 lb yellow marzipan

75 ml/5 tbsp apricot jam, warmed and sieved

black food colouring

1 Preheat a 180°C/350°F/Gas 4 oven. Grease and flour a 900 g/2 lb pudding basin. Spoon in the cake mixture and smooth the surface. Bake in the centre of the oven for 40–45 minutes or until a skewer inserted into the centre of the cake comes out clean. Leave the cake in the basin for about 5 minutes, then turn out on to a wire rack and leave to cool completely.

2 Cut off 175 g/6 oz of marzipan and set aside, wrapped in cling film (plastic wrap). Knead the remaining marzipan on a work surface dusted with icing (confectioners') sugar, then roll it into a long, thin sausage. If it breaks when it gets too long, make more than one sausage. Place the cake, dome-side up, on a cake board and brush the surface with the warmed apricot jam.

3 Starting at the back of the base, coil the marzipan sausage around the cake, keeping it neat and tight all the way to the top. Make any joins neatly at the back of the cake.

4 Cut an arched doorway at the front of the cake. Remove the cut-out section and cut away some of the cake inside to make a hollow. Brush the crumbs away from the doorway.

5 To make up 6 bees, divide the reserved marzipan in half and colour 1 portion black. Divide both the black and the yellow marzipan into 12 small balls. To make a bee, pinch 2 balls of each colour together with a little water. Repeat to make up the remaining bees. Using small scissors, cut a piece of rice paper to make 6 pairs of wings, then stick them to the bees with a drop of water. Twist a length of florist's tape around florist's wire, cut it into pieces and use it to pierce the bees from underneath. Press the other ends of the wires into the cake in various places. Remove the wires before serving.

Perfect Home Skills

Creating the right ambience at home is a question of adding the personal touch. Hints on how to set the mood when you're entertaining, whether it's an intimate dinner party or a huge birthday celebration, are accompanied by innovative tips on decorating tables and arranging flowers. Making your own curtains and drapes, cushion covers and bed linen help to add a special atmosphere, and houseplant and floral displays provide the finishing touches.

SOFT-FURNISHING FABRICS

Most ready-made items of soft furnishing are expensive, but you can make them just as well at home and much more cheaply. Curtains and drapes, blinds and shades, cushion covers and bed linen require the minimum of sewing skills and little in the way of equipment beyond a sewing machine and an iron.

The choice of fabric plays a major part in setting the style of a room, creating accents of colour to enliven a neutral décor or co-ordinating different elements. Colour is an important consideration when furnishing a room – light shades will tend to open it out, while dark and vivid shades will generally close it up. Many people play safe by choosing neutral shades which, although easy to live with, can look rather dull and impersonal.

The ideal colour scheme is usually a basically harmonious one, with interest added by the judicious use of contrasting or complementary colours for some elements of the design. Soft furnishings, such as cushions or blinds and shades, chosen in fabrics to contrast with the overall colour scheme, can add just the right amount of colour to brighten up a room.

Making soft furnishings at home is the perfect way to experiment with colour and make a visual statement. Most items require a few metres (yards) of fabric at the most. A good point to bear in mind when selecting fabric is that there are no hard-and-fast rules, apart from trying not to mix too many different colours and patterns in one setting. Most good stores will supply swatches of furnishing fabrics without charge for colour matching at home.

Another consideration is that the chosen fabric should be suitable for the intended purpose – for example, heavyweight cloths will make up into good curtains and cushion covers, but will be too stiff and unyielding to make a successful bed valance.

Cotton is the fabric most commonly used for soft furnishings, often with small amounts of synthetic fibres added for strength and to improve crease resistance. Linen is extremely strong, although expensive and inclined to crease badly; the addition of both cotton for economy and synthetics to help prevent creasing is usual. Both cotton and linen shrink when laundered, and you should take this into account when estimating the amounts that you require. Some furnishing fabrics are pre-shrunk during manufacture, and you should also always check this when purchasing.

Man-made fibres have different properties, depending on their composition, but the majority resist creases and shrinking. Their most common use for soft furnishings, apart from being added to cotton and linen blends, is for making easy-care nets and sheer curtains (drapes) which are lightweight and launder well.

ABOVE Neutral tones – beiges, creams and browns – used both for the soft furnishings and for the wall and ceiling decoration create a colour scheme that is attractive and restful on the eye in this living room.

BELOW Nothing succeeds in creating a feeling of cosiness as well as a red/pink colour scheme for soft furnishings – here complemented by the warm red wall covering.

Fabrics suitable for making soft furnishings are as follows:
Brocade: cotton, cotton/synthetic blend or acetate with a woven self-pattern created by areas of different weaves. Used for making formal curtains and drapes and cushion covers.
Calico: inexpensive, medium-weight woven cotton, either dyed or printed, or sold unbleached. Used for curtains and blinds (shades), in particular.
Chintz: glazed, medium-weight furnishing cotton, traditionally printed with patterns of roses and other flowers, birds and animals.
Gingham: inexpensive checked fabric woven from cotton or cotton/polyester blends. Often used for making soft furnishings for kitchens.
Hand-woven fabric: heavyweight or medium-weight cotton with an irregular, rather rough weave. Used for curtains and drapes, cushion covers and bedspreads.
Linen union: hardwearing, heavyweight fabric made from linen with some added cotton, often printed with floral designs. Suitable for curtains and covering upholstery.

ABOVE Bright, cheerful soft-furnishing fabrics make an excellent foil to a plain floor covering.

Madras: hand-woven pure cotton originating from Madras in India. Usually dyed in brilliant colours, often with a woven pattern of checks, plaids and stripes.
Poplin: a lightweight or medium-weight cotton, either plain or printed.
Sateen: cotton or cotton/synthetic fabric with a slight sheen. Curtain lining is usually made of lightweight cotton sateen.
Sheeting: extra-wide fabric for making bed linen. Usually woven from a mixture of 50 per cent cotton and 50 per cent polyester or other man-made fibre, making it easy-care.
Ticking: heavy woven cloth with narrow stripes. Originally used for covering pillows, mattresses and bolsters, but today used as a decorative fabric in its own right.
Velvet: heavy fabric made from cotton or cotton/synthetic blends with a cut pile, used for formal curtains and cushion covers. Corduroy (needlecord) is similar, but here the cut pile forms regular ridges down the cloth.
Voile: light, semi-transparent cotton or synthetic fabric. Used for sheer curtains and bed drapes.

ABOVE Luxurious fabrics used for curtains or drapes, cushions and upholstery are often the ideal medium for adding patterned elements to a room's décor.

BELOW Blues and greens are naturally cool, receding colours, ideal for well-lit south-facing rooms, but can be warmed by splashes of contrast in orange and yellow.

MAKING LINED CURTAINS AND DRAPES

Curtains and drapes are the largest items of soft furnishing to make and, although they may appear difficult, they in fact require only the minimum of sewing skills. The secret of successful curtain-making lies in accurate measuring, estimating and cutting out. There is a wide range of ready-made curtain-heading tapes available, which will create different effects ranging from a narrow ruched band (standard tape) to an intricately pleated border (smocked tape). Stitch the tape along the top of the fabric, following the manufacturer's instructions, then gather or pleat the fabric by simply pulling up the cords in the tape. A series of pockets suspends the curtain from rings or hooks attached to the curtain (drapery) track or pole.

Lined curtains are suitable for most windows, but you may prefer unlined ones for the kitchen and bathroom, as these are easier to launder. To make unlined curtains, simply omit the lining steps shown below and turn and stitch a narrow double hem along the side edges before attaching the heading tape.

RIGHT Lined curtains and drapes hang well and the lining also acts as a barrier to sunlight, preventing fabric colours from fading.

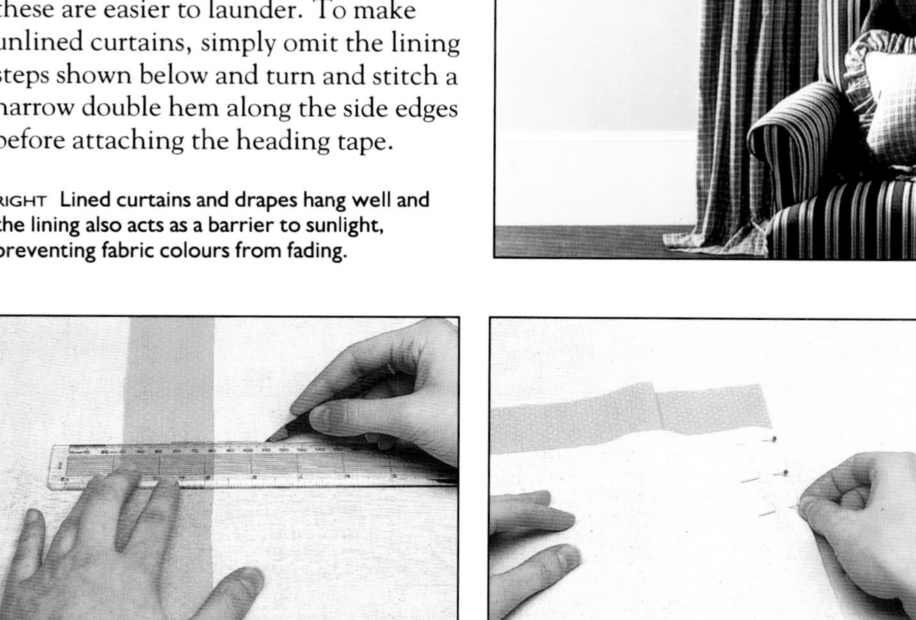

1 Place the lining on the fabric that you have chosen for the curtain (drape) with the right sides together and the lower raw edges aligning. Mark the centre point of the curtain on both the fabric and the lining, using a dressmaker's pencil.

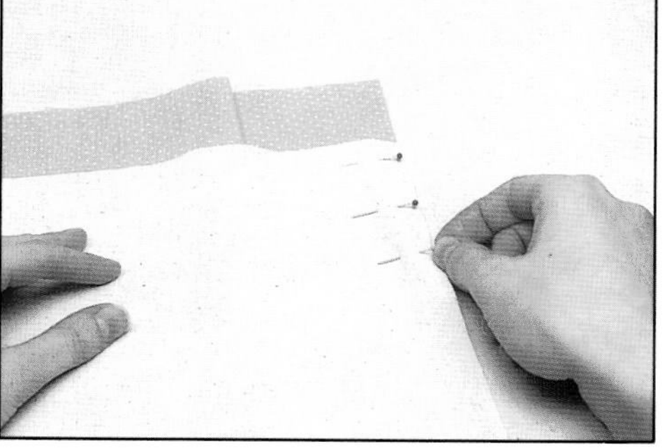

2 With the right sides of the fabric and lining still facing, pin them together along the side edges, taking care that the lower edges of both the fabric and lining are still aligned. At the top, the lining should be 4 cm/1½ in shorter than the fabric.

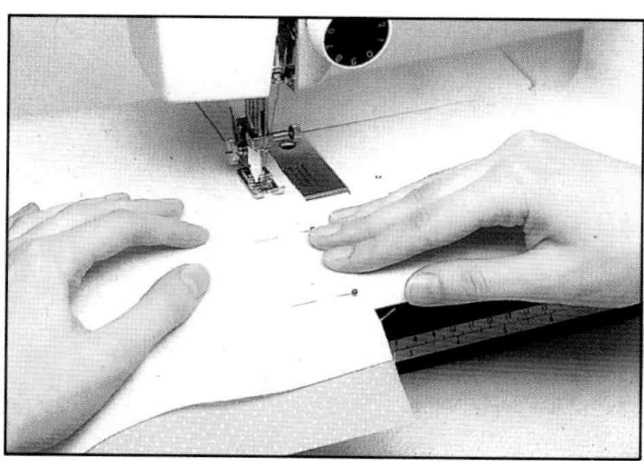

3 Mark the finished length of the curtain and the sewing line for the hem on the lining with a dressmaker's pencil, taking into account the 15 cm/6 in hem allowance. Stitch along the side edges 12 mm/½ in from the raw edge, stitching from the top of the lining to about 10 cm/4 in from the hem sewing line.

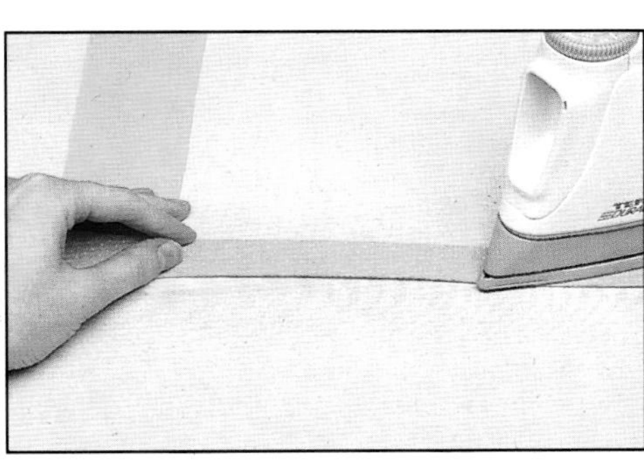

4 Turn to the right side. Press the side edges, making sure that the fabric pulls over to the wrong side by about 2.5 cm/1 in. Matching the marked points at the top of both fabric and lining, fold 4 cm/1½ in of fabric over on to the wrong side and press.

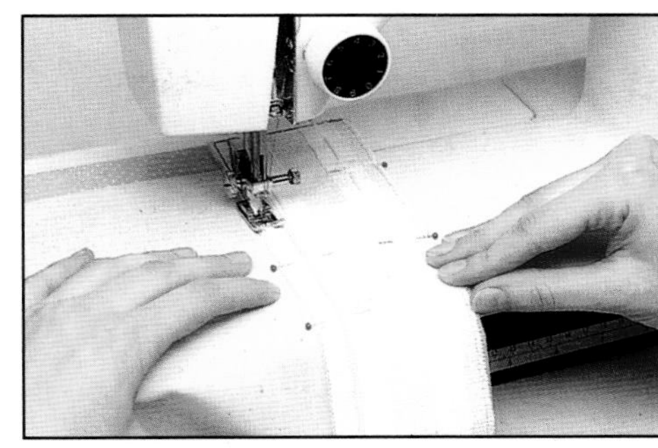

5 Tucking under the raw edges, pin the heading tape in position just below the top of the fabric. Following the manufacturer's instructions, machine stitch the tape to the curtain, taking care to stitch each long side in the same direction to avoid puckering.

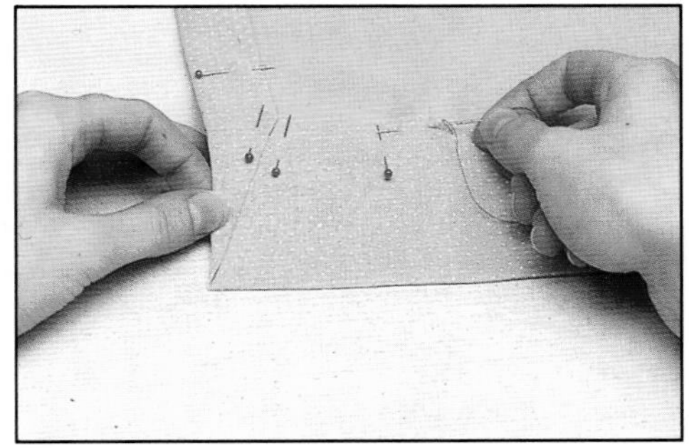

6 Fold over a double 7.5 cm/3 in hem along the lower edge of the fabric and press in place. If you are using heavyweight fabric, fold the corners over to form a mitre and then carefully trim away the surplus cloth. Tack (baste) along the hem.

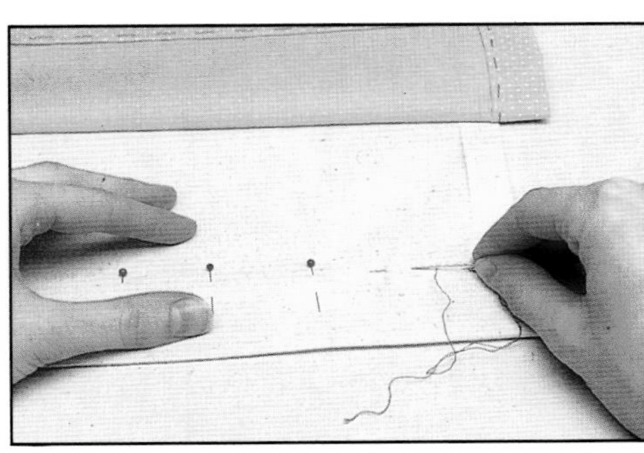

7 Turn up and pin a double hem along the lower edge of the lining so that the hem edge will hang about 20 mm/¾ in above the finished fabric hem. Trim away any surplus lining and then tack along the hem to hold it in place.

8 Pulling from the centre of the heading tape, pull up the cords until the curtain is the correct width. Knot the cords loosely at the centre of the curtain. Hang the curtain for a few days to allow the fabric to settle, then slip stitch both the cloth and lining hems. Finally, slip stitch the lining to the fabric down the remainder of the side.

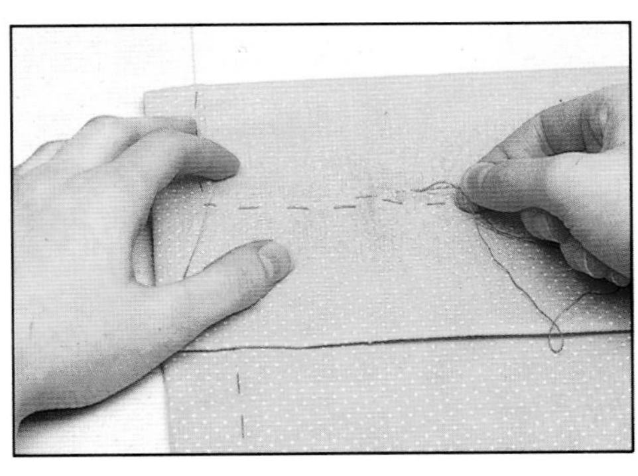

CURTAIN AND DRAPE STYLES

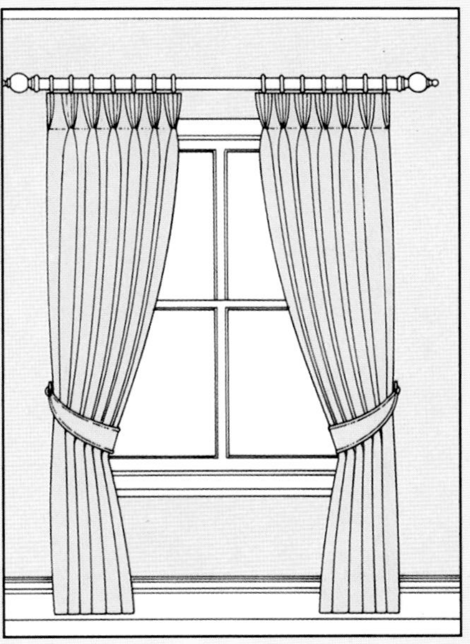

Floor-length curtains can add the illusion of height to square windows. Accentuate the effect by holding the curtains back at window-sill level, using a pair of tie-backs.

With a narrow window, extend the curtain (drapery) track or pole at each side so that, when open, the curtains do not obscure the window.

CALCULATING FABRIC REQUIREMENTS

To calculate the width of fabric, multiply the width of the curtain (drapery) track or pole by the amount of fullness needed for the chosen heading tape (usually between 1½ and 2½ times the width of the window), and allow 3.5 cm/1⅜ in for each side hem. Divide the curtain width required by the width of the fabric, rounding up as necessary. Allow 3 cm/1¼ in for each join that is needed.

To calculate the length, measure downwards from the track or pole to the required curtain length, then add on 4 cm/1½ in to accommodate the heading tape and 15 cm/6 in for the bottom hem.

To calculate the total amount of fabric, multiply the length by the number of widths required.

If you are making lined rather than unlined curtains, you will need almost the same amount of lining as curtain fabric, with just 5 cm/2 in less in the width and 4 cm/1½ in less in the length.

MAKING A PELMET (VALANCE) AND TIE-BACKS

The pelmet (valance) was originally used as a means of keeping curtains and drapes free from dust, and is now very popular simply as a decorative feature. Tie-backs are both attractive and practical, holding back curtains to let in the maximum light.

A fabric-covered pelmet is quick and simple to make with a special PVC (vinyl) material that is self-adhesive on one side and lined with velour on the other. The adhesive is covered with backing paper, which is printed with ready-to-cut pelmet patterns to suit most styles of decoration. Attach the finished pelmet to a batten (furring strip), with the returns secured to the wall above the curtain (drapery) track with angle irons. The batten should be 5 cm/2 in longer than the curtain track at each side of the window.

Plain-shaped tie-backs are easily made with the help of buckram shapes coated with iron-on adhesive. The buckram is available in kit form, pre-cut in several sizes to suit the curtain width. Attach the tie-backs to the wall with rings and hooks. Experiment with the position of the hooks, before fixing, to assess the most pleasing effect.

LEFT A fabric-covered pelmet (valance) provides the perfect finishing touch to this window treatment and echoes the shape of the wallpaper border.

MAKING A PELMET (VALANCE)

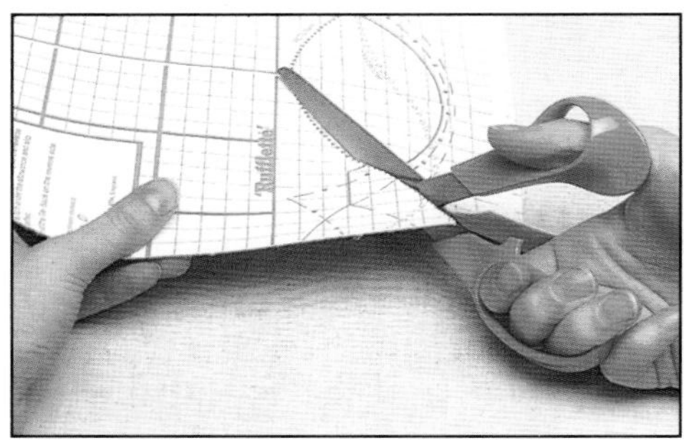

1 Measure the batten (furring strip) and the returns. Cut out the PVC (vinyl) pelmet material to this length, taking care to centre the chosen pattern. Cut out the shaped edge of the pelmet material along the correct line for the required shape. Cut out a piece of fabric about 3 cm/1¼ in larger all around than the pelmet material.

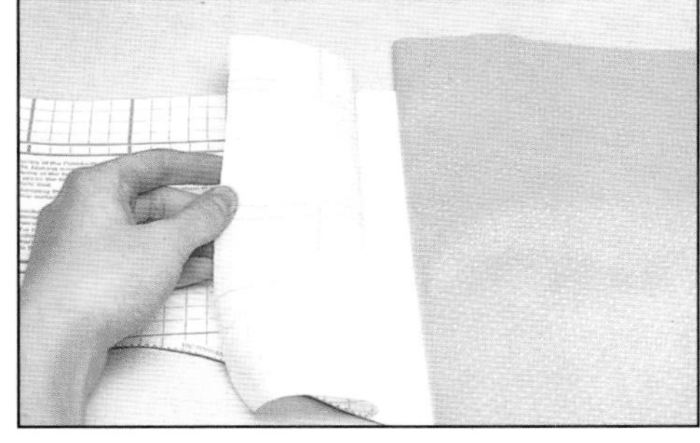

2 Lift the backing paper at the centre of the pelmet material, cut across it and peel back a small amount on either side. Matching the centre of the fabric with the centre of the pelmet material, press the fabric on to the exposed adhesive. Keeping the fabric taut, peel away the backing and smooth the fabric on to the adhesive.

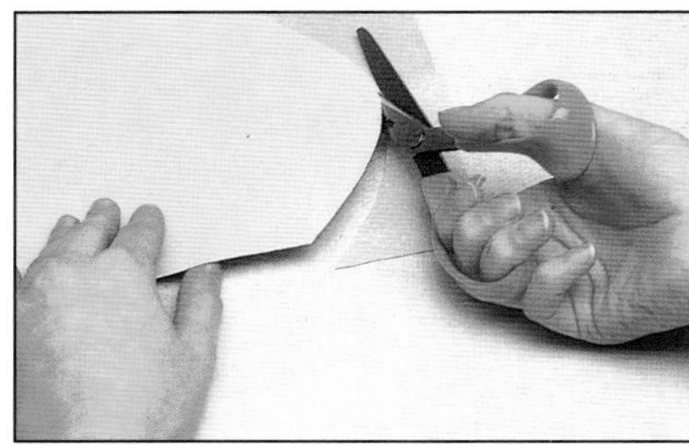

3 Turn the pelmet material so that the velour backing is facing upwards. Using a sharp pair of scissors, carefully cut away the surplus fabric around the edge of the pelmet material.

PELMET (VALANCE) STYLES

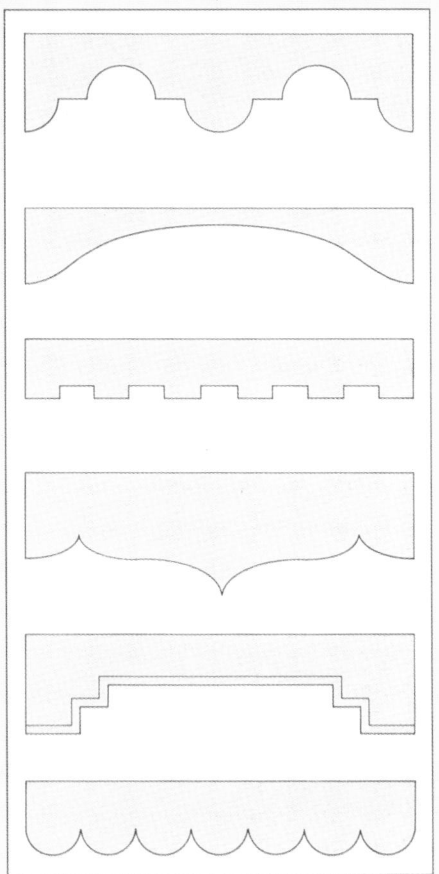

Pelmet styles can be plain or fancy, scalloped or stepped. Choose a style to suit your chosen fabric and the general décor of the room.

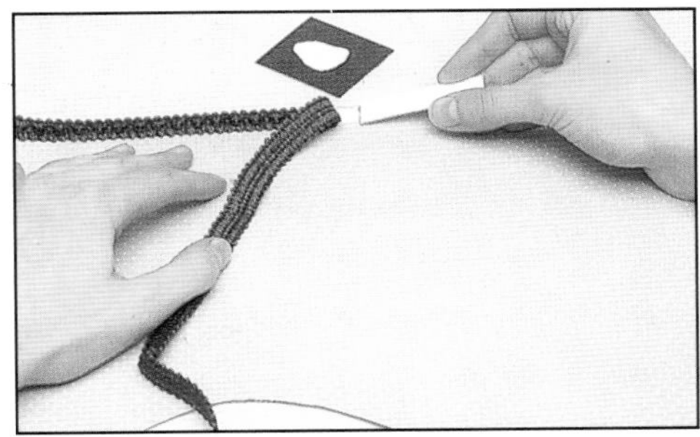

4 For a neat finish, glue a length of braid around the edge of the pelmet using a suitable craft adhesive. Attach strips of touch-and-close fastener to the batten with staples or tacks – use the hooked part only, as the velour backing of the pelmet material acts as the looped part of the fastener. Press the pelmet in position on the batten.

MAKING A SHAPED TIE-BACK

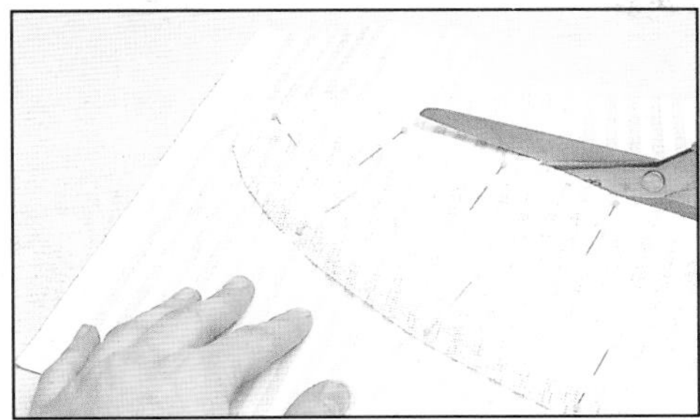

1 To make the back of the tie-back, pin the buckram shape on to the fabric and cut out around the edge of the shape. Lay this on the wrong side of the fabric to make the front, and, using a dressmaker's pencil, mark a line on the fabric 12 mm/½ in all around the outside of the buckram shape. Cut out the larger front piece.

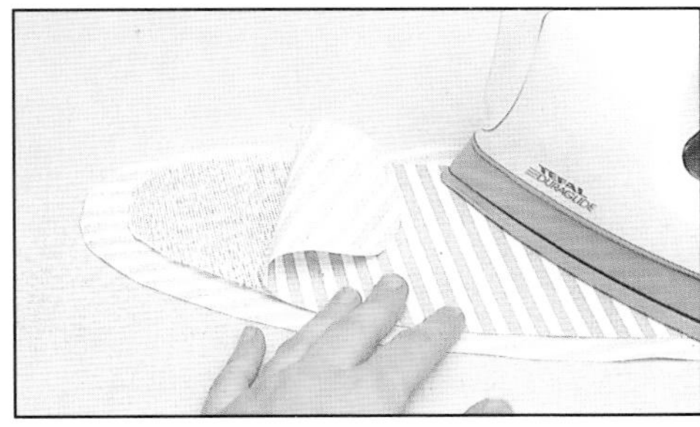

2 With the wrong sides together, sandwich the buckram between the front and back pieces. Press with a hot, dry iron to fuse all the layers together, taking care not to scorch the fabric.

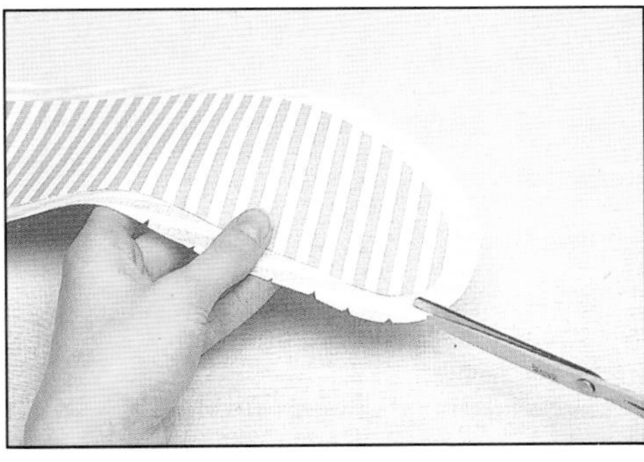

3 Snip into the edge of the surplus fabric all around the tie-back. This will help the fabric to lie neatly without puckering when you turn it over to the wrong side.

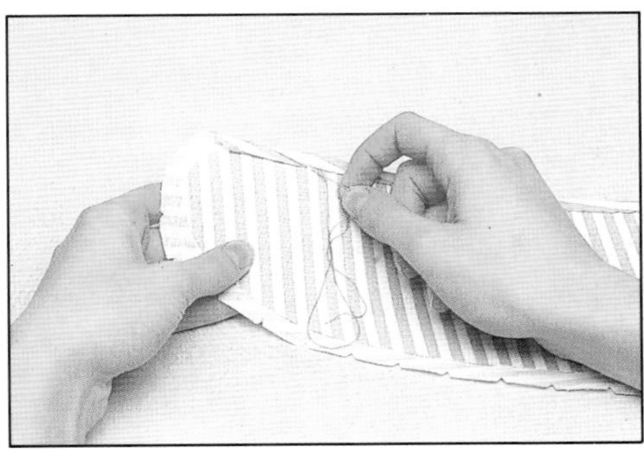

4 Fold the surplus fabric over to the wrong side of the tie-back and turn under the raw snipped edge. Using matching sewing thread, stitch the folded edge neatly in place, taking care that the stitches do not go through to the right side. Stitch a brass ring on to each end of the tie-back.

TIE-BACK VARIATIONS

It is easy to vary the look of plain tie-backs by adding narrow frills or by binding the edges with bias strips of contrasting fabric.

A strip of wide, ornate ribbon or braid makes an unusual tie-back – simply apply iron-on interfacing on the wrong side to stiffen the ribbon and cover the back with a strip of lining fabric in a toning colour. Turn under the raw edges, and slip stitch together around the edge.

RIGHT **Position tie-backs about two-thirds of the way down a short curtain for maximum effect, but do experiment with the positioning before making the final fixing.**

MAKING BLINDS AND SHADES

Blinds are becoming a very popular alternative window-dressing to a pair of curtains (drapes). The styles of blind described here, although made using very similar techniques, create very different effects – choose the softly ruched Austrian blind for a pretty, feminine window treatment and the smartly pleated Roman blind for a room with a modern décor.

Use a light- or medium-weight fabric to make an Austrian blind – anything from lightweight voile or sheer to standard cotton curtain fabric will be suitable. Avoid heavy brocades and handwoven cottons, as these are too thick to drape well. You will need a special type of track to hang and mount the blind; this is known as Austrian-blind track, and is widely available.

A Roman blind, on the other hand, will benefit from being made in a reasonably substantial fabric. You can line this type of blind if you wish, to add body to the pleats and also to retain the warmth of a room. You will need a batten (furring strip) and angle irons to mount the blind. Use strips of touch-and-close fastener to hold the blind in place on the batten.

MAKING A ROMAN BLIND (SHADE)

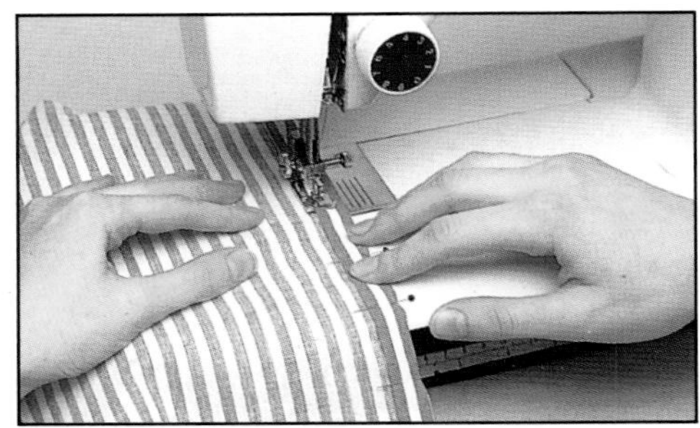

1 Cut out the fabric. Turn, pin and stitch double 12 mm/½ in side hems. Turn, pin and then machine stitch a double 2.5 cm/1 in hem along the top of the fabric. Press all the hems.

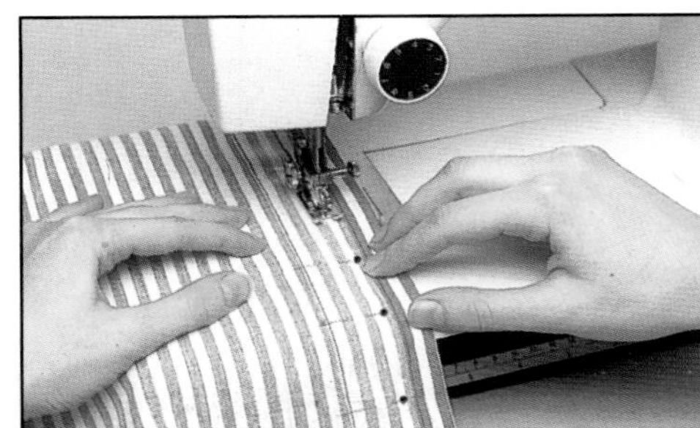

2 Pin and stitch a strip of Roman-blind tape close to the side edge, turning under 9 mm/⅜ in at the top. Stitch another strip along the remaining edge, then attach further strips at intervals across the blind, 25–30 cm/10–12 in apart.

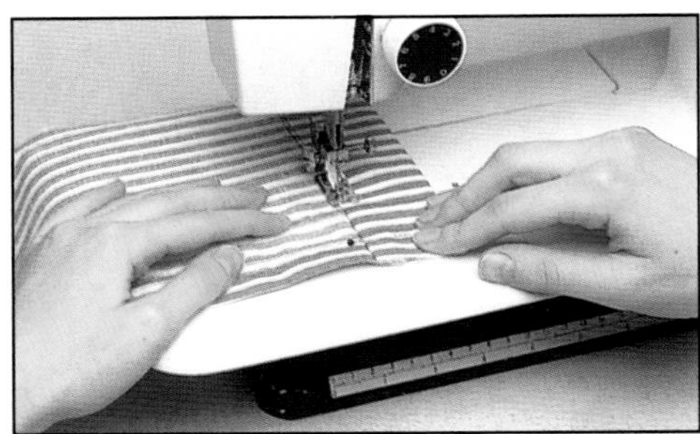

3 At the bottom of the blind, turn over 9 mm/⅜ in and press, then turn over a further 5 cm/2 in to enclose the ends of the tape. Pin and stitch the hem close to the inner fold, leaving the sides open.

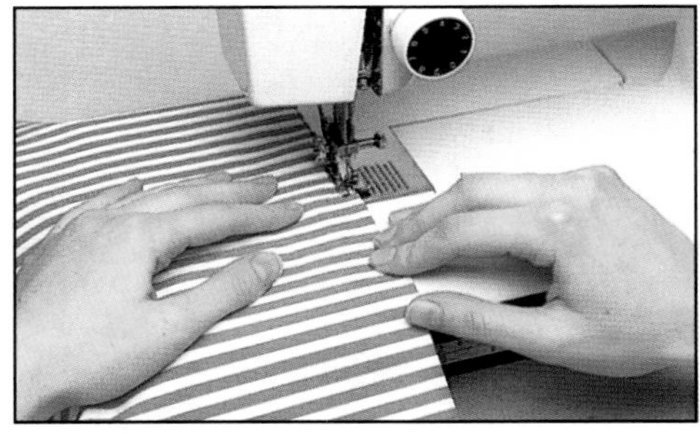

4 Stitch narrow tucks across the width of the blind to correspond with alternate rows of loops or rings on the tape. Make the first tuck level with the second row of loops or rings from the bottom of the blind. To make the tucks, fold the fabric with the wrong sides facing, and stitch 3 mm/⅛ in from the fold.

LEFT A tailored Roman blind (shade) is the perfect answer for a window or décor that demands a simple treatment.

Making an Austrian Blind (Shade)

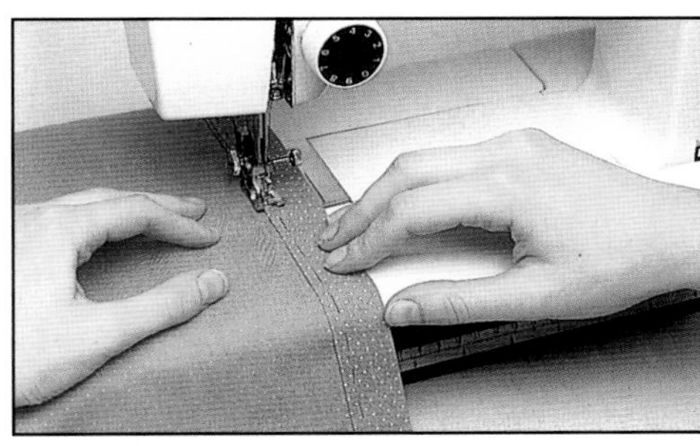

1 Cut out the fabric. Turn, pin, tack (baste) and stitch double 20 mm/¾ in side hems. Turn, pin, tack and stitch a double 20 mm/¾ in hem along the bottom of the fabric. Press all the hems.

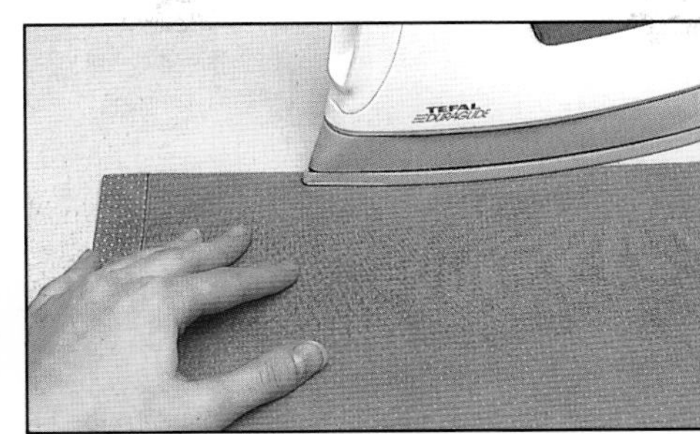

2 Fold the fabric, with the right sides together, vertically like a concertina at approximately 60 cm/24 in evenly spaced intervals and press. The resulting folds mark the positions of the vertical tapes.

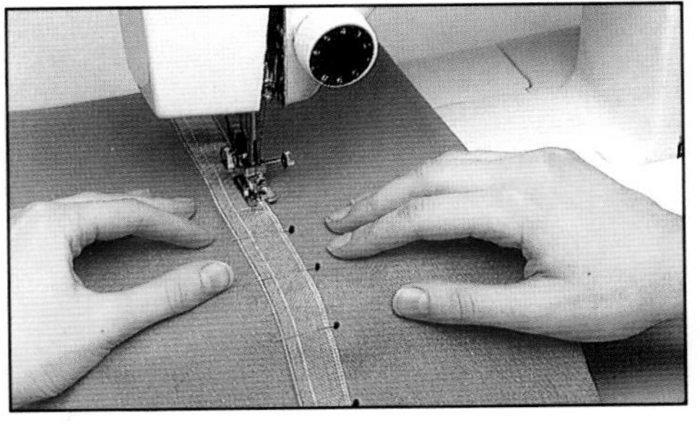

3 Pin and stitch a strip of Austrian-blind tape close to one of the side hems, turning under 12 mm/½ in at the bottom to neaten. Stitch another strip along the remaining side hem, then attach further strips vertically at regular intervals across the blind, aligning one edge of the tape with the pressed folds.

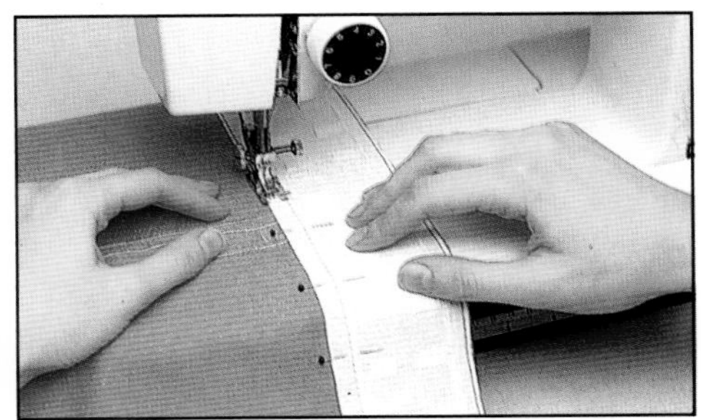

4 Turn over 20 mm/¾ in at the top of the blind and press. Pin the heading tape in position, folding under the raw edges, and stitch in place.

Mounting a Roman Blind (Shade)

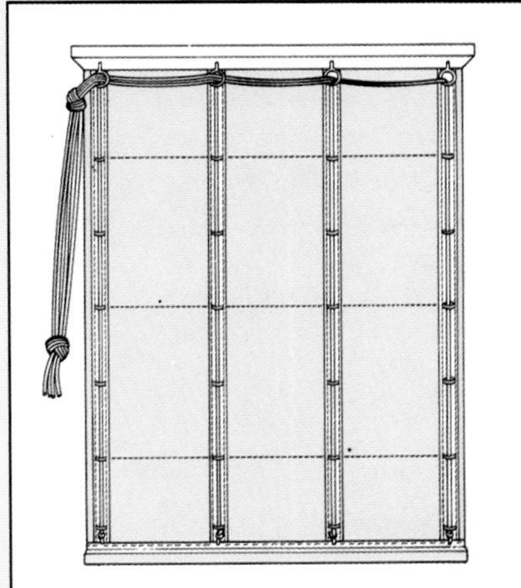

Attach the blind to the top of the batten with strips of touch-and-close fastener. Cut each length of cord to twice the length of the blind plus the distance of the right-hand edge. Thread each cord through the loops in the tape. Knot each length securely on the bottom loop and thread the other end through the corresponding screw eyes on the batten, ending with all the cord ends on the right-hand side of the blind. Knot the cords at the top, cut the ends off level and knot them again.

Austrian blinds are mounted in much the same way, with the cords threaded through rings attached to the track.

Calculating Fabric Requirements

Austrian blind (shade)
To calculate the length, measure the window drop and add 11 cm/2¼ in for hem allowances.

For the width, measure the width of the window and multiply by 2 to 2½ depending on the type of heading tape used. Add 8 cm/3 in for side hems.

You will need enough heading tape to extend across the width of the fabric, plus extra for turnings. You will also need sufficient strips of Austrian-blind tape to position at 60 cm/24 in intervals across the width of the blind. Each strip should be the length of the blind plus 12 mm/½ in; make sure there is a loop or ring 12 mm/½ in up from the bottom of each strip so that they will line up across the blind.

Roman blind (shade)
To calculate the length, measure the window drop, add 14 cm/4½ in for hem allowances and a little extra for the horizontal tucks.

For the width, measure the window and add 6 cm/2 in for side hems.

You will need sufficient strips of Roman-blind tape to position at 25–30 cm/10–12 in intervals across the width of the blind. Each strip should be the length of the blind plus 12 mm/½ in; make sure there is a loop or ring 12 mm/½ in up from the bottom of each strip so that they will match across the blind.

ABOVE An Austrian blind makes a feminine, very decorative window treatment.

MAKING CUSHION COVERS

Cushions add comfort and a stylish touch to most rooms. Newly covered cushions are also a relatively inexpensive way of enlivening a monotone colour scheme, as they require little fabric compared with curtains (drapes) or blinds (shades). Simple shapes such as squares and circles show off strong colours and patterns to the best advantage, and both shapes can be decorated with frills, piping or both combined.

Both types of cushion shown here have a zip (zipper) inserted in the back seam – a neater method than making the opening in a side seam. A zip is the most convenient method of fastening a cushion cover, making it easy to remove for laundering. If you prefer, however, you can close the opening with a row of slip stitches, which you will need to remove and then replace whenever you launder the cover.

MAKING A SQUARE CUSHION COVER

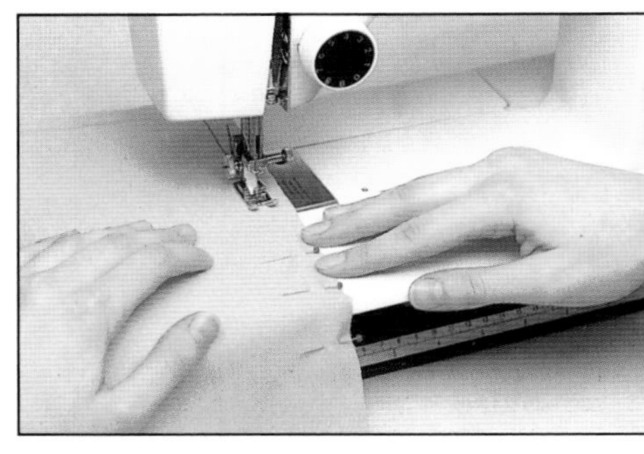

1 Measure the cushion pad, and add 12 mm/½ in all around for ease plus 12 mm/½ in for seam allowances. Do not forget to allow an extra 3 cm/1 in for the centre-back seam. Cut out the front and two back pieces. Pin and stitch the centre-back seam 12 mm/½ in from the raw edges, making sure to leave an opening large enough to accommodate the zip (zipper). Press open the seam.

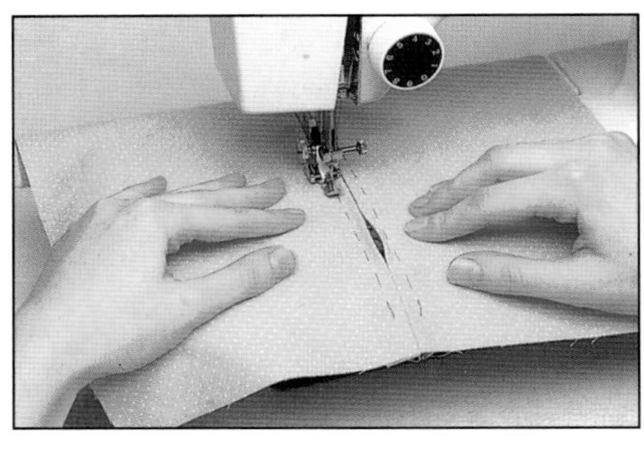

2 Pin and tack (baste) the zip in position along the opening, allowing the fabric to meet centrally over the zip teeth. Using a zip foot on the machine, carefully machine stitch the zip in place.

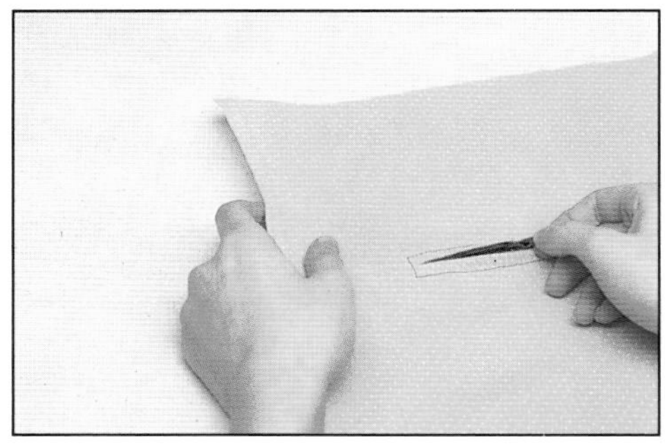

3 Press the seam allowances around the zip. Open the zip, making sure that the fabric does not catch in the teeth and that the ends are stitched securely. With the zip still open, place the front and back pieces together so that the right sides are facing.

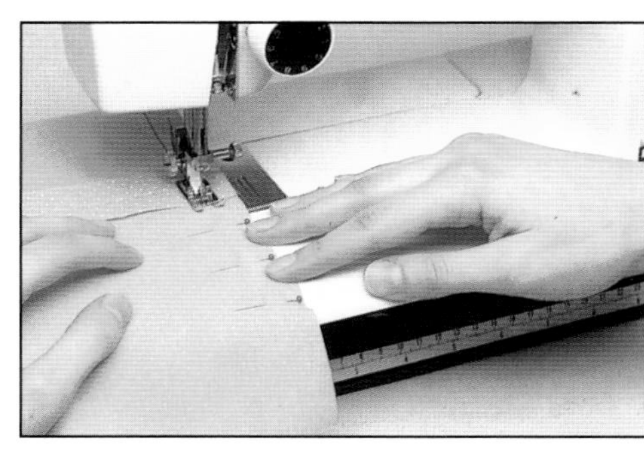

4 Pin and machine stitch twice around the edge, about 12mm/½ in from the raw edges. Carefully clip away the surplus fabric close to the stitching at the corners, in order to reduce the bulk. Press the seams and turn the cover to the right side through the zipped opening. Press the seams, insert the cushion pad and close the zip.

BELOW Frills and piping in matching or contrasting fabric add interest and a nice finishing touch to round and square cushion covers.

MAKING A FRILL

For this you will need a piece of fabric that is twice the depth of the finished frill plus 3 cm/1¼ in, and between 1½ and 2 times the outside measurement of the cover (you may have to join several strips together).

1 Join the ends of the strips together with a flat seam. Fold the strip in half lengthways with the wrong sides facing. Make one or two rows of running stitches along the raw edges of the strip, taking the stitches through both layers and leaving a long end of thread at one end of each row.

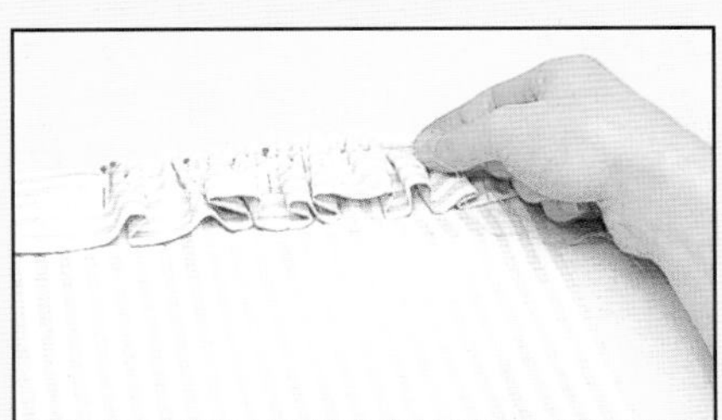

2 Gather the frill by pulling up the long threads until the frill is the correct size to fit around the cushion front. Wind the long threads around a pin to secure them and then even out the gather with your fingers.

To add a frill to either a square or round cushion, align the raw edge of the frill with the raw edge of the front cover, right sides together. Tack (baste) and sew the frill in place, then make up the cover in the usual way.

MAKING A ROUND CUSHION COVER

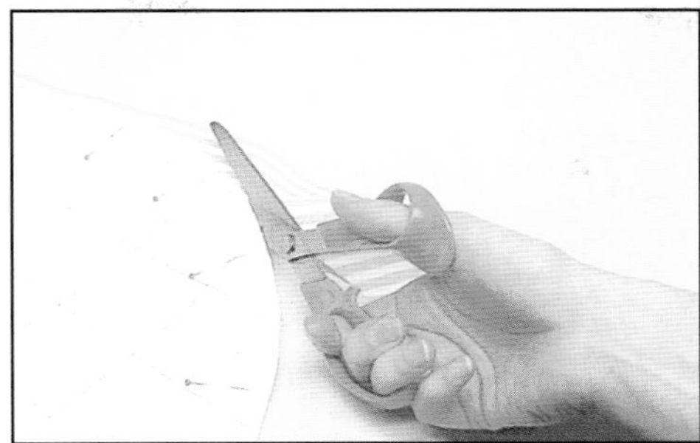

1 Measure the diameter of the cushion pad, and add 12 mm/½ in all around for ease plus 12 mm/½ in for seam allowances. Make a paper pattern to this size using dressmaker's pattern paper. Pin this on to the fabric and cut out one piece for the front of the cover.

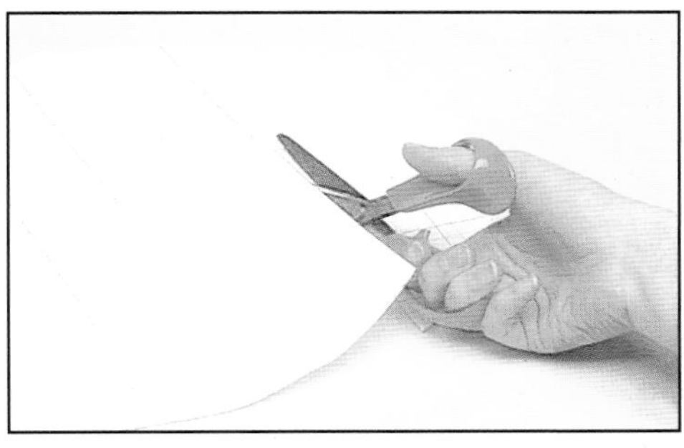

2 Rule a line across the paper pattern to mark the position of the back seam. The line should measure approximately 12.5 cm/5 in longer than the zip (zipper). Cut the paper pattern in 2 along this line.

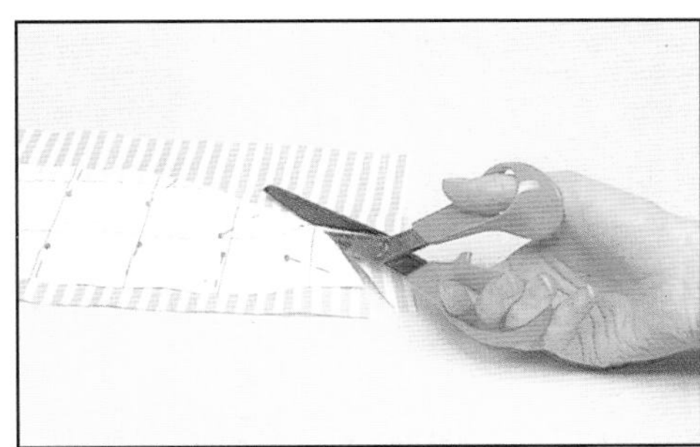

3 Pin both pattern pieces on to the fabric and cut them out, remembering to allow an extra 12 mm/½ in for the seam allowance on the straight edge of each piece.

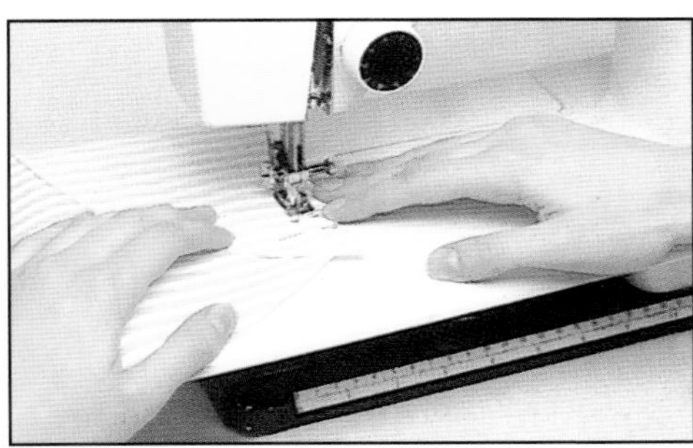

4 Pin and stitch the back seam, leaving an opening long enough to accommodate the zip. Finish off the cover in the same way as the square cover (see opposite page).

RIGHT **Choose sumptuous fabrics for cushion covers to complement curtains and wall coverings for a harmonious decorating scheme.**

PIPING

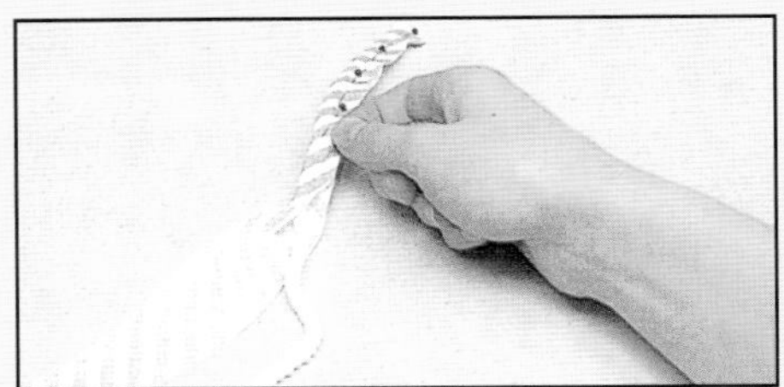

1 Fold a piece of fabric in half diagonally and press the fold. Open out the fabric and mark out strips parallel to the fold about 4–5 cm/1½–2 in apart. Cut out the strips. Join the strips with a flat seam to make the required length. Place the piping cord along the centre of the strip, fold it over and pin. Tack (baste) and stitch close to the cord.

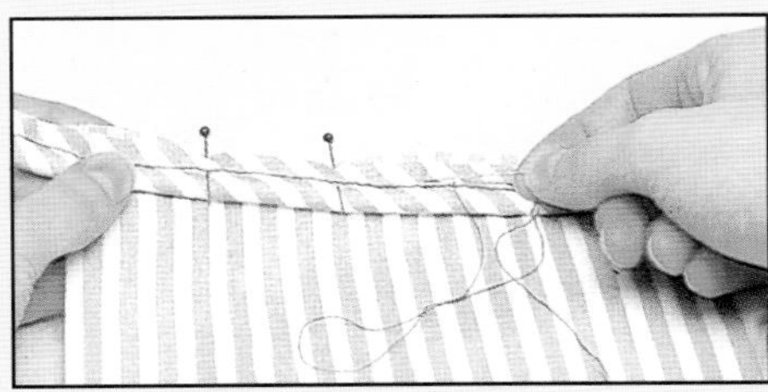

2 Lay the covered cord on the right side of the fabric, with raw edges aligning, and tack in place. Cover with a second piece of fabric, right-side downwards and with the raw edges matching. Stitch the layers together along the seamline using a zip (zipper) foot on the machine. Remove the tacking stitches. Make up the cover in the usual way.

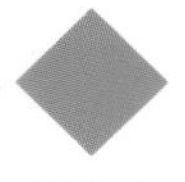

MAKING BED LINEN

Be imaginative when choosing colour schemes and pattern combinations for bed linen. A matching duvet cover and valance looks stylish, particularly when the fabric co-ordinates with the curtains or drapes and other bedroom furnishings. Sheeting is extra-wide fabric sold for making bed linen, and is available in a good range of both plain colours and patterns.

The duvet cover is simply a large bag made from 2 pieces of fabric joined together around the four sides, with an opening left in the bottom edge to allow the duvet to be inserted. Close the opening with a strip of either touch-and-close fastener or press-stud tape. A valance is ideal for covering up an unattractive bed base. It fits over the base, underneath the mattress, and has a frill around 3 of the sides, reaching right down to floor level.

RIGHT **A matching gathered valance finishes off this arrangement perfectly. Lace edging sewn around the pillow cases and duvet cover adds a feminine touch.**

MAKING A DUVET COVER

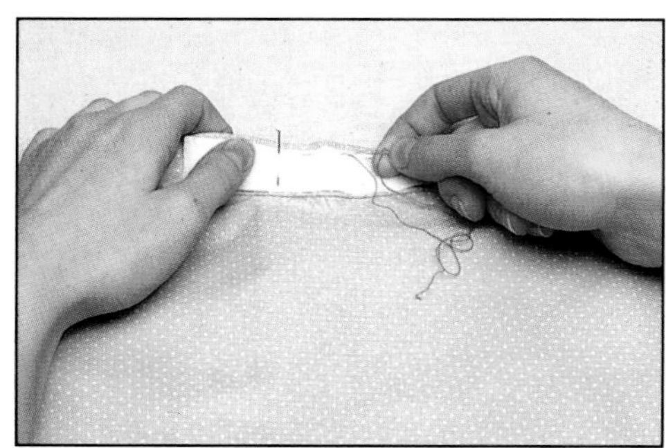

1 Measure the length of the duvet – usually 200 cm/78 in – and add 7 cm/2¾ in for hem and seam allowances. Measure the width and add 4 cm/1½ in for seam allowances. Cut out two pieces of fabric. Turn and stitch a double 2.5 cm/1 in hem along the bottom of each piece. Cut a length of touch-and-close fastener 3 cm/1¼ in longer than the desired opening, separate the strips and pin 1 to the right side of the hem on each piece. Machine stitch around the edge of each strip.

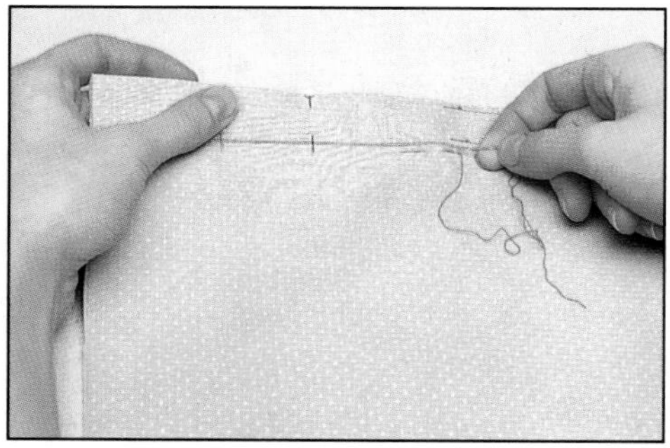

2 Place the 2 fabric pieces with the right sides together so that the fastener strips close. Tack (baste) along the bottom hem from 3 cm/1¼ in inside the strip of fastener and up to each corner.

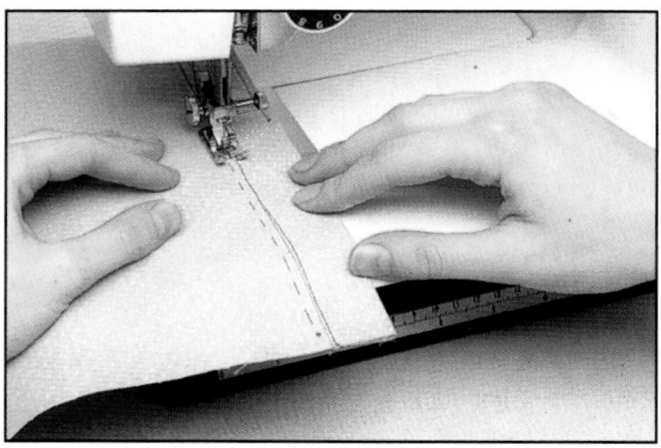

3 Machine stitch through both layers at right-angles to the hem and 3 cm/1¼ in inside the fastener strip, to enclose the raw edges. Pivot the fabric and continue stitching along the tacked line to the edge of the fabric. Repeat at the other corner.

Making a Valance

1 Measure the mattress top and add 3.5 cm/1½ in to the length and 3 cm/ 1¼ in to the width. Cut out 1 piece of fabric to this size for the panel. Round off the 2 bottom corners of the panel by drawing around a large plate and then cutting around the curves.

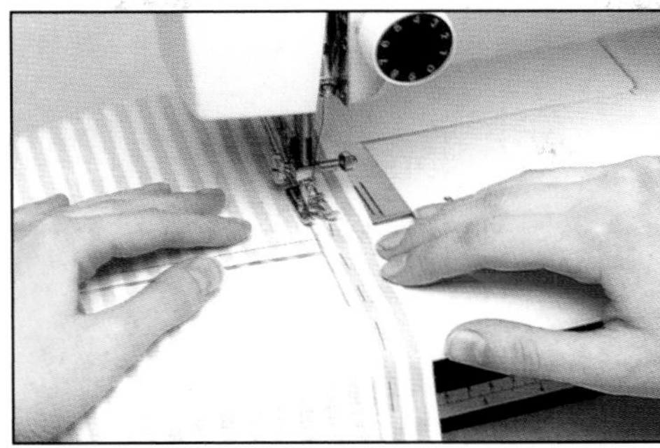

2 For the frill, you will need sufficient pieces of fabric wide enough to reach from the top of the bed base to the floor, plus 6.5 cm/2½ in, to make a long strip 4 times the mattress length plus twice its width. Join the strips with French seams (see Making a Duvet Cover, step 4) and press. Turn a double 2.5 cm/1 in hem along the lower edge. Pin, tack (baste) and stitch.

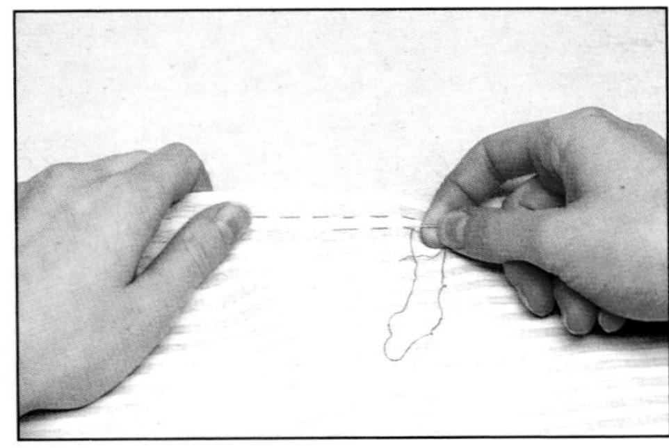

3 Divide the frill into 6 equal sections and mark with pins along the top edge. Work 2 rows of gathering stitches between the pins, leaving long thread ends.

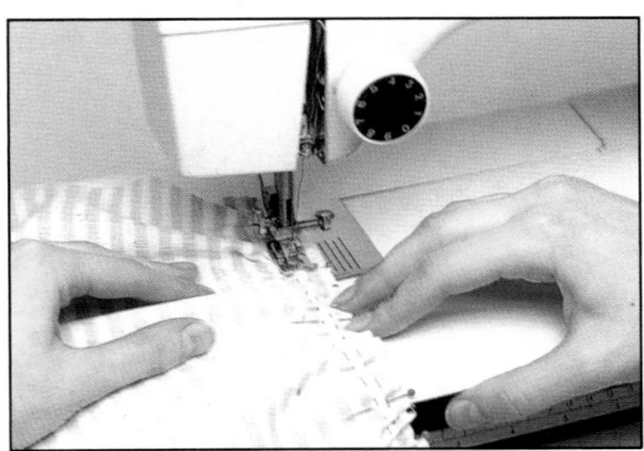

4 Divide the sides and bottom edge of the panel into 6 equal sections and mark with pins. Pull up the gathering stitches in each frill section until it fits the corresponding panel section. Pin each section in place with the right sides facing. Stitch the frill in place 12mm/½ in from the raw edge. Stitch again close to the first line of stitching and neaten the raw edges with machine zigzag. Press the seam allowance towards the panel. Turn a double 12 mm/ ½ in hem along the remaining raw edges of the frill and panel. Pin and stitch.

Choosing Fabric for Bed Linen

The best choice for bed linen is specially woven sheeting, either in pure cotton or a polyester-and-cotton blend. Although pure cotton is cooler in the summer, synthetic blends do have the advantage of needing little or no ironing. Sheeting is very wide, so joins are not necessary, and it is available in a large range of pastel and strong colours.

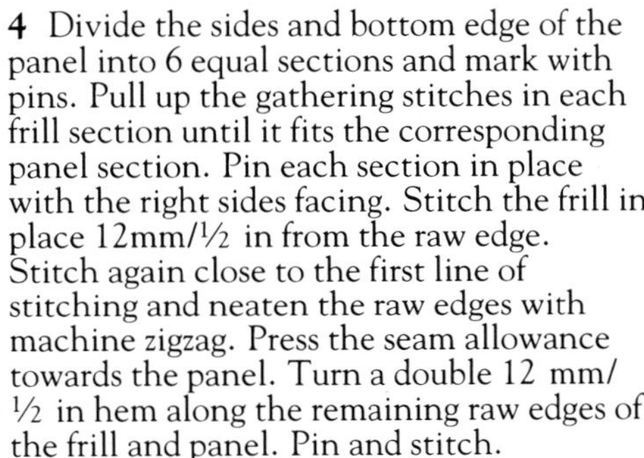

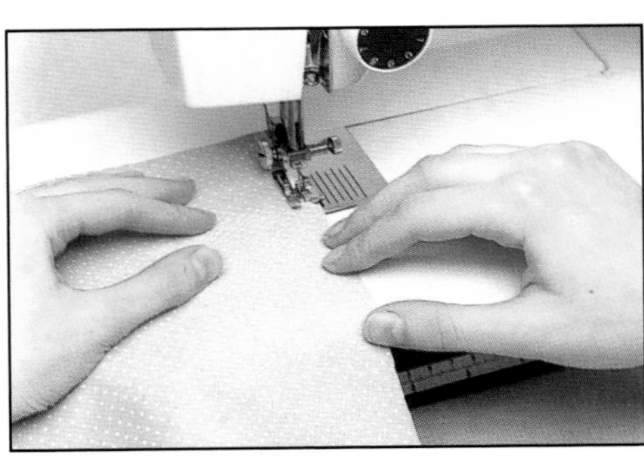

4 Turn so that the wrong sides are facing. Make a French seam around the remaining three sides, as follows. Pin and stitch 6 mm/¼ in from the raw edge. Trim the seam close to the stitching, then open the fastener and turn the cover so that the right sides are facing. Stitch around the three sides again to enclose the raw edges and complete the seam. Turn the cover to the right side and press.

LEFT A crisply checked duvet cover and pillow cases accentuate the light and airy feel of a country bedroom.

BEAUTIFUL TABLE SETTINGS

The first sight of the table plays a keynote for any meal, so it is essential that the setting is just right for the occasion. Whether crisp and sophisticated, softly flowing with lace and flowers, warm and homely, or refreshingly bright, the table should complement the décor of the room and form a focal point. In a contemporary living/dining room or at a buffet party the table is on display throughout; if people happen to pass an open dining-room door as they pass through the hallway before dinner, the merest glimpse of arrangements should hint at the quality of the meal to come.

Table linen

There is an enormous variety of table linen available, most of it far removed from traditional white linen. There are no 'rules' about what is acceptable or otherwise, the only qualification being that the choice should complement the colour scheme of the room, and should suit the occasion.

White linen, the traditional choice for table linen, is both versatile and practical, and there is nothing quite like crisply starched, large napkins on a dinner-party table. Heavy, white-damask table cloths and napkins are expensive, but they will last for years. It is always worth looking out for good-quality secondhand linen at auctions, flea markets and in antique or junk shops – as long as the fabric is not badly marked, worn or torn, it is a good buy.

BELOW The table setting is a central feature of any occasion. Here, the plain but elegant dinner service and glasses complement the stunning red napkin and festive tablecloth.

RIGHT Traditional white-damask table linen adds elegance to a formal dinner.

FAR RIGHT Combine clean lines and black-and-white chinaware and table linen for a strikingly modern look.

Although plain white linen is unsuitable for casual table settings, it does not always have to form the basis of formal arrangements. Introduce a contemporary air with your choice of flowers or table centrepieces; instead of traditional white candles, go for coloured ones; or use colourful napkin ties or ribbons with small flowers or suitable trimmings to pick up on the rest of the table decorations.

Good linen in delicate pastel shades can be as formal as traditional white table settings. Deep colours can be more dramatic but just as stylish, depending on the overall presentation. Strong colours can also make an eye-catching base for flamboyant themes, particularly if you are preparing an ethnic meal, or for a buffet party.

Smart checks and stripes are useful for informal picnics, barbecues, patio meals, breakfasts and brunches. Colourful hand-embroidered linen is ideal for breakfast cloths, and for table coverings for brunches, family teas and high tea.

Themed settings

There are times when it is fun to go for something strikingly different in the way of setting arrangements. White and pastels tend to be favoured colours for table settings, but strong colours make a dramatic impact. A blue-and-gold setting, for example, could have a deep blue cloth and napkins, matching candles and an arrangement of blue flowers, such as hydrangeas, hyacinths, delphiniums, lavender or cornflowers. Wire dried autumn leaves and spray them gold, then use these with the fresh flowers.

Alternatively, try creating a lush green table using a white linen cloth as the base and limiting the other colour to green, including candles. Make a central arrangement of leaves: as well as cuttings from shrubs, take leaves from indoor plants, such as Japanese aralia and grape ivy. Create interest by using leaves of different sizes and shapes.

A pretty lace setting is ideal for a celebratory lunch party, for a small wedding lunch party or for a large buffet table. Lay a plain-coloured cloth or fabric over the table – pink is ideal for this theme. Lay a lace cloth over the plain cloth so that the colour shows through. Set conventional place settings. Roll the napkins and tie them with satin ribbon and large bows. Draw up the lace cloth at the corners of the table and at intervals around the edge (between place settings), then pin it in place so that it hangs in swags. Prepare small posies of roses and tie them with flamboyant bows of satin ribbon to match the place settings. Pin the flowers on the cloth.

ABOVE Brightly coloured table linen, tied casually with string and decorated with a dried red chilli to match the table mat, completes a colourful place setting for an informal dinner.

BELOW Checked linen is ideal for a casual meal such as a picnic, or for an informal table setting.

NAPKIN FOLDING

Crisp, freshly laundered napkins are an essential feature of every well-set table. You can simply press them in large, plain squares and lay one at each place setting with the minimum of fuss. Alternatively, you can fold napkins in a variety of ways to complement the food, the table layout and the occasion.

Regardless of the simplicity of the meal, fabric napkins must be spotlessly clean and well-pressed. Plain white linen napkins are generally best folded very simply for an elegant effect. If they have a monogram or other decorative embroidery, fold them to display this. Press embroidered napkins on the wrong side to make the pattern stand out attractively.

Decorative napkins, trimmed with embroidery or lace or with a prominent self-pattern, should also be folded very simply; plain fabric napkins or those with a small decorative border are more suitable for elaborate folding.

If you are preparing a meal for a comparatively small number – that is, under about 15 guests – it is a good idea to use fabric napkins if possible. The fabrics do not have to be the same, and you can in fact make a virtue of their differences by combining contrasting colours or patterns to create an attractive arrangement. It is a nice idea to allow 2 or 3 different-coloured napkins for each place setting, perhaps fanned out simply, as shown on the opposite page.

For a larger gathering, especially when you are serving finger foods, or when there are a lot of children around, it is an advantage to use disposable paper napkins.

ABOVE Neatly pressed and folded napkins add elegance to a dinner table when accompanied by sparkling cutlery (flatware) and glasses.

BELOW A tartan bow holds a neatly rolled napkin and spoon for a dessert course.

Elaborate folding methods are not used for buffet presentation as the emphasis is mainly on the practicalities of carrying a plate, napkin and cutlery (flatware). There are a number of standard options for placing napkins, all of which are practical for a buffet: roll a knife and fork in each napkin (do not roll cutlery for dessert in the napkin – you should offer this separately); stack a napkin on each plate; fold the napkins diagonally to make triangles and overlap these on one side of the buffet table; roll the napkins and stand them in a wide-necked jug; or arrange them in a rustic basket.

Tips for successful folding

For folding purposes, heavy linen is best, as it becomes firm and crisp when starched. Plain dinner napkins measuring 45–50 cm/18–20 in square, or more, are best, and are essential for many complicated folding techniques. The napkins must be cut square and the fabric must be cut straight on the weave so that the napkins will not pull out of shape easily.

Starch linen napkins after washing, using traditional starch, which you mix with boiling water (follow the manufacturer's instructions for this). You should use this method if at all possible, as spray starch will not give a really good, crisp finish. Iron the napkins while still damp, and dampen napkins which have already dried before ironing. When ironing, gently pull the napkins back into shape if necessary to ensure that they are perfectly square again. It is best to iron napkins on a large surface; an ironing-board can be too narrow when pressing large napkins. Protect the surface with a folded thick towel covered with a piece of plain white cotton.

Simple presentation

To form a neat square, press the napkin, making sure that all the corners are perfectly square. Fold the napkin into quarters, pressing each fold carefully. Lay a large quarter-folded napkin squarely between the cutlery (flatware) at each place setting, or turn it by 90 degrees.

To make a simple triangle, fold the square in half diagonally and press the resulting triangle neatly. Lay the folded napkin on a side plate, with the long side nearest the place setting. The triangle may also be laid on top of a plate in the middle of the setting.

For a simple rectangle, fold a square napkin in half again. This is an ideal way of displaying a decorative corner on the napkin. Plain napkins may be folded and pressed into quarters, then the sides folded underneath and pressed to make an oblong shape. Lay the hemmed edge on the short side at the bottom of the place setting.

Keep rolled napkins in place with napkin rings, or tie them with ribbon or cord. Alternatively, if you roll the napkins carefully and lay them with the ends underneath, they will usually sit quite neatly.

Spreading Fan

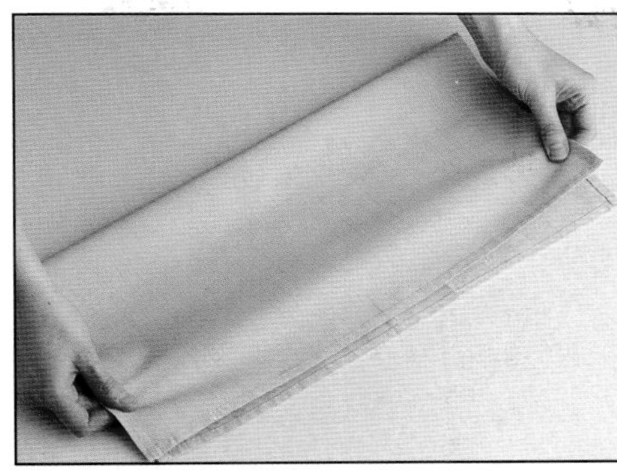

1 This is an elegant yet simple design that would be suitable for any occasion. To begin, fold up the napkin edge nearest to you to meet the top edge.

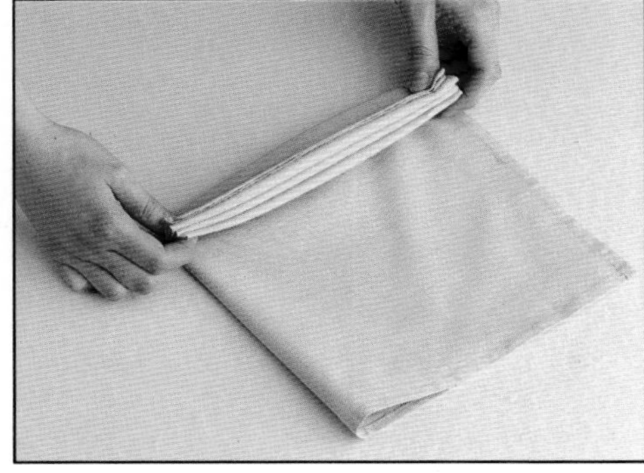

2 Rotate the napkin so that the folded edge is on your right, then make equal-sized 'accordion' pleats all the way up to the top of the napkin.

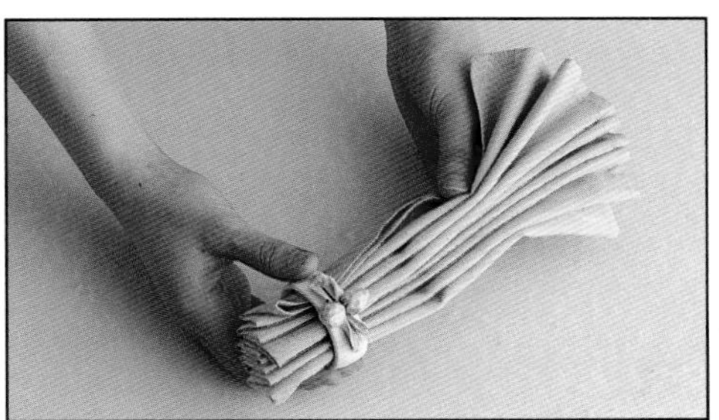

3 Insert the end of the napkin into a ring, or tie it with ribbon or cord.

4 Spread out the pleats neatly to make the fan shape, and lay the napkin on a plate. Here, 2 small napkins of different colours have been folded together to match the colours of the setting perfectly.

NAPKIN FOLDING (continued)

FOLDED WINGS

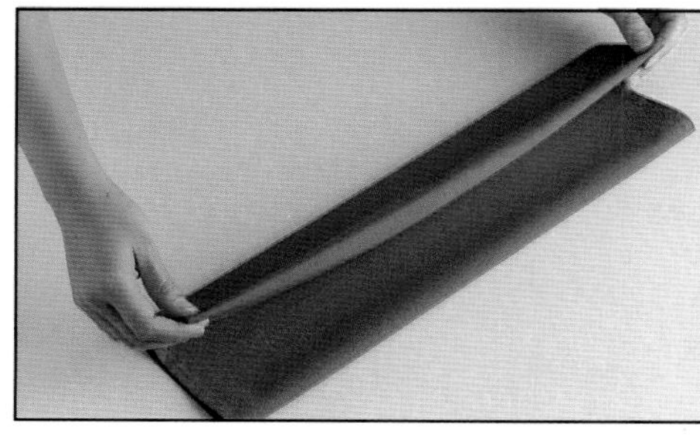

1 This design works best with a stiff cotton napkin. Fold the bottom and top edges of the open napkin into the centre. Bring the bottom fold up to the top.

2 Fold in the left side of the napkin by exactly one-third.

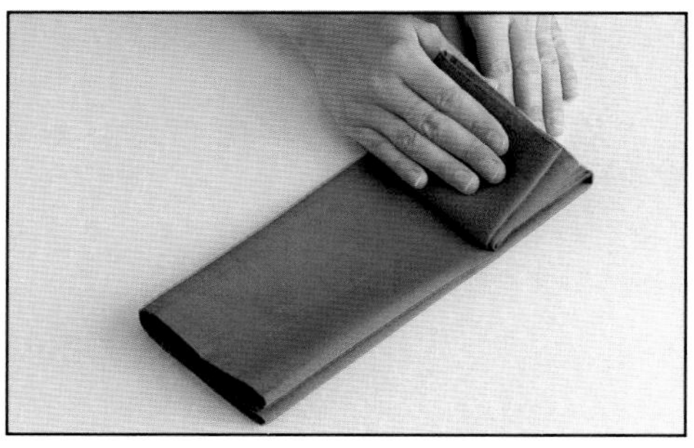

3 Fold this side back on itself to align with the outside edge again.

4 Repeat with the right side. Lift the top layers on both sides and curl them back under into their folds to form the wings.

IRIS IN A GLASS

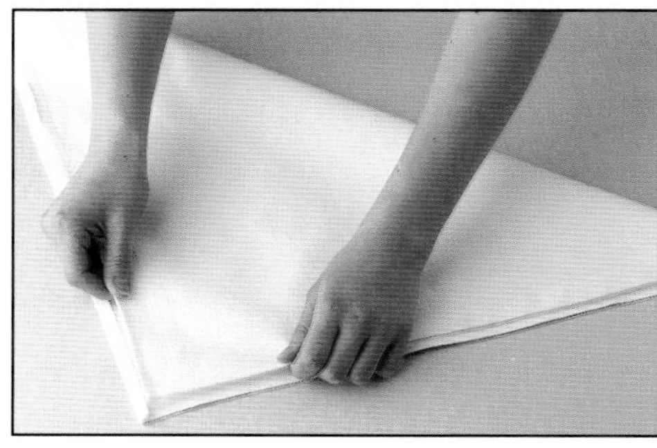

1 This design creates a very striking display if folded with a large, colourful napkin. Starting with the corners of the open napkin top and bottom in the form of a diamond, bring the point nearest to you up to the top point to form a triangle.

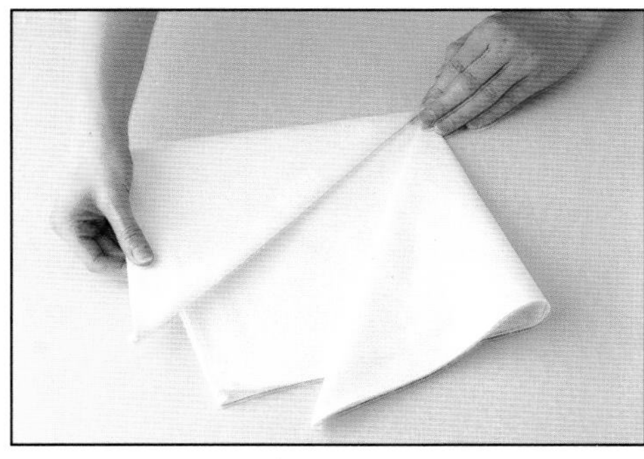

2 With a finger at the centre of the fold line, fold up the 2 corners nearest to you so that they are level with the centre-top point and slightly to each side of it.

3 Fold the newly formed bottom point part-way up towards the top point.

4 Make accordion pleats across the napkin from left to right. Position the napkin in the glass and fan out the petals of the iris.

ELF'S BOOT

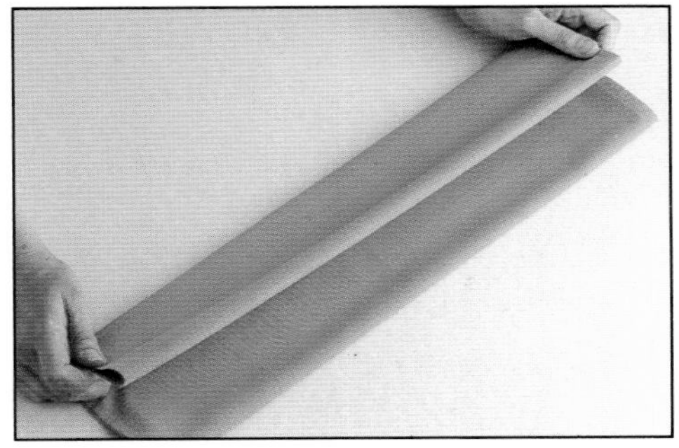

1 Use a fabric napkin for this fun design. Fold the top and bottom edges to meet in the middle. Bring the bottom edge to meet the top edge, folding the rectangle in half.

2 With a finger at the centre bottom, fold up both sides away from you so that the edges meet in the middle.

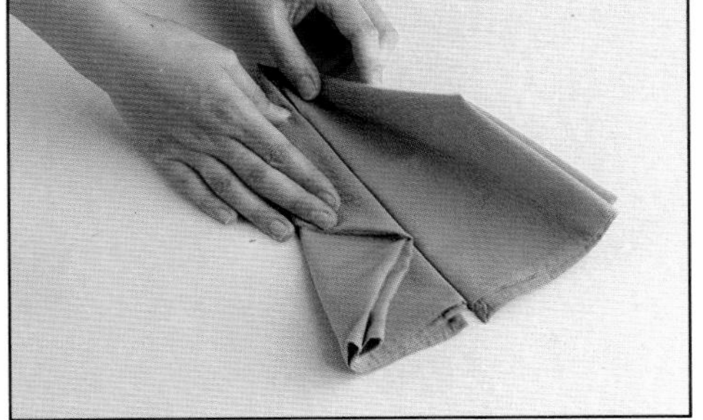

3 Fold the right and left sides closest to you into the centre to form a sharper point.

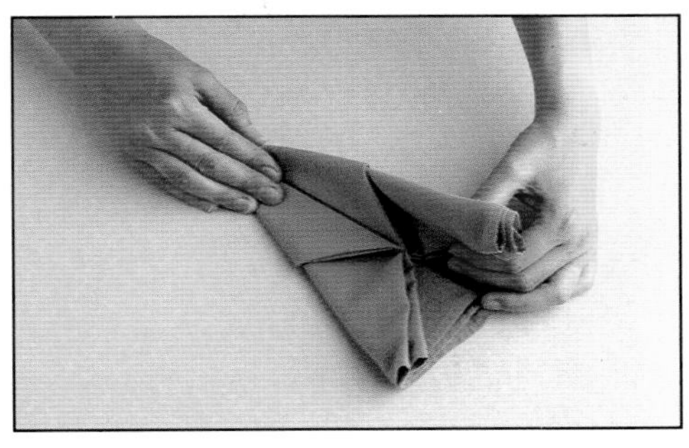

4 Fold the left side of the napkin over on to the right side.

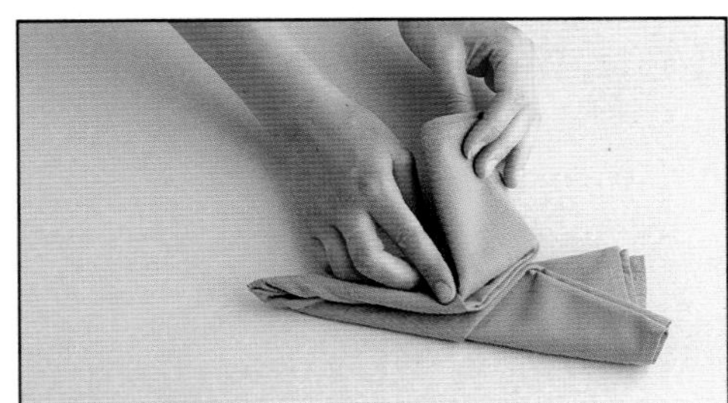

5 Move the napkin round so that the bottom point now faces to your right. Fold the top-left tail down towards you.

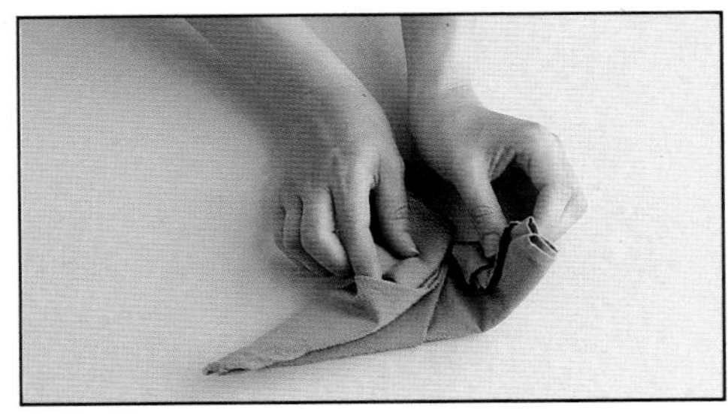

6 Fold the bottom edge of the other left tail upwards, and tuck the tail securely into the pocket of the tail on the right.

DECORATING WITH CANDLES

An elegant array of candles adds the finishing touch to any table setting, creating an atmosphere that cannot be equalled by any other form of lighting. Their use does not stop at tables, however – candles can be used in all areas of the home and in all kinds of containers, to marvellous effect.

At Christmas time, for instance, you may like to incorporate candles into a large, deep swag filling a wide window sill or mantelpiece, using thick, stubby candles raised on flowerpots concealed among the greenery. Position tall candles to taper from a forest of twigs and pine-cones, or trim plain altar candles, beautiful in their simplicity, with evergreens, berries and bows to stand as a sign of welcome in a window.

At other times of the year, flowerpots make practical if somewhat rustic holders for candles of all kinds – from the highly-textured beeswax candles to those in traditional colours. Select the most earthy and weatherbeaten flowerpots you have, and plant the candles in heavy holding material such as gravel chippings concealed under (for safety reasons) damp moss or hay. A garland of ivy trailing around the top of the flowerpot, held in place with unobtrusive blobs of clay, will add to the pastoral look, while a large green and white gingham bow will add a touch more elegance.

A variety of household items, including pottery mugs and tumblers, casseroles and glass dishes, are ideal for holding candles of all shapes and sizes. Bargain-shop candlesticks can also be transformed with a simple verdigris look-alike technique using acrylic paints. You can even use hollowed-out vegetables – pumpkin-shaped gourds have a wonderful shape and colour – as bases for candles. Arrange these in a cluster on a dining table, a sideboard or in the kitchen, or use them as party decorations. Remember never to leave lit candles unattended.

PAINTING A CANDLESTICK

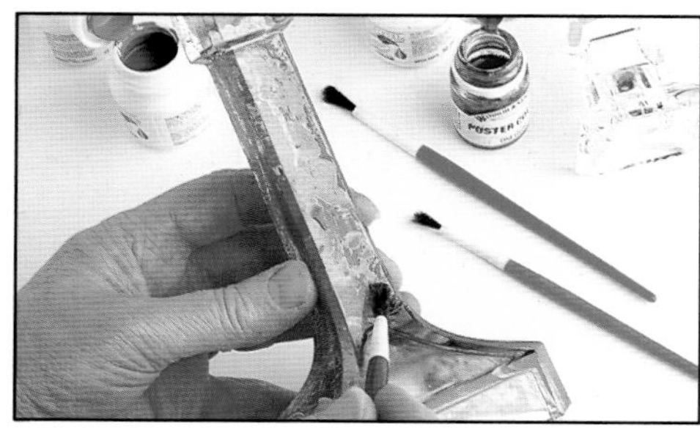

1 Paint the candlestick with a base coat of bronze acrylic paint, using criss-crossing brushstrokes for an uneven, textured finish. Allow the paint to dry.

2 Daub the bronze-coloured surface with green acrylic paint. If you prefer a more transparent finish, thin the paint with turpentine (methylated spirits) first. Leave to dry for 10 minutes, then daub on gold acrylic paint in uneven patches.

3 A verdigris-style candlestick makes an elegant flower stand. Fix a small foam-holder and a piece of soaked stem-holding foam to the top of the candlestick with florist's tape, and arrange a colourful combination of flowers and foliage.

CHRISTMAS CANDLES

1 Cut short lengths of evergreens and holly and bind them into bunches using silver wire. Place a few stems against a candle and bind them on with silver wire. Add more bunches, binding them on all around the candle, and secure the wire. Hook on false berries, if you wish. Tie ribbon around the stems to conceal the wire. Trim the other candles in a similar way.

2 Place the candles in appropriate holders and arrange them in the centre of a dining table or on a window sill among cuttings of mixed evergreens.

Vegetable Candle Holders

1 To make gourd candle holders, first break off the stalks. If the gourds are soft enough, gouge out a shallow hole from each one that is wide enough to hold a candle, using a sharp knife. If the gourds are too hard to do this – and dried ones may well be – fix the candles securely in the indentations using a little florist's adhesive clay.

2 Arrange the gourds to make an attractive group. Here, trailing stems of Chinese lanterns (winter cherry) wind through the gourds, an element that could be repeated in neighbouring flower arrangements.

Dish of Candles

1 Fill a shallow dish two-thirds full of clean sand, and place a tall candle in the middle. Position shorter candles around it.

2 Arrange a variety of pretty shells around the candles, pressing them into the sand.

3 Check that all the candles are securely positioned before lighting them.

TABLE DECORATING WITH FLOWERS

A garland is a lovely way to decorate a table – indoors or out – for a special occasion such as a wedding or christening reception, a birthday, or any other celebration. You can make the garland to loop across the front of the table, to encircle the rim, or to drape on all four sides of a free-standing table. Long, leafy stems work extremely well for this type of decoration – smilax (*Asparagus asparagoides*) has been used here. With its pliable stem and mass of bright green leaves, this forms a natural garland, and makes an attractive instant decoration, even without the addition of flowers.

Smilax is usually sold to order in bundles of 5 stems. Keep the stem ends in water until just before you assemble the garland, and the foliage should stay fresh for several days. Mimosa, gypsophila and spray chrysanthemums all make a good accompaniment for a bright, summery look.

GARLAND TIPS

Floral and foliage garlands are very simple to make and as they are almost invariably composed of short-stemmed plant materials, they can utilize clippings from larger designs. Side shoots of delphinium cut from stems arranged in a pedestal design; individual spray-chrysanthemum flowers that formed too dense a cluster; florets and leaflets that would come below the water level in a vase – you can form them all into posies and bind them on to a garland using silver wire.

Garlands can be composed on a central core. According to the weight of the plant materials, this may vary from tightly coiled paper ribbon, thin string, twine or wire, to thick rope or even a roll made of wire-mesh netting filled with offcuts of absorbent stem-holding foam. This latter core has the advantage of providing fresh flowers in a garland with a source of moisture.

1 Gather together your chosen flowers and foliage, and the other materials you will need: a roll of florist's silver wire, florist's scissors, 2.5 cm/1 in wide ribbon and pins for fixing the ribbon in place on the cloth.

2 It will save time just before the event if you make up the posies in advance. Choose materials that will contrast well with the bright foliage of the garland. Cut the flower stems short, using 5 or 6 pieces of gypsophila, 2 small snippings of mimosa, and either 1 or 2 spray chrysanthemums, according to their size. Gather the stems together and bind them with silver wire.

3 You can space the posies as close together or as wide apart on the garland as you wish, so make up as many as you will need. As a general rule, the smaller the table, the smaller the gap should be between the flowers. Once you have assembled the posies, place them in a shallow bowl of water before attaching them to the garland.

4 Measure the length of garland needed for the side drapes and mark the centre. With the stems of the first posy towards the end of one of the lengths of foliage, bind the posy to the main stem with silver wire. Bind on more posies in the same way, reversing the direction of the stems when you reach the centre of the draped garland. Repeat the decoration with the remaining lengths of garland, but without reversing the direction of the flowers of the side trails.

5 Pin the garland to the cloth, adjusting the fall of the drape so that it is equal on all sides, and pin on the side trails. Check that the garland hangs well. Sometimes the weight of the posies will cause it to twist, with the flowers facing inwards. If this happens, pin the garland to the cloth at intervals. Pin lengths of ribbon to the corners, and tie more lengths into bows and attach to the centres of the drapes.

RIGHT A garland of dried flowers, wired on to paper ribbon and finished off with an extravagant bow, makes a beautiful table decoration. The garland will retain its crisp and colourful appearance throughout the day, and can be carefully packed away and used another time.

MAKING A WREATH

Through the centuries, wreaths have been regarded as symbols of protection, love, friendship and welcome. Most are composed of a central core, although you can twist and weave supple stems of foliage such as clematis or hops into wreaths that are decorative in their own right, or construct a simple wreath base from supple grass or other stems and then decorate it with flowers.

With the revival of interest in decorative rings, it is now possible to buy a wide variety of wreath bases from florists and department stores. Dried-stem rings, vine wreath forms and twisted willow rings can all be adorned with posies of fresh flowers and foliage, or with dried plant material for long-term display. Pre-formed rings of absorbent stem-holding foam encased in a plastic base provide fresh flowers with a moisture source and can be used throughout the year for wall hangings or table decorations. They are, however, unattractive to look at, so you must plan your decoration to include an all-concealing cover – a handful of ivy leaves or other foliage would be ideal.

MAKING A FRESH-FLOWER WREATH

1 Gather up your materials: a pre-formed foam ring of 25 cm/10 in diameter, a selection of flowers such as sweet peas, roses, spray carnations, Peruvian lilies and gypsophila, evergreen foliage such as ivy, and florist's scissors. Arrange a ring of ivy leaves around the inside and outside of the ring form to frame the flowers. Cut each sweet-pea flower on a short stem and arrange at intervals around the ring.

2 Complete the ring of sweet peas and arrange more ivy leaves between the flowers, to give the design a natural and 'countrified' look.

3 Cut individual roses, Peruvian lilies and spray carnations and arrange them between the sweet peas. Insert short sprays of gypsophila around the ring.

4 Use the floral circlet to decorate a table top, a low shelf or a buffet table, where it would make an unusual centrepiece.

IDEAS FOR FOAM RINGS

Outline a foam ring with periwinkle leaves, fill it with some short-stemmed daffodils, tulips and pansies, and then embellish it with a cluster of lighted tapers for an Easter table decoration; cover a small ring with lady's mantle and cornflowers, and then stud it with strawberries pierced with cocktail sticks (toothpicks) for a midsummer party piece; or define a large ring with ivy leaves, fill in with sweet peas, Peruvian lilies and roses, and cover it with delicate gypsophila.

MAKING A POT-POURRI WREATH

1 Gather up the materials you will need: a dried-stem ring of 20 cm/8 in diameter, about 115 g/4 oz pot pourri, a hot-glue gun, dried flowers such as rosebuds and sea lavender, a roll of florist's silver wire, half a stub wire (floral pin), satin ribbon and a pair of scissors.

2 Spurt the glue on to the ring a little at a time, and press the pot pourri on to it. Take care not to burn your fingers when using hot glue. Allow to cool for a few seconds before pressing on the petals.

3 Work all around the ring, gluing and pressing on the petals until you have covered the form on top, both inside and outside. If there are any gaps, spurt on a little more glue and add more petals. Glue some of the most colourful petals on top to give the ring a bright appearance.

4 Arrange the dried flowers to make a small posy. Cut short the stems and bind them with silver wire. Bend the stub wire in half to make a U-shape, loop it over the stems and press the ends of the wire into the ring to secure the posy.

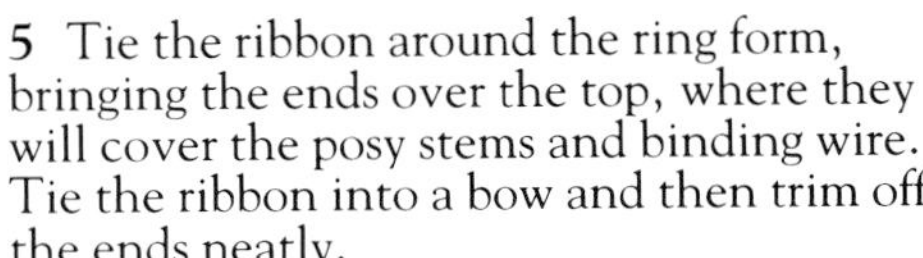

5 Tie the ribbon around the ring form, bringing the ends over the top, where they will cover the posy stems and binding wire. Tie the ribbon into a bow and then trim off the ends neatly.

PLANNING A PARTY

Many parties celebrate an event such as an annual feast, birthday, wedding, christening or anniversary; they can also take place for no special purpose at all other than to see friends. Whatever the occasion, it is most important to have a clear outline of the form of entertaining before you begin to work on any of the preparations – planning is the cornerstone of success.

Annual festivities, such as Thanksgiving, Christmas, New Year and Easter, often follow a traditional structure, but this does not mean that there is no need to plan ahead; it simply means that there will be fewer decisions to make and that they will all fall into an existing framework. For all other occasions, a decision on the type and size of celebration is the starting point, and the usual pre-arranging has to follow. Begin by considering your budget, then outline what sort of party you are planning within your financial restrictions. Work through all of the following points to establish a structure for planning all the details.

ABOVE Planning ahead will leave you time to add finishing touches such as flower arrangements.

Degree of formality

If you decide on a formal party, this will provide you with a set of clear-cut rules to follow. You may opt for complete informality, in which case you need to work out your own pattern of rules. However, many occasions tend to fall somewhere between these extremes.

The important thing is to decide exactly how you want to entertain, let everyone know what to expect and to stick to your decision by planning accordingly. Think in terms of dress, how you expect guests to participate and the type of refreshments, and pass all this information on to your guests.

The style of celebration will also dictate whether you need outside help. Caterers, waiting staff and bar staff may be hired for formal occasions, such as weddings, and may also be employed for any large party or even for formal dinner parties. These aspects of any party should always be planned at the outset, not as afterthoughts.

The guests

Bringing people together for small parties such as dinner parties is not always easy, and deciding on the group of people to invite to larger gatherings can also be difficult. Nevertheless, this is an essential and important first step in good planning. If you organize a dinner party for people who are strangers to one another, it is important to mix individuals who are likely to get on well together, or at least to express an interest in one another. When inviting friends to larger gatherings, always ensure that there are groups who will know or can relate to one another.

Think back over your own social experiences, and you will probably recall occasions when certain guests in the minority have obviously lingered on the fringe of a gathering, awaiting the first polite opportunity to take their leave. Having made the point, it is equally important to stress that there are exceptions – outstanding social successes do sometimes occur with the most unlikely groups of people.

Numbers

Although it may seem an obvious point, it is vital to make sure that you can cope with the numbers for the type of party that you are planning. This is

RIGHT A buffet can work as well as a more formal sit-down arrangement – perhaps in a marquee (closed-sided party tent) in the garden if numbers are too large for the house.

BELOW A traditional British cream tea provides an ideal opportunity for entertaining friends informally at home.

largely a matter of space. For example, it is not practical to arrange a formal dinner party for 8 guests if you can only sit 7 around the table: the eighth person who is perched on a stool at the corner of the table will make everyone else feel thoroughly uncomfortable. The same applies to a barbecue for 50 when you have one small grill; a cosy kitchen brunch for 10 in an area that is cramped with 6 people; or a children's party for 25 in a house that is overfilled when half-a-dozen children are invited and where there is only a small garden. Remember, however, that the equation can work the other way, and that, for some types of gatherings, success depends on having the party area fairly tightly packed with people.

Food and drink

Whether the gathering is small or large, it is important to decide on the level of refreshments – snacks, finger food, some form of buffet or a proper sit-down meal – and to make sure that the food and drink you provide are suited to the occasion. You need to think about this in relation to the time of day, numbers invited and your budget. Do not be afraid to make an unusual decision about the form of food, but do make sure that it is adequate and that you can cope with the preparation, or that caterers, if you are using them, do not need facilities that are not available.

Invitations

Whether printed, handwritten or extended by word of mouth, invitations should convey certain important information clearly to the recipients. They should state the names of those invited, your own name(s), the occasion and the reason for it, the place, the time and an address to which replies should be sent. Written invitations often include the formula 'RSVP' in one corner, which stands for the French '*Répondez, s'il vous plaît*' ('Please reply'), to remind guests that an answer is required. You should give details of any special form of dress on the bottom of the invitation.

Ready-made cards on which you write in the details yourself are available in styles ranging from formal to fun. You can also have cards printed for a special occasion.

GIVING A DINNER PARTY

A proper dinner party can be fun, as well as formal, especially if you know your guests well. This is an opportunity to lay the table with your best table linen and chinaware, to make your home look beautiful with flowers and other decorations, and to prepare dishes that are special and out of the ordinary. Plan to have all the cooking calmly under control and to allow yourself a period of all-important relaxation before your guests arrive, so that you can enjoy the occasion too.

To ensure that everything goes smoothly on the night of the party, draw up a checklist of things that you need to do, starting with jobs that you can easily complete a few days before the event, such as the shopping and cleaning. Try to prepare as much as possible in advance: make and freeze suitable dishes or, with dishes that cannot be frozen, make them the day before if possible and store them in the refrigerator. Leave only the finishing touches to be done on the day, to avoid a last-minute rush.

ABOVE **A bouquet of fresh flowers completes an elegant dinner-party table.**

MENU REMINDERS

Menus for dinner parties are best kept simple, and cook-ahead dishes are ideal, as most will not spoil if your guests linger over pre-dinner drinks.

Simple first courses often make the most memorable appetizers – opt for prime-quality ingredients and serve them attractively. You might try avocadoes and chopped walnuts with an oil-and-vinegar dressing, melon with Parma ham (prosciutto), fresh figs served with a twist of freshly ground black pepper, or perhaps something hot, such as Scallops wrapped in Parma Ham (Prosciutto) – see page 149.

Classic casseroles such as Coq au Vin or Boeuf Bourguignon make practical and versatile dinner-party fare, as do simple but delicious meat dishes such as Boned Pork Loin with Apple-cream Sauce (see page 135), or Pot-roast Chicken with Sausage Stuffing (see page 139). For the latter, you can prepare the stuffing the day before, making the dish very simple to put together and cook on the day of the party. Lightly spiced curries, such as the Simple Chicken Curry on page 141, are also most acceptable and often benefit from being cooked a day ahead so that the flavours mingle.

Even if you plan an elaborate dessert, it is a good idea to offer a simple alternative. Do not dismiss fresh fruit – pineapple and different types of melon (see page 158), as well as other fruits, can be presented in eye-catching ways. Fruit ices and sorbets are also wonderfully refreshing to the palate at the end of a meal.

A formal dinner party

Serving a meal of many courses can be an excellent way of entertaining, particularly when guests appreciate the nuances of different foods and subtle flavours. As lighter eating has become the norm, the most acceptable way of serving such a feast is to present small portions throughout the meal. Serve good-quality bought or home-made appetizers with drinks before dinner. The meal itself may consist of 4 or 5 courses, or more. Supper dishes and single-pot dishes are usually avoided on very formal occasions in favour of carefully sauced dishes with separate vegetables or side salads.

The simplest of formal dinner-party menus should include soup or a first

Making Place Cards

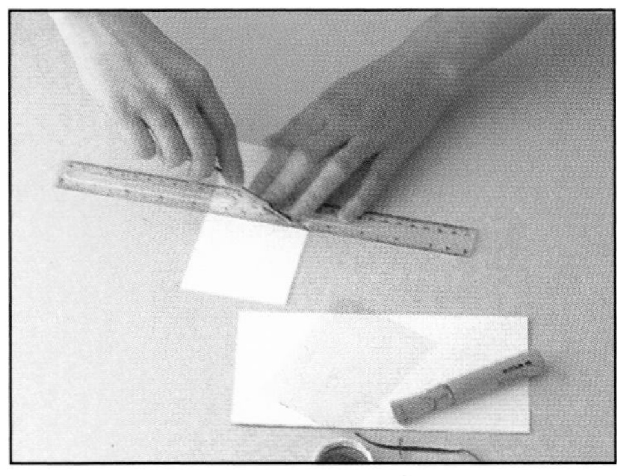

1 Place cards are always laid at formal or large dinners. Simple, elegant cards are best for such occasions. First cut a strip of card (cardboard) measuring 15 × 7.5 cm/6 × 3 in. Mark a fold across the centre and a 2.5 cm/1 in fold at each end of the strip. Using a craft knife, lightly score the folds.

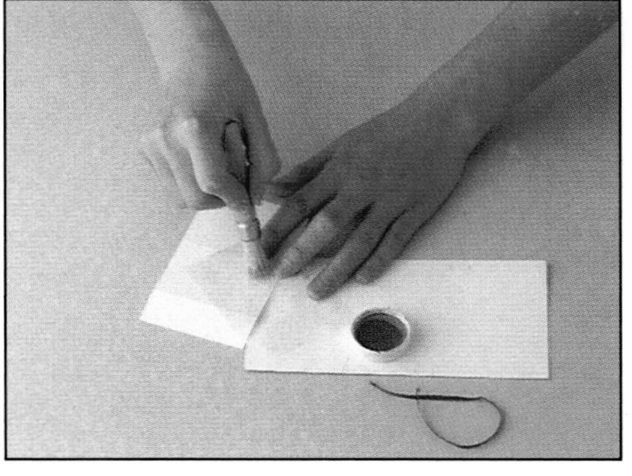

2 Draw a simple stencil design on to a sheet of acetate using a waterproof felt-tip pen, and cut it out using a craft knife. Lightly load a stencil brush with gold paint. Hold the stencil firmly in position on the card (cardboard) and dab the paint through it, keeping the brush vertical.

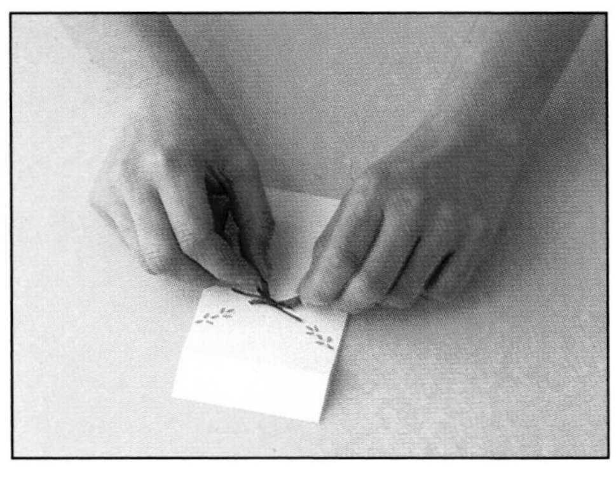

3 To attach the ribbon, mark and then cut 2 small slits in the card. Thread the ribbon through and tie it into a bow. Trim the ends of the ribbon if necessary.

4 Lay the finished cards in suitable positions on the table, such as on side plates or with the napkins.

course, a main course and dessert. In Europe it is also usual to serve a cheese course towards the end of the meal. A fish course or light appetizer may be served after the soup or a refreshing sorbet may be served between the first and main courses, and a savoury dish may be served instead of cheese.

An informal dinner party

Although the style of an informal party will differ from that of a more formal occasion, your aim should still be to provide well-prepared and beautifully presented food. 3 or 4 courses are usually served at a party of this kind. The opening course may be a starter (appetizer), salad or soup, and the main course will be followed by either dessert or cheese, or both. An informal dinner party can feature a more extensive menu, if you wish, even though the general approach to the evening is very casual. If the informal nature of the evening refers more to dress than to food, you may wish to offer 4 or more courses of less 'classic' food, with supper-style dishes (such as pasta or risotto), perhaps with a national theme, included on the menu.

PERFECT *PETITS FOURS*

Individual servings of *petits fours*, attractively arranged, will round off any meal. Arrange the *petits fours* in small fluted paper or foil cases. Try the following ideas:

- Dip the ends of brandysnaps in melted white and plain chocolate.
- Use a standard meringue mixture to pipe button-sized meringues, and dry them out in the coolest possible oven. Sandwich them in pairs by dipping their bases in melted plain chocolate.
- Stuff fresh dates with marzipan (almond paste) and roll in caster (superfine) sugar.
- Sandwich pecan or walnut halves in pairs with marzipan.

PREPARING FOR A BUFFET PARTY

ABOVE China plates add style to a buffet table, but plastic plates make a good alternative.

Preparing a buffet is the practical and fun answer to most types of home entertaining when more than about 8 people are invited. A buffet can, of course, be just as impressive as a sit-down menu, if you give some thought both to the presentation and display of the food. A buffet table also provides the perfect excuse for impressive settings, perhaps with swags of flowers or greenery (see opposite page) as well as a large main decoration. All the food should be decorative, too, and it must be arranged for ease of access when guests serve themselves.

Depending on the size and shape of your room, you could either place the buffet against a wall so that guests move along in front of the table and serve themselves, or situate it in the middle of a room (or with space all around) so that guests move around the table. Whichever system you use, there should be an obvious starting point for serving, indicated by a pile of plates.

If you decide to set the buffet against a wall, the main decoration should be at the rear of the table and positioned centrally. If guests walk all around the table, place the decoration in the centre for maximum effect.

Make sure that all the dishes are easy to reach and that there are serving spoons nearby. If there is a ham or other food to be carved, set it in a position to one side of the table so that guests do not obstruct access to other dishes while they carve. It should be someone's task to check the availability of foods, topping up dishes and tidying the buffet occasionally.

ABOVE Streamers and brightly coloured napkins and tableware enliven an informal buffet table.

Set napkins and cutlery (flatware) separately on a side table. Large paper napkins are usually used for informal buffets. If you use disposable plates, they should be sturdy and of good quality, as thin plates sag miserably and make eating difficult. Buffet-style plates are now available which include a holder for a wine glass. Alternatively, keep a large number of good-quality, large plastic plates, which are ideal for entertaining in large numbers. They are easier to rinse, stack and wash than china plates, and are ideal for outdoor parties as well as for informal buffets.

Be sure to site the buffet in a cool, well-ventilated place, away from radiators, and cover the table with a protective cloth before adding the decorative linen as there are always spills when guests serve themselves. The buffet should be set with savoury food for the main part of the meal. If you are serving a starter (appetizer), you can bring it to the buffet at the beginning of the meal, and assist the guests with it.

Serve desserts and cheese from the buffet once you have removed the main dishes. If, at a large gathering, you set out the desserts and cheese before clearing the main course, prepare a side table for them.

Always make sensible arrangements for receiving the used dishes and cutlery (flatware) when preparing a buffet. At a large gathering some guests may not feel inclined to bring their dishes out to the kitchen, so it is a good idea to set up a trolley (cart) where these may be placed out of the way.

Making a Greenery Chain

1 Join lengths of foliage together with plastic-covered or florist's wire cut into manageable strips.

2 Wire sprigs of herbs such as bay leaves, rosemary and thyme, and stitch them to the chain using a needle and thread.

3 Pin 1 end of the chain to a corner of the table. Work along the length of the chain, pinning it to the table at each of the sprigs of herbs to form looped swags. Tie bows in wide green satin ribbon, and use them to trim the herb sprigs.

ABOVE A selection of cheeses for the buffet table is always welcome, as is plenty of fresh fruit.

Avoiding Buffet Pitfalls

- Have dishes which are easy to serve – otherwise guests may feel inhibited about helping themselves.
- Avoid offering foods which really must be cut with a knife for easy eating.
- Avoid putting a first course on the buffet with all the main dishes so that everyone advances on all the food at once: if you want to keep a dish as a first course, make sure that you serve it yourself, otherwise guests will pile on the salads and other food, too.
- Arrange savoury and sweet foods on dishes at different levels, rather than in flat dishes, and 2 or 3 rows deep on the table. Use cake stands and stemmed dishes to full advantage so that the food creates a splendid display.
- Serve salad dressing separately for guests to help themselves, to avoid being left with a lot of dressed salad which has to be thrown out.

ORGANIZING A LARGER PARTY

Whatever the scale of the party you decide to give, the same principle applies, in that meticulous planning is essential. Decide first on the type of party you wish to give and think carefully about the date, then issue your invitations as soon as possible – this is particularly important at busy social times of year such as Christmas.

Make an inventory of your glasses, cutlery (flatware) and china, and the cooking and serving dishes that you have, so that you are alerted well in advance to any shortfall. If you only need a few extra items, you could probably borrow from friends, otherwise you would be best advised to use an outside supplier. Some wine merchants will lend glasses for a party, and some also offer a sale-or-return service. If your stock of tableware is inadequate for the numbers involved, you could consider good-quality disposable plates as an alternative to hiring (renting).

RIGHT Push back sofas and chairs to the edges of the room and cover them if necessary to avoid damage from spillages. A table left in the centre for people to put down food and drinks may be a good idea, but a plant left in this position would almost certainly be knocked over and should be removed to a safe place.

PARTY TIPS

- Clear the floor in the largest room to allow space for dancing. Set chairs aside but make sure that there are some comfortable areas where less-lively guests can congregate and talk.
- Subdued lighting always casts a flattering glow, so arrange table lamps around the room. The food and drinks tables should be well-illuminated.
- Lay a thick cloth on the drinks table for protection and pile plenty of clean towels and rolls of absorbent paper towels nearby in case of spillages. Place waste bags under the table.
- If you are short of chilling space, particularly for beer, use a clean dustbin (trash can) and tip a large bag of ice into it. Pour in a couple of buckets of cold water. Stand the dustbin conveniently outside the back door and place all the unopened bottles and cans in it. Knot a few towels on the dustbin handles for wiping off chilled bottles and cans.
- Be sure to supply plenty of alcohol-free drinks: mineral water, soda water, lemonade, tonic, fruit juices, alcohol-free beer and low-alcohol wine.
- Make large chunks of ice for chilling punches: they do not melt as quickly as small cubes, so they dilute the punch more slowly. Use margarine tubs or similar containers for this.
- Make colourful ice cubes for mixed drinks and cocktails by freezing cherries and pieces of orange, lemon or lime in water in ice-cube trays.

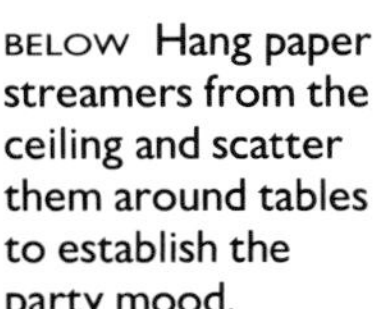

RIGHT A platter of crudités and a dip makes quick-and-easy party food.

BELOW Hang paper streamers from the ceiling and scatter them around tables to establish the party mood.

ESTIMATING DRINKS

This is a general guide to the numbers you can expect to serve, giving a standard measure, from a standard bottle:

Drink	*Glasses per bottle or carton*
Table wine, 70–75 cl	6–8
Champagne and other sparkling wines, 75 cl	6–7
Gin, whisky, vodka and other spirits served as cocktails, or with 'mixers', 70–75 cl	30
Tonic water, ginger ale or dry ginger, soda water and other 'mixers', 500 ml/18 fl oz	4–5
Vermouth, 70 cl	12–14
Liqueurs, 70 cl	30
Tomato juice, 1 l/1¾ pts	10–12
Orange, pineapple and other fruit juices, 1 l/1¾ pts	8–10
Fruit cordials (add 3.5 l/6 pts water to each bottle)	16–18

Calculate the quantities of food that you will need, and check that your pantry is stocked with all the long-lasting items that you are likely to use for cooking, to save time on shopping later. Then make a shopping list of the fresh foods that you will need to buy nearer the time, and the flowers and foliage to compose any decorations.

If necessary, clean and de-frost your refrigerator days in advance and clear space for the party food, soft drinks and wines. Make quantities of ice cubes and fancy ice shapes, and store them in plastic bags in the freezer.

If it is to be a large gathering and your 'reception-room' space is limited, pack away any valuable ornaments to avoid damage and, on the day of the party, re-arrange or move back the furniture to make easy 'traffic' routes. Set out the drinks at one end of the room and organize a table with the food at the other end, or in a separate room.

How much food you make is up to you, but there should be sufficient refreshments to balance the alcohol intake. Preparing canapés, hors d'oeuvres and snacks for a party is deceptively time-consuming, so a better option may be to make a large potful of something wholesome and to serve it accompanied by a great bowl of rice or a stack of baked potatoes. As most guests will find themselves a seat on the floor if the party atmosphere is informal enough, presenting food that needs to be eaten with the assistance of a knife is rarely a problem.

With your plans made in advance and put into operation smoothly, remember to build in enough time to get ready, as it is your welcoming and relaxed smile that will put your guests immediately at their ease.

ENTERTAINING AT CHRISTMAS

The celebration of Christmas is deeply woven into the fabric of home and family life. Much of the activity is centred on the kitchen which, as the culinary preparations get under way in the run-up to Christmas, more than ever becomes the heart of the home. The smooth running of the Christmas catering programme calls for a fair amount of advance planning and, nearer the day, meticulous timing, particularly if you have guests staying.

Entertaining over the Christmas period is a special pleasure, but there is no denying that it involves extra work and responsibility, as you will want to ensure that guests not only enjoy the highlights of their stay, but the quiet moments too.

For your own busy schedule and peace of mind, prepare guest bedrooms well in advance. Check that there are plenty of basic requirements such as fluffy towels, tissues, cotton wool (absorbent cotton) and guests' soap.

If you have the facilities, it is a good idea to take a leaf from the hoteliers' book and provide coffee- and tea-making equipment, something that is especially welcomed by those who wake up at unsociably early hours. Arrange a tray with an electric kettle, a small cafetière and a jar of ground coffee (or just supply instant coffee, if it is easier), a teapot and a choice of two tea blends. Add wrapped sugar and a decorative tin of biscuits (cookies), with milk and fresh fruit to be replenished daily.

ABOVE A bright wreath of evergreens, holly and berries gives a traditional sign of welcome.

Make a small selection of books and magazines for friends who like to travel light. Check that there are bulbs in the reading lamps, and provide an electric torch (flashlight) or plug in extra nightlights to help with night-time navigation to the bathroom.

Flowers help to make a room more welcoming. If there are plenty of Christmas decorations in the other rooms, flowers can bring a breath of spring or summer to the guest rooms. Dried-flower arrangements are a pretty option that also have the advantage of being long-lasting, preventing the need for last-minute preparation.

When your guests arrive, be sure to show them such essentials as where the light switches and sockets (receptacles) are to be found, and which cupboard (closet) space is available. Such extra thoughtfulness has an advantage for you too, as it will give you a chance to get on with household tasks while guests enjoy the warmth of your hospitality.

Sugared flowers and fruits

Sparkling under a light dusting of sugar as though tinged with frost or snow, sugared sweetmeats are a Christmas delicacy that add a lovely touch when displayed in bowls in guest bedrooms or in a living or dining room. You can prepare them several days ahead of the festivities and, once they are dry, store them in an airtight tin.

Not all flowers are edible, although many are – consult a reliable source if you are in any doubt. Marigolds, nasturtiums and pansies were all favourites in Victorian times, and offer an attractive variety of colour and shapes. Sugared fruits also look beautiful. Use small fruits, such as cherries, cranberries, strawberries and raspberries, whole. Peel and segment larger fruits such as oranges and tangerines, halve or quarter figs, according to their size, and halve and stone (pit) plums and apricots. You can also use sugared leaves with fruit and flowers, if you wish, to add contrast.

OPPOSITE Spoil your guests with breakfast in bed. Although the preparation is simple (coffee, orange juice and croissants warmed in the oven) the presentation is cheerful and welcoming – bright blue china is offset by flowers in complementary yellow.

RIGHT A plate is fitted with absorbent stem-holding foam for this pretty arrangement. Be careful to use freesias only in moderation in arrangements intended for bedrooms – their heavy scent, although lovely, may be oppressive to some guests.

SUGARING FLOWERS AND FRUITS

1 Hold fruits or flowers from a stem if possible, or pierce with a cocktail stick (toothpick), and dip into a bowl of lightly beaten egg white.

2 Lightly dust each petal, flower, fruit or leaf with caster (superfine) sugar to cover the whole surface.

3 Place on a wire rack covered with a sheet of greaseproof (waxed) paper, and leave to dry thoroughly.

Flower Arranging

FLORAL DISPLAYS FOR THE HOME

Just as each room in the home serves a different function, so different floral displays in appropriate styles will enhance their environment.

The dining room has a high profile in flower-arranging terms, as it becomes the centre stage whenever the family gathers for a leisurely meal – at Sunday lunchtime, perhaps – or when entertaining friends. If you have more than one arrangement in the room, it is a good idea to compose them with a linking theme. You could choose similar flowers, but in different colours: deep-pink Peruvian lilies, for example, in one case and the palest of pinks in another. A tall pitcher of white iris on the sideboard could be interpreted by floating similar flowers in a glass bowl on the dining table, by placing a single flower in a specimen vase at each place setting, or by blending white iris in an arrangement with anemones or roses.

In the living room, the well of the fireplace forms a dramatic arch for a flamboyant arrangement of seasonal plant materials chosen according to the colour and texture of the fireplace surround: a large earthenware jug of horse-chestnut buds in spring, a cool blend of blues and greens in summer, and the fiery hues of red, orange and yellow as winter approaches.

In summer, fresh flowers – especially if placed on a sunny window sill – are vulnerable and will fade quickly. In these circumstances, achieve the best of both worlds and choose the brightest and boldest of containers to display sun-bleached seedheads; fill a large white jug with a burst of fresh or dried gypsophila and strawflowers; pack a basket full of wild oats and decorative grasses, and wrap it with a brightly coloured paper-ribbon bow; or arrange some arching stems of translucent, dramatically back-lit foliage.

Flower arrangements for a bedroom or guest room are unashamed tokens of indulgence, and should be both romantic and restful. Try filling a pretty jug with a handful of fully opened roses or a nosegay of roses, lilies and larkspur in muted colours. Arrange a posy for a dressing table with spray carnations and daisy chrysanthemums in apricot and

ABOVE The vertical outline of irises combined with hosta (plantain lily) leaves makes an elegantly proportioned window-sill decoration.

RIGHT Spring flowers are complemented perfectly by a rustic basket in this simple arrangement.

FAR LEFT Bright tulips, daffodils, irises and hyacinths create a wonderfully colourful corner in a traditional-style kitchen.

LEFT Arranged in glorious profusion, dried flowers are a sophisticated and long-lasting choice for a dining-room centrepiece.

peach tints, or compose a miniature group of moody blues with forget-me-nots and cornflowers tumbling over the side of a blue-glass pitcher.

In a bathroom, take account of the likely temperature and humidity changes, and select the sturdiest and most long-lasting of blooms. These include chrysanthemums of all kinds, marigolds, carnations, spray carnations, lilies and tulips.

For a dried-flower bathroom arrangement, choose, again, from the most good-tempered examples, which include all the everlastings – strawflowers, rhodanthe, and acroclinium – statice, honesty, Chinese lanterns (winter cherry), and other seedheads. Or protect more delicate flowers under glass: an arrangement composed in dry foam on a board and covered with a glass dome – a modern cheese dish (see pages 238–9) or an upturned preserve jar – satisfies both aesthetic and practical considerations.

The kitchen is another room that is subject to rapid temperature changes, so many of the same ground rules apply as for the bathroom. A jug of marigolds on the kitchen table signals a cheery early-morning greeting; a pot of herbs on the window sill has both decorative and culinary properties; and a hanging basket of foliage plants, or grains and grasses, lifts floral décor to a high level.

BELOW Well-chosen colours provide a seasonal feel, as in this side-table arrangement of flowers, foliage, fruit and nuts.

CREATING A CENTREPIECE

A design that is destined to be seen from all angles, as it would be in the centre of a dining table or occasional table, for example, must be an all-round attraction. It should also look as good when seen from above – dome shapes, low pyramids and both regular and irregular all-round shapes, as here, are all effective. Turn the arrangement round one-quarter of a circle as you compose it, and give it a final check to make sure that it looks well-balanced from all viewpoints.

In order to create a lush and luxurious look for this semi-formal centrepiece, a colour scheme in the rich, warm colours of velvet has been used; choose the flowers for your arrangement from a selection such as anemones, roses, *Euphorbia fulgens* and flowering shrub, and foliage such as eucalyptus. Here, a wide-necked, bulbous pot was painted to give a feeling of nineteenth-century opulence, but a brass, copper or pewter pot, or any container in black, dark red, deep blue, purple or forest green would be equally suitable. A surface of polished wood makes the perfect complement to this jewel-bright arrangement.

1 Gather together the flowers and foliage, pot and all the materials that you will need: a piece of plastic-covered florist's wire-mesh netting, narrow florist's adhesive tape, scissors and florist's scissors.

2 Crumple the wire-mesh netting into a neat ball and press it into the top of the container. Secure it in place by threading 2 strips of florist's adhesive tape through the wire, criss-crossing them in the centre and sticking them to the top of the pot (see the box on the opposite page), where the ends will be concealed by the overhanging plant materials. Arrange the foliage to make a full shape all around the pot. Turn the container to check that the leaves are distributed evenly on all sides.

3 Work on one-quarter of the arrangement at a time. Place short stems of euphorbia to arch over the side of the container at different levels. Next, position the anemones all around the centre, alternating their colours to heighten the interest, and the spray carnations fairly close to the container rim. Position the fully opened roses at the heart of the design.

4 Compose the opposite side in a similar way, and fill in the gaps with short sprays of variegated foliage to separate the rich, deep colours of the flowers.

5 Turn the container around and repeat the design on the reverse, matching the first side in essence if not in detail. When you feel that the arrangement is complete, give it a final inspection and make any minor adjustments as necessary.

Fixing Florist's Wire-mesh Netting

Preparing a container in this way helps to anchor stems of fresh or dried flowers in a casual and informal design.

1 Gather your materials: a container with a large aperture, plastic-covered florist's wire-mesh netting, wire-cutters, narrow florist's adhesive tape and scissors.

2 Crumple the wire netting into a ball and place it in the neck of the container. If you wish to position some of the stems to slant at a low angle, ease the wire so that it forms a mound extending slightly above the level of the container rim. Remember that you will have to position the lowest of the plant materials so that they conceal this holding material from view.

3 Cut 2 lengths of tape slightly longer than the diameter of the container's opening. Thread the first strip under the wire in 2 places, take it across the container, and stick it to the rim on each side. Cross the second strip at right-angles to the first and fix it in the same way. Threading the tape under the wire will ensure that the ball of wire does not slip down into the container.

MAKING THE MOST OF COLOUR

Your choice of flowers for the home will generally take into account the furnishings of a room, the background against which the arrangement will be seen, and the effect that you wish to create – subtle and restful, or bold and eye-catching. When 2 colours that oppose each other on the colour wheel, such as mauve and yellow, are arranged together, the result can be dazzling.

Add to the impact of the design by using a scooped-out melon, with its deeply ridged texture, as an unusual container. Watermelons, pumpkins and marrows (squash), or oranges and lemons also make interesting short-term flower holders. You can dry the shells in an oven at a low temperature for a longer-lasting display.

Choose flowers that contrast dramatically with each other in size, shape and texture for this arrangement, such as huge, glossy yellow lilies and tiny, fluffy mimosa flowers, as well as yellow roses, mauve Singapore orchids and carnations. Eucalyptus foliage makes an attractive accompaniment.

OTHER CONTAINER IDEAS

You can use all kinds of baskets, pots, jugs, teapots and even decorated food cans as unusual holders for flowers. Rustic baskets always look attractive, either left plain or painted to harmonize with a particular colour scheme. If you are using soaked absorbent stem-holding foam in a basket, line the basket with a sheet of plastic, or fit a plastic container inside.

1 Gather together the materials you will need: a scooped-out melon or other container, a knife, a dessertspoon, a plastic foam-holding saucer, a cylinder of absorbent stem-holding foam, pre-soaked in water, narrow florist's adhesive tape, scissors and florist's scissors.

2 Cut a thin slice from the top of the melon, and a sliver from the base so that it will stand steadily. Using the spoon, scoop out the melon seeds into a bowl. Scoop out the melon flesh into a second bowl, taking care not to pierce and damage the shell.

3 Press the plastic saucer over the top of the melon and press the soaked foam into the indent. Criss-cross 2 lengths of adhesive tape over the foam and saucer and down on to the melon shell. Arrange stems of mimosa to make an irregular shape.

4 Arrange the orchids to make a triangular outline, the tallest one in the centre and 2 slightly shorter stems at the sides. Position the carnations to give weight to the design at the top and sides. Cut the lily stems and position them at the heart of the design, where the fully opened flowers will be seen head-on.

5 Add the cream roses, positioning some at the back so that they will be viewed through the more prominent flowers, and one low at the right. Complete the design with light sprays of foliage, placing some on the left of the arrangement to balance the rose. Keep the foam permanently moist, adding water at least once a day.

Fixing a Saucer of Stem-holding Foam

Preparing a container in this way allows you to use a tall vase, carafe or jug as a pedestal, positioning flower and foliage stems to slant both downwards and horizontally, or in any direction you choose. You will need a tall container, a strip of florist's adhesive clay, a plastic foam-holding saucer, a cylinder of stem-holding foam (either absorbent or dry according to the materials to be arranged), narrow florist's adhesive tape and scissors.

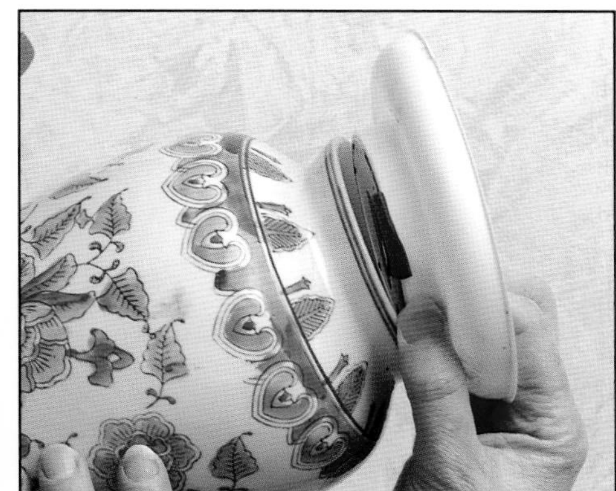

1 Cut small lengths of adhesive clay and press them on to the underside of the plastic saucer, where they will come into contact with the top of the container. Press the saucer firmly in place to hold it securely.

2 Soak the foam if it is to hold fresh flowers and foliage. Press the foam cylinder into the indent in the saucer. Cut 2 lengths of adhesive tape long enough to go over the foam, across the saucer and down on to the container rim. Stick them in place, criss-crossing them on top of the foam.

FLOWERS FOR A SPECIAL OCCASION

A basket of roses and Peruvian lilies makes a beautiful gift – perhaps for a special birthday, anniversary or Mother's Day. It would also add a lovely touch of colour and interest to a window sill, a fireplace or an otherwise dull corner that you feel needs cheering up. The basket, painted to tone with the flowers, would be ideal to use afterwards as a container for yarns, sewing materials or bath preparations.

1 Gather together your materials: a shallow basket with a handle, a waterproof liner such as a plastic box, a block of absorbent stem-holding foam (soaked beforehand), narrow florist's adhesive tape, scissors, long-lasting foliage such as eucalyptus and flowering shrub, flowers such as roses and Peruvian lilies, florist's scissors, secateurs (pruning shears), paper ribbon and a stub wire (floral pin). Prepare the basket to co-ordinate with the flowers that you are using, if you wish; the one shown here was painted in stripes of pink gloss paint, to add a touch of sparkle to the arrangement.

2 Put the liner in the basket and place the block of foam in it. Cut 2 strips of adhesive tape and criss-cross them over the foam and down on to the sides of the basket, to hold the foam firmly in place. Arrange the tallest stems of foliage to make a fan shape at the back of the basket. Cut progressively shorter stems for the centre and front, positioning them so that they droop and trail over the rim.

3 Arrange the roses to make a gently rounded shape in the basket, alternating the colours (pink and pale yellow were used here) so that each complements the other to create an attractive effect.

4 Add the Peruvian lilies, cutting some individual flowers on short stems and positioning them close against the foam. Fill in the gaps with short sprays of flowering shrub.

5 Unfurl the twisted paper ribbon by pulling it out gently from one end. You need about 1 m/1 yd to make a full, generous bow.

6 Cut the length of ribbon required and tie it into a bow. Gently ease the loop until it looks neat, and trim the ribbon ends by cutting them at a slant. Thread the stub wire through the back of the loop, and twist and insert the 2 ends into the foam at the front of the basket. Spray the flowers with a fine mist of cool water, and keep the foam moist by adding a little water to it at least once a day.

ARRANGING DRIED FLOWERS

Most of the equipment and techniques used for fresh-flower arrangements can be applied to dried-flower designs as well. You can fit a jug or vase with a block of stem-holding foam and hold it in place with florist's adhesive tape, or use a purpose-made saucer if you wish (see page 233), so that stems may be angled in any direction, or you can bind stems with florist's silver wire, as shown in this arrangement.

A hanging bunch of dried flowers, the interior-design version of a posy, makes a charming wall decoration for any room in the home, especially when complemented by a pretty floral paper ribbon. This design was created for a girl's bedroom, where it is displayed with a collection of Greek pottery.

1 Collect up dried flowers such as larkspur, lady's mantle, marjoram, sea lavender, strawflowers, rosebuds and hydrangea, and some dried grasses, in colours to blend with the proposed site for the decoration. Those to be placed at the back of the bunch will need long stems. Collect the other materials that you will need: a roll of florist's silver wire, florist's scissors, paper ribbon and scissors.

2 Compose the flower bunch on a table. Place the longest stems (the grasses) so that they will fan out at the back. Cover them with blue larkspur, the tips widely spaced and the stems close together.

3 Arrange stems of pink larkspur over the blue ones. Position marjoram stems in the centre and shorter sprays of lady's mantle from side to side. Place pink roses in the centre, and then strawflowers at varying heights. Place short stems of sea lavender so that they will fan out at the sides.

DRYING IN WATER

Although it seems a contradiction in terms, some delicate plant materials such as hydrangea, as well as cornflowers and statice (used in the project overleaf) may be air-dried with their stems standing in a little water. The principle is that the water gradually evaporates as it is absorbed by the stems and, over a week or 10 days, the plant material dries naturally. Other flowers in this category include gypsophila and mimosa.

4 Bind the stems with silver wire. Before pulling the wire tight, re-arrange the stems until the shape is pleasing. Tuck in a few short stems of hydrangea.

5 Unfurl the length of paper ribbon from each end but leave the centre section tightly furled. Wrap the centre section tightly around the stems and tie in a knot. Tie the ends into a bow, adjusting the ribbon to make a full, rounded shape, and then cut the ends at a slant.

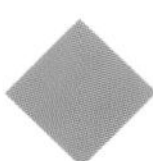

Wiring Dried Flowers

1 To bind flowers that have a reasonable length of stem, such as the air-dried rose and the delphinium shown above, place a stub wire (floral pin) close against the stem and then bind the 2 together securely using a length of silver wire.

2 To wire a dried flower that has a very short stem, such as the ranunculus shown above, place a stub wire close against the short stem length and then bind it and the stem together securely with silver wire. Bind the false wire stem with a length of gutta-percha (floral) tape (available from most good florists).

3 To wire a dried flower that has no stem – strawflowers are a frequent example – push a stub wire through the flower from the base. Bend a short hook in the top of the wire and pull it down so that the hook is concealed within the flower centre. Bind the false wire stem securely with a length of gutta-percha tape.

DRIED FLOWERS FOR A BATHROOM

A dried-flower arrangement may seem paradoxical in a hot and steamy bathroom, breaking all the rules about displaying dried flowers in a dry, airy environment. If the flowers are under permanent protection, however, as with this arrangement, they will stay beautiful indefinitely. The design, a modern version of a Victorian flower dome, is created on the pine base of a cheese dish and covered with the glass lid. Select dried flowers in sharply contrasting colours so that they do not blend into an unidentifiable mass.

1 Collect together the materials you will need: a glass-covered dish, florist's adhesive clay, scissors, a plastic prong, a cylinder of dry stem-holding foam, a knife, a selection of dried flowers such as helichrysum, statice, lady's mantle, cornflowers and rosebuds, and florist's scissors.

2 Press a small strip of adhesive clay to the base of the plastic prong and press it on to the centre of the base. Cut the foam to the size and shape required and press it on to the prong. Arrange a ring of white statice around the base, positioning the stems horizontally in the foam. Make a dome shape with yellow rosebuds. Put on the glass cover to check that the stems are not too tall to fit inside, then remove the cover again. If the stems are too long, carefully extract them from the foam and trim the ends as necessary, using the florist's scissors. Replace the stems as before.

KITCHEN COVER-UP

You need not confine this type of flower decoration to a bathroom. The frequently changing and sometimes steamy environment of a kitchen would be another area in which a covered arrangement would be ideal – perhaps on a dresser or in the centre of the table. The glass cover will not only shield the flowers from changes in temperature, but will also provide excellent protection from dust and dirt. Many kinds of dried flowers are suitable for displaying in this way, although small flowerheads look the most effective.

3 Arrange short stems of blue and yellow statice between the rosebuds and, to soften the effect, add some short sprays of helichrysum and lady's mantle.

4 Position cornflowers evenly throughout the design. Turn the base around slowly and check that it is equally well-covered and attractive from every angle.

5 Once the cover is in place, the dried flowers will be well-protected from any steam. To make a complete seal, press a narrow strip of modelling clay such as Plasticine all around the rim of the base, and scatter a few highly absorbent silica-gel crystals among the dried flowers. These crystals, which are available from some chemists (drugstores), florist's shops and camera retailers, are very effective in drawing away any moisture from the surrounding air. Press the cover on to the clay to complete the seal.

CHOOSING PLANTS FOR THE HOME

By using houseplants as ornaments, focal points and as integrated decorations in the home, you will derive even more pleasure from your plants than you would by regarding them merely as botanical specimens. Although plants are constantly changing – they grow, die, or simply alter their shape – this very lack of stability can be turned to your advantage. Unlike any other decorative element that you can place and forget, and eventually even take for granted, plants have a dynamic existence. You have to move them, re-arrange them, even re-pot them into different containers, all of which gives them an extra dimension and vitality that other kinds of ornaments lack.

Many evergreens are tough enough for the more difficult positions around the home, such as a draughty hallway. They will be far more robust than plants with thin or papery leaves, feathery and frondy ferns, or even those with hairy leaves. You need these other leaf textures, as well as flowering plants, to add variety of shape and form, and a touch of colour, but it makes sense to use the toughest evergreens as the basis of your houseplant displays. Ivies are ideal if you need a tough climber or trailer, and there are lots of varieties to choose from, with a wide choice of leaf shape, size and colour.

Palms are the epitome of elegance and will add a touch of sophistication to your home. Many are slow-growing, and, consequently, large specimens are often expensive. But do not be deterred from trying palms; if you provide the right conditions, even small plants will gradually become very impressive specimens. The most common mistake is to regard all palms as lovers of hot sunshine and desert-dry air. They often have to cope with both in countries where they grow outdoors, but as

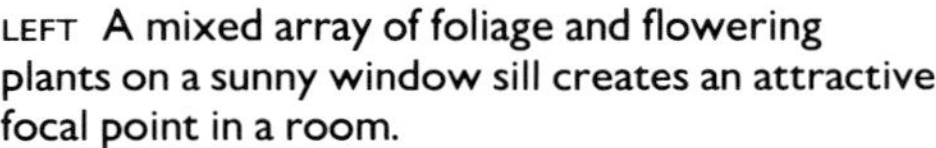

LEFT A mixed array of foliage and flowering plants on a sunny window sill creates an attractive focal point in a room.

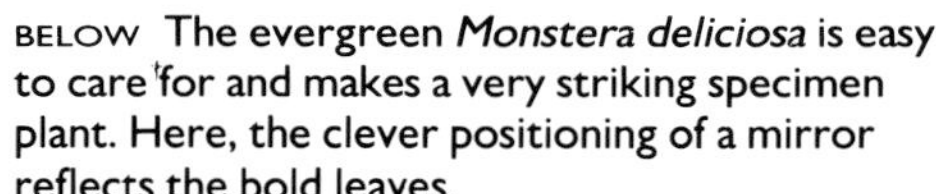

BELOW The evergreen *Monstera deliciosa* is easy to care for and makes a very striking specimen plant. Here, the clever positioning of a mirror reflects the bold leaves.

OPPOSITE A tall, elegant plant such as this palm is best positioned in a large, open area such as a conservatory to show it off to best effect.

RIGHT The fern *Nephrolepis exaltata* is one of the best ferns for a pedestal or table-top display. It needs frequent misting with water to keep it in peak condition.

GERBERA

Although it will flower less profusely than when planted out in the garden, a gerbera can be grown successfully in a pot and makes a delightful houseplant. Ideally, place a gerbera in a sunny position, although, if you plan to discard it after flowering, you can use it to brighten up dull spots too.

houseplants you want them to remain in good condition with unblemished leaves. Brown leaf tips are usually caused by over-dry air, and yellowing leaves by underwatering.

Ferns are grown mainly for the grace and beauty of their fronds. The majority of ferns will thrive in shade or partial shade, conditions that are easily provided in any home. Unfortunately they also require a lot of moisture and high humidity, both of which are in short supply in the average living room. Although most of the ferns sold as houseplants come from tropical regions, central heating spells death to many of them unless you counteract the dry air by taking measures to increase the humidity. The ideal place for ferns is in a conservatory, porch or garden room where it is easier to establish a moist atmosphere. If you wish to grow the delicate types with feathery fronds, try planting them in a bottle garden (see page 251), where they will thrive.

Although generally short-lived in the home, flowering houseplants will bring a wonderful splash of colour and vibrancy. They also add an element of seasonal variation that ordinary foliage houseplants lack. The most rewarding flowering houseplants are those that grow bigger and better each year, with each subsequent blooming crowning another year of good cultivation and care. Flowers that you should be able to keep growing in the home from year to year include beloperones, bougainvillaeas, *Campanula isophylla*, clivias, gardenias, hoyas, *Jasminum polyanthum*, *Nerium oleander*, pelargoniums, saintpaulias, spathiphyllums and streptocarpus.

ABOVE A year-round chrysanthemum makes an excellent short-term houseplant, and will flower for several weeks.

Many flowering pot plants are difficult to keep permanently in the home and are best discarded when flowering has finished (or placed in a greenhouse if you have one). You should therefore really regard them as long-lasting cut flowers. A lot of them are annuals (in other words, they live for only 1 year) and can, therefore, be inexpensively raised from seed. Try browallias, calceolarias, cinerarias and exacums, which all make bright and cheerful plants for the home.

WATERING AND HYDROCULTURE

No plant can survive without water, yet more plants probably die from overwatering than from underwatering. Getting to grips with this apparently simple procedure is one of the essentials of good plant care in the home.

There are no fixed 'rules' about watering. How much a plant needs, and how often, depends not only on the plant but also the kind of pot (clay pots need watering more often than plastic ones), the compost (potting soil), (peat-based composts retain more water than loam-based), and the temperature and humidity of the environment.

When you water, fill the pot to the brim – dribbles are not sufficient. If the root-ball has completely dried out, water may run straight through, down the inside of the pot, in which case stand the pot in a bucket of water until the air bubbles stop rising. After watering, always check whether surplus water is sitting in the saucer or cache-pot. This will not matter if there are pebbles or marbles to keep the bottom of the pot out of contact with the moisture, but otherwise you must tip out the extra water. Failure to tip out standing water is the most common cause of problems. With just a few exceptions, if you leave most ordinary houseplants standing in water for a long period, they will probably die.

Examine the pots daily if possible – appearance alone can be a guide. Loam-based composts look paler when dry than when moist. A dry surface does not mean that the compost is dry lower down, but, if it looks damp, you will know that you do not need to water.

The touch test is useful for a peat-based compost. Press a finger into the surface – you will know immediately if it feels very dry or very wet. The bell test is useful for clay pots. Push a cotton reel on to a garden cane and tap the pot: a dull thud indicates moist compost; a clear ring suggests dry compost.

Tap water is far from ideal for watering, but most houseplants will tolerate it. If the water is hard (has a high calcium or magnesium content), however, you need to make special arrangements for plants that react badly to alkaline soil or compost. These include aphelandras, azaleas, hydrangeas, orchids, rhododendrons and saintpaulias. Rain water is usually recommended for these plants, but a good supply is not always available. If your tap water is only slightly hard, simply filling the watering cans and allowing the water to stand overnight may be sufficient. For harder water, try boiling it: part of the hardness will be deposited in the form of scale, and you can use the water once it has cooled.

HOLIDAY-CARE TIPS

- Porous wicks are sold for insertion into the base of a plant pot, which is then stood above a reservoir of water. You can make your own porous wicks by cutting a piece of capillary matting (available at all good garden centres) into strips, as shown above. Make sure that the wicks and compost (potting soil) are moist before you go on holiday, and that the wick is pushed well into the compost.
- If it is summer, stand as many plants as possible outdoors. Choose a shady, sheltered position, and plunge the pots up to their rims in the soil. Apply a thick mulch of chipped bark or peat over the pots to keep them cool and to conserve moisture. Provided that you water them well before you leave, most plants will survive a week like this.
- Move plants that are too delicate to go outdoors into a few large groups in a cool position out of direct sunlight.

For easy and convenient watering, choose a watering can that is well-balanced to hold and has a long, narrow spout that makes it easy to direct the water to the compost (potting soil) rather than over the plant.

Just a few plants tolerate standing with their roots in water, like this cyperus. With these you can add water to the saucer or outer container, but never do this unless you know the plant grows naturally in marshy places.

If you find watering a chore, self-watering pots may be the answer. The moisture is drawn up into the compost (potting soil) through wicks from a reservoir below, and you will need to water much less frequently.

Starting Off a New Plant

Hydroculture

Watering correctly is an acquired skill, but, with practice, you will come to learn exactly how much or how little water your plants need. If you do find watering difficult or time-consuming, however, other alternatives would be to use self-watering containers, or to try the technique of hydroculture (also known as hydroponics) which will enable you to grow plants successfully with the minimum of attention. Hydroculture is a method of growing plants without soil or compost (potting soil). Watering is normally only necessary every fortnight, and feeding is only a twice-yearly task.

You can buy plants that are already growing hydroponically, but, once you realize how easy hydroculture plants are to look after, you will probably want to start off your own plants from scratch. Not all plants respond well to hydroculture, so you may need to experiment, but the range of suitable plants is surprisingly wide, and includes amaryllis, aspidistra, some begonias, ficus, saintpaulia and yucca, as well as cacti and succulents.

Routine care is very simple. Wait until the water indicator (see step 3) registers minimum, but do not water immediately. Allow an interval of 2 or 3 days before filling again. Always use tap water because the special ion-exchange fertilizer used for hydroculture (available from garden centres) depends on the chemicals in tap water to function effectively. The water must be at room temperature. As there is no compost (potting soil), cold water has an immediate chilling effect on the plant – a common cause of failure with hydroculture. Make a note of when you replace the fertilizer, and renew it every six months. Some systems use the fertilizer in a 'battery' fitted within the special hydroculture pot, but otherwise you can just sprinkle it on to be washed in with a little water.

1 Choose a young plant and wash the roots free of all traces of compost (potting soil). Place the plant in a suitable-sized container with slatted or mesh sides.

2 Pack expanded clay granules around the roots, being careful to damage the roots as little as possible.

3 Insert the inner pot into a larger, watertight container, first placing a layer of clay granules on the base to raise the inner pot to a level of about 12 mm/½ in below the rim. Insert a water-level tube (available from garden centres). If you cannot find one specially designed to indicate the actual water level, use one that indicates how moist the roots are.

4 Pack with more clay granules to secure the inner pot and water indicator. Sprinkle special hydroculture fertilizer (available from garden centres) over the granules.

5 Wash the fertilizer down as you water to the maximum level on the indicator. If the indicator does not show an actual level, add a volume of water equal to one-quarter of the capacity of the container – and only water again when the indicator shows dry.

6 A few months on and the houseplant is flourishing.

POTTING PLANTS

Never be in too much of a hurry to pot on a plant into a larger container. Plants do not appreciate having their roots disturbed, and any damage to them will result in some check to growth. Some types of houseplants also prefer to be in small pots.

Re-potting should never simply be an annual routine. It is a job to be thought about annually, but should not actually be done unless a plant needs it. Young plants require potting on much more frequently than older ones. Once a large specimen is in a big pot, it may be better to keep it growing by re-potting into another pot of the same size, by top-dressing (see below right), or simply by additional feeding.

When re-potting is necessary

The sight of roots growing through the base of the pot is not in itself a sign that re-potting is immediately necessary. If you have been watering the plants through a capillary mat, or have placed the pot in a cache-pot, some roots will inevitably have grown through the base to seek the water.

If you are in doubt, knock the plant out of its pot. To remove the root-ball easily, invert the pot and knock the rim on a hard surface while supporting the plant and compost (potting soil) with your hand. It is normal for a few roots to run around the inside of the pot, but if there is also a solid mass of roots it is time to pot on. There are several ways to re-pot a plant, but the 2 methods described here are among the best.

WHEN TO RE-POT

A mass of thick roots growing through the bottom of the pot (top) is an indication that it is time to move the plant into a larger one. Equally, a mass of roots curled around the edge of the pot (above) is a sign that it is time for a larger container.

The vast majority of plants on sale are grown in plastic pots, which are inexpensive, light and remain largely free of algae. Plastic pots do become brittle with age, however, and even a slight knock can break them, whereas a clay pot will not break unless you actually drop it on a hard surface.

POT-IN-POT METHOD

1 Prepare the new pot as in step 1 of the Traditional Method if you are using a clay pot. However, if you are using a plastic pot and you intend to use a capillary watering mat, do not cover the drainage hole at all.

TOP-DRESSING

Once plants are in large pots, perhaps 25–30 cm (10–12 in) in diameter, continual potting on into a larger pot may not be practical. Try removing the top few centimetres (inches) of compost (potting soil), loosening it first with a small hand fork. Replace this with fresh potting compost of the same type. This, plus regular feeding, will enable most plants to be grown in the same pot for many years.

2 Put in a little dampened compost (potting soil). Insert the existing pot (or an empty one of the same size), ensuring that the soil level will be 12 mm/½ in below the top of the new pot when filled.

3 Pack more compost firmly between the inner and outer pots, pressing it down gently with your fingers. This will create a mould when you remove the inner pot.

4 Remove the inner pot, then take the plant from its original container and place it in the hole formed in the centre of the new compost. Gently firm the compost around the root-ball, and water thoroughly.

TRADITIONAL METHOD

1 Prepare a pot that is either 1 or 2 sizes larger than the original and, if the pot is a clay one, cover the drainage hole with pieces of broken pot or a few pieces of chipped bark.

2 Water the plant to be re-potted, and leave it for a few minutes. Remove the root-ball from the old pot, either by pulling gently on the plant, or by inverting the pot and tapping the rim on a hard surface.

3 Place a little compost (potting soil) in the base of the new pot, then position the root-ball so that it is at the correct height. If it sits too low or too high, adjust the amount of compost in the base.

4 Trickle more compost around the sides, turning the pot as you work. It is a good idea to use the same kind of compost – peat- (peat-moss) or loam-based – as used in the original pot.

5 Gently firm the compost with your fingers. Make sure that there is a gap of about 12 mm–2.5 cm (½–1 in) between the top of the compost and the rim of the pot, to allow for watering. Water thoroughly.

POTTING ON, POTTING UP, RE-POTTING

Potting up is what happens the first time a seedling or cutting is given its own individual pot.
Potting on is the action of re-planting the root-ball in a larger pot.
Re-potting is sometimes taken to mean replacing the plant in a pot of the same size, but with the bulk of the compost replaced, if the plant cannot be moved into a larger pot.

TAKING STEM AND LEAF CUTTINGS

Many houseplants can be raised from stem cuttings and leaf cuttings. The techniques are easy, and you will gain even more pleasure from your plants by seeing them grow from the start.

Taking stem cuttings

Most houseplants can be propagated from softwood cuttings taken in spring, and many of the shrubby plants root from semi-ripe cuttings taken later in the year. The method of taking softwood cuttings is similar to that of semi-ripe cuttings (see right), but choose the ends of new shoots. Take softwood cuttings after the first flush of spring but before the shoots have become hard, and follow the same procedure as for semi-ripe cuttings. Geranium (pelargonium) softwood cuttings root readily, and are therefore good to try if you are a beginner.

Softwood cuttings – especially easy ones such as coleus and impatiens – can often be rooted in water. Fill a jam-jar almost to the top with water and fold a piece of wire-netting (chicken wire) over the top. Take the cuttings in the normal way but, instead of inserting them into compost (potting soil), rest them on the netting, with the ends of the stems in water. Top up the water as necessary. When roots have formed, pot up the cuttings into individual pots.

Taking leaf cuttings

Some of the most popular houseplants, such as saintpaulias, foliage begonias, streptocarpus and sansevierias, can be raised from leaf cuttings, using a variety of methods. For leaf-petiole cuttings, you need to remove the leaves with a length of stalk attached. For square-leaf cuttings, instead of placing a whole leaf on the compost (medium), cut it into squares and insert these individually. With leaf-midrib cuttings, slice the long, narrow leaves of plants such as streptocarpus into sections and treat them as for square-leaf cuttings.

TAKING SEMI-RIPE STEM CUTTINGS

1 Make the cuttings 10–15 cm/4–6 in long, choosing the current season's growth after the first flush of growth but before the whole shoot has become hard. Fill a pot with a cuttings compost (medium) or use a seed compost, and firm it to remove any large pockets of air.

2 Trim the cutting just below a leaf joint, using a sharp knife, and remove the lower leaves to produce a clear stem to insert into the compost.

3 Dip the cut end of the cutting into a rooting hormone. If using a powder, moisten the end in water first so that it adheres. Make a hole in the compost with a small dibber or a pencil, and insert the cutting so that the bottom leaves are just above the compost. Firm the compost gently around the stem to remove large air pockets. You can usually insert several cuttings around the edge of a pot.

4 Water the cuttings, then label and place in a propagator, or cover the pot with a clear plastic bag, making sure that it does not touch the leaves. Keep in a light place, but out of direct sunlight. If a lot of condensation forms, reverse the bag or ventilate the propagator until excess condensation ceases to form. Do not allow the compost to dry out. Pot up the cuttings once they have formed a good root system.

USING ROOTING HORMONES

Some plants, such as impatiens and some tradescantias, root readily even without help from a rooting hormone. Others, and especially semi-ripe cuttings, will benefit from the use of a rooting hormone. Rooting hormones are available as powders or liquids, and their use usually results in more rapid rooting and, in the case of the trickier kinds of plants, a higher success rate.

Taking Leaf-petiole Cuttings

1 Use only healthy leaves that are mature but not old. Remove the leaf with about 5 cm/2 in of stalk, using a sharp knife or razor blade. Fill a tray or pot with a suitable rooting compost (medium), then make a hole with a dibber or pencil.

2 Insert the stalk into the hole, angling the cutting slightly, then press the compost gently around the stalk to firm it in. The base of the blade of the leaf should sit on the surface of the compost. You should be able to accommodate a number of cuttings in a seed tray or large pot. Water well, preferably with the addition of a suitable fungicide, and then allow any surplus moisture to drain away.

3 Place the cuttings in a propagator, or cover with a clear plastic bag. Make sure that the leaves do not touch the glass or plastic, and remove condensation periodically. Keep the cuttings warm and moist, in a light place out of direct sunlight. Young plants usually develop within a month or so and can then be potted up individually, but leave them until they are large enough to be handled easily.

Taking Square-leaf Cuttings

1 First cut the leaf into strips about 3 cm/1¼ in wide, in the general direction of the main veins, using a sharp knife or razor blade (be sure to handle the latter very carefully). Cut across the strips to form small, even-sized squares of leaf.

2 Fill a tray with a rooting compost (medium), then insert the squares on edge, with the edge that was nearest to the leaf stalk facing downwards. Once the young plants are well-established, after a month or so, pot them up individually.

Plants to Grow from Leaf Cuttings

Leaf-blade cuttings
Begonia rex
Leaf-petiole cuttings
Begonias (other than *B. rex*)
Peperomia caperata
Peperomia metallica
Saintpaulia
Leaf-midrib cuttings
Gesneria
Sansevieria
Sinningia speciosa (gloxinia)
Streptocarpus

Taking Leaf-midrib Cuttings

1 Remove a healthy, undamaged leaf from the parent plant – ideally one that has only recently fully expanded.

2 Place the leaf face-down on a firm, clean surface, such as a sheet of glass. Cut the leaf into strips no wider than 5 cm/2 in.

3 Fill a pot or tray with a rooting compost (medium), and insert the cuttings 2.5 cm/1 in apart, with the end that was nearest the stalk downwards. Pot up the plants when they are large enough to handle.

DEALING WITH PLANT PROBLEMS

Not all plant disorders are caused by pests and diseases. Sometimes physiological problems such as chills and cold draughts, or nutritional deficiencies, can be the cause. Tracking down a physiological problem calls for a bit of detective work. The following descriptions of some common problems will help to pinpoint some potential causes, but be prepared to look for anything that has disturbed the usual routine – has the plant been moved, watered more or less heavily, has the weather become much colder, or have you turned the central heating on but not increased humidity or ventilation? By piecing together the various clues you can often deduce probable causes, and thereby work out what you can do to avoid a repetition.

Temperature

Most houseplants will tolerate cool but frost-free temperatures if they have to. It is sudden changes of temperature or icy draughts in a warm room that cause most problems. If leaves drop, it may be due to low temperature. This often happens with newly bought plants that have been on display outdoors or chilled on the way home. Leaves that look shrivelled and slightly translucent may have been touched by frost.

Hardy plants such as *Euonymus japonicus* may drop their leaves if kept too warm in winter, and berries are also likely to fall prematurely.

Light and sun

Light is usually beneficial, but direct sunlight, intensified through glass, will often scorch leaves – the effect will be brown, papery areas on the leaf. Plants that need a high light intensity in order to grow properly will become elongated and drawn if the illumination is poor, and leaves and flower stalks will be drawn towards the window. Lopsided growth is another indication of inadequate light.

ABOVE This plant is clearly showing signs of neglect and lack of nutrients. It may be best to discard a plant in this state.

ABOVE RIGHT Yellowing lower leaves are often a sign of overwatering, but may also be due to a chill. This is a *Fatshedera lizei* beginning to show signs of overwatering.

RIGHT Plants that are not adapted to grow in very strong light are easily scorched by strong sunlight intensified by a glass window. This dieffenbachia is suffering from scorch.

Humidity

Dry air can cause leaf tips to turn brown and papery on vulnerable plants.

Feeding

Pale leaves and short, stunted growth may be due to lack of fertilizer in the compost (potting soil). Try liquid feeding for a quick boost.

Bud drop

Bud drop is often caused by dry compost (potting soil) or dry air. Some plants also resent having to re-orientate their buds to light from a different direction if they are moved.

Wilting and collapse

Plants usually wilt for the following reasons: too much water; too little water; or insects or a disease affecting the roots. The first of the problems will usually be obvious, but, if the compost seems neither overwatered nor underwatered, check the base of the plant. If the stem looks black or rotten, a fungal disease is the likely cause and the plant is best discarded.

If none of the above symptoms is present, remove the plant from its pot. If many of the roots are soft or black and decaying, a root disease is likely to be the problem. It will be very difficult to revive a plant with a severe root rot, but you can try drenching the compost (potting soil) with a fungicide, then after a couple of hours letting it dry out

First Aid for a Dry Plant

1 If the leaves of a plant have started to wilt like this, the compost (potting soil) is probably too dry. Feel it first – overwatering also causes wilting.

2 Stand the pot in a bowl or bucket of water and leave it until the air bubbles have ceased to rise. It will take some hours for the water to revive the plant. In the meantime, help it further by misting the leaves with water from time to time.

3 Once the plant has revived, remove it from the bowl and stand it in a cool place out of direct sunlight for at least a day.

First Aid for a Wet Plant

1 Knock the plant out of its pot. If it does not come out easily, invert the plant while holding the compost (potting soil) in with one hand, and knock the rim of the pot on a hard surface.

2 Wrap the root-ball in several layers of absorbent paper.

3 Stand the plant in a warm place, out of direct sunlight, with more absorbent paper wrapped around the root-ball. Change the paper periodically if it is still drawing moisture from the compost. Re-pot and water very cautiously for the next week.

on absorbent paper. If the root system is badly damaged, re-pot the plant in sterilized compost before treating it.

Some soil pests, such as root aphids, can be controlled if drenched with an insecticide. Wine weevil grubs and other serious soil pests are not so easy to control. Try shaking the old soil off the roots, dusting them with an insecticidal powder, then re-potting in fresh, sterilized compost. The plant may survive once it makes new growth.

Other Possible Causes of Collapse

Plants may collapse for one of the following physiological reasons:

- Cold air at night may cause plants to collapse, especially if they have been warm during the day.
- Strong, hot sunshine through glass will make many plants wilt. They will usually recover when given cooler, shadier conditions.
- Hot, dry air will have a similar effect on some plants, such as the more delicate ferns.
- Poor light will eventually cause a plant to exhaust itself. This is likely to be a gradual process, however – much less rapid than the collapse caused by watering problems or by soil pests such as root aphids.

CREATING PLANT DISPLAYS

Small plants can be displayed more creatively than just in individual pots. Plant them in groups in planters or baskets, or in a shallow container on a pedestal. You can even create a miniature garden in a large bottle. An advantage of grouping plants is that you can get away with less-than-perfect specimens: a plant with lopsided growth, or one that is bare at the base, can be arranged so that its defects are hidden by other plants.

Grouped plants also benefit from the microclimate created when plants are grown together. The local humidity is likely to be a little higher as the leaves tend to protect each other from drying air and cold draughts, and it is easier to keep the compost (potting soil) evenly moist in a large container than a small one. Groupings are ideal for self-watering containers and for plants grown hydroponically, and simply ensuring a steady and even supply of moisture produces better growth.

Pedestals make good bases for plant displays. If you have an attractive pedestal, use short trailers that will cascade over the pot but will not completely hide the pedestal under a curtain of leaves. Plants with an arching rather than a cascading habit are also ideal for a pedestal where you want to show off both pot and pedestal.

Another display idea is a *pot-et-fleur* arrangement. This makes an ideal centrepiece, and gives plenty of scope for artistic presentation.

The still, protected and humid environment of a sealed bottle garden, with moisture re-circulating as it condenses and runs down the glass, makes it possible to grow many small jungle and rainforest-type plants that would soon die in a normal room environment. Yet, if you leave the top off and water very carefully, a bottle garden can also be a pretty way to display those plants that enjoy less-humid conditions.

PLANTING A PEDESTAL ARRANGEMENT

1 Fill a wide, shallow, stable container with a layer of compost (potting soil). Choose a mixture of flowering and foliage plants for a spectacular display. Try them for position while still in their pots, until you are happy with the arrangement.

2 Remove the plants from their pots for final planting. Set those at the edge at an angle so that they tumble over the side.

3 Water, then sit the container in a saucer and position it on the pedestal.

CREATING A *POT-ET-FLEUR* WITH FOAM

1 If you are using a basket, line it with plastic to ensure that it is waterproof.

2 Position your foliage plants first, preferably in shallow pots.

3 Cut a block of absorbent stem-holding foam (this should be soaked overnight in water first) into pieces of the size required. Pack the pieces of foam between the pots to fill up all the gaps and hold the pots securely in position.

4 Insert your flowers (and some additional cut foliage if you wish) into the moist foam. Stand back from the arrangement and view it from a distance to see whether you are happy with the result, and add more flowers and foliage if necessary.

5 Place the arrangement in a fairly cool position, and replace the flowers and cut foliage as necessary (adding water to the foam will help to preserve them). If any of the foliage plants deteriorate in time, simply replace them with fresh ones.

PLANTING A BOTTLE GARDEN

1 Place a layer of charcoal and gravel or expanded clay granules in the bottom of a thoroughly clean, fairly deep bottle. Add compost (potting soil), using a funnel or cone made from a sheet of thick paper or thin cardboard as a guide.

2 If necessary, remove a little of the compost from the plants to make insertion easier. Unless the neck of the bottle is very narrow, you should be able to insert the plants without difficulty. If you cannot get your hand into the bottle, use implements such as those shown to lower the plants into position. Add another layer of charcoal and gravel or expanded clay granules around the bases of the plants.

3 After tamping the compost around the roots (use a cotton reel on the end of a cane if necessary), mist the plants and compost. If necessary, direct the spray to remove compost adhering to the sides of the bottle. This type of open-topped bottle will require careful watering. Place it in good light, but away from direct sun as the plants may easily be scorched through the glass.

Main Index

Recipe Index

A

B

C

D

E

F

G

I

ACKNOWLEDGEMENTS

Special photography and illustrations © Anness Publishing Limited
Photography: David Armstrong – pages 185, 189; James Duncan – pages 192/193, 207–211, 213 cl bl br, 218–223, 224 b, 225; John Freeman – pages 10–67; 86–101, 194–205; 240–251; Nelson Hargreaves – pages 4, 68–85, 102–118, 120, 121, 123–131, 206, 212, 213 tl tr, 214–217, 226–239; Amanda Heywood – pages 132–177; Tim Hill – pages 178–184, 186–188, 190, 191; Vyner Street Studio – pages 79 bc, 119, 122, 125 b.
Illustrations: Andrew Green – pages 13, 26, 27, 49, 61, 197, 199, 201; Keith Jackson – pages 79, 81, 83, 84, 85, 117, 126, 127; Beverley Lees – pages 70–75.

The publishers would also like to thank the following for additional images used in this book: Addis Ltd – page 63 b; Laura Ashley – pages 196 t, 199 br, 202 bl, 205 br; Richard Burbidge Ltd – page 53; Concord Lighting Ltd – page 15 tr b; Cristal (H & R Johnson Tiles) Ltd – pages 38, 63 c; Crown Paints – page 29; Crucial Trading Ltd – page 44 b; Cuprinol Ltd – pages 16 b, 45 b; Dulux – pages 2, 8/9, 10 b, 11 tl, 16, 17 t, 52, 67 t, 194 t; Fired Earth Tiles plc – page 39 tl; Forbo-CP (Fablon) Ltd – pages 3, 10 t, 14, 120 t; Forbo Kingfisher Ltd – page 28; Forbo-Nairn Ltd – pages 39 tr, 45 t; Harlequin Wallcoverings Ltd – pages 1, 195 bl, 203 br; Harrison Drape – page 194 b; Hayloft Woodlock – pages 11 b, 63 t; Junckers Ltd – pages 13 cr, 51 t; Mazda Lighting – pages 12, 13 tr tl cl, 15 tl; Peter McHoy – pages 243, 248 tr br; MFI – pages 11 tr, 62 l; Monkwell Fabrics and Wallpapers – page 195 br; Sanderson – pages 198 t, 204 t; Silver Lynx Products – page 118 t; Spur Shelving Ltd – page 62 r; Today Interiors – page 195 t; Mr Tomkinson – page 44 t; Elizabeth Whiting and Associates – page 201 bl; Wicanders – page 39 b.